Women and Leadership
in the European Union

Women and Leadership in the European Union

Edited by

HENRIETTE MÜLLER
INGEBORG TÖMMEL

OXFORD
UNIVERSITY PRESS

OXFORD
UNIVERSITY PRESS

Great Clarendon Street, Oxford, OX2 6DP,
United Kingdom

Oxford University Press is a department of the University of Oxford.
It furthers the University's objective of excellence in research, scholarship,
and education by publishing worldwide. Oxford is a registered trade mark of
Oxford University Press in the UK and in certain other countries

Published in the United States of America by Oxford University Press
198 Madison Avenue, New York, NY 10016, United States of America

British Library Cataloguing in Publication Data
Data available

Library of Congress Control Number: 2021941491

ISBN 978-0-19-289621-6

DOI: 10.1093/oso/9780192896216.001.0001

Printed and bound by
CPI Group (UK) Ltd, Croydon, CR0 4YY

*To all the women advancing the cause of European integration
in the past, present, and future*

Acknowledgments

Women's leadership matters. This sentence may seem trivial and blatantly self-evident. However, when we started to study women and leadership in the European Union in spring 2018, it felt like a journey into unknown scholarly territory, as very little systematic research existed on this topic. Since Ursula von der Leyen and Christine Lagarde assumed the top positions in the EU as president of the European Commission and president of the European Central Bank, respectively, the issue of women leaders in Europe has generated wide public attention. Signaling a deep transformation of the European Union in and beyond its leadership structures, these developments felt like the reality caught up with our research in a powerful way.

When we began the project, it was far from obvious that research on women and leadership in the EU, situated at the crossroads of EU studies, leadership studies, and gender studies, would attract broad scholarly interest. Yet precisely because of this opportunity to explore a novel issue, all the contributors to this edited volume joined our initiative with great enthusiasm. We would therefore first and foremost like to thank our contributors for their dedication, diligence, and unwavering support. Without them, this book would not have been possible.

We are also very grateful to the Fritz Thyssen Foundation, which provided this project with generous funding. As a result of its support, we were able to convene an international author conference at the University of Osnabrück, Germany, between 9 and 11 January 2020. In this regard, we would also like to thank the University of Osnabrück for hosting and administering the event and Susanne Hölscher for her outstanding administrative assistance.

We are equally indebted to New York University Abu Dhabi and the NYUAD Humanities Research Fellowship Program for their generous financial support both concerning our conference and the extensive internal copy-editing process. In particular, we would like to thank Reindert Falkenburg for his enthusiastic encouragement and backing of the project from the beginning, as well as Alexandra Sandu for her exceptional administrative support.

The conference in January 2020 was central to the success of this project, since it enabled all participants to deeply engage with each other's expertise in the areas of EU studies, leadership studies, and gender studies in order to establish an integrative theoretical and methodological approach. Each contributor in some way had to step out of their comfort zone, engaging not only with new perspectives but often also new fields of study and bodies of literature. The conference was a unique journey, forging new scholarly collaborations and friendships. It is also a cherished memory since it was for many participants the last "normal" academic event before the COVID-19 pandemic changed the world.

We are also grateful to our excellent student and research assistants who have contributed to our work and the success of this project in numerous ways. We would especially like to thank Sophie Haas for her great support in preparing and coordinating the conference as well as for her invaluable contribution in collecting and collating the material for the book's Appendix. We would further like to thank Tiril Hoye Rahn for her fantastic work in the process of data collection and the coding of speeches related to the agenda-setting analysis in Chapter 16. Finally, we are very grateful to Inês Damas Pacheco Lobato Santos for her meticulous review and formatting of all chapters during our internal copy-editing process.

We also thank the editorial team from Oxford University Press for their excellent work throughout the book's production. A unique expression of gratitude goes to Dominic Byatt for his faith in our project and his unwavering support of this edited volume from the very start. We would also like to thank the two anonymous reviewers for their valuable comments and constructive feedback that further contributed to improving the manuscript. Special thanks also goes to Dan Geist for his outstanding copy-editing, diligently improving the style and writing of each chapter and thus the final typescript.

From the outset, the goal of our initiative was to make an intervention into the field. We hope that our volume will live up to this aspiration and that it will open new perspectives and avenues to its readers. We understand it as a starting point for new scholarly inquiry and research, since the study of women's leadership in the European Union has only just begun.

Table of Contents

VII. LOOKING AHEAD: WOMEN AT THE TOP OF THE EU

List of Figures and Tables

Figures

Tables

List of Abbreviations

AA	Auswärtiges Amt [Foreign Office]
AAR	Annual Activity Report
AEA	American Economic Association
AfD	Alternative für Deutschland
AG	Advocate General
AGRI	European Parliament Committee on Agriculture and Rural Development
AGs	Advocates General
ALDE	Alliance of Liberals and Democrats for Europe Political Group
ANCOVA	Univariate Analysis of Covariance
BAME	Black, Asian, and minority ethnic
BMWi	Bundesministerium für Wirtschaft und Energie [Ministry for Economic Affairs and Energy]
BRA	Better Regulation Agenda
BUDG	European Parliament Committee on Budgets
CDU	Christlich Demokratische Union Deutschlands [Christian Democratic Union of Germany]
CFI	Court of First Instance
CJEU	Court of Justice of the European Union
CMC	Crisis Management Concept
CoJ	Court of Justice
Coreper	Committee of Permanent Representatives
COVID-19	Coronavirus disease of 2019
CSDP	Common Security and Defence Policy
CSU	Christlich-Soziale Union in Bayern [Christian Social Union in Bavaria]
CSV	Christian Social People's Party
CULT	European Parliament Committee on Culture and Education
DG	Directorate General
DG AGRI	Directorate General for Agriculture and Rural Development
DG BUDG	Directorate General for Budget
DG CLIMA	Directorate General for Climate Action
DG COMM	Directorate General for Communication
DG COMP	Directorate General for Competition
DG CONNECT	Directorate General for Communications Networks, Content and Technology
DG DEVCO	Directorate General for International Cooperation and Development
DG DIGIT	Directorate General for Informatics
DG EAC	Directorate General for Education and Culture
DG ECFIN	Directorate General for Economic and Financial Affairs

DG ECHO	Directorate General for European Civil Protection and Humanitarian Aid Operations
DG EMPL	Directorate General for Employment, Social Affairs and Inclusion
DG ENV	Directorate General for Environment
DG FISMA	Directorate General for Financial Stability, Financial Services and Capital Markets Union
DG GROW	Directorate General for Internal Market, Industry, Entrepreneurship and SMEs
DG HOME	Directorate General for Migration and Home Affairs
DG HR	Directorate General for Human Resources and Security
DG JRC	Directorate General Joint Research Centre
DG JUST	Directorate General for Justice and Consumers
DG MARE	Directorate General for Maritime Affairs and Fisheries
DG MOVE	Directorate General for Mobility and Transport
DG NEAR	Directorate General for European Neighbourhood and Enlargement Negotiations
DG REGIO	Directorate General for Regional and Urban Policy
DG RTD	Directorate General for Research and Innovation
DG SANTE	Directorate General for Health and Food Safety
DGT	Central Services for Translation
DG TAXUD	Directorate General for Taxation and Customs Union
DG TRADE	Directorate General for Trade
DUP	Democratic Unionist Party
ECB	European Central Bank
ECE	East Central European
ECJ	European Court of Justice
ECON	European Parliament Committee on Economic and Monetary Affairs
ECR	European Conservatives and Reformists Political Group
EEAS	European External Action Service
EFDD	Europe of Freedom and Direct Democracy Political Group
EMI	European Monetary Institute
EMPL	European Parliament Committee on Employment and Social Affairs
ENF	Europe of Nations and Freedom Political Group
ENVI	European Parliament Committee on the Environment, Public Health and Food Safety
EP	European Parliament
EPG	European Party Group
EPP[G]	European People's Party Political [Group]
ERG	European Research Group
ERI	European Recovery Instrument
EU	European Union
EUBAM Libya	EU Border Assistance Mission in Libya
EUFOR Libya	EU Military Operation in Libya
EUROSTAT	European Statistical Office
FAC	Foreign Affairs Council

FI	Feminist institutionalism
GC	General Court
GDP	Gross Domestic Product
GDPR	General Data Protection Regulation
Greens/EFA	Greens/European Free Alliance Political Group
GUE/NGL	European United Left/Nordic Green Left Political Group
Heads	Heads of state and government
HoD	Head of delegation [European Parliament]
HR	High Representative of the Union for Foreign Affairs and Security Policy
IA	Impact Assessment
ID	Identity and Democracy Political Group
ILO	International Labour Organization
IMCO	European Parliament Committee on the Internal Market and Consumer Protection
IMF	International Monetary Fund
INTA	European Parliament Committee on International Trade
ITRE	European Parliament Committee on Industry, Research and Energy
JURI	European Parliament Committee on Legal Affairs
LCI	Leadership Capital Index
LH	Lower Houses
LI	Liberal intergovernmentalism
LIBE	European Parliament Committee on Civil Liberties, Justice and Home Affairs
MANCOVA	Multivariate analysis of covariance
MEP	Member of European Parliament
MFF	Multiannual Financial Framework
MHH	Hanover Medical School
MLG	Multilevel governance
MP	Member of Parliament
N.A.	Not available
NGEU	Next Generation EU
NGO	Nongovernmental organization
NI	New institutionalism
NPD	National party delegation [European Parliament]
OLAF	European Anti-Fraud Office
PA	Public administration
PFCA	Political Framework for a Crisis Approach
PLP	Parliamentary Labour Party
PM	Prime minister
PR	Public relations
PR	Proportional representation
PSC	EU Political and Security Committee
RCI	Rational choice institutionalism
Renew	Renew Europe Political Group
S&D	Socialists and Democrats Political Group

SCIC	Service Commun Interprétation-Conférences [Central Services for Interpretation]
SecGen	Secretariat General
SG	Secretary general
SI	Sociological institutionalism
SPD	Sozialdemokratische Partei Deutschlands
SPP	Strategic Planning and Programming
SURE	Support to Mitigate Unemployment Risks in an Emergency
TEU	Treaty on European Union
TFEU	Treaty on the Functioning of the European Union
TNC	Transitional National Council
TRAN	European Parliament Committee on Transport and Tourism
UK	United Kingdom
UN	United Nations
UNOCHA	UN Office for the Coordination of Humanitarian Affairs
UNSC	United Nations Security Council
US	United States
USA	United States of America
VP	Vice-president

About the Contributors

Gabriele Abels is Jean Monnet Chair of European Integration at the Institute of Political Science, University of Tübingen. She was president of the German Political Science Association (2012–2015). Her areas of interest cover democracy in the EU system, the role of parliaments and regions, integration theories, and gender studies. Key publications include *Routledge Handbook of Gender and EU Politics* (coedited with Andrea Krizsán, Heather MacRae, and Anna van der Vleuten; 2021); *Gendering European Integration Theory: Engaging New Dialogues* (coedited with Heather MacRae; Barbara Budrich, 2016); *Gendering the European Union: New Approaches to Old Democratic Deficits* (coedited with Joyce M. Mushaben; Palgrave Macmillan, 2012).

Maria Giulia Amadio Viceré is a Marie Skłodowska-Curie Fellow at Robert Schuman Centre for Advanced Studies/European University Institute (RSCAS/EUI). She is also an Adjunct Professor of Political Science at LUISS University and a Research Associate at Istituto Affari Internazionali (IAI). Before that, she has been a Post-Doctoral Fellow at LUISS University and an Assistant Professor at the University of Leiden. Dr. Amadio Viceré has held visiting positions at: Harvard University's Center for European Studies (Cambridge, MA, USA); the RSCAS/EUI (Florence, IT); the Henry M. Jackson School of International Studies at the University of Washington (Seattle, WA, USA); and the Policy Institute at King's College (London, UK). She published the book *The High Representative and EU Foreign Policy Integration: A Comparative Study of Kosovo and Ukraine* (Palgrave Macmillan, 2018). Her articles have appeared in journals such as *Contemporary Security Policy; Conflict, Security and Development Journal; European Security; Global Affairs*; and *Journal of European Integration*.

Karen Beckwith is the Flora Stone Mather Professor in the Department of Political Science at Case Western Reserve University. Her research concerns the comparative politics of gender, with a focus on the USA and West Europe; her work on gender and comparative political parties, party leadership, and cabinet formation has been published in a wide range of scholarly journals. Her most recent publications include *Cabinets, Ministers, and Gender* (Oxford University Press, 2019) and "Feminist Approaches to the Study of Executive Politics" (*Oxford Handbook of Executive Politics*, 2020).

Agnes Blome is Postdoctoral Research Fellow at the Cluster of Excellence "Contestations of the Liberal Script" and Lecturer at the Otto Suhr Institute of Political Science (OSI) at Freie Universität Berlin. At the OSI, she teaches classes on comparative social policy, comparative political institutions, and gender and politics. Before joining the OSI, she was senior research fellow at the WZB Berlin Social Science Research Center. She is the author of *The Politics of Work-Family Policy Reforms in Germany and Italy* (2016, Routledge). Her work appeared in *Comparative Politics, Socio-Economic Review, Journal of Social Policy, Parliamentary Affairs*. She is presently studying social policy responsiveness, the politics of care, and the causes and consequences of gender inequalities in political representation.

Michelle Cini is Professor of European Politics at the University of Bristol, where she has been based since 1991. She was Head of the School of Sociology, Politics, and International Studies at the University of Bristol between 2017 and 2021. From 2010 until mid-2017, she was editor-in-chief (with Amy Verdun) of *JCMS: Journal of Common Market Studies*. She has held a number of visiting positions, including at the EUI (Jean Monnet Fellow, 1999–2000), New York University and Columbia University (1999), Nanjing University (2008); Harvard University (2014). She has published extensively in the field of EU politics, and particularly on the European Commission, competition policy and EU public ethics. Her research interests include EU institutional politics, EU policymaking and organizational reform, public ethics, and lobbying regulation in the EU.

Sarah C. Dingler is Assistant Professor for empirical gender research at the University of Innsbruck. She was a postdoctoral researcher at the Geschwister-Scholl-Institute of Political Science at the Ludwig-Maximilians-University (Munich), and received her PhD from the University of Salzburg in May 2019. Her main areas of research include the analysis of political institutions on women's representation and the role of women as political actors in legislatures and the executive. In her dissertation, she studied how recruitment procedures of political parties affect the representation of women in national parliaments in Europe. Related work has appeared in the *Journal of European Public Policy, Parliamentary Affairs, Government and Opposition, Electoral Studies*, and the *Journal of Elections, Public Opinions and Parties*.

Sandra Eckert currently holds a Marie Skłodowska-Curie COFUND Fellowship to conduct research as Associate Professor at the Aarhus Institute of Advanced Studies (AIAS) in Denmark, and is on leave from Goethe University Frankfurt/Main. Sandra previously held positions at the universities of Berlin, Darmstadt, Mannheim, Osnabrück, and at the Robert Schuman Centre of the European University Institute in Florence. She received her PhD in political science from Free University Berlin. In her research, Sandra studies issues related to European integration, comparative public policy, and international political economy.

Christoph Erasmy is a security professional and independent researcher. He holds a BA in liberal arts and sciences from the University College Utrecht and a MSc in countering organized crime and terrorism from the University College London. First sparked during his undergraduate studies, he has a keen interest in security, leadership, and the European refugee crisis. Parts of his contribution to this book were inspired by research conducted during his studies in Utrecht. Erasmy currently works in the private sector and supports leaders in their crisis management decision-making.

Jessica Fortin-Rittberger is Professor of Comparative Politics at the University of Salzburg and co-lead editor of the *European Journal of Politics and Gender*. Her main areas of research include political developments in former communist countries, political institutions with particular focus on electoral rules, women's political representation, as well as the impact of state capacity on democratization. Her work has appeared in *Comparative Political Studies*;

European Journal of Political Research; *European Union Politics*; *Journal of European Public Policy*.

Charlotte Galpin is Associate Professor in German and European Studies at the University of Birmingham (UK). Previously, she taught and researched at the Goethe University Frankfurt, University of Bath, and the University of Copenhagen. Her research is concerned with European identities, EU citizenship, Euroscepticism, and the European public sphere. She is the author of *The Euro Crisis and European Identities: Political and Media Discourse in Germany, Ireland and Poland* (Palgrave Macmillan, 2017).

Jessica Guth is the Head of School of Law at Birmingham City University with research interests in legal education and in the feminist and queer approaches to law and legal study. She has a background in law and social science subjects and combines the two in her teaching and research. Jess is currently developing two aspects of her work. The first relates to academic identity and how that is experienced in UK law schools. The second is an analysis of the Court of Justice of the European Union and its work from a gender perspective. The latter project has so far led to a book (coauthored with Sanna Elfving; Routledge, 2018).

Miriam Hartlapp is Professor of Comparative Politics: Germany and France, at the Freie Universität Berlin (FUB). Before joining the FUB in April 2017 she held chairs at Leipzig (2014–2017) and Bremen University (2013–2014) and worked at the Max Planck Institute for the Study of Societies in Cologne, the ILO in Geneva and the WZB Berlin Social Science Center. She is co-author of 'Complying with Europe: The Impact of EU Minimum Harmonisation and Soft Law in the Member States' (CUP 2005) and 'Which policy for Europe?: Power and conflict inside the European Commission' (OUP, 2014). Her research focuses on governance in the EU multilevel system, particularly the European Commission and the role of France and Germany in the EU; implementation, (non-)compliance and enforcement; as well as regulation of economic and social policies. Currently she is researching "Effects of EU Soft Law Across the Multilevel System" with an ANR-DFG grant.

Eva G. Heidbreder is Professor of Political Science/Multilevel Governance in Europe at the Otto von Guericke University Magdeburg in Germany. Her research tackles questions of effective and legitimate governance from a public policy and public administration perspective. She has worked on various issues of EU governance that include the evolution of EU competences in the context of enlargement, the handling of the Brexit negotiations, the development of the EU's multilevel administration and civil society participation in EU policymaking. Since completing her PhD at the European University Institute in Florence, she has held positions at the Heinrich Heine University Düsseldorf, the Hertie School of Governance, Free University, and Humboldt University in Berlin and the University of Konstanz.

Johanna Kantola is Professor of Gender Studies in the Faculty of Social Sciences at Tampere University (Finland). Her research centers on gender, power, and politics—political parties and institutions, gender equality policies in Finland and in the EU, and theoretical questions about the state, representation, and intersectionality. She is the director of the ERC Consolidator Grant—research project *Gender, Party Politics and Democracy in Europe: A Study of the European Parliament's Party Groups* (EUGENDEM, 2018–2023). She is also the director of the Academy of Finland-funded research project *Gender and Power in Reconfigured*

Corporatist Finland (GePoCo, 2016–2020). Her books include *Gender and Political Analysis* (with Emanuela Lombardo; Palgrave, 2017); *Gender and the European Union* (Palgrave, 2010); *Feminists Theorize the State* (Palgrave, 2006). She is the editor of Palgrave Macmillan's Gender and Politics book series with Sarah Childs.

Heather MacRae is Associate Professor of Politics at York University, Toronto. She held a Jean Monnet Chair of European Integration (2014–2017). She is president of the European Community Studies Association Canada (2018–2021). Her areas of interest are Europeanization and EU gender politics, EU politics and German politics. Key publications include *Routledge Handbook of Gender and EU Politics* (coedited with Gabriele Abels, Andrea Krizsán and Anna van der Vleuten; 2021), *Gendering European Integration Theory: Engaging New Dialogues* (coedited with Gabriele Abels; Barbara Budrich, 2016); "Does European Union Studies Have a Gender Problem? Experiences from Researching Brexit" (coauthored; *International Feminist Journal of Politics* 20(2), 2018).

Cherry Miller is a Postdoctoral Research Fellow on the EUGenDem project at Tampere University (Finland). Her research encompasses areas such as gender, parliaments and legislatures, political parties and institutions, and the methodological development of parliamentary ethnography. She is author of *Gendering the Everyday in the UK House of Commons: Beneath the Spectacle* (Palgrave MacMillan, 2021). Her research has appeared in journals such as *Journal of Common Market Studies; European Journal of Politics and Gender; Parliamentary Affairs* and *Political Studies Review*.

Henriette Müller is Visiting Assistant Professor of Leadership Studies at New York University Abu Dhabi (NYUAD). Her research encompasses the comparative study of political leadership and executive politics both at the national and international level, as well as across regime types and diverse cultural regions. She is the author of *Political Leadership and the European Commission Presidency* (Oxford University Press, 2020). She is the editor of two special issues on *The Role of Leadership in EU Politics and Policy-Making* (*West European Politics*, 2020 43/5) together with Femke A. W. J. van Esch, and *Women Opposition Leaders: Pathways, Patterns and Performance* (*Politics & Governance*, forthcoming 2023 11/1) together with Sarah C. Dingler and Ludger Helms. Furthermore, her research has been published in *Hawwa Journal of Women of the Middle East and the Islamic World*, *Politics & Governance*, *Journal of European Integration* and *West European Politics*.

Pamela Pansardi is Associate Professor of Political Science at the University of Pavia (Italy) and Principal Investigator of the two-year research project "Gender and Power in Italian Politics", which focuses on the investigation of gender inequalities in power and representation in Italy in comparative perspective. She is founding chair of the standing group on Gender and Politics of the Italian Political Science Association (SISP) and member of the executive board of the IPSA Research Committee on Political Power. Her work lies at the intersection of political theory, gender and politics, EU politics, and methods in text analysis, and has appeared in journals such as *European Journal of Political Research, Journal of European Social Policy, Journal of European Integration, Parliamentary Affairs, Journal of Political Power*.

Giulia Tercovich is Assistant Director of the Centre for Security, Diplomacy and Strategy (CSDS) and Assistant Professor in International Affairs at the Brussels School of Governance (BSoG), Vrije Universiteit Brussel, Belgium. She has a double-doctoral degree in Politics and International Studies from the University of Warwick (UK) and Université Libre de Bruxelles (Belgium). She was Erasmus Mundus PhD Fellow in the GEM PhD School in Globalization, the EU and Multilateralism. She has worked for the United Nations Liaison Office for Peace and Security (UNLOPS), the European External Action Service in the Crisis Response and Operational Coordination Department and for the Italian Permanent Representation to the EU, assisting the delegate to the Committee for Civilian Aspects of Crisis Management (CivCom). Her research focuses on EU foreign and security policy, political leadership, EU-Indo-pacific relations, EU inter-organizational relations (UN and NATO), as well as innovative and active education. She has published peer-reviewed articles, special issues and edited volumes in high-standing journals and with internationally recognized publishers. Recent publications on the EU High Representative include a special issue on "Assessing the post-Lisbon High Representatives: from treaty provisions to Europe's multiple crises" (with Amadio Viceré and Carta; *European security*, 29(3)) and a peer-reviewed article on "The High Representative and the Covid-19 Crisis" (with Amadio Viceré; *Global Affairs*, 6(3), 287–299).

Ingeborg Tömmel , Dr. habil., is Professor Emeritus in International and European Politics and Jean Monnet Chair at the University of Osnabrück. Earlier, she held positions at the Free University of Berlin and the Radboud University of Nijmegen (Netherlands) and was a visiting professor in Canada and Egypt. She is holder of the John F. Diefenbaker Award of the Canadian Council (2005–2006). Her research focuses on the political system of the EU, European governance and policymaking, policy implementation in the member states, and political leadership in the EU. Recent publications include *The European Union: What It Is and How It Works* (Palgrave Macmillan, 2014); a special issue "Political Leadership in the EU" (with Amy Verdun; *Journal of European Integration* 39(2), 2017), and "Political leadership in times of crisis: the Commission presidency of Jean-Claude Juncker" (*West European Politics* 2020, 43/5).

Femke A. W. J. van Esch is Professor of European Governance and Leadership at the Utrecht School of Governance, and coordinator of the interdisciplinary, double-degree Master European Governance at Utrecht University. She has expertise in European governance, political leadership, and the method of cognitive mapping. Over the years, Van Esch has obtained various prestigious research grants and published in high-standing journals on EU politics and leadership like the *Journal of European Public Policy*; *West European Politics*; *Journal of Common Market Studies*. In addition to her academic work, Femke was a member of the Committee European Integration of the Advisory Council of International Affairs of the Dutch Ministry of Foreign Affairs (2011–2019).

Amy Verdun is Professor in the Department of Political Science of the University of Victoria (UVic), BC Canada, where she has worked since 1997 and been full professor since 2005. Her research deals with European integration, governance, and policymaking, political economy, as well as comparisons between the EU and Canada. Her recent book is a coedited student textbook (with Achim Hurrelmann and Emmanuel Brunet-Jailly), *European Union Governance and Policy Making: A Canadian Perspective* (University of Toronto

Press, 2018). She was the recipient of the 2009 Craigdarroch Silver Medal for Excellence in Research of the University of Victoria, the prestigious Lansdowne Distinguished Fellow Award in 2017 and the European Community Studies Association–Canada teaching award in 2018. From 2018–2020 she was Professor of European Politics and Political Economy at Leiden University, she has been guest professor since. From 2010–2017 she was coeditor (with Michelle Cini) of the *JCMS: Journal of Common Market Studies*. At UVic she served as Founder and Director of the European Studies Program (1997–2005); Graduate Adviser (2007–2009); and Chair (Head) of the Department (2010–2013).

A Programmatic Introduction

Women's Leadership in the European Union

Henriette Müller and Ingeborg Tömmel

I.1 Introduction

In 2019, to the surprise of many, the European Council nominated women for two of the highest positions in the European Union (EU), Ursula von der Leyen for office of Commission president and Christine Lagarde for the presidency of the European Central Bank (ECB). In addition, Laura Codruta Kövesi was appointed the EU's first anti-fraud prosecutor. Yet the increase in female firsts, from politicians to managers and experts, at the top of the Union—as significant as it is—cannot obscure the fact that gender equality has far from been achieved and women's representation in the European institutions is still very unequally distributed. At the same time, scholarship on women leaders, the pathways by and conditions under which they obtain leadership positions, and women's performance and agency in European decision-making and governance remains remarkably scarce. Who are the women leaders in the European institutions past and present? What have been the specific opportunities and challenges for women in accessing top-level EU positions? How do women exercise leadership in the Union and with what impact? To what extent, if any, do women practice different leadership styles than men in EU institutions?

In response to this vast research lacuna, this edited volume takes on the study of women's leadership in the EU. It provides a coherent analytical framework with which women leaders for the first time are thoroughly studied across EU institutions both in their pathways to top-level positions and in their exercise of leadership. In doing so, it integrates three distinct streams of scholarship that have thus far remained separate: EU studies, leadership studies, and gender studies.

The introduction to this volume proceeds in four steps. First, it provides an overview of the history and development of women leaders in European institutions, pointing at women's continued underrepresentation in EU leadership positions. Second, it sheds light on the analytical framework that unites the 16 chapters of this volume. The exploration of that framework, derived from the theoretical

Henriette Müller and Ingeborg Tömmel, *A Programmatic Introduction: Women's Leadership in the European Union.*
In: *Women and Leadership in the European Union.* Edited by Henriette Müller and Ingeborg Tömmel,
Oxford University Press. © Oxford University Press (2022). DOI: 10.1093/oso/9780192896216.003.0001

and empirical cross-fertilization of the three aforementioned (sub)disciplines, demonstrates how they relate to and inform each other. Third, the introduction sets forth the structure of the volume, outlining each chapter's research focus and contribution. Finally, it discusses the overarching conclusions that we draw from the variety of individual analyses presented herein.

I.2 Women Leaders in EU Institutions: Past and Present Trends

Despite the substantial efforts to increase women's representation and participation at the European level, gender equality continues to vary significantly from one EU institution to another and overall equity has not been achieved. EU institutions, whether supranational or intergovernmental, have by and large not been front runners in women's representation in leadership and often still fail to meet their declared aspirations and self-imposed regulations.

In the European Parliament (EP), often cited as the primary advocate for gender equality among the EU institutions, the share of female representatives increased only slightly, from 3% to 5.5%, between 1958 and 1978. The major leap forward took place in 1979, with an increase to 16% due to the first direct elections to the EP. Since then, the growth of female representation in the EP has been relatively steady, reaching a share of almost 40% in 2019. Between the member states, however, the figures vary widely. As a result of the 2014 elections, for example, 76.9% of the delegates from Finland were women, whereas Bulgaria sent 17.6% (Shreeves et al. 2019: 2). Simone Veil was the first woman to serve as president of the EP, from 1979 to 1982; her lone female successor to date has been Nicole Fontaine (1999–2002). The first female leader of a party group in the EP did not emerge until the 1990s (Pauline Green, leader of the Socialist Group, 1994–1999). Today, women remain substantially underrepresented in the EP's leadership positions, for example, as presidents, vice-presidents, party group leaders, or committee chairs (see the Appendix to this volume).

The European Commission admitted its first woman commissioner, Christiane Scrivener, in 1989, meaning that between 1952 and 1989 there were no female members of the High Authority or the Commission at all. Over the past 30 years, women's representation in the Commission's top-level positions has seen first a slow and then steep increase, culminating in the nomination and election of Ursula von der Leyen in 2019. The number of female commissioners reached parity (13 female to 14 male commissioners) in 2020 with the nomination and election of Irish Commissioner Mairead McGuinness. The share of women in the position of director general has increased to near parity (Hartlapp et al. 2021). While the first female vice-president of the European Commission did not take office until 1999, Viviane Reding (1999–2014) was nonetheless the longest-serving commissioner and also vice-president of the Commission. Of the eight secretaries general in the history of the Commission, only two have been women, with both, again, only in the past two decades.

At the other supranational EU institutions, the Court of Justice of the European Union (CJEU) and the ECB, women's representation in top-level positions has been even more lacking. In 1981, the French lawyer Simone Rozès-Ludwig became the first female judge at the Court, but it was not until 1999 that more women followed. The share of female judges and advocates general has increased only slowly over the years and now barely surpasses 18% (Guth and Elfving 2018: 41). The ECB's record is even worse than that of the CJEU. Female senior managers remain particularly scarce at the top of the institution, meaning that—apart from the current president, Christine Lagarde—there have often been no women represented in the highest decision-making bodies of the bank, the Executive Board and the Governing Council (see the Appendix to this volume).

Turning to the intergovernmental institutions, the European Council and Council of Ministers are the least gender-balanced institutions, since the Council is constituted by member states' delegations and women's representation in executive politics is low in many EU countries. For example, in 2019, Finland had a cabinet comprising 58% women, Spain's and Sweden's had about 50% representation, while Malta (9%), Greece (10%), Estonia (13%), and Hungary (14%) were at the other end of the scale (Eurostat 2020). Considered as a group, the EU member states have never had more than four women as heads of government at the same time (15%; Eurostat 2020). The first President-in-Office of the rotating Council presidency was Margaret Thatcher in 1981 and 1986, who was followed by German Chancellor Angela Merkel in 2007 and 2020. In total, only eight women (if one counts Thatcher and Merkel twice) versus 136 men have presided over the Council (1958–2021). Crucially, Catherine Ashton (2009–14) and Federica Mogherini (2014–2019) have been the first two women to be nominated by the European Council to one of the EU's high-level political executive positions, the High Representative of the Union for Foreign Affairs and Security Policy (HR).

In sum, women's representation in EU leadership positions, while having significantly improved in recent years, remain highly unequally distributed across the Union's institutions. Huge differences persist between member states, with a few front runners, especially the Scandinavian countries, compensating to an extent for the low representation of females among the many laggards. At the same time, the EU seems not only to pose obstacles to women who aspire to leadership but also to offer distinct opportunities, rooted in specific circumstances. For example, due to the historically less intense competition for seats in the EP, women entered it in significant numbers well before they did the legislatures of most of the member states. While the EU is an evolving polity with marked divergences among national governments, political parties, and citizenries, this set-up seems to create specific windows of opportunity for women to take the lead, such as with the politically delicate position of HR.

The questions of whether and to what extent these windows of opportunity are short-lived or starting points for enduring structural transformations demand thorough investigation. The same applies to the variety of factors hindering the access of women to high-level offices in the EU. For example, what role does the persistence of traditional gender regimes in the member states play in women's career progression? To what extent do women's career paths differ between high-ranking administrative and expert posts in comparison to political positions? Most importantly, what role do gender stereotypes (still) play in the EU leadership context? Unsurprisingly, due to the lack of research on women's access to EU leadership positions, studies that examine women's performances in leadership offices have also remained scarce, leaving further questions to be investigated. To shed light on these varied questions, an analytical framework that combines the study of access to and the exercise of leadership is called for to enable systematic research of women and leadership in the EU.

I.3 The State of Research and a New Analytical Framework

To date, no scholarly works have combined perspectives and insights from the three relevant (sub-)disciplines, EU studies, leadership studies, and gender studies.

Scholars at the intersection of gender studies and EU studies have so far mainly focused either on the state and implementation of gender equality, gender representation, and gender mainstreaming in the EU member states (see, for example, Bego 2015; Müller-Rommel and Vercesi 2017; Kantola and Lombardo 2018; Dingler et al. 2019), or on the nature and varieties of gender regimes in the Union (Walby 2004). The works at this intersection have also paid particular attention to EU directives and policies that contribute to gender equality, and, more broadly, to the role of gender in EU policies (Hoskyns 1996; Guerrina 2005; van der Vleuten 2007; Abels and Mushaben 2012; Jacquot 2015; MacRae and Weiner 2017; Ahrens 2017; Ahrens and van der Vleuten 2019). The role of gender in EU institutions and the European integration process, as well as gender representation in European decision-making and its organizational proceedings, have also been studied (see, for example, Kantola 2010; MacRae 2010; Guth and Elving 2018; Haastrup et al. 2019; Berthet and Kantola 2020; Gill and Jensen 2020; Abels et al. 2021). In sum, although the role of leadership and agency has recently gained traction in EU studies (Hayward 2008; Cramme 2011; Helms 2017; Van Esch 2017; Tömmel and Verdun 2017; Müller 2020; Müller and Van Esch 2020a),[1] there has been very little

---

[1] See also the special section on European leadership in *European Political Science* (2017, 1), the special issue of *Journal of European Integration* on European leadership (2017, 39 [2]), and the special issue of *West European Politics* on EU leadership (2020, 43 [5]).

research that focuses specifically on women's agency, access to, and exercise of leadership in the political or administrative-managerial domains of the European institutions.

The recent crises affecting the Union have created a new urgency for scholars of leadership research and EU studies to share their knowledge and thoroughly investigate European leadership. Research on leadership in the realm of the EU is still relatively new, as European studies have long been predominantly institution-focused and often neglected to analyze the role of agency (Tallberg 2006; Bulmer and Joseph 2016; Nielsen and Smeets 2018; Smeets and Beach 2020). Research on European leadership largely consists of single-case and comparative case studies exploring the actions of key—mainly male—members of the European elite and their effects on EU policy making. Among those, the Commission presidents have by far received most of the scholarly attention (see, for example, Ross 1995; Endo 1999; Drake 2000; Cini 2008; Kassim et al. 2013; Tömmel 2013, 2020; Brummer 2014; Olsson and Hammargård 2016; Müller 2016, 2017, 2020). Other studies focus on the Council president (Dinan 2017; Tömmel 2017) or the ECB president (Verdun 2017; Tortola and Pansardi 2018). The role of leadership has also been studied with regard to particular EU policy areas, most notably environmental policy and foreign policy (Parker et al. 2017; Aggestam and Johannson 2017; Koops and Tercovich 2020), as well as from the perspective of how national and European leaders engage in collaborative leadership (Müller and Van Esch 2020b).

This means that despite a valuable list of publications on the most famous European female leaders and their national achievements, such as Margaret Thatcher (King 2002; Simms 2008; Dyson 2009; Cannadine 2017) or Angela Merkel (Mushaben 2017; Helms and Van Esch 2017; Helms et al. 2019), there has been only limited research on the agency of national women leaders in the European arena (Van Esch 2017) and hardly any comparative or case study research on female commissioners, MEPs, or other officeholders in the highest echelons of European politics. Although women in their capacities as leading politicians, managers, and administrators have shaped the process of European integration, governance, and decision-making, research on their accession to leadership positions, their agency, and their leadership has remained scarce. The disconnect between EU studies, leadership studies, and gender studies has in turn reinforced the image of the EU as an overly male-dominated environment to this very day.

To integrate and cross-fertilize the three (sub)disciplines and thus allow for a comprehensive analysis of a variety of women actors in EU leadership positions, this volume conceptualizes their pathways to power and their performances through two complementary analytical approaches. First, we distinguish between *positional* and *behavioral* leadership. The concept of positional leadership addresses women's access to high-level positions. It highlights the multiplicity of social and at times institutional barriers both visible and invisible that inhibit women's access to leadership positions in ways that may be distinct from their effect on women's general representation in European institutions. The concept of behavioral leadership focuses on the exercise of leadership, while taking it that in principle women's performances do not differ from those of men—in other words, that there is overall a greater diversity of personal attributes within each sex than there is, on average, between the sexes. However, social and role expectations based on assumptions and stereotypes about gender tend to expose women leaders in certain cases and circumstances to a double bind that can lead to differing leadership performances and evaluations thereof, often negatively impacting women's exercise of leadership.

Second, we categorize the leadership positions of the European institutions into *political, administrative,* and *expert* leadership offices. The analysis of women's positional leadership across the three types of EU offices compares and contrasts the multiplicity of challenges but also specific opportunities that women encounter in accessing any of these positions. Political offices (for example, EU commissioners, the HR, members of the Council and European Council, and MEPs) are generally attained via political party careers and largely determined at the member-state level. By contrast, administrative offices (for example, director general or secretary general in various EU institutions) are accessed via career paths within the EU civil services. Expert leadership positions, such as with the ECB or the CJEU, involve mixed career paths but require in any event expertise and prior officeholding experience in the relevant field. The analysis of women's behavioral leadership across the three types of high-level EU positions examines their performance in the respective offices and in fulfilling the offices' functions. It focuses on their leadership styles as well as their achievements and impact. While every chapter of this volume can be situated within this overarching methodological framework, each chapter also provides a tighter, more detailed analytical focus that matches the concrete research topic, whether that is a particular EU institution, the performance of an individual leader, or the comparative analysis of leadership.

By integrating the three distinct (sub)disciplines—EU studies, gender studies, and leadership studies—into one coherent analytical approach, this edited volume systematically studies women's access to EU leadership positions, as well as their behavior, leadership styles, and impact on European governance. In doing so, it focuses on three central research questions: *(1) How have women accessed leadership positions across EU institutions? (2) How have they performed the official functions of their offices? (3) To what extent have they achieved significant successes and lasting impact?* Integrating theoretical and empirical insights from these three (sub)disciplines, this collection makes possible a deeper understanding of the role and significance of women in the evolution of European integration and the process of European governance.

I.4 Structural Synopsis and Findings of the Chapters

The chapters of this volume, all original contributions, together cover all of the Union's high offices across its executive, legislative, judicial, expert, and administrative branches. In addition, our selection of case studies on individual women leaders involves examples from divergent member states and varying situational contexts.

The chapters have revealed deep insights into the institutional and situational challenges and constraints that women encounter on their path to top-level positions and when exercising leadership once they arrive. At the same time, they show the institutional and situational opportunities that enable women to ascend to and exercise leadership in the EU, and what personal capacities are paramount to seizing these opportunities and performing successfully in positions of power.

Part I opens the volume with two chapters aimed at developing the general conceptual framework for the study of women's leadership and a deeper theoretical understanding of women's agency in the European context. Müller and Tömmel, exploring the manifold hurdles that women encounter on their paths to and when in power, distinguish analytically between positional and behavioral leadership, as well as political, administrative, and expert leadership. Both theoretically and with an empirical overview of the Union, the authors show that these distinctions are essential to understanding the various obstacles but also opportunities that women face on their way to and in top-level EU offices.

Focusing on European integration theory, Abels and MacRae further strive to connect insights from integration theories, gender studies, and leadership studies. Since theoretical reflection on the role of leadership and its intersection with gender is still rudimentary within European integration theory, the authors emphasize that the concept of agency and those integration theories having inbuilt concepts of agency provide the best inroads to a more comprehensive theoretical understanding of women and leadership in the EU.

Part II of the volume is dedicated to the analysis of positional leadership in the Union. Hartlapp and Blome show that women's access to leadership positions—both political and administrative—in the European Commission occurred very late and slowly; only recently has women's share of representation in the Commission passed 40%. And hurdles remain. Women leaders more often bear responsibility for portfolios considered to be "soft" or less prestigious, though this is slowly changing as well. In a framework of demand and supply, the authors discuss various explanations for the quantitative and qualitative (under)representation of women in the Commission.

Dingler and Fortin-Rittberger reveal similar, even more striking findings regarding the EP. Much earlier than the Commission and most national legislatures, the European assembly reached a significant level of female representation.

Even today, however, women encounter high hurdles in ascending to EP leadership positions such as committee chair, party group leader, or president/vice-president. Moreover, when acting as committee chairs, they mostly preside in traditionally "feminine" portfolios. The authors conclude that continuing biases, prejudices, and structural factors hamper women's access to influential positions in the EP.

Part III of the book examines various aspects of behavioral leadership in the Commission and the EP. Cini provides a thorough case study of Viviane Reding's performance as commissioner and MEP, emphasizing how different institutions require different styles of leadership. As commissioner, Reding achieved significant successes due to her independent and assertive leadership style. However, this style provoked much contestation and did not result in successes in the EP. Cini concludes that Reding's proactive leadership fits well with the Commission's role of proposing policies, but less well with the EP, where collective leadership is required.

Amadio Viceré and Tercovich compare the leadership of the two first post-Lisbon HRs, Catherine Ashton and Federica Mogherini. The chapter shows that gender stereotypes and power dynamics played a central role in both women's ascents to the position. In office, the women exercised different leadership styles, with Mogherini being more successful than Ashton. Mogherini's performance indicates that proactively anticipating member states' preferences and gaining support from different audiences creates leverage in EU foreign politics.

The chapters by Müller and Pansardi and by Kantola and Miller add a cross-gender comparative angle to the study of leadership. Müller and Pansardi study the rhetoric of female vice-presidents of the European Commission, comparing them to all other commissioners (male and female) and male vice-presidents and presidents between 1999 and 2019. Using charisma as a proxy for rhetorical skillfulness, female vice-presidents and commissioners consistently outperform their male counterparts. The chapter corroborates that women speakers, though very diverse, are affected by contradictory socially and culturally constructed expectations that seem to oblige them more than men to engage in highly skilled forms of speechmaking.

Kantola and Miller show that gender composition in the leadership of the political groups of the EP, including political, policy, and administrative positions, continues to matter. Hidden structures, especially concerning national party delegations, remain heavily dominated by men. Access to leadership positions in political groups is influenced by power politics, trust networks, and the prioritization of seniority, factors that are also apparent in many national contexts. The authors conclude that gendered norms and practices continue to shape the conditions of leadership in the EP.

Part IV of the book draws attention to the national level, studying women's political and behavioral leadership as prime ministers and the effects on EU politics and governance. Focusing on positional leadership, Beckwith underscores that women have rarely and only recently ascended to prime ministerial office. Looking at party leadership as a step toward premiership, Beckwith finds that left- and right-wing parties equally fail to promote women as party leaders and, consequently, prime ministers. The dearth of female prime ministers has restricted women's presence in the European Council as well as their ascendance to EU leadership positions post-premiership, confirming that the member states are hardly at the front lines of advancing women, either domestically or in the EU.

Van Esch and Erasmy study the crisis management of German Chancellor Angela Merkel during two crises affecting the EU: the refugee and COVID-19 crises. Using the leadership capital index as an analytical tool, the chapter shows fundamental differences in Merkel's performance. While in the refugee crisis she acted unilaterally and lost leadership capital, during the COVID-19 crisis she fostered solidarity and cooperation across the EU. This increased her leadership capital and shows that acting in the interest of the EU as a whole does not necessarily imply losing political support domestically.

Eckert and Galpin also examine women's leadership during a crisis: In a situation where opportunities for success were low, British Prime Minister Theresa May attempted to implement Brexit. Comparing May's self-representation of leadership with media perceptions of her performance, the chapter shows a huge discrepancy. While May purposefully presented herself as both a caring and strong leader, she was confronted with extremely gendered media evaluations, criticizing her as both too weak and timid and too stubborn and inflexible. This double bind, which women leaders often face, contributed to the perception of her failure.

Part V of the book studies women's administrative leadership both in the EU and in national ministerial departments where EU policy is coordinated. Tömmel analyzes the behavioral leadership of Catherine Day as secretary general of the European Commission: her strategies in reforming decision-making, shaping the political agenda, closely collaborating with the president, and mediating in intra- and interinstitutional settings. The chapter concludes that Day not only excelled in performing the multifaceted functions of her office, she succeeded as well in transforming the Secretariat General into a presidential office, centralizing leadership at the heart of the Commission, and expanding the strategic resources of the Commission beyond her tenure.

Heidbreder studies the impact of the EU multilevel system on women's leadership in national public administration (PA). She argues that the need for transnational coordination of EU policies implies new functional demands in the multilevel system that clash with prototypical virtues promoted in standard PA, but are positively addressed by feminist counterimages. Taking the expectation that women might better match these new demands as a starting point, the chapter, using data from two ministries in Germany, indeed reveals that women are overrepresented in the respective coordinative leadership functions.

Part VI of the volume zooms in on women's expert leadership in EU institutions. Guth focuses on positional leadership in the CJEU. Despite recent advances, women remain severely underrepresented as judges and particularly as Advocates General in both branches of the CJEU, the Court of Justice and the General Court. The share of women is, unsurprisingly, slightly higher in the less prestigious General Court. In addition to the usual barriers that women face in accessing leadership positions, the chapter attributes their underrepresentation in the CJEU to the appointment procedures in the member states.

Complementary to Guth, Verdun examines women's positional leadership in the ECB. She shows that socially constructed stereotypes and performance expectations specific to the field of macroeconomics and central banking are pivotal in women's extreme underrepresentation in the institution. Despite recent affirmative action that advanced more women into the bank's higher administrative ranks, the top-level governing positions remain male dominated, as member states continue to nominate almost exclusively men to these offices. A first assessment of Christine Lagarde's performance as president of the ECB shows that she practices a more political and communicative leadership style than her predecessors.

Part VII concludes the volume by looking at the future of women's leadership in the EU. Müller and Tömmel offer a first comprehensive account of Ursula von der Leyen's positional and behavioral leadership at the top of the Commission. The chapter shows that von der Leyen's personal capacities—political ambition and determination, resolve in the face of conflict, and party-political independence—are vital to both ascending to the presidency and leading the Commission. Despite tremendous institutional and situational constraints, heightened by the COVID-19 crisis, von der Leyen has succeeded in expanding the role of the European Commission and the Union as a whole into new political directions.

I.5 Conclusions of the Volume and Implications for the European Union

The rich findings of the individual chapters allow us to draw far-reaching conclusions about women and leadership in the EU, which in turn may inspire future research.

Regarding positional leadership, women accessed top-level offices in the EU only late and at different paces. The first institution they accessed was the EP, which, however, offered less prestigious positions and exposed aspirants to less political competition. After some delay, the European Commission followed, not least due to pressure from the Parliament. Having entered the EP early on in significant numbers, women have contributed to transforming the assembly into a strong advocate of fair gender balance in high-level EU offices. In contrast to the Parliament and Commission, the intergovernmental institutions, the Council and European Council, constituted by the national executives, lag far behind. This is likewise true of the CJEU and the ECB, where nominations to the top-level leadership positions come from the member states' governments. In sum, women have more easily accessed the political functions of the supranational institutions, while those of the intergovernmental bodies remain difficult to access. Access to administrative functions within EU institutions has grown only slowly, and expert functions pose particularly high hurdles to women.

Regardless of these differences between offices, in all these functions and across all EU institutions women face challenges in accessing more prestigious positions. They are still exposed to adverse gender stereotypes and social biases against women in leadership positions, resulting in and reinforcing hidden structures of gendered power. Although women's representation has overall been strong in the EP, it has been difficult for women to access the Parliament's leadership positions, in which they remain extremely underrepresented, particularly in the most prestigious positions and committee portfolios. Regarding the Commission, although women have successfully advanced to the position of commissioner, they have nonetheless again encountered major hurdles and delays in accessing the more senior and powerful portfolios and positions such as president. Despite the presence of self-imposed gender equality regulations since the early 1990s, administrative leadership positions nonetheless opened up only slowly for women in the Commission, particularly in the prestigious portfolios.

And, as we've observed, leadership positions in the Court and the ECB are even more difficult to access. Continued gender stereotypes and prejudices in the still male-dominated fields of law and economics often lead to disparaging evaluations of women's capacity and suitability for positions within the Court and the ECB. If women attain leadership positions in these two institutions, it seems to be solely through competence and expertise in the respective fields, rather than, for example, profession-based networks. What is more, women's career paths to high-ranking positions in these institutions also tend to be atypical, as in the case of Christine Lagarde and top-level ECB administrators (see the Appendix to this volume). This confirms that the professions of law and particularly economics are still relatively closed to women in Europe.

Yet it is the political functions in the intergovernmental bodies that are most difficult to access as women's representation in these bodies is dependent on their presence in the national executives, in which most countries are still far from a fair gender balance. Female prime ministers and national ministers have remained few and highly unequally distributed across Europe and, again, across portfolios. Here, it is also important to note that many women, most notably Angela Merkel and Theresa May, have entered these positions in "glass cliff" situations or circumstances of deep transformation within either their own party or the national context more broadly. Such circumstances have also been apparent to varying degrees in the nominations of Ursula von der Leyen and Christine Lagarde. It seems that situational contexts of crisis or profound transformation tend to favor the nomination of women for high-level offices; at the same time, they also heighten the risk of failure, as the case of Theresa May shows.

Looking at behavioral leadership, those women who have attained top-level leadership positions perform extremely well overall (Catherine Day, Theresa May, Federica Mogherini, Viviane Reding, Ursula von der Leyen). We might even assume that women outperform men, as some chapters reveal. Women in these positions are particularly successful if they practice both considered feminine and masculine leadership styles, that is, if they act assertive and conciliatory at the same time. Deviations such as a more one-sidedly assertive approach as practiced by Reding confirm this insight. Meanwhile, the case of Theresa May, despite her performance of a simultaneously assertive and conciliatory leadership style, indicates that a highly polarized political sphere constitutes an extremely difficult context for women's exercise of leadership.

This is not to say that women are the better leaders. While women's leadership in the EU has been characterized by both collaboration and consensus as well as domination, authority, and ambition, there are hardly any indications that women perform differently from men per se. The variations that occur in some situations and circumstances seem to derive from specific factors that women are exposed to more strongly than men in their ascendance to and exercise of leadership. First, women leaders for the time being are much more subject to severe selection processes and intense public and professional scrutiny. The few who reach top-level positions across the political, administrative, and expert spheres are thus highly qualified.

Second, assuming that combined leadership styles are more recent phenomena in Western democracies (Helms 2016), women leaders as latecomers in top-level positions are likely to more often engage in such styles. By contrast, men, traditionally accustomed to the exercise of leadership in various top-level functions, seemingly more often practice one-sided leadership styles. Of course, there are wide variations among male leaders, depending on the political systems and cultures of their home countries, the demands of their office, the situational context, and their personal characteristics and capacities.

Turning to the EU, we may assume that this evolving polity with its manifold checks and balances is particularly in need of cooperation and collaboration between a multitude of national and supranational leaders as well as institutions. A more consensus-driven and collaborative leadership approach seems to better fit the EU political system than traditional forms of leadership (Müller and Van Esch 2020b: 1119). It is important therefore to acknowledge that in the European context men who practice combined leadership styles are also more successful. The leadership performance of Commission President José Manuel Barroso, whose style was domineering and top-down oriented, was less than successful, while his successor Jean-Claude Juncker, with a more conciliatory and consensus-oriented style, achieved major successes (Müller 2020; Tömmel 2020).

This raises the question of whether the EU, with its fragmented institutional structure and, hence, multitude of institutionalized leadership positions, constitutes a specific political system, demanding collaboration and consensus-building to a greater extent than do nation states. Indeed, the Union, as a system primarily concerned with mediating highly divergent interests among its member states, peoples, and constituencies, not only demands sophisticated strategies of consensus-building, but also elaborate forms of cooperative and at the same time determined leadership. This may explain why women, with their generally combined leadership styles, have recently accessed top-level EU positions in greater numbers and why they achieve significant successes in these positions. Yet research on the exercise of leadership in modern democracies indicates that national political systems also increasingly require more inclusive leadership styles that can effectively address and overcome the "complex and difficult-to-solve 'wicked problems'" of contemporary societies (Helms 2016: 467). In this sense, the EU may earlier than states display the evolving contours of new, more complex leadership forms and styles, and research on these forms and styles may reveal insights that point to political transformations that by far transcend the subject of analysis.

The insights of this volume indicate that we are witness to a time of deep transformation of the leadership context both with regard to exercising leadership and the study thereof. Overall, women seem to adapt to and fulfill the changing leadership demands more quickly than men. While the needs of individual countries vary widely, the EU is clearly in need of leadership that seeks consensus and compromise. The case of Theresa May negatively confirms this point. As the British political system was extremely polarized and demanding domineering leadership, her simultaneously conciliatory and authoritative style was not appreciated, but evaluated very unfavorably. At the same time, while the success of a combined leadership style is well evidenced across the different EU institutions, it also seems to be about time for both the perception and analysis of leadership to move beyond narrow gender dichotomies and open new doors for comprehensive research on leadership and agency in the EU and beyond.

References

Abels, Gabriele, Andrea Krizsán, Heather MacRae, and Anna van der Vleuten, eds. 2021. *The Routledge Handbook of Gender and EU Politics*. Abingdon, UK, and New York: Routledge.

Abels, Gabriele, and Joyce Marie Mushaben, eds. 2012. *Gendering the European Union: New Approaches to Old Democratic Deficits*. New York: Palgrave Macmillan.

Aggestam, Lisbeth, and Markus Johansson. 2017. "The Leadership Paradox in EU Foreign Policy." *Journal of Common Market Studies* 55 (6): 1203–1220.

Ahrens, Petra. 2017. *Actors, Institutions and the Making of EU Gender Equality Programs*. London: Palgrave Macmillan.

Ahrens, Petra, and Anna van der Vleuten. 2019. "Fish Fingers and Measles? Assessing Complex Gender Equality in the Scenarios for the Future of Europe." *Journal of Common Market Studies* 58 (2): 292–308.

Bego, Ingrid. 2015. *Gender Equality Policy in the European Union: A Fast Track to Parity for the New Member States*. London: Palgrave Macmillan.

Berthet, Valentine, and Johanna Kantola. 2020. "Gender, Violence and Political Institutions: Struggles over Sexual Harassment in the European Parliament." *Social Politics* 28 (1): 143–167.

Brummer, Klaus. 2014. "Die Führungsstile von Präsidenten der Europäischen Kommission." *Zeitschrift für Politik* 61 (3): 327–345.

Bulmer, Simon J., and Jonathan Joseph. 2016. "European Integration in Crisis? Of Supranational Integration, Hegemonic Projects and Domestic Politics." *European Journal of International Relations* 22 (4): 725–748.

Cannadine, David. 2017. *Margaret Thatcher: Life and Legacy*. Oxford: Oxford University Press.

Cramme, Olaf. 2011. "In Search of Leadership." In *The Delphic Oracle on Europe*, eds. Loukas Tsoukalis, and Janis A. Emmanouilidis, 30–49. Oxford: Oxford University Press.

Cini, Michelle. 2008. "Political Leadership in the European Commission: The Santer and Prodi Commissions, 1995–2005." In *Leaderless Europe*, ed. Jack Hayward, 113–130. Oxford: Oxford University Press.

Dinan, Desmond. 2017. "Leadership in the European Council: An Assessment of Herman Van Rompuy's Presidency." *Journal of European Integration* 39 (2): 157–173.

Dingler, Sarah C., Corinna Kroeber, and Jessica Fortin-Rittberger. 2019. "Do Parliaments Underrepresent Women's Policy Preferences? Exploring Gender Equality in Policy Congruence in 21 European Democracies." *Journal of European Public Policy* 26 (2): 302–321.

Drake, Helen. 2000. *Jacques Delors: Perspectives on a European Leader*. London: Routledge.

Dyson, Stephen Benedict. 2009. "Cognitive Style and Foreign Policy: Margaret Thatcher's Black-and-White Thinking." *International Political Science Review* 30 (1): 33–48.

Endo, Ken. 1999. *The Presidency of the European Commission under Jacques Delors: The Politics of Shared Leadership*. Oxford: Macmillan Press.

Eurostat. 2020. "1 in 3 Parliament and Government Members Are Women." https:// ec.europa.eu/eurostat/web/products-eurostat-news/-/EDN-20200308-1 (accessed February 6, 2021).

Gill, Rebecca D., and Christian Jensen. 2020. "Where Are the Women? Legal Traditions and Descriptive Representation on the European Court of Justice." *Politics, Groups, and Identities* 8 (1): 122–142.

Guerrina, Roberta. 2005. *Mothering the Union: Gender Politics in the EU*. Manchester: Manchester University Press.

Guth, Jessica, and Sanna Elfving. 2018. *Gender and the Court of Justice of the European Union*. Abingdon, UK: Routledge.

Haastrup, Toni, Katharine A. M. Wright, and Roberta Guerrina. 2019. "Bringing Gender In? EU Foreign and Security Policy after Brexit." *Politics and Governance* 7 (3): 62–71.

Hartlapp, Miriam, Henriette Müller, and Ingeborg Tömmel. 2021. "Gender Equality and the European Commission." In *The Routledge Handbook of Gender and EU Politics*, eds. Gabriele Abels, Andrea Krizsán, Heather MacRae, and Anna van der Vleuten, 133–145. Abingdon, UK, and New York: Routledge.

Hayward, Jack, ed. 2008. *Leaderless Europe*. Oxford: Oxford University Press.

Helms, Ludger. 2016. "Democracy and Innovation: From Institutions to Agency and Leadership." *Democratization* 23 (3): 459–477.

Helms, Ludger. 2017. "Introduction: Leadership Questions in Transnational European Governance." *European Political Science* 16 (1): 1–13.

Helms, Ludger, and Femke A. W. J. van Esch. 2017. "Turning Structural Weakness into Personal Strength: Angela Merkel and the Politics of Leadership Capital in Germany." In *The Leadership Capital Index: A New Perspective on Political Leadership*, eds. Mark Bennister, Paul 't Hart, and Ben Worthy, 27–45. Oxford: Oxford University Press.

Helms, Ludger, Femke A. W. J. van Esch, and Beverly Crawford. 2019. "Merkel III: From Committed Pragmatist to 'Conviction Leader'?" *German Politics* 28 (3): 350–370.

Hoskyns, Catherine. 1996. *Integrating Gender: Women, Law and Politics in the European Union*. New York: Verso.

Jacquot, Sophie. 2015. *Transformations in EU Gender Equality: From Emergence to Dismantling*. London: Palgrave Macmillan.

Kantola, Johanna. 2010. *Gender and the European Union*. London: Palgrave Macmillan.

Kantola, Johanna, and Emanuela Lombardo, eds. 2017. *Gender and the Economic Crisis in Europe. Politics, Institutions and Intersectionality*. London: Palgrave Macmillan.

Kassim, Hussein, John Peterson, Michael W. Bauer, Sara Connolly, Renaud Dehousse, Liesbet Hooghe, and Andrew Thompson. 2013. *The European Commission of the Twenty-First Century*. Oxford: Oxford University Press.

King, Anthony. 2002. "The Outsider as Political Leader: The Case of Margaret Thatcher." *British Journal of Political Science* 32 (3): 435–454.

Koops, Joachim A., and Giulia Tercovich. 2020. "Shaping the European External Action Service and Its Post-Lisbon Crisis Management Structures: An Assessment of the EU High Representatives' Political Leadership." *European Security* 29 (3): 275–300.

MacRae, Heather. 2010. "The EU as a Gender Equal Polity: Myths and Realities." *Journal of Common Market Studies* 48 (1): 155–174.

MacRae, Heather, and Elaine Weiner, eds. 2017. *Towards Gendering Institutionalism. Equality in Europe*. London: Rowman & Littlefield International.

Müller, Henriette. 2016. "Between Potential, Performance and Prospect: Revisiting the Political Leadership of the EU Commission President." *Politics and Governance* 4 (2): 68–79.

Müller, Henriette. 2017. "Setting Europe's Agenda: The Presidents and Political Leadership." *Journal of European Integration* 39 (2): 129–142.

Müller, Henriette. 2020. *Political Leadership and the European Commission Presidency*. Oxford: Oxford University Press.

Müller, Henriette, and Femke A. W. J. van Esch. 2020a. "The Contested Nature of Political Leadership in the European Union: Conceptual and Methodological Cross-Fertilisation." *West European Politics* 43 (5): 1051–1071.

Müller, Henriette, and Femke A. W. J. van Esch. 2020b. "Collaborative Leadership in EMU Governance: A Matter of Cognitive Proximity." *West European Politics* 43 (5): 1117–1140.

Müller-Rommel, Ferdinand, and Michelangelo Vercesi. 2017. "Prime Ministerial Careers in the European Union: Does Gender Make a Difference?" *European Politics and Society* 18 (2): 245–262.

Mushaben, Joyce M. 2017. *Becoming Madam Chancellor: Angela Merkel and the Berlin Republic.* Cambridge: Cambridge University Press.

Nielsen, Bodil, and Sandrino Smeets. 2018. "The Role of the EU Institutions in Establishing the Banking Union: Collaborative Leadership in the EMU Reform Process." *Journal of European Public Policy* 25 (9): 1233–1256.

Olsson, Eva-Karin, and Kajsa Hammargård. 2016. "The Rhetoric of the President of the European Commission: Charismatic Leader or Neutral Mediator?" *Journal of European Public Policy* 23 (4): 550–570.

Parker, Charles F., Christer Karlsson, and Mattias Hjerpe. 2017. "Assessing the European Union's Climate Change Leadership: From Copenhagen to the Paris Agreement." *Journal of European Integration* 39 (2): 239–252.

Ross, George. 1995. *Jacques Delors and European Integration.* Cambridge: Polity Press.

Shreeves, Rosamund, Martina Prpic, and Eulalia Claros. 2019. *Women in Politics in the EU: State of Play.* Briefing, EPRS European Parliamentary Research Service, PE 635.548. Brussels: European Parliament.

Simms, Marian. 2008. "Are women leaders different? Margaret Thatcher and Helen Clark." In *Public Leadership: Perspectives and Practices*, eds., Paul 't Hart and John Uhr, 275–285, Canberra: ANU E Press.

Smeets, Sandrino, and Derek Beach. 2020. "Political and Instrumental Leadership in Major EU Reforms: The Role and Influence of the EU Institutions in Setting up the Fiscal Compact." *Journal of European Public Policy* 27 (1): 63–81.

Tallberg, Jonas. 2006. *Leadership and Negotiation in the European Union.* Cambridge: Cambridge University Press.

Tömmel, Ingeborg. 2013. "The Presidents of the European Commission: Transactional or Transforming Leaders?" *Journal of Common Market Studies* 51 (4): 789–805.

Tömmel, Ingeborg. 2017. "The Standing President of the European Council: Intergovernmental or Supranational Leadership?" *Journal of European Integration* 39 (2): 175–189.

Tömmel, Ingeborg. 2020. "Political Leadership in Times of Crisis: The Commission Presidency of Jean-Claude Juncker." *West European Politics* 43 (5): 1141–1162.

Tömmel, Ingeborg, and Amy Verdun. 2017. "Political Leadership in the European Union: An Introduction." *Journal of European Integration* 39 (2): 103–112.

Tortola, Pier Domenico, and Pamela Pansardi. 2018. "The Charismatic Leadership of the ECB Presidency: A Language-Based Analysis." *European Journal of Political Research* 58 (1): 96–116.

Van der Vleuten, Anna 2007. *The Price of Gender Equality: Member States and Governance in the European Union.* Burlington, VT: Ashgate.

Van Esch, Femke A. J. W. 2017. "The Paradoxes of Legitimate EU Leadership. An Analysis of the Multi-level Leadership of Angela Merkel and Alexis Tsipras during the Eurocrisis." *Journal of European Integration* 39 (2): 223–237.

Verdun, Amy. 2017. "Political Leadership of the European Central Bank." *Journal of European Integration* 39 (2): 207–221.

Walby, Sylvia. 2004. "The European Union and Gender Equality: Emergent Varieties of Gender Regime." *Social Politics* 11 (1): 4–29.

PART I
CONCEPTUAL APPROACHES TO WOMEN AND LEADERSHIP IN THE EU

1

Women and Leadership in the European Union

A Framework for Analysis

Henriette Müller and Ingeborg Tömmel

Despite a recent increase in female leaders in the European Union (EU), scholarship on their performance and agency in European decision-making and its organizational processes remains limited. Against this background, this chapter focuses on gender and leadership in the EU. First, it conceptualizes the leadership of women at the intersection of leadership and gender studies; second, by applying this concept to the Union, it studies the opportunities and challenges that female politicians, managers, and experts face on their paths to leadership positions and when exercising leadership in EU institutions.

Concerning the first theme, the chapter questions whether women face structural hurdles in ascending to leadership positions; whether women practice different leadership styles than men; and, if so, when and why this might be the case. Regarding the second theme, the chapter examines the specific opportunities for and constraints on women's ascent to different leadership positions within the EU system and, having reached such positions, whether and in what ways women actually exercise leadership.

In doing so, this chapter provides a framework for the analysis of leadership that is based, on the one hand, on the distinction between *positional* and *behavioral* leadership and, on the other, that between *political, administrative*, and *expert* leadership in EU offices and functions. Integrating theoretical and empirical insights at the intersection of contemporary EU studies, leadership studies, and gender studies allows us to comprehensively study women's leadership and empowerment in European institutions.

Henriette Müller and Ingeborg Tömmel, *Women and Leadership in the European Union: A Framework for Analysis.*
In: *Women and Leadership in the European Union.* Edited by Henriette Müller and Ingeborg Tömmel,
Oxford University Press. © Oxford University Press (2022). DOI: 10.1093/oso/9780192896216.003.0002

1.1   Women and Leadership: Conceptual Approaches

The study of women's leadership has been dominated by two debates: first, over the hurdles that women encounter in their access to and representation in positions of power and authority, and second, over the question of whether women lead differently from men (Eagly and Carli 2007). The first debate refers to *positional* leadership, while the second addresses *behavioral* leadership (see Figure 1.1). Considering leadership as a positional attribute, the definition of a leader is simple and straightforward: "a person who exercises authority over other people" (Eagly and Carli 2007: 8). This definition encompasses both formal and informal positions within groups, organizations, and institutions (Rhode and Kellerman 2007: 1). Focus on leadership as behavior or performance, however, and the concept becomes more complex and multifaceted.

While definitions of behavioral leadership in modern societies and democratic political systems vary widely, scholars agree on three constitutive characteristics. First, leadership is seen as a reciprocal process between leaders and their followers (Burns [1978] 2010; Elgie 2015). Second, this process is characterized by striving for goals that both leaders and followers embrace (Burns [1978] 2010). Third, instead of using coercion, leaders mainly achieve these goals through influence, mobilization, and persuasion (Blondel 1987; Burns [1978] 2010; Cronin and Genovese 2012).

Power and authority do indeed play central roles in leadership, yet they are not exercised unidirectionally but rather embedded into the reciprocal relationship between leaders and followers (Müller 2020; Kellerman 1984). Individuals, groups, or institutions may act as leaders, and their followers may vary from the inner circle of the leader(s) or the active participants in decision-making to the leader's constituency or the general public (Tömmel 2020). The performance of leaders may vary from transactional to transforming leadership (Tömmel 2013; Burns [1978] 2010). The former refers to the "basic, daily stuff of politics, the pursuit of change in measured and often reluctant doses"; the latter involves "basic alterations in entire systems" and "radical change in outward form or inner character" (Burns 2003: 24–25). This in turn implies that "leaders and followers raise one another to higher levels of motivation and morality" (Burns [1978] 2010: 83).

The extent to which leadership can be exercised depends not only on individual capacities but also on the institutional as well as situational opportunities of and constraints on a given office (Blondel 1987; Elgie 1995). The interplay between the *institutional setting*, the *situational factors*, and the *personal qualities* of the incumbent is thus decisive for the exercise of leadership (for the EU, see Endo 1999; Müller 2020; Nugent 2001; Tömmel 2013). In this sense, successful leadership, in contrast to the mere holding of an office, depends on a leader who, faced with a certain environment of institutional and situational resources and constraints, "attempts and succeeds to go *beyond* them, expanding and creating

Type of Leadership	Behavioral Leadership	
Positional Leadership	+	–
+	++ (Position of authority; exercise of leadership)	+– (Position of authority; no exercise of leadership)
–	–+ (No formal position of authority; exercise of leadership)	–– (no formal position of authority; no exercise of leadership)

Fig. 1.1 Relationship between positional and behavioral leadership (own model)

resources and opportunities," thereby motivating followers to embrace and achieve mutually desired goals (Endo 1999: 26; emphasis in original; see also Figure 1.1).

A gender perspective on this schema reveals variations in both positional and behavioral leadership (Ridgeway 2001: 641). Eagly and Carli have argued that "men have predominated in leadership roles for so long" that leadership positions and performance, as well as stereotypes thereof, are considered to be outright masculine (2007: 84; see also Rhode and Kellerman 2007: 6). As fundamental aspects of human identity, gender and sex are central signifiers in the creation of stereotypes at both the conscious and unconscious levels (Rhode 2003: 7–8; Diehl and Dzubinski 2017: 275). Gender hierarchies tend to ascribe women caring, domestic roles, while associating men with vocational roles, privileging the latter (Ridgeway 2001: 637). As a result, "[p]rejudice against women leaders [usually] flows from a mismatch between people's mental associations about women and leaders" (Eagly and Carli 2007: 96).

The conscious and unconscious societal role associations of women and men have nurtured double standards and double binds regarding women and leadership. Overall, men are still more readily accepted as leaders, and often "what is [considered] assertive in a man can appear abrasive in a woman, and female leaders risk appearing too feminine or not feminine enough" (Rhode and Kellerman 2007: 7). In the pursuit and exercise of leadership positions, women thus face challenges that men usually do not.

For example, a meta-analysis by Eagly et al. showed that women are consistently devalued in their leadership performance relative to their male counterparts "if they intrude on traditionally male domains by adopting male-stereotypic leadership styles, or by occupying male-dominated leadership positions" (1992: 18; see also Eagly and Karau 2002). In addition, women often internalize these devaluations and gender stereotypes, creating self-imposed psychological barriers to attaining leadership positions (Rhode and Kellerman 2007: 8; Diehl and Dzubinski 2017: 281). This means that women tend to engage less in assertive behavior, self-promotion, or network building and underevaluate their own performance (Rhode 2017: 10; see also Maranto et al. 2019).

Finally, the continued underrepresentation of women contributes to the continuation of gender biases, since the "few" are often exposed to higher levels of scrutiny (Diehl and Dzubinski 2017: 275). As stereotypes and unconscious bias mostly operate at a non-overt level, their impact is often hard to assess.

Women's Leadership as a Positional Concept

Societal barriers to women's attainment of leadership positions have often been the focus of gender studies analyses, usually examined through metaphors such as "the concrete wall," "the glass ceiling," and more recently "the labyrinth" (Eagly and Carli 2007: 2). The "concrete wall" represents the fact that in the early phases of state systems in Europe, women were legally excluded from voting and obtaining political or other high offices. The lack of political equality encompassed all societal domains, inhibiting women's educational, economic, and social self-determination and representation. The cultural assumption that women's rightful realm was the home and household meant that they were denied prestigious careers and positions of leadership across almost every social domain. This method of exclusion changed only slowly.

In the postwar period and particularly since the 1970s, the gradual shift away from visible barriers involved both the continuation and erection of new, invisible ones (Eagly and Carli 2007: 4). This qualitative change in societal barriers to women's career progress is reflected by the "glass ceiling" metaphor, which aims to capture the persistent, though less visible influence of gender stereotypes and role expectations (Ridgeway 2001: 652; Diehl and Dzubinski 2017: 272). The result is that women have considerably more access to lower-level leadership positions, while they often remain excluded from most positions in the higher echelons of politics, the economy, and society more broadly (Eagly and Carli 2007: 5).

Since the turn of the twenty-first century, leadership opportunities for women have further increased. Leadership equality, however, remains elusive. "The labyrinth metaphor symbolizes the complexity of the causes of women's current situation as leaders" (Eagly and Carli 2007: 8). Persistent gender assumptions, unconscious and conscious bias against women in leadership positions, and stereotypes continue to play important roles in the context of women's positional leadership. In the political realm, this social bias is reflected in the fact that women often obtain "softer socio-cultural ministerial positions rather than [ones in] the harder and politically more prestigious areas such as economic planning, national security and foreign affairs" (Kantola 2010: 69). Women are also often confronted with leading in vulnerable or uncertain situations, navigating so-called "glass cliff" leadership positions (Elliott and Stead 2008: 162). Male-dominated political and economic cultures and networks, women's individual perceptions of their own abilities, unequal access to key resources and political networks, unequal family responsibilities, the absence of a variety of female role models, as well as intersectional barriers are among the many impediments that continue to constrain women's access to and perseverance in a diverse range of leadership positions (Rhode 2017: 2; Rhode 2003: 7; Diehl and Dzubinski 2017: 273ff.).

In sum, while women have indeed obtained more leadership positions in recent decades, they have frequently been in precarious, "glass cliff" situations. The context of women's positional leadership continues to be a complex environment of often invisible barriers and circumstances that contribute to women's prolonged underrepresentation and diversity in leadership positions across the various arenas of the economy, politics, and society.

Women's Leadership as a Behavioral Concept

"It is a common belief that women lead in a more collaborative and democratic manner than men" (Eagly and Carli 2007: 119). This socially constructed notion is another product of gender biases. Overall, no statistically relevant principal differences between male and female leadership styles have been found, especially in experimental studies, that would exceed the differences between two women leaders (Eagly and Carli 2007: 121; Carless 1998: 898). Referring back to positional leadership, the perceptions of differences in performance based on social constructions about gender thus also impact women's pathways to power and often determine the positions they are able to obtain. For example, "gender norms tend to steer male leaders toward a task-oriented style, and female leaders toward an interpersonally oriented style," thus creating "implicit performance expectations" (Eagly and Carli 2007: 124; see also Ridgeway 2001: 652; Eagly and Johannesen-Schmidt 2001: 789).

How do gender stereotypes impact leadership performance? Women are stereotypically considered communal, selfless, and caring, whereas leadership is often associated with being agentic, ambitious, and forceful. "Leadership is ordinarily conflated with men and masculinity," coinciding with notions of dominance, authority, and ambition (Eagly and Carli 2007: 90; Ridgeway 2011: 3, ch. 2; Setzler 2019: 716). However, if women emphasize these characteristics, they are often penalized and evaluated negatively—by both men and women—for being *too* assertive (Rhode 2017: 11; Ridgeway 2001: 649, 2011: 4, 24 ch. 2; Eagly and Johannsen-Schmidt 2001: 790). In other words, women are faced with a double bind, in which they have to fit masculine ideals of leadership while upholding traditional preconceptions of femininity (Rhode 2017: 41).

Although in general no significant gender-based performance differences between male and female leaders have been found, some studies have argued that "female leaders are more participatory, democratic, and interpersonally sensitive than male leaders" (Rhode 2017: 5). This means, for example, that "women tend to use a transformational style because it relies on skills associated with women, and because more autocratic approaches are viewed as less attractive in women than in men" (Rhode 2017: 5; see also Helms 2010: 360; Eagly and Carli 2007: 5). However, "success in leadership generally require[s] a combination of traditionally masculine and feminine traits, including vision, ethics, interpersonal skills, technical competence, and personal capabilities such as self-awareness and self-control" (Rhode 2017: 6; see also Adler 1997). In fact, the core characteristics of the prototypical charismatic leader incorporate both nominally masculine and feminine traits, linking vision and collective goals (Antonakis et al. 2016: 295).

Toward the end of the twentieth century, a trend of overemphasizing women's leadership capabilities—as being superior to those of men—gained traction (Pittinsky et al. 2007). Under the rubric of a "great women theory of leadership," scholars characterized female leaders as "sincere, nurturing, relational, communal, collaborative," as Pittinsky et al. critically observed (2007: 94). Such stereotypes of female leadership suggest that women might be by gender the better leaders, while individual leadership performances, specific leadership contexts, and particular leadership functions appear to hardly play a role. It is important to note, as well, that there is little evidence of a specific "female leadership style"; rather, positive stereotypes reproduce gender demarcations (Pittinsky et al. 2007: 98; see also Elliott and Stead 2008: 163; Helms 2010: 353).

As pointed out by Pittinsky et al., the aim here is not to dismiss women's specific contributions to leadership; yet "women are not a monolithic group, possessing a set of specific traits and styles exclusive to women that qualify them as better leaders" (2007: 99; see also Adler 1997). Overcoming gendered leadership polarization allows for all leaders a greater scope of styles and expectations. Since the similarities between the genders outweigh the differences, leadership performance and its effectiveness need to be considered from a functional point of view (Pittinsky et al. 2007: 115): What is it that leadership needs to accomplish? What are the functions of a specific office, how can they be exercised, and how are they in fact exercised by a given officeholder? Conclusively, from this perspective, the term "female leadership" is more a social construction than a behavioral reality.

To sum up, this section has demonstrated that women's leadership can be conceptualized through two complementary analytical approaches—one focused on positional leadership, the other on behavioral leadership. The former addresses the multiplicity of socially intersecting barriers both visible and invisible that inhibit women's access to and diversity in leadership positions. The latter focuses on the exercise of leadership, arguing that women's performances do not differ from those of men per se; yet social and role expectations based on assumptions and stereotypes about gender place women leaders in a double bind that can lead in certain circumstances to differing leadership performances and evaluations thereof—often negatively impacting women's exercise of leadership.

1.2 Women's Leadership in the European Union

Despite the manifold hurdles women face on their career paths, they increasingly access leadership positions in the EU and proactively perform the functions of their offices. Yet little is known about these women: how they have accessed their positions, how they have performed their respective functions, what leadership style(s) they have practiced, and whether they have achieved significant successes. This section conceptualizes the contextual factors that affect female (under)representation in EU institutions and provides a preliminary empirical overview of the behavior and performance of selected women leaders in European affairs. In other words, it explores both women's positional and behavioral leadership in the EU.

Women's Positional Leadership—Why Underrepresentation?

EU institutions provide three types of leadership positions with distinctive career paths: political, administrative, and expert leadership offices. Of course, leaders in administrative and expert offices may also act politically; this is not their primary role, however, but either a side effect of their functions or a deliberate effort to transcend them (Burns [1978] 2010; Blondel 1987).

Political offices—e.g., commissioner, member of the Council or European Council, or Member of the European Parliament (MEP)—are generally attained via political party careers and largely determined at member-state level. By contrast, administrative offices—e.g., director general in the Commission or a high-level position in the Council or the European Parliament's (EP) secretariat—are generally accessed via career paths within the EU civil services. Expert leadership positions—e.g., president of the European Central Bank (ECB) or the Court of Justice of the European Union (CJEU)—involve mixed career paths, but are in any event based on prior expertise and experience in offices of the respective issue areas. Women aspiring to high-level EU offices thus face diverse institutional hurdles.

Regarding *political leadership* positions in the EU, political parties and particularly the governing parties in the member states decide on the delegation of candidates. The nomination of women to such positions thus largely depends on the varying gender regimes and party politics in the member states. Member states' gender regimes display enormous differences, ranging from systems that have almost reached gender equality to ones still characterized by male domination.

Party politics differ as well, with parties of the center and left in general being more attentive to gender-equality policies in their own ranks, while conservative and right-wing parties often ignore such policies.

Career routes to *administrative leadership* positions in the EU have resulted in mainly male high-level administrators. Yet since the late 1980s, the Commission (as well as the other EU institutions) initiated a series of action programs aimed at increasing female representation at the senior staff level (A grade) and also in leadership positions (Hoskyns 1996; Hartlapp et al. 2021).

Expert leadership positions to a large extent depend on nominees' earlier careers in related policy or issue areas, often in jobs outside the Union. Nominations for such positions in the EU are made by national governments, either individually, for example, when appointing representatives to the board of governors of the ECB or judges to the CJEU, or collectively through the European Council, as is the case with the presidents of the ECB. The presidents of the CJEU are elected by the judges.

These different career paths and the specific hurdles each entail for women have resulted in varied patterns of female representation in high-level functions across the EU. The EP was the first body to feature a significant percentage of female members, while the Commission started to increase women's representation much later, not least because of persistent pressure from the EP. Only quite recently have the Council secretariat and other EU institutions followed the trend of bringing women into their higher ranks.

For election to the EP, national political parties nominate candidates, and the elections are held separately in each member state for its allocated seats. The national delegations range in size from 96 seats (Germany) to just six (Malta, Luxembourg) (Art. 14(2) TEU). This suggests that the leading political parties of large member states have the greatest influence on the composition of the EP and, hence, the gender balance within it. Regionally, the Scandinavian countries usually send the highest share of women to the EP, while the Eastern European states often send the lowest.[1] Furthermore, gender policy tends to vary across the left–right dimension—with liberal and left parties sending higher percentages of females to the EP, while conservative and especially right-wing parties clearly privilege men (Kantola 2010: 65; Kantola and Rolandsen Agustín 2019; Fortin-Rittberger and Rittberger 2015: 13–14).

Since 1995, the EP has had a substantially higher percentage of women in its ranks than most of the member states' national legislatures (European Parliament 2018). This points to specific factors favoring female representation in the Parliament. For a long time, the EP was considered to play a mainly advisory role and, hence, to be of minor significance (Kantola 2010: 61). This perception, irrespective

---

[1] http://www.europarl.europa.eu/news/en/headlines/society/20190226STO28804/women-in-the-european-parliament-infographics (accessed November 17, 2019).

of the fact that the EP's authority was significantly expanded with every treaty amendment since the Single European Act (in force since 1987), lasted more or less until the adoption of the Lisbon Treaty (in force since 2009), which elevated the EP to a full-fledged legislature alongside the Council. Ambitious politicians thus long ranked a seat in the EP as less beneficial to a path to higher office than similar functions at national level; this meant women had a greater chance to access the EP (Kantola 2010: 61). The glass ceiling that women normally encounter in attempting to access legislative positions turned out to be more permeable in the case of the EP. Yet within the EP, women again encounter the usual barriers that inhibit their access to and diversity in leadership positions. They are under-represented in such positions as committee chair, president of party group, and vice president of the European legislature. Most notably, only twice to date have women accessed the office of EP president (see the Appendix to this volume).

While the nomination of Commission members overall displays similarities with the EP, significant variations are also at play. National governments, and thus the ruling parties, are entitled to nominate the commissioners. As with the EP, individual politicians long considered Commission seats to be of only minor benefit to their careers and reputations. This, however, did not result in increased access for women. On the contrary, senior and post-career politicians were often rewarded with commissioner posts (MacMullen 2000: 35), effectively excluding women, as the number of post-career female candidates has long been low in most member states.

It was only with the pressure exercised by the EP in 1995 that female commissioners came into office in substantial numbers (Hartlapp et al. 2021). The Maastricht Treaty (in force in 1993) for the first time gave the EP a vote of consent on the Commission as a whole (Art. 17(7) TEU). The EP used this new power by calling on the member states to ensure "a balanced distribution of Commissioner posts between men and women"—specifically, that at least 25% of the commissioners be women (European Parliament 1994). The pressure worked as intended; five member states nominated a female candidate. Since then, the number of women commissioners has steadily increased, reaching 13 in the current College of 27 (see the Appendix to this volume).

The *president of the European Commission* used to be nominated by the heads of state or government in the European Council by unanimous vote. Until recently, this resulted without exception in the nomination of men. Since 1995, the nominees have all been former prime ministers and, as such, members of the European Council. The Lisbon Treaty fundamentally changed the nomination procedure, giving the EP the right to elect the Commission president while the European Council "shall propose to the European Parliament a candidate" (Art. 17(7) TEU). The EP interpreted this rule in its own favor by introducing the so-called *Spitzenkandidaten* procedure (Christiansen 2016). This procedure envisages that the party groups, ahead of elections to the EP, will nominate lead candidates for the Commission presidency; the candidate of the party group winning the largest percentage of votes—assuming he or she can win the support of an absolute majority in the assembly—is elected president. The procedure worked in 2014, as the lead candidate was again a former prime minister—Jean-Claude Juncker of Luxembourg—and the two biggest party groups quickly reached an agreement to elect him (Cloos 2019).

Following the 2019 European elections, however, none of the top party-group candidates was able to attract a majority in Parliament. This gave the European Council the opportunity to turn the procedure back to its advantage, by nominating its own candidate: Ursula von der Leyen. The choice of a woman was clearly motivated by the fact that the European Council's candidate had to be approved by an absolute majority in the EP. Since the Parliament had long pushed for more women in high-level positions, a positive vote for a female candidate appeared more likely. Specific circumstances and strategic considerations thus brought the first woman into the office of Commission president.

The Commission president decides on the allocation of portfolios to the individual commissioners, though often under strong pressure from national governments, which strive to get an important portfolio for "their" man or woman in Brussels. In the past, female commissioners were mostly charged with "soft" portfolios, such as education, social policy, or environmental policy. However, this too has changed recently. Portfolios considered among the most important, such as competition and trade, have increasingly been held by women, often from small, Northern member states (e.g., Neelie Kroes [2004–2010], Margrethe Vestager [2014–present], Cecilia Malmström [2014–2019]). Furthermore, during the last decade, the commissioners for foreign affairs, who since the Lisbon Treaty serve at the same time as High Representatives of the Union for Foreign Affairs and Security Policy, have been women (Catherine Ashton [2009–2014], Federica Mogherini [2014–2019]). The European Council decides on these positions (Art. 18(1) TEU), and it was due largely to pressure from the EP that the heads of state and government have nominated women for this office.

High-level administrative positions within the Commission are nominated internally, either by the Commission president (as with the secretary general) or the individual commissioners (as with the directors general) (Bauer and Ege 2012: 413). This has resulted in increased representation of women in the higher echelons of the Commission bureaucracy. Apart from Catherine Day (2005–2015), who served as secretary general of the Commission, the percentage of female directors general has steadily increased, reaching almost 42% under Commission President Juncker. This sends a clear signal that the Commission now seriously strives for gender balance in its own ranks (Hartlapp et al. 2021; see also the Appendix to this volume).

Obviously, the Council of the EU and the European Council are the institutions where women have faced the greatest difficulty in gaining access to power, as positions in these bodies depend completely on the politics of the member states and their governing parties (Kantola 2010: 72; see also the Appendix to this volume). With conservative parties currently heading the majority of governments across Europe, male incumbents tend to dominate the ministerial offices. The few female heads of state or government past and present, who have mostly been members of conservative parties, often obtained their positions in "glass cliff" situations, e.g., Angela Merkel during the crisis of the CDU (1999–2000) and Theresa May in the aftermath of the Brexit referendum (2016). At the ministerial level, liberal or left-wing parties have played a major role in broadening female access to high office. And again, there is a wide range in the gender balance in governmental offices between the member states, with the Scandinavian countries featuring the highest levels of female representation. Finally, as far as women are represented in the Council of Ministers, they mostly head ministries seen as having minor significance (Kantola 2010: 72).

Access to most expert high-level positions in the EU, like those with the CJEU or the ECB, likewise depends on nominations by the heads of state or government, based heavily on nominees' earlier career paths. Women are clearly disadvantaged in this respect by their underrepresentation in the relevant sectors, particularly banking and financial affairs. Nevertheless, the European Council recently nominated Christine Lagarde as president of the ECB. Although she is not an economist by training, she has held many leadership positions in the financial realm, such as minister of finance in France and president of the International Monetary Fund (IMF). In the CJEU, meanwhile, a steady increase in female judges and advocates general has brought their share to about 18% (Guth and Elfving 2018: 41; see also the Appendix to this volume).

In sum, the positional leadership of women in the EU has significantly improved in recent years, though a fair gender balance and diversity in high-level positions have not yet been reached. Huge differences persist between the member states, with a few front runners compensating to an extent for the low representation of females among the many laggards. The factors hindering the access of women to high-level offices in the EU are manifold: the persistence of traditional gender regimes in the member states; the lack of consistent gender policies within political parties; the customarily long career pathways to high-ranking administrative and expert posts, especially in economic and financial affairs; and the still prevalent view that women are less suited than men to performing leadership functions.

For all that, the EU has not only posed obstacles to women who aspire to leadership; it has also offered opportunities, rooted in specific circumstances. First, due to the historically less intense competition for seats in the EP, women entered it in significant numbers well before they did the legislatures of most of the member states. Second, this resulted, together with the generally more open, cosmopolitan attitude of a majority of EP members, in transforming the assembly into a strong advocate of fair gender balance in high-level EU offices. This induced, third, the Commission to implement a gender-balance policy in its own ranks and the European Council to more often nominate women for high-level positions. Finally, fourth, it seems that "glass cliff" situations occur more often in the EU, as it is an evolving polity, characterized by deep divergences among national governments, political parties, and increasingly also the European citizenry. Whether these specific circumstances are short-lived windows of opportunity or starting points for enduring structural transformations remains to be seen.

Women's Behavioral Leadership—Exploring Performances

Detailed studies on women's behavioral leadership in EU high-level positions are largely lacking. This section therefore explores a few examples of women's performances in the core institutions of the EU, highlighting their behavior, leadership style, and achievements. It raises questions about what the functions of specific offices are, how they can be exercised, and how in fact they are exercised by various officeholders.

The *functions* of a political leadership position in the Commission entail agenda-setting and initiating policies that are relevant to European integration or to the citizens of the EU (Müller 2020). Mobilizing followers for the corresponding proposals and surveying due implementation of EU policies in the member states are relevant functions as well (Tömmel 2020). By contrast, ministers or heads of state or government as members of the Council or the European Council are expected to act in the interest of the Union as a whole, while also championing their national interests. Particularly when holding the presidency of the Council, they are expected to broker compromises among the member states. Holding an administrative leadership position in EU institutions entails providing administrative–managerial support to those in political positions as they duly perform their functions. Finally, the functions of experts in leadership positions are more narrowly defined by the objectives of their respective institutions, as laid down in the EU treaties (see, for the CJEU Arts. 251–281 TFEU; for the ECB Arts. 282–284 TFEU).

The successful *exercise of these functions* depends to a large extent on an office's particular institutional and situational resources and constraints, and how the officeholder deals with the strategic choices at hand (Tömmel 2013; Müller 2020). As indicated above, successful leadership means creating resources and opportunities within a certain institutional–situational environment to achieve mutually desired goals (Endo 1999: 26). While the few women who gained access to Commission leadership positions in the past were mostly allocated "soft" portfolios, the case of Viviane Reding shows that women in such situations can nonetheless excel as leaders.

Reding served in the Commission for three legislatures (1999–2014), starting with a portfolio where the EU has hardly any competences. In her second and third terms, she held offices with greater prominence. Throughout her entire time in the Commission, regardless of portfolio, Reding succeeded in setting up important policy initiatives, despite strong opposition from national governments and, at times, the business community. Her achievements included implementing the Jean Monnet and Erasmus Mundus Programmes, the abolishment of all roaming charges for mobile telephones across the Union (Cini and Šuplata 2017), the initiation of a gender equality policy beyond the workplace, and fundamental reform of data protection. Overall, Reding, even when holding relatively "soft" portfolios, provided strong leadership.

Within the Commission administration, women successfully exercise leadership in high-level offices. Several female directors general have recently held influential portfolios and performed extremely well, for example, Nadia Calviño, who was director general for budget before she became a minister in the Spanish government in 2018. The most prominent case of women's successful leadership in the Commission administration is that of Catherine Day, who served for ten years as secretary general, the body's highest administrative position.

Colleagues within the Commission and outsiders alike describe Day as an extremely smart and competent person. She improved the coordinative and policy functions of the Secretariat General, framed to a significant extent the Commission agenda, mediated opposing views in the Commission, while also fostering consensus-building across the core EU institutions.

To date, women have rarely had the opportunity to exercise political leadership in the European Council. Yet Angela Merkel, particularly when holding the body's presidency (in 2007 and again in 2020), displayed an outstanding capacity for brokering compromises among the member states. In 2007, she put the renegotiation of the Constitutional Treaty—rejected in 2005 by referenda in France and the Netherlands—on the agenda. After intense consultations and negotiations with the heads of state and government, she forged a consensus on the future EU treaties, preserving most of the regulations envisioned in the Constitutional Treaty. The most contested aspects of the reform had thus already been settled before the intergovernmental conference under Portuguese presidency started its work, resulting in the adoption of the Lisbon Treaty. In 2020, Poland and Hungary threatened to veto the Multiannual Financial Framework 2021–2027 and the proposed European Rescue Fund in the event that the Council adopted a regulation making EU funding to the member states conditional on respect for the rule of law. In response to this stalemate, Merkel succeeded in reaching a deal with the two governments, promising them only minor concessions, so that both the MFF with its Rescue Fund and the regulation concerning respect for the rule of law could smoothly be adopted.

Yet in other situations, Merkel was not able to provide leadership in the European Council, let alone to broker compromises, in spite of her power position as German chancellor. Particularly at the beginning of the financial and sovereign debt crisis (2010), national interests and the interest of the Union as a whole fell far apart. In this situation, she mainly advocated German national interests, constraining her capacity to act as a credible broker in European affairs (Van Esch 2017).

Do women practice different leadership styles than men? As yet, there is hardly any indication, let alone confirmation of such differences in the context of the EU. Only one study, based on interviews with Commission officials, claims that the increasing number of women in high-level managerial positions has resulted in a change in leadership style (Ban 2013: 190–191). According to these findings, women in the Commission administration have introduced a more cooperative, less "gladiatorial" mode. It is questionable, though, whether this change came about as a consequence of the increasing inflow of women into managerial functions or a broader trend toward more cooperative forms of leadership, as highlighted in many studies, independent of a specific gender perspective (Helms 2017; Müller and Van Esch 2020; Smeets and Beach 2020). The EU system, with its highly fragmented institutional setting, manifold checks and balances, and strong veto powers, appears to favor and even reward a cooperative and consensual leadership style among both men and women. This might offer women an additional window of opportunity to successfully perform as leaders in this realm.

In sum, the exploration of women's behavioral leadership in the EU has shown that there are more and more cases of strong and successful leadership in both political and administrative or managerial functions. Women leaders have provided proactive leadership in agenda-setting, decision-making, brokering compromises, and policy implementation; behaviorally, their leadership has been characterized by both collaboration and consensus-building, but also authority and ambition.

1.3 Conclusion

Although the study of leadership and agency has recently gained traction in EU studies, the role of women, their leadership performance, and impact are still highly under-researched. Against this background, this chapter first conceptualized leadership of women at the intersection of leadership and gender studies, defining both a positional and a behavioral perspective. Gender equality in positional leadership is not simply a matter of political will, but rather involves a multitude of societal factors, such as the persistence of gender roles, conscious and unconscious biases against women in leadership positions, male-dominated political and economic cultures and networks, women's individual perceptions of their own abilities, unequal access to key resources, unequal family responsibilities, diversity and intersectional barriers, and the dearth of female role models.

Women face these pervasive gender-based obstacles not only in accessing leadership positions but also—and even more so—in their exercise and performance of leadership. However, as similarities outweigh the differences in men's and women's exercise of leadership and evidence for "female leadership" as such has not been found, we have demonstrated that leadership needs to be analyzed from a functional rather than a gender-based point of view. Central questions that research on EU leadership thus needs to address include: What is it that leadership needs to accomplish? What are the functions of a specific office, how can they be exercised, and how in fact are they exercised by various officeholders?

Second, we studied the specific opportunities for and constraints on women's access to leadership positions in the EU as well as selected examples of women's performance as leaders across European institutions. The analysis illustrated that women increasingly access leadership positions and proactively perform the functions of their offices. Furthermore, it showed that rather than focusing only on the barriers to leadership, we need to turn our attention to why and under what conditions women become leaders within the EU and how they perform the functions of their offices.

In sum, the analysis of women's positional and behavioral leadership in the EU reveals that the European polity, even though a relative latecomer to gender equality, also provides windows of opportunity for women on their pathways to power and in exercising leadership in their respective functions. In this context, the following factors are particularly relevant. First, the complex institutional structure, where no individual institution or actor dominates, favors, or even rewards a more collaborative and consensual leadership style; second, the relative distance of the Commission, as well as the ECB and the CJEU, from party politics favors both nominations and performances based on expertise; third, the EP, being independent from a government at European level and holding a critical mass of female MEPs, can successfully campaign for more women in leadership positions. We do not assume that these features of the EU particularly favor women in accessing leadership positions and successfully performing in such positions, yet they seem to open windows of opportunity for women in both positional and behavioral leadership. The chapters of this volume provide ample and detailed evidence for this conclusion.

References

Adler, Nancy J. 1997. "Global Leadership: Women Leaders." *MIR: Management International Review* 37 (1): 171–196.

Antonakis, John, Nicolas Bastardoz, Philippe Jacquart, and Boas Shamir. 2016. "Charisma: An Ill-Defined and Ill-Measured Gift." *Annual Review of Organizational Psychology and Organizational Behavior* 3: 293–319.

Ban, Carolyn. 2013. *Management and Culture in an Enlarged Commission*. London: Palgrave Macmillan.

Bauer, Michael W., and Jörn Ege. 2012. "Politicization within the European Commission's Bureaucracy." *International Review of Administrative Sciences* 78 (3): 403–424.

Blondel, Jean. 1987. *Political Leadership: Towards a General Analysis*. London: Sage.

Burns, James MacGregor. [1978] 2010. *Leadership*. New York: HarperCollins.

Burns, James MacGregor. 2003. *Transforming Leadership: A New Pursuit of Happiness*. New York: Atlantic Monthly Press.

Carless, Sally A. 1998. "Gender Differences in Transformational Leadership: An Examination of Superior, Leader, and Subordinate Perspectives." *Sex Roles* 39 (11/12): 887–902.

Christiansen, Thomas. 2016. "After the Spitzenkandidaten: Fundamental Change in the EU's Political System?" *West European Politics* 39 (5): 992–1010.

Cini, Michelle, and Marián Šuplata. 2017. "Policy Leadership in the European Commission: The Regulation of EU Mobile Roaming Charges." *Journal of European Integration* 39 (2): 143–156.

Cloos, Jim. 2019. "Spitzenkandidaten: A Debate about Power and about the Future Development of the EU." *European Policy Brief* (Egmont Royal Institute for International Relations), no. 56.

Cronin, Thomas E., and Michael A. Genovese. 2012. *Leadership Matters: Unleashing the Power of Paradox*. Boulder, CO: Paradigm Publishers.

Diehl, Amy B., and Leanne Dzubinski. 2017. "An Overview of Gender-Based Leadership Barriers." In *Handbook of Research on Gender and Leadership*, ed. Susan R. Madsen, 271–286. Cheltenham, UK: Edward Elgar Publishing.

Eagly, Alice H., and Linda L. Carli. 2007. *Through the Labyrinth: The Truth about How Women Become Leaders*. Cambridge, MA: Harvard Business School Press.

Eagly, Alice H., and Mary C. Johannesen-Schmidt. 2001. "The Leadership Styles of Women and Men." *Journal of Social Issues* 57 (4): 781–797.

Eagly, Alice H., and Steven J. Karau. 2002. "Role Congruity Theory of Prejudice toward Female Leaders." *Psychological Review* 109 (3): 573–598.

Eagly, Alice H., Mona G. Makhijani, and Bruce G. Klonsky. 1992. "Gender and the Evaluation of Leaders: A Meta-analysis." *Psychological Bulletin* 111 (1): 3–22.

Elgie, Robert. 1995. *Political Leadership in Liberal Democracies*. New York: Palgrave Macmillan.

Elgie, Robert. 2015. *Studying Political Leadership. Foundations and Contending Accounts*. Basingstoke, UK: Palgrave Macmillan.

Elliott, Carole, and Valerie Stead. 2008. "Learning from Leading Women's Experience: Towards a Sociological Understanding." *Leadership* 4 (2): 159–180.

Endo, Ken. 1999. *The Presidency of the European Commission under Jacques Delors: The Politics of Shared Leadership*. Oxford: Macmillan Press.

European Parliament. 1994. *Report of the Committee on Women's Rights on Women in the Decision-Making Process; Rapporteur: Mrs. Jessica Larive. PE 205.666/fin.* Luxembourg: Office for Official Publications of the European Communities, January 27.

European Parliament. 2018. *Women in the European Parliament.* Brussels: European Parliament. https://www.europarl.europa.eu/RegData/publications/2018/0001/P8_PUB%282018%290001_EN.pdf (accessed November 17, 2019).

Fortin-Rittberger, Jessica, and Berthold Rittberger 2015. "Nominating Women for Europe: Exploring the Role of Political Parties' Recruitment Procedures for European Parliament Elections." *European Journal of Political Research* 54 (4): 767–786.

Guth, Jessica, and Sanna Elfving. 2018. *Gender and the Court of Justice of the European Union.* London: Routledge.

Hartlapp, Miriam, Henriette Müller, and Ingeborg Tömmel. 2021. "Gender Equality and the European Commission." In *The Routledge Handbook of Gender and EU Politics*, eds. Gabriele Abels, Andrea Krizsán, Heather MacRae, and Anna van der Vleuten. Abingdon, UK, and New York: Routledge.

Helms, Ludger. 2010. "Political Leadership und die 'Gender Challenge': Eine explorative Kritik." *Österreichische Zeitschrift für Politikwissenschaft* 39 (3): 351–366.

Helms, Ludger. 2017. "Introduction: Leadership Questions in Transnational European Governance." *European Political Science* 16 (1): 1–13.

Hoskyns, Catherine. 1996. *Integrating Gender: Women, Law and Politics in the European Union.* New York: Verso.

Kantola, Johanna. 2010. *Gender and the European Union.* London: Palgrave Macmillan.

Kantola, Johanna, and Lise Rolandsen Agustín. 2019. "Gendering the Representative Work of the European Parliament: A Political Analysis of Women MEPs' Perception of Gender Equality in Party Groups." *Journal of Common Market Studies* 57 (4): 768–786.

Kellerman, Barbara. 1984. "Leadership as a Political Act. Leadership." In *Leadership: Multidisciplinary Perspectives*, ed. B. Kellerman, 63–89. Englewood Cliffs, NJ: Prentice-Hall.

MacMullen, Andrew. 2000. "European Commissioners: National Routes to a European Elite." In *Studies of the European Commission*, ed. Neill Nugent, 28–50. Basingstoke, UK: Palgrave Macmillan.

Maranto, Robert, Manuel P. Teodoro, Kristen Carroll, and Albert Cheng. 2019. "Gendered Ambition: Men's and Women's Career Advancement in Public Administration." *American Review of Public Administration* 49 (4): 469–481.

Müller, Henriette. 2020. *Political Leadership and the European Commission Presidency.* Oxford: Oxford University Press.

Müller, Henriette, and Femke A. W. J. van Esch. 2020. "The Contested Nature of Political Leadership in the European Union: Conceptual and Methodological Cross-Fertilisation." *West European Politics* 43 (5): 1051–1071.

Nugent, Neill. 2001. *The European Commission.* Basingstoke, UK: Palgrave Macmillan.

Pittinsky, Todd L., Laura M. Bacon, and Brian Welle. 2007. "The Great Women Theory of Leadership? Perils of Positive Stereotypes and Precarious Pedestals." In *Women and Leadership: The State of Play and Strategies for Change*, eds. Barbara Kellerman and Deborah L. Rhode, 93–126. San Francisco, CA: Jossey-Bass.

Rhode, Deborah L. 2003. "The Difference 'Difference' Makes." In *The Difference "Difference" Makes*, ed. Deborah L. Rhode, 3–52. Stanford, CA: Stanford University Press.

Rhode, Deborah L. 2017. *Women and Leadership.* Oxford: Oxford University Press.

Rhode, Deborah L., and Barbara Kellerman. 2007. "Women and Leadership: The State of Play." In *Women and Leadership: The State of Play and Strategies for Change*, eds. Barbara Kellerman and Deborah L. Rhode, 65–92. San Francisco, CA: Jossey-Bass.

Ridgeway, Cecilia L. 2001. "Gender, Status, and Leadership." *Journal of Social Issues* 57 (4): 637–655.

Ridgeway, Cecilia L. 2011. *Framed by Gender: How Gender Inequality Persists in the Modern World*. Oxford: Oxford University Press [accessed via Oxford Scholarship Online].

Setzler, Mark. 2019. "Measuring Bias against Female Political Leadership." *Politics & Gender* 15 (4): 695–721.

Smeets, Sandrino, and Derek Beach. 2020. "Political and Instrumental Leadership in Major EU Reforms: The Role and Influence of the EU Institutions in Setting-up the Fiscal Compact." *Journal of European Public Policy* 27 (1): 63–81.

Tömmel, Ingeborg. 2013. "The Presidents of the European Commission: Transactional or Transforming Leaders?" *Journal of Common Market Studies* 51 (4): 789–805.

Tömmel, Ingeborg. 2020. "Political Leadership in Times of Crisis: The Commission Presidency of Jean-Claude Juncker." *West European Politics* 43 (5): 1141–1162.

Van Esch, Femke A. W. J. 2017. "The Paradoxes of Legitimate EU Leadership: An Analysis of the Multi-level Leadership of Angela Merkel and Alexis Tsipras during the Euro Crisis." *Journal of European Integration* 39 (2): 223–237.

2

Searching for Agency

Gendering Leadership in European Integration Theory

Gabriele Abels and Heather MacRae

2.1 Introduction

Approximately 25 years ago, Anita Gradin, then newly appointed Swedish commissioner, expressed her dismay at the dominance of "grey-suited men" in the upper levels of the European Commission (quoted in Hoskyns 1996: 1). Although men still dominate the hallways of Berlaymont, women are entering the upper echelons in unprecedented numbers (see Chapter 3 in this volume). At the time of writing (July 2020), the Commission has its first ever female president. Additionally, about 40% of commissioners and parliamentarians are women. Even the European Council of heads of state and government has seen a small increase in women leaders (currently four out of 27). Although it is not clear how this numerical rise may affect legislative focus, deliberation, negotiation, and policy outcomes in the EU, there is general consensus that gender diversity does "make a difference" (Rhode 2017: 5). Importantly, the increase in women's leadership coincides with what may be referred to as an EU in crisis. Commission President Jean-Claude Juncker has used the term "polycrisis" to describe multiple and interconnected crises: economic and fiscal crises, the migrant crisis, institutional crises emerging from Brexit, and most recently the COVID-19 health crisis. Clearly, at a time like this, leadership is essential and offers a unique opportunity to examine women's increasing leadership in the EU. To do this from a theoretically sound position, we suggest bringing integration theories into conversation with both gender insights and theories of leadership studies.

Recently, linkages have been discussed between various pairs of the three strands: gendering integration theories (Abels and MacRae 2016a; Kronsell 2012), leadership in the EU (e.g. Helms 2017; Müller and Van Esch 2020; Tömmel 2013, 2017; Tömmel and Verdun 2017; Van Esch 2017), and gender and leadership (Genovese 2013; Sykes 2014). We search for connections between the *three* strands and make these productive for investigating gender and leadership in the EU.

Gabriele Abels and Heather MacRae, *Searching for Agency: Gendering Leadership in European Integration Theory*. In: *Women and Leadership in the European Union*. Edited by Henriette Müller and Ingeborg Tömmel, Oxford University Press. © Oxford University Press (2022). DOI: 10.1093/oso/9780192896216.003.0003

We contend that integration theories can offer insights into some of these emergent trends, but that these must be expanded through a gender lens. We assume that the conceptualization of agency is vital for exploring such connections.

First, we must briefly look at the individual strands, starting with integration theories. Today, an incredible array of theories tries to make sense of the process, evolution, nature, and future of European integration. While some theories emphasize agency-related factors, others focus on structures as driving forces. For a leadership focus, it is paramount to identify potential actors and supporting structures. Nevertheless, integration theorists have seldom adopted a leadership perspective. This becomes evident when searching through the indexes of established textbooks. While "leader" and "leadership" are listed in some general introductory textbooks and handbooks, the terms are missing in integration theory textbooks. Even if it is obvious that politicians have played a major role in European integration, bringing together leadership and integration theories is not a straightforward endeavor. It requires us to begin with the ways in which integration theories approach questions of structure and agency to grasp how they understand leadership and leaders. Many theories implicitly consider leaders to be (groups of) states rather than individuals. Insofar as they do look to the role of specific actors, integration theories are notoriously gender-blind and there is seldom consideration of the gendered nature of these actors and the ways in which they operate within gendered leadership structures. Thus, to understand gender, which we assume to be a socially constructed category establishing sex differences (presumed male and female characteristics) and hierarchies in gender relations, and leadership from within the integration theories, we need to bring together three very different literatures: integration theories, leadership studies, and gender theories.

We propose EU gender studies as a junction. Feminist EU scholars have put forth gender-sensitive analyses of mainstream schools as well as critical strands in integration theories. Gender analyses have typically emphasized women's agency and gendered structures in European integration. Even here, however, female agency is usually not addressed through a leadership lens. For instance, the impact of female heads of state and government—i.e., of de facto national leaders—and members of government is still under-researched despite the growing number of women in top executive offices.

In the following, we set out what we see as the most salient points of these three literatures and look for synergies. We focus on how various integration theories conceptualize (gendered) agency, what assumptions they hold about leadership (if any) as a specific kind of agency, and what kinds and types of leadership the various theories consider. The final section discusses how leadership studies and European integration theory can be more strongly interlinked and how the resulting insights can profit from a gendered interpretation. Our main argument is that gendering both integration theories and leadership studies creates spaces to bring these three literatures together. The gendered lens allows us to better understand the role of gendered agency and how it interacts with gendered structures in European integration, because leadership is always contextual—that is, from a gender lens it is exercised in a "gender-specific environment shaped by 'masculinist' norms and expectations" (Sykes 2014: 691). This is important for assessing if gendered leadership can be transformative.

2.2 Gendering Agency and Leadership in EU Studies

First of all, we need to clarify some key concepts and the ways in which we, and others, use them. Specifically, what do we mean by leaders and leadership? How does this differ from agency? What happens to these core concepts when considered through a gendered lens?

Leadership itself is an ambiguous term and concept, especially in the EU context. If leadership is interpreted as meaning "hegemony" (Müller and Van Esch 2020: 1051), then it has been a prominent topic in EU studies since at least the early 1990s. While some scholars have looked to individual states (e.g., Germany as a "hegemon"), others have looked at power blocs (such as the Franco-German tandem) as "leaders," especially in the creation of "grand bargains." EU institutions such as the European Council or the Commission can also be conceptualized as leaders due to their constitutional position in the EU polity, or the European Central Bank (ECB) with regard to monetary policy. We understand leaders to refer, not so much to institutions, but rather more specifically to *individual* actors. These individuals occupy specific positions, which gives them the power and ability to act. Their power is likely both derived and constrained by the position they hold, but it is the way that a particular individual navigates this position that interests us. Holding office is thus a precondition, but not sufficient, for exercising leadership. We consider both positional and behavioral leadership as outlined in Chapter 1 of this volume.

Leadership, interpreted in this way, has been absent from integration theories. Lately, much of the literature has actually focused on the lack of leadership, the crisis of leadership and the inability of the European states to "lead," and the problematic ways in which the EU can be seen as leading at the expense of others. This sense of a lack of leadership has only been amplified of late, as leadership is more intensely called for in times of crisis. And "crisis leadership differs from leadership in routine times," because its "stakes are much higher, the public is much more attentive, its mood more volatile, and institutional constraints on elite decision making are considerably looser" (Ansell et al. 2014: 418f.). In times of crisis, leadership also requires more investment in sense making and meaning making (Ansell et al. 2014). In other words, leaders are responsible for interpreting, defining, and transmitting a particular understanding of the crisis. This role places leaders at the center of crisis management, not only in terms of actions, but also framing those actions for the general public, thus helping to define how the EU can or should react. Depending on the kind of crisis, different leadership qualities are required and appreciated. During the COVID-19 pandemic crisis, there was speculation that "there may be a relationship between women's leadership and their handling of a crisis like this (with a greater degree of effectiveness and compassion)" (Kathleen Gersen, quoted in Somvichian-Clausen 2020).

For some scholars, the EU's lack of leadership is not surprising, but rather a direct consequence of the institutional structures in place to prevent the concentration of power and the ascent of a single, powerful leader. Ludger Helms (2017: 2) has suggested that the EU is actually an "anti-leadership environment" in which the complex institutional setup results in an inability to identify a focal point of leadership. Jack Hayward (2008) speaks of "leaderless Europe," emphasizing the difficulties caused by having too many leaders and a fragmented leadership structure. Müller and Van Esch (2020: 1055), in contrast, perceive the EU as an "intensely 'leaderful' polity" and "purposely designed as such." Based on these analyses, it is essential to link leadership to the conceptualization of agency. If we understand leaders as individuals, rather than institutions or states, then it is obvious that leadership must be associated with a few specific offices such as the presidents of the various bodies, and political leaders such as heads of state and governments of member states, as well as national ministers.

Nonetheless, leaders are not simply individuals who occupy a specific office nor are they defined only by their ability to wield power (Della Sala 2014: 307). What defines leaders is the mutually beneficial relationship with their followers (see Müller and Van Esch 2020: 1053). Thus, we understand leadership as a collective and relational endeavor, which depends on leaders' actions and followers' consent. Leaders use influence and persuasion to achieve goals viewed as mutually desirable (see Chapter 1 in this volume; Müller and Van Esch 2020).

Typically, integration theories have sought to understand the bigger pictures around the process of integration, policymaking, and the distribution of power. For the most part, integration theories have not dug down to the micro level of analysis to think about the role of individual leaders. There are, of course, some exceptions. Studies on, for example, the role of presidents of EU institutions utilize a micro level of analysis and investigate the role of an individual leader (see Tallberg 2010; Tömmel 2013, 2017). These studies, though, have seldom relied on integration theory per se. As a result, leadership and integration theory have hardly crossed.

To find places where leadership might be incorporated, we propose to look at the different approaches to agency in integration theory. "Agency," a common concept in social and political sciences, refers to the ability of an actor (individual or institution) to influence decision-making. The ability of agents to exercise their decision-making power, depending on the theoretical perspective, may be viewed as partially constrained by the structures shaping the political and social systems.

Simply put, an actor who possesses agency is presumed to have the capacity to deliberate and is empowered to act without (or in spite of) structural constraints—often in cooperation with others. Therefore, although not all agents are leaders, all leaders exercise agency.

Although there are clear links, there is little overlap of leadership and agency in the theoretical literature. Helms, reflecting on Dimitrakopoulos's observations about collective leadership in the EU, notes that "agency-related factors—which should be expected to be at the heart of thinking about leadership—are not even mentioned" (Helms 2017: 5). Helms suggests that if we understand leadership as an "agency-driven process" then there is no reason to prioritize studies of institutions, rather than individuals, as most theoretical approaches do. He proposes the term "structured agency" to characterize the ability of leaders to work within structures to facilitate change.

We are thus pressed to ask why some individuals or agents are considered leaders and others are not. Does the type of follower matter in our understanding of a leader? What assumptions do integration theories make about leaders and agents? These questions are, at least partially, addressed by gender scholars in their interrogation of the contemporary leadership literature, but this does not necessarily intersect with the integration literature. Through a gendered approach to integration theories, we may create spaces in which to pose new questions. While there are few scholars who have advanced a gendered critique of the leadership literature within the context of the EU, we can take some of the broader gender critiques of European studies and of the leadership literature to address some concerns.

The gender critiques of leadership studies tend to highlight a few key points in the mainstream literature. Four key themes run through the literature, two of which focus on representation. First, there is a relatively large body of scholarship on the (under-)representation of women in leadership positions. That paucity in turn explains the relative lack of (quantitative) studies on women and leadership (Sykes 2014: 691). In the context of the EU, this theme may prompt researchers to ask questions about the individuals who are leaders, both of the European institutions and in key positions within the member states. Second, and related to this, are studies investigating the obstacles to the increasing representation of women in leadership roles. "The careers of successful women can illustrate the extent to which gender itself, directly or indirectly, is a limiting condition in a particular society" (Genovese 2013: 4). These include the inability to balance personal and career responsibilities, an unequal and gendered sharing of family responsibility between partners, and gendered stereotypes around the qualities associated with leadership. "Regardless of how she [the female leader] handles the internal impact of gender roles, she must also develop strategies for dealing with them as a strategic aspect of her career, because others may react to her in terms of gender" (Genovese 2013: 5).

The other two themes encourage us to consider how women lead, whether their leadership styles differ from men's, and how these differences may contribute to different outcomes or the prioritizing of "women's issues" (Sykes 2014). These questions do not, at first glance, appear to have much in common with those posed by integration theories. However, there may be some room for overlap and mutual learning.

2.3 Searching for (Gendered) Agency in Integration Theories

How do integration theories conceptualize (gendered) agency? What are the assumptions they hold about leadership (if any) as a specific kind of agency and about different kinds and types of leadership? Müller and Van Esch (2020: 1053) identify four key ways in which EU studies have brought leadership into the broader debates: leadership as hegemony; the impact of specific leaders; leadership as soft power; and the interaction between leadership and context. As we navigate through integration theories, we consider how they may be linked to these different dimensions.

Overall, the reference to leadership is, at best, implicit. While a number of integration theories focus on either structure *or* agency, many try to balance both factors, leaving room for investigating leadership. In our discussion of agency, we include gender approaches and gendered variants of integration theories. The key contribution of gender approaches is that they "bring to the fore both feminist and masculinist agency and its role in challenging and reproducing gendered structures" (Locher and Prügl 2009: 196). A feminist approach "requires us to consider structures of power, agency, social mobilization and activism as well as relationships among various actors and levels of governance" (Abels and MacRae 2016b: 27). This combined focus will drive our investigation of integration theories. Given the mushrooming of theories, we only address some of the more prominent ones.

"Grand" Theories

Over the past decade, we have seen a revival of schools of integration theories: neofunctionalism, intergovernmentalism, and postfunctionalism. These theories do, albeit only implicitly, address the dimension of "interaction between leadership and context" within leadership studies (Müller and Van Esch 2020: 1053). *Neofunctionalism*, developed by Ernst Haas in the late 1950s (Haas 1958), for instance, links European integration to functional forces and minimizes the role of individual agency. Haas emphasizes the role of social and political elites as potentially collective leaders. He postulated that as institutions at the European level—in particular, the European Commission (called the High Authority in the early days)—become empowered in a wider scope of policy areas, the elites will shift loyalties from the national to the European level. As they do, the broader public will also begin to identify more closely with the European level. This can be conceptualized as collective elite leadership. Thus, neofunctionalism has room to consider leadership, but it engages only peripherally with the idea of followers. Haas tended to ignore followers and referred to the elites or leaders as driving forces. Yet the public can be seen as followers. For Haas, the nature and individual personalities of the elites was not important. Rather, "elites" were addressed mainly as a monolithic "force." Inserting a gender perspective into neofunctionalism means looking beyond national governments, supranational institutions, and elites as nongendered entities. We thereby could create space for considering *individual* agency, including leaders, such as presidents of EU institutions.

Intergovernmentalism appears to be a more "natural" theoretical fit because of its strong focus on states, and by extension national governments, in integration. In this respect, its perspective is closer to that of "leadership as hegemony." In addition, intergovernmentalism's distinction between high and low politics, and the effect on the likelihood of integration, can be helpful in terms of understanding how different policies need different degrees and kinds of leadership. Stanley Hoffmann's seminal essay on intergovernmentalism (1966) was most explicit about leadership in addressing its contextual dimension and impact. Hoffmann's account was partially prompted by the "empty chair crisis" of the mid-1960s, where it became clear that national leaders played a very strong role in negotiating integration and balancing national versus European interests (in this case, President de Gaulle of France blocked all decisions in the Council of Ministers by not taking the French chair until he forced an accord favoring his country's interests). Hoffmann highlighted a need to analyze the quality of leadership and its impact on policies. In those days, leaders were still exclusively male; possessing leadership was seen as a very masculine trait and exercise. Forty years later, in light of the rising number of women in executive office in Europe, Anna van der Vleuten (2016: 94) suggests that a leadership focus "would open up the possibility of examining the role of gender when more women are in power at the highest levels," for example, in the Council of Ministers and European Council of heads of state and government or as presidents of EU institutions.

In some of its more recent iterations, the intergovernmental school lost this focus on the quality of leadership. Andrew Moravcsik's (1998) *liberal intergovernmentalism* (LI) sees national governments as key, especially in the stage of domestic preference formation and "grand bargains" with other member states' governments over treaty reforms. National governments are thus important in the two-level game of negotiation involving the national and the EU arenas. In addition, some member states (or groups thereof) may be more powerful than others and may dominate negotiations. However, LI does *not* analyze this with reference to leadership. Given that it has become somewhat of a "baseline theory"

(Moravcsik and Schimmelfennig 2019: 64) in EU studies, it is essential to insert a—gendered—leadership perspective. Lastly, *new intergovernmentalism* (Bickerton et al. 2015) emphasizes ongoing integration, yet without supranationalization. In contrast to the community method, the "union method," developed in response to crisis, happens at the expense of the Commission. Control remains in the hands of national governments, which make increasing use of non-majoritarian "de novo bodies" (e.g., the ECB and EU regulatory agencies). This is, however, not so obvious, as Smeets and Beach (2020) illustrate in their critical discussion of "new institutional leadership" in the "machine room" of crisis management. Again, the study of individual leaders in national governments as well as in these de novo institutions (e.g., the role of Christine Lagarde as the ECB president since 2019) remains a gap in the literature, which gender scholars are beginning to address (see Chapter 15 in this volume).

Today, *postfunctionalism* is seen as part of the "grand theories of the twenty-first century" (Hooghe and Marks 2019). Its development is crisis triggered. Liesbet Hooghe and Gary Marks (2009) argue against the neofunctionalist assumption of "permissive consensus," in which citizens tacitly consent to integration by virtue of their lack of contestation and general disinterest. Instead, they emphasize that rising Euroscepticism among national publics is increasing the salience of EU politics—culminating in a "constraining dissensus" on integration. This approach emphasizes the role of national governments in "steering" politicization across different levels. For example, in the eurozone crisis, governments were more successful in keeping this politicization at bay and fostering the creation of new instruments to preserve the eurozone, which was key to national interests. Simultaneously, with its emphasis on public discourse, postfunctionalism is the first integration theory to intentionally bring in the role of followers. This is essential, because—based on James Burns's classic 1978 definition—studying leadership must include the study of followers and their goals, values, and expectations about leaders that they choose to follow, as well as the study of different types of leadership and the ways in which different leadership styles influence policy outcomes.

The EU is considered to be a difficult environment for leaders *and* for followers. As Van Esch (2017: 35) demonstrates, leadership in the EU is in crisis and the "marked decline in legitimacy" challenges the concept of followers. "Followership," much like leadership, is fragmented along territorial and functional lines. With regard to territory, the member states are still a relevant forum for public debate and the evaluation of leadership by constituents. Different kinds and degrees of Euroscepticism and "Euro-optimism" in the national publics and among social groups illustrate this well. In functional terms, leadership is about "attaining goals that are mutually desired" (Müller and Van Esch 2020: 1053) by leaders and followers. But whose goals? Some initial studies illustrate that these are often male-dominated goals. We find gender differences in Euroscepticism, just as there are gender gaps in voting behavior. This is, to some extent, linked to a knowledge gap, but the gender differences in support for the EU go beyond that (Fortin-Rittberger and Ramstetter 2021). Given the multilevel EU structure, it is difficult to identify and attain desired goals or simply to choose not to follow. In fact, today the desirability of EU-wide goals and the feasibility of accomplishing these goals has become increasingly contested among different social groups. Thus, while postfunctionalism does not speak about leaders, it does—without using the term itself—speak about the problem of followers and, thereby, implicitly addresses leadership. While this offers some possibilities, it remains insufficient for the purposes of generating a gender-aware perspective on leadership as well as on followers in EU integration.

In sum, while none of the grand theories speaks explicitly about leadership, they do sometimes bring in relevant concerns for a leadership perspective. And these need to be reinvestigated through a gender lens.

Critical Approaches

Since the mid-1990s, we observe a shift toward more critical and normative approaches in integration theories. Such "dissident voices" (Manners and Whitman 2016) have become much louder and bring in a variety of perspectives (see Bigo et al. 2020). These approaches can be linked—in different ways—to various strands in leadership studies. From a gender perspective, these theories are particularly interesting. In fact, gender approaches are part of this critical choir. Gender approaches exist as stand-alone theories, but they are also infused into a number of other critical perspectives (see Abels and MacRae 2016a, 2020). We cannot attend to all of these approaches, so select those that appear most promising and open toward a leadership perspective.

One of the key newcomers is *multilevel governance* (MLG). While not a theory in the strict sense, MLG is at least a coherent approach to conceptualizing the EU. The main assumption is that power is dispersed among levels and actors, who share an interest in problem-solving via policy networks. In the EU, power is not clearly hierarchical but rather more polycentric, with interweaving levels of authority. Even national governments, considered natural leaders in other theories, are "in the MLG world view … far from omnipotent" (Pagoulatos and Tsoukalis 2012: 65). Skeptical of both structural hierarchy and natural leadership from the member states, MLG appears to be, at first sight, an unlikely case for leadership. Yet it is compatible with gender analysis, partly because it is open to the involvement of nonstate actors and their networking across levels, thereby potentially including social (feminist) movements (Abels 2016). Simona Piattoni (2010) argues that the MLG approach is essentially about understanding political mobilization at and across different levels. This motivates questions of who mobilizes whom, how, and to what ends. This line of questioning can subsequently open up our analysis of leadership to include more numerous and heterogeneous collective actors (including NGOs and EU agencies), representing a broad range of interests. Thus, despite its own built-in bias against hierarchical leadership, this pluralistic perspective surprisingly offers the opportunity to bring in concepts of leadership and, potentially, followers as well.

Furthermore, we find a broad array of approaches in the *new institutionalist* (NI) tradition. Typically, these have been concerned more with structures (or in their words, institutions) than with agents and leaders. Their focus on individuals and actors is limited to a concern with how institutions constrain and promote their actions and thus contribute to institutional change and continuity (Gains and Lowndes 2014). Some NI strands clearly offer more entry points to a leadership analysis than others. *Rational choice institutionalism* (RCI), for instance, recognizes the role and importance of leaders particularly in times of crisis or change. However, leaders are simply understood to be rational actors seeking to maximize their own position or that of their institution. It is assumed that any rational individual occupying the position of leader would act the same way. Thus, there is no real room to consider leaders' personalities, backgrounds, and individual characteristics within RCI. In contrast, *sociological institutionalism* (SI) offers an interesting opening through its concern with formal and informal rules, norms and values. SI is particularly interested in how individuals shape and interpret these norms, placing an important focus on the role of individual actors. SI is generally interested in individuals, however, not necessarily leaders. *Feminist institutionalism* (FI), which may draw from many NI strands, has much more to offer as this approach uses a gender lens to ask questions about how rules and institutions come to be—implicitly and explicitly—looking to see what role women played in shaping institutions (MacRae and Weiner 2021). For FI scholars, it matters if social and political institutions are constructed by individuals who self-identify or are identified by others as female (or male). While FI scholars have researched women leaders in other regions, there are surprisingly few studies on the EU that draw explicitly on FI and focus specifically on women's agency (MacRae and Weiner 2017). Although there is room to bring leadership into the NI and FI approaches, scholars have so far paid mostly implicit attention to agents and their relationship to institutions.

Closely linked to SI is, finally, *social constructivism*, a meta-theoretical school which has become quite prominent in EU studies. In analogy to Alexander Wendt's famous claim "anarchy is what states make of it," we can claim: leadership is what followers make of it. Müller and Van Esch (2020: 1052) emphasize that leadership is "a collective and reciprocal interaction among (multiple) leaders and their followers." Investigating such interactions through a social constructivist lens is particularly fruitful, even in the case of the EU, where the supply of leadership and the lack of followers is problematic. Tömmel and Verdun (2017: 109) argue that leadership in the EU is rather a "complex interplay between a multitude of leaders or leading organizations with diverging powers and prerogatives, objectives and constituents or followers." Regarding "followership," we have already illustrated certain problems with regard to postfunctionalism. The famous turn from "permissive consensus" to "constraining dissensus" (Hooghe and Marks 2009) implicitly addresses the leader–follower relationship. Social constructivism offers the possibility to scrutinize how this interaction is constructed based on diverging norms, rules, and power relations, and how this can be linked to gender.

2.4 Gender and the Social Construction of Leadership

As illustrated, some integration theories offer venues for including a leadership perspective and allow—to different degrees—these to be combined with the necessary gender lens. We maintain that the social constructivist school is the most promising from a leadership lens and, simultaneously, for a gendering of leadership. Lombardo and Kantola (2021) demonstrate that "social constructivism and gender approaches are potentially good allies" in terms of how they contribute to integration theory. They "both address the EU as a socially constructed reality, the former with an emphasis on the social construction of institutions, processes, and actors, as well as the effects of social norms and institutions on individuals, and the latter with a focus on the gendering of such social construction and effects, with particular attention to roles, norms, and power between the people" (Lombardo and Kantola 2021: 43–44). This complementarity also makes these approaches most fruitful for investigating leadership. Agents, norms, and structures are presumed to be gendered. One can look at the gender of agents in leadership position and find that men still dominate in EU and national institutions—the famous "glass ceiling" for women politicians still exists. The first women in leadership positions—e.g., the first female chancellor in Germany, the first female Commission president—are assigned a high symbolic value, especially if gender equality is seen as an important democratic norm. In this sense, leadership studies can be linked to political representation, which is an established field within gender studies. This is an easy part of the gendering exercise.

In addition, one has to question the male-as-norm assumption. Traditionally, leaders are imagined as lone heroes. These "hero-leaders" (Müller and Van Esch 2020: 1054) are often associated with qualities such as determination, energy, rationality, ambition, and drive. All of these are stereotypically defined as masculine traits and behavior whereas qualities labeled feminine—warmth, gentleness, compassion, emotionality, cautiousness, etc.—are not generally associated with leadership (see Sjoberg 2014: 75f.). In times of crisis (especially in times of war), this association between (good) leadership and masculinity may even be stronger. Given the context of masculine norms, the question is: How do women leaders exercise leadership? What traits are seen as appropriate and which behavior is considered suitable by their followers? How do women leaders overcome and/or neutralize gender barriers? Female politicians always struggle with ambivalences and conflicting expectations of masculinity and femininity. They have, as Laura Sjoberg (2014: 76) argues, the "burden of proof to demonstrate masculine capacity" to their followers, while simultaneously "remaining female."

Ann Tickner argued early on that narratives about political leadership in international politics "reinforce the belief, widely held … by both men and women, that military and foreign policymaking are arenas of policymaking least appropriate for women" and that these beliefs "limit both women's access and the influence of femininity in politics" (quoted in Sjoberg 2014: 73). This, in principle, applies also to European politics. Yet, with rising numbers of women in top executive positions in many EU member states and in EU institutions (see also Chapters 3 and 4 in this volume), with the EU seeing itself as a soft, normative power rather than a military power, and, finally, due to experiences with leadership in crisis, these gendered expectations might change. For example, do expectations about leadership in the economic crisis differ from those in the COVID-19 health crisis? We must consider not only the leaders but also the followers through a gender lens. Do expectations, values, and goals differ between (groups of) men and women? How gendered are their ideas about leadership and leaders' traits? Gender gaps in voting behavior indicate that differences can exist. But what role do these differences play, in turn, for the leaders?

Besides agents and norms, it is important to acknowledge that structures themselves are gendered. Power relations among institutions or processes are essential parts of such structures. Against this background, the proposal by Michelle Cini and Marián Šuplata (2017) is interesting. They speak of "policy leadership" as a combination of agency and capacity; the latter relates to the Commission's unique role in policy initiation and output, and the conditions under which this policy leadership can be successfully exercised. Building coalitions—or relations to followers—is an important aspect. This policy focus is exciting because it opens the opportunity for constructivist framing analyses: How are policies framed, by whom, and for what purpose? Gender studies is most interested in the EU's policy dimension and makes frequent use of framing approaches. Mieke Verloo (2007), for instance, has demonstrated the value of "critical frame analysis" in analyzing EU gender-equality policies.

2.5 Conclusion and Outlook: Where Does This Lead Us?

In this final section, we reiterate some of the key difficulties and posit possible ways forward. As we have illustrated, integration theories, overall, have been oblivious to both leadership and gender, and certainly to gendered leadership. This needn't be the case. The dynamic and peculiar nature of the EU polity provides researchers with an excellent opportunity to investigate the correlation between leadership and its gendered nature and to consolidate their findings with theories of European integration. Agency is a good starting point. Vincent Della Sala briefly alludes to the relationship between leader and agency and considers power to be the conceptual overlapping point. He argues that the dynamic relationship between leader and followers "is why leadership is associated with power—institutional, economic and military—but it also implies more complex ways in which some have the capacity to effect change while others do not" (Della Sala 2014: 307). Incorporating a gendered understanding of leadership into existing theories can lead to more nuanced understandings of power and institutional interactions.

A first key insight is that none of the integration theories speak explicitly in leadership terms. Neither the term "leader" nor "follower" is used in the theories reviewed. This may be partially a result of their primary level of analysis. Classical integration theories typically operate at a macro or even meta level, searching for common patterns and universal statements of truth that could explain the progress (and lack thereof) that is characteristic of European integration. Given their focus on the broad process, it is perhaps not surprising that they do not attend to the role of individual actors and thus do not really make space to bring in a leadership perspective. Where these theories do see leadership, they tend to focus on the institution rather than the individual occupying the role at any given time. At best, we can see that postfunctionalism at least allows for the possibility to integrate followers into the analysis. Critical approaches, in contrast, tend to operate more at the micro or meso level of analysis, and could therefore be presumed to be more open to a leadership perspective. However, these too are surprisingly unaware of how a leadership perspective could augment their understanding of power relations in European governance. Of these approaches, those drawing on social constructivist principles appear to be most promising for addressing issues of leaders *and* followers.

Second, integration theories as well as leadership studies need to be revisited with a gender lens. The very idea of leadership is linked to power, even if the conceptualization of what makes a leader powerful differs. Gender approaches are interested in unpacking power relations. This is indeed at the heart of gendering integration theory, as Annica Kronsell (2012: 40) argues: "The strength of feminist analysis lies in its understanding of how power hierarchies rooted in gender are operationalized in political practices and thus 'permanently' embedded in institutions. Such critical approaches to power can contribute significantly to EU integration studies in the future." They thus offer a fruitful opportunity to consider power relations between leaders and followers and the ways in which individual characteristics shape integration.

Third, when we do bring agency—as leadership by individuals—into the integration theories, we must recognize that many of the existing narratives about leadership are clearly gendered. By this, we mean that all leaders, regardless of biological sex, act in ways that may reinforce or undermine existing gendered norms and assumptions. It is thus important to study both male *and* female leaders as gendered. With rising numbers of women leaders, there is a chance that leadership will no longer be recognized as "naturally masculine" and that its gendered nature will itself be questioned. Expectations about qualities of leaders and what is considered "good leadership performance" in specific circumstances can change and move away from "male-as-norm" or become "remasculinized." Finally, an equally important task is to gender the analysis of followers. In a pluralistic society, social groups have divergent interests in European integration. Gender as a key social category impacts upon these interests—along with other social categories such as class and race. This diversity of followers requires attention to understand the role of leaders and publics in integration.

Neither leaders nor followers, nor norms, nor institutions, nor power relations are nongendered. Gendered approaches recognize that it is not only the institution or office that matters, but that the "nature" of officeholders—their identification as male, female, or nonbinary—matters for leaders and for followers as well. The male-as-norm is a pervasive construction in leadership. A first step to bringing in a leadership perspective is thus to make integration theory more gender aware. This allows for questions of power, agency, and relationships, which, in turn, open space for the leadership focus on individual powers, relationships, and ideas.

References

Abels, Gabriele. 2016. "Multi-level Governance: Tailoring a 'Favourite Coat' to the Needs of 'Gender Fashion.'" In *Gendering European Integration Theory*, eds. Gabriele Abels and Heather MacRae, 99–121. Opladen: Barbara Budrich.

Abels, Gabriele, and Heather MacRae, eds. 2016a. *Gendering European Integration Theory*. Opladen: Barbara Budrich.

Abels, Gabriele, and Heather MacRae. 2016b. "Gendering European Integration Theory: Introduction." In *Gendering European Integration Theory*, eds. Gabriele Abels and Heather MacRae, 9–37. Opladen: Barbara Budrich.

Abels, Gabriele, and Heather MacRae, eds. 2020. "Gender Approaches." In *The Routledge Handbook of Critical European Studies*, eds. Didier Bigo, Thomas Diez, Evangelos Fanoulis, Ben Rosamond, and Yannis A. Stivachtis, 112–124. Abingdon, UK, and New York: Routledge.

Ansell, Chris, Arjen Boin, and Paul 't Hart. 2014. "Political Leadership in Times of Crisis." In *The Oxford Handbook of Political Leadership*, eds. R. A. W. Rhodes and Paul 't Hart, 418–433. Oxford: Oxford University Press.

Bickerton, Christopher J., Dermot Hodson, and Uwe Puetter, eds. 2015. "The New Intergovernmentalism: European Integration in the Post-Maastricht Era." *Journal of Common Market Studies* 53 (4): 703–722.

Bigo, Didier, Thomas Diez, Evangelos Fanoulis, Ben Rosamond, and Yannis A. Stivachtis, eds. 2020. *The Routledge Handbook of Critical European Studies*. Abingdon, UK, and New York: Routledge.

Burns, James M. 1978. *Leadership*. New York: Harper & Row.

Cini, Michelle, and Marián Šuplata. 2017. "Policy Leadership in the European Commission: The Regulation of EU Mobile Roaming Charges." *Journal of European Integration* 39 (2): 143–156.

Della Sala, Vincent. 2014. "Leaders and Followers: Leadership amongst Member States in a Differentiated Europe." In Oxford Handbook of the European Union, eds. Erik Jones, Anand Menon, and Stephen Weatherill, 306–317. Oxford: Oxford University Press.

Fortin-Rittberger, Jessica, and Lena Ramstetter. 2021. "The Privilege of (Defining) Knowledge. Gender Differences in Political Knowledge across Europe." In *The Routledge Handbook of Gender and EU Politics*, eds. Gabriele Abels, Andrea Krizsán, Heather MacRae, and Anna van der Vleuten, 208–221. Abingdon, UK, and New York: Routledge.

Gains, Francesca, and Vivien Lowndes. 2014. "How Is Institutional Formation Gendered, and Does It Make a Difference?" *Politics and Gender* 10 (4): 524–548.

Genovese, Michael A. 2013. "Women as Political Leaders: Does Gender Matter?" In *Women as Political Leaders*, eds. Michael A. Genovese and Janie S. Steckenrider, 1–13. New York: Routledge.

Haas, Ernst B. 1958. *The Uniting of Europe*. Palo Alto, CA: Stanford University Press.

Hayward, Jack, ed. 2008. *Leaderless Europe*. Oxford: Oxford University Press.

Helms, Ludger. 2017. "Introduction: Leadership Questions in Transnational European Governance." *European Political Science* 16 (1): 1–13.

Hoffmann, Stanley. 1966. "Obstinate or Obsolete?: The Fate of the Nation-State and the Case of Western Europe." *Daedalus* 95: 862–914.

Hooghe, Liesbeth, and Gary Marks. 2009. "A Postfunctionalist Theory of European Integration: From Permissive Consensus to Constraining Dissensus." *British Journal of Political Science* 39 (1): 1–23.

Hooghe, Liesbeth, and Gary Marks. 2019. "Grand Theories of European Integration in the Twenty-First Century." *Journal of European Public Policy* 26 (8): 1113–1133.

Hoskyns, Catherine. 1996. *Integrating Gender: Women, Law and Politics in the European Union*. London: Verso.

Kronsell, Annika. 2012. "Gendering Theories of European Integration." In *Gendering the European Union*, eds. Gabriele Abels and Joyce M. Mushaben, 23–40. Basingstoke, UK: Palgrave Macmillan.

Locher, Birgit, and Elisabeth Prügl. 2009. "Gender and European Integration." In *European Integration Theory*, eds. Antje Wiener and Thomas Diez, 2nd ed., 181–197. Oxford: Oxford University Press.

Lombardo, Emanuela, and Johanna Kantola. 2021. "Gendering Integration Theory: Social Constructivism." In *The Routledge Handbook of Gender and EU Politics*, eds. Gabriele Abels, Andrea Krizsán, Heather MacRae, and Anna van der Vleuten, 43–55. Abingdon, UK, and New York: Routledge.

MacRae, Heather and Elaine Weiner. 2021. "Feminist Institutionalism." In *The Routledge Handbook of Gender and EU Politics*, eds. Gabriele Abels, Andrea Krizsán, Heather MacRae, and Anna van der Vleuten, 56–67. Abingdon, UK, and New York: Routledge.

MacRae, Heather, and Elaine Weiner, eds. 2017. *Towards Gendering Institutionalism: Equality in Europe*. Lanham, MD: Rowman & Littlefield.

Manners, Ian, and Richard Whitman. 2016. "Another Theory Is Possible: Dissident Voices in Theorising Europe." *Journal of Common Market Studies* 54 (1): 3–18.

Moravcsik, Andrew. 1998. *The Choice for Europe: Social Purpose and State Power from Messina to Maastricht*. Ithaca, NY: Cornell University Press.

Moravcsik, Andrew, and Frank Schimmelfenning. 2019. "Liberal Intergovernmentalism." In *European Integration Theory*, eds. Antje Wiener, Tanja A. Börzel, and Thomas Risse, 3rd ed., 64–84. Oxford: Oxford University Press.

Müller, Henriette, and Femke A. W. J. van Esch. 2020. "The Contested Nature of Political Leadership in the European Union: Conceptual and Methodological Cross-Fertilisation." *West European Politics* 43 (5): 1051–1071.

Pagoulatos, George, and Loukas Tsoukalis. 2012. "Multilevel Governance." In *The Oxford Handbook of the European Union*, eds. Erik Jones, Anand Menon, and Stephen Weatherill, 62–75. Oxford: Oxford University Press.

Piattoni, Simona. 2010. *The Theory of Multi-level Governance*. Oxford: Oxford University Press.

Rhode, Deborah L. 2017. *Women and Leadership*. Oxford: Oxford University Press.

Sjoberg, Laura. 2014. "Feminism." In *The Oxford Handbook of Political Leadership*, eds. R. A. W. Rhodes and Paul 't Hart, 72–86. Oxford: Oxford University Press.

Smeets, Sandrino, and Derek Beach. 2020. "Intergovernmentalism and Its Implications: New Institutional Leadership in Major EU Reforms." *Journal of European Public Policy* 27 (8): 1137–1156.

Somvichian-Clausen, Austa. 2020. "Countries Led by Women Have Fared Better against Coronavirus: Why?," *The Hill*, April 18, 2020 (cited May 2, 2020). Available from https://thehill.com/changing-america/respect/equality/493434-countries-led-by-women-have-fared-better-against.

Sykes, Patricia L. 2014: "Does Gender Matter?" In *The Oxford Handbook of Political Leadership*, eds. R. A. W. Rhodes and Paul 't Hart, 690–704. Oxford: Oxford University Press.

Tallberg, Jonas. 2010. "The Power of the Chair: Formal Leadership in International Cooperation." *International Studies Quarterly* 54 (1): 241–265.

Tömmel, Ingeborg. 2013. "The Presidents of the European Commission: Transactional or Transforming Leaders?" *Journal of Common Market Studies* 51 (4): 789–805.

Tömmel, Ingeborg. 2017. "The Standing President of the European Council: Intergovernmental or Supranational Leadership?" *Journal of European Integration* 39 (2): 175–189.

Tömmel, Ingeborg, and Amy Verdun. 2017: "Political Leadership in the European Union: An Introduction." *Journal of European Integration* 39 (2): 103–112.

Van der Vleuten, Anna. 2016. "Intergovernmentalism: Gendering a Dinosaur?" In *Gendering European Integration Theory*, eds. Gabriele Abels and Heather MacRae, 77–97. Opladen: Barbara Budrich.

Van Esch, Femke A.W.J. 2017. "The Nature of the European Leadership Crisis and How to Solve It." *European Political Science* 16 (1): 34–47.

Verloo, Mieke. 2007. *Multiple Meanings of Gender Equality: A Critical Frame Analysis of Gender Policies in Europe*. Budapest: Central European University Press.

PART II

ACCESSING POSITIONAL
LEADERSHIP IN EU INSTITUTIONS

3

Women's Positional Leadership in the European Commission

When, Where, and How?

Miriam Hartlapp and Agnes Blome

3.1 Introduction

Much of the literature on the role of women in EU policymaking focuses on the European Parliament (EP) and the Council (Freedman 2002; Norris and Franklin 1997; Stockemer and Sundström 2019; Naurin et al. 2019; Naurin and Naurin 2018) or explores policy initiatives, programs, and implementation strategies involving issues associated with women's interests regarding equal pay, employment equality, antidiscrimination, and gender mainstreaming (Kantola 2010; Jacquot 2015; Mazey 1988; Ahrens 2019; Hafner-Burton and Pollack 2009).[1] There is, however, a lack of scholarship that looks specifically at the EU Commission and how women work and exert powers in its leadership positions. This is astonishing for at least two reasons. First, the European Commission is a central institution of EU policymaking. In the EU political system, it holds a quasi-monopoly to propose legislation and oversees member states' implementation of EU policies. The Commission's leadership positions are extremely powerful and it is expected that they play central roles in policymaking. Second, beyond exploring how the rise of the number of female politicians in politics matters for the adoption of women-friendly policies, much national-level research has demonstrated the importance of female critical actors in decision-making bodies more generally (Blome 2017; Brunsbach 2011). Neglecting the role of women in the Commission's leadership positions gives an incomplete picture of how the representation of women is

[1] An earlier version of this chapter was presented at the "Women and Leadership in the European Union" workshop at the University of Osnabrück in January 2020. We wish to thank the participants and in particular Michelle Cini, Henriette Müller, and Ingeborg Tömmel for helpful comments, Antonia Fidler for research assistance, and our students for inspiration in our teaching about and discussing women in politics.

Miriam Hartlapp and Agnes Blome, *Women's Positional Leadership in the European Commission: When, Where, and How?* In: *Women and Leadership in the European Union.* Edited by Henriette Müller and Ingeborg Tömmel, Oxford University Press. © Oxford University Press (2022). DOI: 10.1093/oso/9780192896216.003.0004

accomplished, while a systematic analysis of women in the EU Commission could improve our understanding of policymaking. This chapter seeks to contribute toward closing the existing gap with a systematic and original account of women in the Commission.

The Commission has a political and an administrative top. Commissioners make decisions in the College of Commissioners and give political guidance to their portfolios, the Directorates General (DGs). Most DGs are organized in sectoral responsibilities to develop, implement, and manage EU policies. Besides service, DGs deal with tasks such as translation. Each DG is headed by a director general reporting to the responsible commissioner. Since the first Hallstein Commission in 1958, a total of 201 commissioners and 229 directors general have worked in the Commission. Yet the first 30 years of integration saw neither a female commissioner nor a female director general. Numbers started to rise in the late 1980s only. From the Delors II Commission onward, more and more women have been found in the highest positions. Some of them have received scholarly attention as individuals, e.g., Catherine Day (see Chapter 12 in this volume; Kassim et al. 2013: 193–197) and Margot Wallström (MacRae 2012: 305). Certainly, these women have been important leaders in their own right. Yet, with more than 60 women working at the top of the Commission, female representation merits more systematic consideration. When, where, and how do women enter leadership positions in the Commission?

In addressing this question, we take up the concept of positional leadership. We are interested in "women's access to and representation in positions of power and authority" (see Chapter 1 in this volume). We thus focus on political and administrative leadership positions in the Commission as an organization. Where appropriate, we add insights on more nuanced understandings of leadership that take into account agency, in particular the question of critical mass and women's alliances in positions of power and authority. Based on original data, we provide the first systematic and comprehensive analysis of women at the top of the Commission. We find that women have long been underrepresented but that their number has significantly increased over time. The analysis reports well-known patterns of sectoral gender divides, with women more frequently filling positions of power in "feminine" portfolios. In contrast to horizontal gender divides at the national level, however, female EU commissioners also occupy "masculine" and more prestigious policy areas, such as budget and external affairs. We describe how the organizational setup, appointment procedures, and personnel policy of the Commission create two distinct paths to leadership in the Commission: an administrative and a political path. Along these paths, we argue, individual factors like prior qualification and nationality play out differently, leading to the observed patterns in positional leadership.

The next section (3.2) develops this argument in more detail before we introduce our data (3.3). The chapter then describes women's leadership in the

Commission over time and across portfolios (section 3.4). It discusses the distinct career paths to political and administrative leadership in light of nationality and prior qualification and argues that, where these two paths meet, there is particular potential for women leaders to demonstrate agency (section 3.5). A brief conclusion (section 3.6) ends the chapter.

3.2 Explaining Positional Leadership: The Potential of Comparative Politics Insights for the Commission

This section sketches a framework for analyzing the "when," "where," and "how" of women's leadership in the Commission. Organizational setup, appointment procedures, and personnel policy provide a first layer of explanations for the state of women's positional leadership in the Commission.

In the EU system, access to the political top of the Commission is based on a formal appointment process. Every country nominates one or two potential candidates. On this basis, the Commission president decides on the allocation of portfolios and negotiates policy field responsibilities in close connection with personnel decisions. This process has changed over time, with implications for women's leadership in the Commission. Historically, commissioners were proposed by their national governments and the list adopted by the Council. The Maastricht Treaty increased the EP's say in the choice of Commission personnel, giving it the power to approve or reject the entire Commission. The Parliament turned this into a powerful instrument to scrutinize nominees in individual hearings on their legal and political fit for the job (Wonka 2007: 169–189). Prodi has been referred to as the first Commission president to "understan[d] at least the rhetoric of balanced participation" (MacRae 2012: 310). He explicitly encouraged member states to put forward women's names. Close scrutiny indicates that the effort to achieve a gender-balanced Commission originates in the EP at least as much as in the Commission itself. For example, in 1995 the EP used its new right of scrutiny and consent to announce that it would accept the Commission only if it encompassed at least 25% female members. The Commission president gained more power to select commissioners with the Lisbon Treaty. The *Spitzenkandidaten* process strengthened the Commission president's ties with Parliament, which had been pushing for more women in the EU institutions. Closely connected, the nomination and selection of commissioners gained public visibility. In sum, these changes rendered the president more assertive vis-à-vis national governments in demanding that candidates meet specific profiles or that a number of candidates be put forward rather than a single choice (see Hartlapp et al. 2021: 137ff.).

The most powerful formal decision-making body in the Commission is the College of Commissioners. Decisions are made by simple majority, but de facto consensus prevails. In this setting, the share of women matters for putting issues on the agenda but also for discourse and alliance formation. Following critical mass theory, a tipping point is reached when roughly one-third of a group is female (Kanter 1977). This allows alliances to mobilize organizational resources and may give room to critical actors to not only shape policies, but also to reform institutions to improve the situation of women within them (Dahlerup 1988; Childs and Krook 2009).

Recruitment into the Commission administration is merit based and focuses on generalist profiles. Besides qualifications, nationality is a key factor both for initial recruitment and when it comes to promotion to higher career positions. Historically, staff regulations contained a commitment to "geographical balance." The allocation of top administrative positions was carried out with an eye to "fair shares" of nationalities (Kassim et al. 2013: 36) and national networks mattered for career advancement within the Commission. Over time, selection became more meritocratic and nationality less important (Kassim et al. 2013: 38–39). We observe a "technocratization" where individuals are increasingly likely to have worked in the Commission administration—on average in two different DGs— before moving to top positions (Kassim et al. 2013: 46, 59). For almost three decades now, staff policies have explicitly aimed at improving gender balance within the Commission ranks. These policies developed hand in hand with legislation and policy initiatives on gender equality, gender mainstreaming, and antidiscrimination directed at member states. Starting in the late 1980s, a number of positive action programs and strategies were adopted. Initially, they aimed at increasing career opportunities for women in the Commission administration through training and recruitment, but moved on to include awareness raising for equal opportunities and later evaluation and monitoring. In the 2000s, concrete measures were added, for example a requirement to build recruitment juries such that female candidates would not face all-male panels as well as systematic training of high-ranking officials in how to ensure gender mainstreaming in their management decisions. More recent measures and developments include gender equality scoreboards to compare advances across DGs, the strengthening of peer networks among senior female staff, and a number of holistic personnel policy programs that focus on broader matters of diversity and inclusion (see Hartlapp et al. 2021: 141ff.).

As nationality makes a difference in the supply of female candidates, we expect it to make a difference also as women seek to advance along the two paths to leadership positions in the Commission. In most countries, women have had considerably more difficulty gaining access to the executive compared to the legislature (Bauer and Tremblay 2011), and female shares in executive branches have tended to follow the dynamics in the legislatures with a substantial time lag (Reynolds 1999: 572). The comparative politics literature typically shows that women's representation in national politics is influenced by a mixture of country-specific political institutions and socioeconomic and cultural factors. Proportional elec-toral systems—in particular the ones involving relatively large, multicandidate districts—together with a gender quota, a high share of women's employment, and a prevalence of progressive gender role attitudes are seen as instrumental in in-creasing the share of women legislators (Stockemer 2007; Paxton et al. 2010; for an overview, see Bauer and Tremblay 2011). In this respect, nationality is a proxy for a number of potentially meaningful differences between countries that affect the supply of female candidates as well as the importance a national government attaches to nominating women.

What is more, gendered differences in prior qualification, networks, and self-selection are likely to structure patterns of women's leadership. A common theme in research on women in national politics is a horizontal gender divide in execu-tive positions (Goddard 2019: 640; Kantola 2010). Krook and O'Brien consider portfolios with "feminine" and "masculine" characteristics[2] and combine them with a measure of portfolio prestige to assess horizontal gender divides (Krook and O'Brien 2012: 844–846). Women typically take executive positions in "softer socio-cultural ministerial positions" (Kantola 2010: 69) such as health, social welfare, education, family, and culture, while men assume ministries such as secu-rity and foreign affairs (Kantola 2010: 69; Goddard 2019: 640). These arguments are supported by cross-national data that shows that family, social affairs, envi-ronment, employment, and culture are those portfolios most frequently held by women.[3] Self-selection into portfolios that are particularly relevant for women's substantive representation (Celis et al. 2008) as well as structural conditions and stronger competition for "harder and politically more prestigious areas such as economic planning, national security and foreign affairs" (Kantola 2010: 69) could drive this. We know, however, that in the EU multilevel system competency trans-fer to the supranational level differs strongly between portfolios. While member states have endowed the Commission with far-reaching direct competences in some areas, other policy areas remain in the hands of member states. A good example is competition policy, where Brussels has a direct say on mergers and decides on the permissibility of state aid. In trade policy, the EU also negotiates on behalf of its members. What is more, areas that are attractive for their redistributive influence at the national level might fail to be so in a context where overall bud-get volume is limited to a very small proportion of national GDP. This is the case for employment and social policies, which in many member states make up the

---

[2] "Feminine" and "masculine" portfolio characteristics refer to the assignment of "primary respon-sibility for affairs in the public sphere to men and a central role in the private sphere to women" (Krook and O'Brien 2012: 842). Women thus often assume ministerial responsibility in areas closely associated with women's issues and the private sphere, i.e., "feminine" portfolios, while men in cabinets are often found in areas associated with the public sphere, i.e., "masculine" portfolios (Krook and O'Brien 2012: 844).

[3] Inter-Parliamentary Union, https://www.ipu.org (last accessed May 18, 2020).

greatest share of public expenditures, while at the EU level social policy spending remains low both in absolute terms and relative to agricultural or regional policy spending. This could affect the attractiveness of portfolios in the EU political system and might result in horizontal gender divides that differ substantially from those at the national level.

In sum, combining insights on the EU political system with arguments about women in national politics, this section has highlighted potential explanations for "when," "where," and "how" women lead in the Commission.

3.3 Data

The empirical analysis in this chapter uses data collected as part of a project on position formation in the European Commission. The project built up a database on all commissioners and directors general from the first Hallstein Commission in 1958 through the von der Leyen Commission (Hartlapp 2019). It covers information about names, dates of birth, gender, nationality, party affiliation, DGs,[4] Commissions, and dates of entry and exit for all positions a person served in the EU Commission as well as information regarding a person's professional background and post-Commission career (as per June 2020). The collected data primarily stems from official organization charts taken from the institution's website and its Historical Archives in Brussels, from Fabio Franchino's dataset on Commission portfolios since 1958, and from personal websites. The data has been complemented with interview material from the oral history project of the Historical Archives in Brussels to gain valuable insights on agency back in time.

When counting women who lead in the Commission, we analyze the material in distinct ways. We consider both the number of women in leadership positions in each Commission term (Figure 3.1) and the overall number of leadership terms served by women per member state (Figure 3.2).[5] Commissioners are appointed for one term but may return, either on the same portfolio or on a different one. The latter is typical for directors general, too. What is more, women in the Commission may be assigned to lead multiple portfolios. An example is Edith Cresson, who at a time led the DGs for Human Resources, for Research and Development, and for Education and Culture. Consequently, the number of women in the Commission differs depending on whether we look at persons, terms, or positions.

---

[4] The von der Leyen Commission functions as the default for DG and Service abbreviations and adjustments are made to allow for timelines. For the analysis, we include all DGs, but exclude central services for interpretation (SCIC), for translation (DGT) and for statistics (EUROSTAT), as well as the European Anti-Fraud Office (OLAF) and Publications Office.

[5] In cases where the person who holds an office changes during a term, we consider the person who served longer and exclude the other; e.g., Kristalina Georgieva is excluded as budget commissioner under Juncker. For the same reason, we do not consider women that served as "acting" director general at the cutoff date in June 2020.

In our data, we present absolute numbers as well as relative shares. Absolute numbers show how the political staff has become more female. Relative numbers provide insight into women's likely impact on decision-making in an evolving institution. The number of commissioners has varied over the integration process. In 2021, there are 27 commissioners—one per member state. Historically, France, United Kingdom, Italy, Spain, and Germany each had two commissioners, but with enlargement the Nice Treaty brought this to an end (2004). Following Eastern enlargement there was a period when some portfolios had double heads. An example is the DG for Health and Food Safety, which was led jointly by Commissioners Meglena Kuneva and Markos Kyprianou during part of the Barroso I Commission. The deepening and widening of integration are visible in the growing number of commissioners after enlargement and shifts in the number of DGs[6] in reaction to competence transfer, emerging policy problems, and related restructuring. These changes are particularly relevant in the interpretation of relative numbers.

3.4 Patterns of Women's Leadership in the Commission

To understand when and where women accessed leadership positions, we start with developments over time before turning to horizontal gender divides.

Dynamics over Time: Growing Slowly toward (Near) Parity

Figure 3.1 plots the absolute numbers as well as the relative share of women over the different Commission terms. Women are clearly underrepresented and have been absent from power positions in the early decades of integration. The first women entered the College of Commissioners with the Delors II Commission in 1989: Vasso Papandreou from Greece and Christiane Scrivener from France. A little later, in 1990, the first female director general, Colette Flesch from Luxembourg, followed on the administrative side. From then on, numbers started to rise. The increase over time is striking—from 12% under Delors II to almost parity today.

Patterns differ substantially between political and administrative positions. In the College of Commissioners, numbers started to rise earlier. There were five women in the Santer and Prodi Colleges. During this period, female commissioners were largely nominated by the big member states, which each had two positions at their disposal. Thus, under Delors, Christiane Scrivener accessed the

---

[6] The number evolves from 24 (Delors II) to 28 (Santer), 26 (Prodi and Barroso I), 31 (Barroso II and Juncker), and, currently, 33 (von der Leyen).

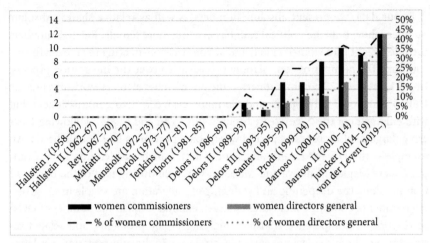

Fig. 3.1 Women at the top of the Commission over time

Notes: Women's terms with N = 87, 52 women commissioners and 35 women directors general, including double entries of persons serving in more than one Commission.
Source: Own compilation (as of June 2020).

Commission on the "second ticket" from France. The same held true for Edith Cresson from France, Emma Bonino from Italy, and Monika Wulf-Mathies from Germany under Santer as well as Loyola de Palacio and Michaele Schreyer under Prodi. This practice ended with the Nice Treaty coming into force in 2004. Thus, where governments once sent women in addition to men, starting with Barroso, women were more often sent instead of men. Yet women's share of commissioners in the two Barroso Commissions and the following Juncker Commission never surpassed 35% (eight, ten, and nine women, respectively). This is partly due to enlargement, as the greater number of commissioners overall (including many new male commissioners) "consumed" the effect of women's greater representation from older members. From the perspective of critical mass theory, this is crucial. It marks a lengthy period of stagnation, before the College moved from being skewed to a more balanced decision-making arena (Kanter 1977). Female empowerment at the political top of the Commission gained traction again with von der Leyen (12 women, 44%).[7] Overall, female access has seen upswings and relative stagnation, with absolute as well as relative figures growing significantly under Santer as well as von der Leyen.

At the administrative top, women's access to the Commission started at a similar moment in time, but shows a different dynamic. Shortly after the first female commissioner was appointed, Colette Flesch followed as the first female director

---

[7] The figures grew to 13 women and 48% when the Irish government replaced Commissioner Philip Hogan with former MEP Mairead McGuinness in September 2020, and von der Leyen reshuffled the Commission.

general. Heading the DG for Communication, she remained the only female director general under Delors III. In fact, the numbers remained exceptionally low over an extended period (two women under Santer, three under Prodi and Barroso I). A steady increase began with Barroso II (five women), continuing under Juncker (eight women) and von der Leyen (12 women). This points to the relevance of structural and systemic change in the Commission administration that affects women's positional leadership. Overall, developments at the apex of the administration were more limited in the beginning. Recently, women have reached absolute numbers and shares in administrative leadership positions that are similar to the figures on the political side.

Horizontal Gender Divides and "Feminine" Portfolios

The following figures show gender divides among Commission portfolios for commissioners and directors general. The Commission, of course, is an evolving institution. DGs have been subject to cuts and reassignments and have thus existed for different time spans—consequently affecting the odds of showing a high or low number of female positions.

Figure 3.2 illustrates that "feminine" portfolios clearly exist in the Commission. Much like at the national level, more women are represented in those portfolios that are considered as "feminine" in the literature (Krook and O'Brien 2012: 844–846): Education and Culture (EAC, seven positions in total), Health and Food Safety (SANTE, six positions in total) and Employment and Social Affairs

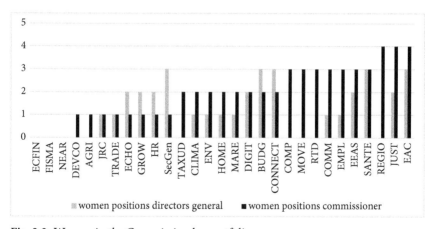

Fig. 3.2 Women in the Commission by portfolio

Notes: Women's positions with N = 92, 35 positions for women directors general and 57 positions for women commissioners, including double entries for persons holding more than one sectoral responsibility in a term. President not counted as she does not hold a sectoral responsibility. *Source:* Own compilation (as of June 2020).

(EMPL, four positions in total). Education, Health, Social, and Employment are comparatively weak EU portfolios as few competences in these fields have been transferred to the supranational level and relevant policymaking is hampered by divergent member-state interests. In contrast, the more powerful Economy (ECFIN) and Financial Affairs (FISMA) portfolios as well as the Enlargement (NEAR) portfolio have never been led by women.

Yet the Commission in other respects shows no clear-cut horizontal gender divide. This is visible not only where women in the Commission have accessed power positions in portfolios that are considered "masculine" (Krook and O'Brien 2012: 844–846) at the national level, but even more so where they lead powerful and prestigious portfolios in the EU political system. Budget is a prime example: Commissioners Michaela Schreyer[8] and Dalia Grybauskaite as well as Directors General Isabella Ventura, Edith Kitzmantel, and Nadia Calviño (BUDG, five positions total) led the powerful portfolio, holding internal veto power on all Commission decisions concerning EU spending (Hartlapp et al. 2014: 256–257). Similarly, the High Representatives Catherine Ashton and Federica Mogherini as well as Secretary General Helga Schmid have led the prestigious European External Action Service since its foundation in 2010 (EEAS, five positions in total).

Turning to differences between administrative and political leadership positions, we note that numerous portfolios have been led by female commissioners while all their directors general remain men. Regional Policy (REGIO, four positions), Research and Development (RTD, three positions), Mobility and Transport (MOVE, three positions), and Competition, with the prominent faces of Neelie Kroes and Margrethe Vestager (COMP, three positions), standing out in this regard. In the EU multilevel system, three of these portfolios can be considered particularly prestigious, as a substantial part of the EU budget runs through regional and research policy while the EU holds strong competences in competition policy. Women commissioners seem more likely to lead these particularly powerful portfolios with hard competences than their female counterparts at the administrative top of the Commission. In contrast, among directors general, many of the portfolios with a higher number of women have few EU competences, like Education and Culture (EAC), Health and Consumer Protection (SANTE), and Communications (CONNECT, three positions each). But even at the administrative top, notable exceptions exist, with strong women's leadership in the powerful portfolio of Budget (BUDG) and the highly prestigious Secretariat General (SecGen, three positions each), widely considered to be the power center of the European Commission (Kassim et al. 2013).

---

[8] Prodi had offered the Research portfolio. Schreyer declined "due to potential conflicts with her ideological Green beliefs" (Hartlapp et al. 2014: 158).

In sum, gender inequality in the Commission was particularly extreme in the early years of European integration. Unlike the EP, where a major breakthrough for women's representation occurred right after the first direct elections in 1979 (Norris and Franklin 1997), women's leadership in the Commission had a slow takeoff. Since then, women's shares have increased to 44% and 36% of the Commission's top political and administrative positions, respectively. Similar to the national level, access frequently runs via "feminine" portfolios. However, in contrast to national politics, women also lead "prestigious" portfolios with strong EU competences, in particular on the political side of the Commission.

3.5 Linking Paths to Power with Women's Individual Characteristics

Administrative and political leadership in the Commission show substantial differences regarding "when" and "where" women access these positions. Section 3.2 provided initial information on the organizational setup, appointment procedures, and personnel policy characterizing the two paths to leadership positions. We now turn to discussing how prior qualifications and nationality play out along the career paths to explain the observed patterns.

The Path to Political Leadership

The prior qualifications of female commissioners help us to understand patterns of "when" and "where" women lead at the political top of the Commission. For each commissioner, we determine prior qualification by assigning a professional group, based on the professional positions the person held previous to their engagement in the Commission. The largest share (62%) held ministerial positions, including one as head of government, before entering the Commission. Some were members of national parliaments or acted as party leaders (21%). National political institutions are clearly arenas important to fostering women's leadership in the Commission. The expertise women gain in national politics could in part explain why horizontal gender divides are less pronounced in the EU's executive than in national politics. Leadership positions in the Commission frequently mark a further step in careers that are already well advanced. Women who started out in "softer" portfolios have frequently moved to more powerful and prestigious positions at the national level. This qualifies them for powerful portfolios at the supranational level, as well. Take the example of Neelie Kroes: she had dealt with the privatization of public services as the Netherlands' minister for transport and communication before entering the Commission on the Competition portfolio. Or consider Margrethe Vestager, who entered Denmark's national government as minister for education, a classical soft portfolio, in 1998. She moved on to become minister for economic affairs and interior in 2011, providing her with valuable experience for the Competition portfolio in the EU Commission.

These individual characteristics then interact with the recruitment process for commissioners. Particularly since the Lisbon Treaty, Commission presidents have signaled to member-state governments that putting forward women might be rewarded with access to more prestigious and powerful portfolios. A case in point is von der Leyen's promise to give the powerful Internal Market portfolio to France on the condition that it nominates a woman for the position. Consequently, France proposed Sylvie Goulard, who had a strong background in EU politics as well as different national executive functions.[9] This example highlights that, while changes in appointment procedures are important to explain "when" women enter the Commission, taking into account differences in these women's experiences in national political systems leads us to a better understanding of "where" they act on leadership positions in the Commission.

Figure 3.3 shows large cross-country differences in the frequency distributions of women's nationality at the political top of the Commission. They range from zero terms for Hungarian and Slovakian women to six terms for female commissioners from Sweden. Low numbers of terms for women are typical among Eastern enlargement countries (Croatia, Estonia, Latvia, Lithuania, Slovakia, Slovenia, and Malta with one term each).[10] On the other side, Swedish commissioners are followed by Danish (five terms) and Bulgarian (four terms), then commissioners from France, Luxemburg, Greece, Germany, and Cyprus (three terms each). The comparative politics literature suggests that these differences are due to a range of national factors impacting on the differences in the supply of potential candidates and the likelihood that specific governments will nominate women. With a larger pool of women in national politics, governments were more easily able to appoint politically experienced female candidates when the demand for female commissioners increased beginning in the 1990s. The Scandinavian countries had cabinets with or close to parity early in the 1980s, while others still lag behind today (Davis 1997: 14).

As countries differ in how long they have been EU members, the figures are particularly remarkable for Sweden and Bulgaria, but also for Poland. Since its accession in 2007, Bulgaria has been represented in the College exclusively by women: Meglena Kunewa (DG SANTE), Kristalina Georgieva (DG ECHO under

---

[9] This condition, however, was later sacrificed when the politically divided EP signaled that it would not accept Goulard (cf. "Von der Leyen Commission Faces Delay after French Nominee's Rejection," *Politico*, October 10, 2019, and "Social Democrats Warn von der Leyen on Gender Balance," *Politico*, November 5, 2019).

[10] Ten new member states entered the EU in 2004 (Czech Republic, Estonia, Hungary, Latvia, Lithuania, Poland, Slovakia, Slovenia, Malta, and Cyprus), two in 2007 (Bulgaria and Rumania), and Croatia in 2013. Consequently, they are less likely to show a high number of women terms.

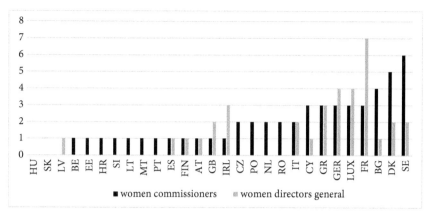

Fig. 3.3 Women in the Commission by country of origin

Notes: Women commissioner terms (N = 52) and women directors general terms (N = 35), including double entries of persons serving in more than one Commission. Note that countries differ in the duration of EU membership.
Source: Own compilation (as of June 2020).

Barroso II and a short stint in DG BUDG under Juncker), and Mariya Gabriel (DGs CONNECT and DIGIT under Juncker and DG EAC under von der Leyen). Similarly, all of Sweden's commissioners since the country entered the EU in 1995 have been female: Anita Gradin (DG JUST), Margot Wallström (DGs ENV under Prodi and COMM under Barroso I), Cecilia Malmström (DGs HOME under Barroso II and TRADE under Juncker), and Ylva Johansson (DG HOME). Along with Wallström (MacRae 2012: 305), Gradin has been hailed as a strong leader in the literature. She was decisive in anchoring women's interests in the Justice and Home Affairs portfolio by pushing trafficking in women onto the wider agenda of European policy cooperation and broadening the debate to include women's perspectives (Kantola 2010: 83). Regarding accession countries, women might thus be especially likely to be represented in "fresh" political settings where no male incumbents occupy positions and where top political positions seem more easily available than in their home countries, where they "struggle with gendered institutions" (Naurin and Naurin 2018: 222).

The Path to Administrative Leadership

Women in positions of power in the Commission administration typically worked in the Commission services before. Among female directors general, the majority were recruited to the Commission early in their careers and moved up the career ladder via a number of different portfolios. Some exceptions to this rule exist, notably for the women who were "parachuted" into leadership positions in earlier periods. Colette Flesch, the first female director general, held high-ranking positions in national politics in Luxembourg before taking up her position, and Edith Kitzmantel was a career bureaucrat in the Austrian Ministry of Finance before becoming director general in DG BUDG. There is only one recent example of this sort of exception. Helga Schmid was a career diplomat in Germany before entering the European External Action Service. This may be attributed to the unusual nature of the EEAS, which is jointly staffed by member states and the Commission.

Those who followed a more typical path through the administrative hierarchy include former Director General Odile Quintin, who came to Brussels as an intern in 1969–1970 before entering the services in 1971,[11] and the influential Secretary General Catherine Day, who arrived at the Commission in 1979. Starting in the DG for Common Market and Industry, she proceeded to work on portfolios as diverse as Competition, External Relations, and Environment before she moved to the administrative top of the Secretariat General (see Chapter 12 in this volume). Many of the current women leading DGs entered the Commission in the 1980s early in their lives (e.g., Irene Souka in 1980, Lowri Evans in 1983, or Monique Pariat in 1987) and worked their way up the career ladder through different DGs in line with the call for mobility in the Commission's personnel policy.

The administrative logic of career-making inside the Commission also affects nationality-related leadership patterns. As Figure 3.3 shows, over a dozen countries have never sent a female director general to the Commission. Among the Eastern enlargement countries, only Bulgaria, Latvia, and Cyprus have been represented by women directors general. In contrast, female leaders from founding member states are particularly well represented at the administrative top, with France counting seven women who have shaped EU policies as directors general. This nationality bias toward women leaders from the founding members suggests that recent increases in the number and share of women at the administrative top build on increasing recruitment at lower-ranking positions that began some time ago. Combining these observations and insights into prior qualification for the administrative path to leadership in the Commission, we can hypothesize that women ascending to leadership positions from countries that only became members in the new century (Eastern Europe) still need time to reach the top. This could explain their underrepresentation in positions at the apex, even though they may have "reached middle management positions significantly more rapidly" (Kassim et al. 2013: 63).

In sum, the organizational setup, appointment procedures, and personnel policy that structure the administrative and the political path to leadership positions in the Commission interact differently with prior qualifications and nationality. Prior career paths differ between commissioners, who typically served in their national executives, and directors general, who customarily worked their way up through

---

[11] Historical Archives of the European Union, Oral History Programme, Entretien avec Odile Quintin, January 31, 2011, p. 4, https://archives.eui.eu/en/oral_history/#ECM2.

the organizational hierarchy. Scandinavian nationalities are overrepresented in the political but not in the administrative branch. This highlights the importance of national differences in the supply of potential candidates for political leadership. At the same time, it underlines that the date of accession particularly matters to women's presence in administrative leadership, as time is needed for women to work their way up the Commission's internal career ladder.

The Potential of Combined Paths for Women's Substantive Representation

Sometimes, in some fields, women co-lead at the administrative and political top. Under Prodi the portfolios of Budget, Environment, and Employment and Social Affairs were jointly led by a female commissioner and a female director general. Similar constellations followed under Barroso I (DG SANTE), Barroso II (DGs JUST and MARE), Juncker (DGs DIGIT, GROW, JUST and EEAS), and von der Leyen (DGs EAC, COMM, CLIMA, HOME, and SANTE; see the Appendix to this volume, for an overview). Compared to the absolute numbers of women in the Commission, these politico-administrative leadership alliances are relatively frequent and seem to have become even more common since a critical mass of female commissioners joined the College (see Figure 3.1). It is possible that women have used their political leadership positions to recruit women to top administrative positions as their directors general. A good example is Environment Commissioner Wallström; looking for a new chief for her DG in 2002, she called Catherine Day, stating that she "would love to have a woman Director General."[12] This underlines that, even more than critical mass, it is the critical agency of women that matters to the mobilization of organizational resources and shaping of leadership positions (Childs and Krook 2009; Dahlerup 1988).

What is more, there is evidence that portfolios with joint women leadership across the politico-administrative branches are particularly likely to shape policies in line with women's interests. A prime example begins with Commissioner for Employment and Social Affairs Anna Diamantopoulou, who pushed through legislation that widened the scope of existing antidiscrimination directives from employment to social protection, including healthcare and social advantages, as well as access to public goods and services (Directives 2000/78/EC and 2004/113/EC). She used her power position in the organizational setup of the Commission to advance policies against opposition from other DGs and member states that feared increased costs. When she left the Commission in 2004, her director general, Odile Quintin, continued to push the agenda and led DG Employment and Social

---

[12] Historical Archives of the European Union, Oral History Programme, Entretien avec Catherine Day, September 9, 2011, p. 11, https://archives.eui.eu/en/oral_history/#ECM2.

Affairs to propose a general framework directive for equal treatment (Hartlapp et al. 2014: 71–77). Similarly, women's leadership alliances across the political and administrative top seem to have affected foreign policy developments, e.g., the 2018 Strategic Approach to Women, Peace and Security to further implement UN Security Council Resolution 1325 and a shift from men/women dichotomies toward more gender-inclusive reasoning in central policy documents (Haastrup et al. 2019: 67–68). The current women leaders are reported "to ensure the gender perspective" in all the meetings in which they mutually participate and to have "launched several initiatives to strengthen the pipeline of women for management positions, by providing trainings and networking opportunities" (Horst 2020). These examples suggest that combined administrative and political leadership could be particularly relevant to the study of agency and to explain with greater precision how descriptive and substantial representation are linked.

3.6 Conclusion

This chapter has described the ascent of women to leadership positions in the Commission. Original data on all women who have worked at the political and administrative top of the Commission shows that women's representation developed late—with virtually no women at the Commission's apex in its first 35 years—rising to almost 45% (commissioners) and 36% (directors general) today. Women partly access leadership positions via "feminine" portfolios (Krook and O'Brien 2012), but at the political top they also occupy powerful and prestigious EU portfolios such as Budget or External Affairs. The organizational setup, appointment procedures, and personnel policy—all evolving over time—interact with individuals' prior qualifications and supply of potential women leaders in national political systems, resulting in a complex process that does not offer one single dynamic or explanatory factor. Instead, different patterns characterize female leadership at the administrative and political top. Regarding the top administrative positions, prospective candidates—women not least—from accession countries need time to reach the top of the career ladder. This means of ascent within the organization is supported by a personnel policy that since the 1980s addressed gender as a staff issue. Women in the highest political echelons typically enter through national executives. In the early years, they were almost exclusively nominated by member states that could appoint two commissioners and chose to name a woman on the second ticket. When the EP and the Commission president demanded more female candidates be put forward for the political top positions from the mid-1990s onward, this was more easily met by governments with higher numbers of experienced female politicians. These experienced women were frequently able to gain access to "masculine" and "prestigious" portfolios (Krook and O'Brien 2012: 846). We have argued that this interaction of demand

and supply across the EU multilevel system helps explain why the horizontal gender divide seems to be less pronounced at the political top of the Commission. At a more general level, the case of the Commission shows how factors used to explain women's representation in national politics are mediated by the specificities of the EU political system. Researchers thus benefit from combining the literatures of comparative politics of gender and EU politics.

How these patterns and causes of descriptive representation affect policymaking is beyond the scope of this chapter. In this respect, we consider agency in the exertion of leadership within alliances a particularly promising aspect for research on positional leadership. Our data helps to identify terms with joint female leadership across the Commission's political and administrative branches. These observations could be developed further in two directions. First, future research could link the issue of alliance formation and critical agency (Dahlerup 1988; Childs and Krook 2009) more systematically to questions of substantial representation. Second, the study of alliances and women's agency could move beyond the Commission and expand to links that run between women in the EP, Council, and Commission (Kantola 2010: 101).

References

Ahrens, Petra. 2019. "The Birth, Life, and Death of Policy Instruments: 35 Years of EU Gender Equality Policy Programmes." *West European Politics* 42 (1): 45–66.

Bauer, Gretchen, and Manon Tremblay. 2011. *Women in Executive Power: A Global Overview*. New York: Routledge.

Blome, Agnes. 2017. *Politics of Work-Family Policy Reforms in Germany and Italy*. New York: Routledge.

Brunsbach, Sandra. 2011. "Machen Frauen den Unterschied? Parlamentarierinnen als Repräsentantinnen frauenspezifischer Interessen im Deutschen Bundestag." *Zeitschrift für Parlamentsfragen* 42 (1): 3–24.

Celis, Karen, Sarah Childs, Johanna Kantola, and Mona Lena Krook. 2008. "Rethinking Women's Substantive Representation." *Representation* 44 (2): 99–110.

Childs, Sarah, and Mona Lena Krook. 2009. "Analysing Women's Substantive Representation: From Critical Mass to Critical Actors." *Government and Opposition* 44 (2): 125–145.

Dahlerup, Drude. 1988. "From a Small to a Large Minority: Women in Scandinavian Politics." *Scandinavian Political Studies* 11 (4): 275–298.

Davis, Rebecca Howard. 1997. *Women and Power in Parliamentary Democracies: Cabinet Appointments in Western Europe, 1968–1992*. Lincoln: University of Nebraska Press.

Freedman, Jane. 2002. "Women in the European Parliament." *Parliamentary Affairs* 55 (1): 179–188.

Goddard, Dee. 2019. "Entering the Men's Domain? Gender and Portfolio Allocation in European Governments." *European Journal of Political Research* 58 (2): 631–655.

Haastrup, Toni, Katharine A. M. Wright, and Roberta Guerrina. 2019. "Bringing Gender In? EU Foreign and Security Policy after Brexit." *Politics and Governance* 7 (3): 62–71.

Hafner-Burton, Emilie M., and Mark A. Pollack. 2009. "Mainstreaming Gender in the European Union: Getting the Incentives Right." *Comparative European Politics* 7 (1): 114–138.

Hartlapp, Miriam. 2019. Position Formation in the EU Commission. Version 1.0.0. doi: 10.7802/1.2130.

Hartlapp, Miriam, Julia Metz, and Christian Rauh. 2014. *Which Policy for Europe? Power and Conflict inside the European Commission*. Oxford: Oxford University Press.

Hartlapp, Miriam, Henriette Müller, and Ingeborg Tömmel. 2021. "Gender Equality and the European Commission." In *The Routledge Handbook of Gender and EU Politics*, eds. Gabriele Abels, Andrea Krizsán, Heather MacRae, and Anna van der Vleuten, 133–145. Abingdon, UK, and New York: Routledge.

Horst, Corinna. 2020. "A Credible and Accountable EU Foreign Service? Not Yet." EUobserver, March 11.

Jacquot, Sophie. 2015. *Transformations in EU Gender Equality. From Emergence to Dismantling*. London: Palgrave Macmillan.

Kanter, Rosabeth Moss. 1977. *Men and Women of the Corporation*. New York: Basic Books.

Kantola, Johanna. 2010. *Gender and the European Union*. Basingstoke: Palgrave Macmillan.

Kassim, Hussein, John Peterson, Michael W. Bauer, Sara Connolly, Renaud Dehousse, Liesbet Hooghe, and Andrew Thompson. 2013. *The European Commission of the Twenty-First Century*. Oxford: Oxford University Press.

Krook, Mona Lena, and Diana Z. O'Brien. 2012. "All the President's Men? The Appointment of Female Cabinet Ministers Worldwide." *Journal of Politics* 74 (3): 840–855.

MacRae, Heather. 2012. "Double-Speak: The European Union and Gender Parity." *West European Politics* 35 (2): 301–318.

Mazey, Sonia. 1988. "European Community Action on Behalf of Women: The Limits of Legislation." *Journal of Common Market Studies* 27 (1): 63–84.

Naurin, Daniel, and Elin Naurin. 2018. "Descriptive Representation and Negotiation: Gender Balance in the Committees of the Council of the European Union." In *Gendering Diplomacy and International Negotiation*, eds. Karin Aggestam, and Ann E. Towns, 213–237. Cham, Switzerland: Palgrave Macmillan.

Naurin, Daniel, Elin Naurin, and Amy Alexander. 2019. "Gender Stereotyping and Chivalry in International Negotiations: A Survey Experiment in the Council of the European Union." *International Organization* 73 (2): 469–488.

Norris, Pippa, and Mark Franklin. 1997. "Social Representation." *European Journal of Political Research* 32 (2): 185–210.

Paxton, Pamela, Melanie M. Hughes, and Matthew A. Painter. 2010. "Growth in Women's Political Representation: A Longitudinal Exploration of Democracy, Electoral System and Gender Quotas." *European Journal of Political Research* 49 (1): 25–52.

Reynolds, Andrew. 1999. "Women in the Legislatures and Executives of the World: Knocking at the Highest Glass Ceiling." *World Politics* 51 (4): 547–572.

Stockemer, Daniel. 2007. "Why Are There Differences in the Political Representation of Women in the 27 Countries of the European Union?" *Perspectives on European Politics and Society* 8 (4): 476–493.

Stockemer, Daniel, and Aksel Sundström. 2019. "Do Young Female Candidates Face Double Barriers or an Outgroup Advantage? The Case of the European Parliament." *European Journal of Political Research* 58 (1): 373–384.

Wonka, Arndt. 2007. "Technocratic and Independent? The Appointment of European Commissioners and Its Policy Implications." *Journal of European Public Policy* 14 (2): 169–189.

4

Women's Leadership in the European Parliament

A Long-Term Perspective

Sarah C. Dingler and Jessica Fortin-Rittberger

4.1 Introduction

The European Parliament (EP) is often touted as a role model of gender parity with its explicit commitments to gender equality and higher levels of women's representation than in the lower houses of its member states. Is this exceptionalism still visible when we peel back the most conspicuous layer and look past who gets to have a seat in Strasbourg? In this chapter, we investigate patterns of representation between countries over time and identify current hurdles to women's access to the EP. We also move beyond presence and investigate how women fare across the hierarchies and policy areas of the EP, contributing to the study of women's positional leadership (see Chapter 1 in this volume) in parliamentary contexts.

Our investigation reveals a paradox. The representation of women in the EP has remained on average higher than that of its member states' parliaments during its entire 40 years of existence. Furthermore, the proportion of female MEPs has steadily increased with each successive election. In this regard, the EP is nothing short of an exceptional success story for the representation of women in elected office: the march toward equal representation shows no sign of slowing down and offers no hint of an invisible or unbreachable barrier that will keep women short of parity in this elected body as is the case in many countries. This is a rare trend even among advanced industrial democracies, where the most gender-equal parliaments feature some 40% women at most. While this 40-year trend at the European level is undeniable, we have yet to find compelling explanations for it.

The absence of an upper limit to presence does not translate into a parallel pattern of vertical mobility. Patterns of positional leadership inside the EP becloud the widely held narrative of EU exceptionalism. Chairmanships and vice-chairmanships remain gendered, mirroring the patterns we find in member countries' lower houses. The proportion of women in leadership positions has

Sarah C. Dingler and Jessica Fortin-Rittberger, *Women's Leadership in the European Parliament: A Long-Term Perspective.*
In: *Women and Leadership in the European Union.* Edited by Henriette Müller and Ingeborg Tömmel, Oxford University
Press. © Oxford University Press (2022). DOI: 10.1093/oso/9780192896216.003.0005

remained below that of men in the EP, with a slower growth rate. Further, the distribution of women in committees follows a gendered pattern as well. The bulk of women are leading or participating in committees that are more "feminine" in substance. The influential committees still tilt in favor of men.

After all, the EP is not so exceptional if we look beyond presence. This opens interesting avenues for research challenging existing theories, which are mainly geared toward explaining descriptive representation. Future contributions should seek to shed light on the mechanisms linking descriptive representation to vertical mobility of women in elected bodies. Understanding how these two relate may, in turn, disentangle factors that are intrinsic to the EP as an electoral arena from the combination of factors unfolding in each country or at the level of individual parties.

4.2 The EP: A Unique Place for Women's Representation

Few will find grounds to challenge the now established conventional wisdom that the EU is a success story in terms of women's representation. All studies of the matter—from the earliest to the most recent—have observed what seems to be EU exceptionalism and sought to account for it (Freedman 2002; Kantola 2010; Vallance and Davis 1986; Norris 1997; Fortin-Rittberger and Rittberger 2014). Sifting through 40 years of history and scholarship, the EP consistently outperforms its member states' parliaments in terms of gender-equal representation. Figure 4.1 illustrates these two parallel, but distinct trends. While both show an upward trajectory, the line representing the percentage of women in the lower houses of national parliaments stubbornly lingers below that of the EP. This gap between national politics and the EP shows no sign of closing since the first European election in 1979: the EP has been and remains a beacon.

The patterns of expansion in women's political representation have often been nonlinear at the national level (Salmond 2006; Matland 1993). In most advanced industrial democracies, growth in women's presence has been S-shaped. The early years after enfranchisement were characterized by low and stable levels of women in parliaments followed by a slow rate of growth. These slow starts were often followed by dramatic upward shifts—resulting from societal modernization of attitudes and the adoption of gender quotas—before smoothing at a relatively high level, ideally parity. For most countries, growth has flattened in the 2000s, in a range just shy of parity, between 30% and 40%. Given that the EP was established long after most of its main constituent countries instated universal voting rights, we cannot expect it to reproduce the traditional pattern, as the 1980s marked for many countries an era of fast representational progress.

The shape of the historical development of women's representation in the EP deserves special attention, as it defies most of the patterns observed in countries.

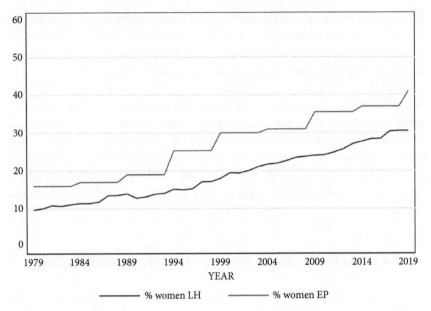

Fig. 4.1 Percentage of women in the European Parliament and the lower houses of the EU member states

This trajectory of progressive growth shows no visible setback so far. The gains in numerical strength in the EP have been incremental: steady increases from election to election, what Hughes and Paxton (2019: 40) call a "high incremental gains trajectory" like that of countries such as Finland and Sweden, where women's representation crossed the 30% threshold in the late 1970s. In the EP, this level was reached in 1999.

This pattern of gradual increases in women's representation over time is interesting given the incredible diversity in women's numerical strength in the lower houses of EU members: from tokenism and minimal representation in Hungary to parity in Sweden. The steady growth is also surprising considering that additional countries have joined the EU over the years, thereby drastically altering the relative national composition of the EP. The latest set of additions to the EU, East Central European (ECE) countries, have not managed to slow down the march toward a more gender-equal EP, despite having substantially lower proportions of women in their national parliaments than most of the older member countries.

Most important, these representational gains imply that the kind of informal barrier that constrains women's advancement in so many professional settings seemingly does not operate in the EP. Such barriers to representation have loomed in almost all organizations, including the parliaments and subnational assemblies of advanced industrial democracies. The EP does not exhibit the patterns of stagnation in shares of female office holders observed in the Netherlands, Denmark, and Germany (Kjaer 1999; Kroeber et al. 2019; Leyenaar 2013), which means that in this arena, at least, by contrast with national and subnational assemblies, the representation of women has generated the self-reinforcing impact outlined in the literature, operating via contagion or coattail effects (Leyenaar 2013; Tremblay and Pelletier 2001; Wolbrecht and Campbell 2007).

Further, the EP has so far been immune to a backlash against women's equality, which could have resulted from the increased visibility of women as leaders (Brescoll et al. 2018; Rudman et al. 2012), a perceived change in the balance between group privilege and disadvantage (Townsend-Bell 2020), or the rising electoral success of radical-right parties with reactionary views of women's position in society (Wodak 2015).

4.3 What Explains Women's Representation in the EP?

The literature has given rise to six complementary explanations to account for the high percentage of women in the EP. The assumption underlying most of these explanations is that the EP produces a different, even unique, competitive environment compared to national parliaments. The first and most common line of argumentation emphasizes the role of electoral institutions, namely that the prevalence of proportional representation (PR) in EP elections benefits women (Vallance and Davis 1986). The second pertains to the assumed lower importance and competitiveness of EP elections in relation to national parliamentary elections (Kantola 2010; Stockemer 2008). Third, a number of studies highlight the supply side and argue that women consider the EP a friendlier environment than their national parliaments (Footitt 2002; Freedman 2002). A fourth set of explanations hinges on the absence of entrenched male hegemony in the EP and the absence of male incumbents to defeat in the first, 1979 elections (Studlar and McAllister 1991; Studlar and Welch 1991), yielding increased opportunities for female candidates to succeed (Kantola 2010). Fifth, some have credited the high level of activism of women's movements in the EU for increasing women's descriptive representation by politicizing the issue of gender-equal representation (Krook 2002). Finally, a more recent branch of research has looked into the interplay of supply of candidates, voters, and parties nominating candidates for EP elections (Fortin-Rittberger and Rittberger 2015; Lühiste and Kenny 2016; Xydias 2016; Aldrich 2020; Lühiste 2015).

While there is merit in all these strands of research, a convincing explanation still eludes researchers. The aggregate representation figures, as illustrated in Figure 4.1, conceal much of the rich variance that exists between countries. Women's representation in each country's lower house compared to the EP exhibit differences that are not readily interpretable through a single pattern. In other words, we should be careful and resist the temptation to assume that elections at the European level are intrinsically distinct electoral contests; for some countries, there are large disparities between national parliaments and the EP, for others, much less. The representational gaps between national lower houses and the EP have been trivial in Cyprus, Italy, Portugal, Spain, Belgium, the Netherlands, and Germany—below five percentage points on average. These cases put a dent in theories holding the European legislature as being a friendlier or less competitive electoral arena across the board. Differences have been much more pronounced in Austria, France, Ireland, and, to a certain extent, the United Kingdom (UK) and Greece. We are hard pressed to determine why this is the case since these countries have little in common. We find the largest representational gaps in the group of new additions to the EU in East Central Europe, where women have been nearly absent from the national parliaments—for many, the difference is more than 15 percentage points between the domestic and EP levels. And still, there is no clear-cut regional trend: in Lithuania and the Czech Republic, representational gaps have fluctuated widely, while in the case of Poland, the representational gap is even inverted, with the Sejm having been more open to women than the EP.

While there certainly are grounds for rejoicing when looking at the status women have achieved in the EP, researchers seeking explanations should keep in mind that these figures are highly aggregated ones. Descriptive representation at the European level is a distal outcome of a combination of factors that include the interaction of national cultural contexts and electoral rules shaping national party systems. These, in turn, are transposed to a different competitive arena for EP elections, often held under quite different districting, consequently affecting both intra- and inter-party competition. In other words, it remains to be demonstrated whether this aggregate higher level of representation is caused by factors intrinsic to the EP as an electoral arena rather than a combination of factors unfolding in each country or at the level of individual parties. If the EP indeed provides a friendlier and more gender-equal environment, we should see better legislative presence translate into better access to leadership positions, including those regarded as the most powerful. As we show in the following section, however, hierarchical mobility of female MEPs has remained limited and there is a persistent pattern of feminized division of labor.

4.4 Women's Leadership Positions within the EP

Significant attention has been dedicated to explaining women's access to the EP at the aggregate level; few studies, however, have looked into the linkage between legislative and executive positions (see Chapter 1 in this volume). While the representation of women in the EP shows no sign of being constrained by an informal barrier, the question as to whether more opportunities for women to access the EP have increased their influence beyond tokenism—in other words, if presence translates into access to leadership positions—has received much less attention. The status of women in parliaments merits serious consideration and what we find is sobering: while women have steadily approached and almost reached parity in the EP, their presence among EP presidents, European party group (EPG) leaders, and committee chairs has not followed the same trend. If we consider gendered patterns of appointments to the kind of leadership positions that are particularly important to careers at the European level, the old adage "the higher, the fewer" still applies.[1]

A number of studies suggest that increasing the number of women in parliament may go hand in hand with women's inclusion in cabinets, executives, or high courts (Jalalzai 2013; Reynolds 1999; Thames and Williams 2013). There are reasons, however, to remain skeptical about whether there is a naturally reinforcing process of women's positional power across different hierarchies, as evidenced by multiple works on the law of minority attrition (Cotter et al. 2001; Putnam 1976; Taagepera 1994). Once in office, women face additional barriers to advancement into leadership positions compared to men. Research focusing on the national level demonstrates that within party organizations, irrespective of their numerical representation, women face more obstacles to achieving positions of leadership (O'Brien 2015; Verge and de la Fuente 2014). Female MPs tend to be sidelined in the agenda-setting process and are less likely to serve as powerful committee chairs (Barnes 2016; Heath et al. 2005). To understand if similar patterns of women's marginalization are also at play in the EP, we investigate whether representational gains have translated into leadership equality (see Chapter 1 in this volume). This section first examines all EP presidents, EPG leaders, and committee chairmanships in the EP. Second, we assess whether women disproportionately obtain leadership positions in committees with relatively little budgetary control and legislative influence or softer "feminine" policy areas that reproduce patriarchal or stereotypical societal roles (Krook and O'Brien 2012).

The most prestigious positions in the EP include the leadership of EPGs and the EP presidency. While these offices are scarce and difficult to attain for any MEP, climbing up the hierarchy to reach these top positions seems to be particularly challenging for women. Of the 153 MEPs that served as chair or cochair of an EPG within the EP since 1979 until the end of the last legislative term, only 32 (21%) were female, and only two women (11%) presided over the EP compared to 16 men. Women fare slightly better in secondary leadership positions, with 27%

---

[1] These positions can be considered especially important to become part of the developing European elite. Previous research demonstrates that MEPs holding the office of president, vice-president of the EP, committee chair, or party group leader are more likely to return to the EP indicating that these positions are an attractive option for a legislative career. In turn, they are important leadership positions for careers within the EP, which increasingly requires EU-specific experience (Whitaker 2014).

of EPG vice-chairs and 23% of EP vice-presidents. Even as the number of leadership positions available increases, a clear gendered hierarchy persists, with men occupying the most influential positions.

The most sought-after position within the EP—albeit not the most prestigious per se—is the role of committee chair.[2] Committee chairs and vice-chairs can structure committee proceedings and contribute to the shaping of legislation. Chairs, in particular, can enhance cohesion and coherence within committees and play a vital role in finding effective solutions to problems, thereby increasing the committee's output substantially (Hix 1999). Additionally, leadership positions provide opportunities to influence legislation and significantly affect visibility— the position of a committee chair is a strong predictor for speech-making in the plenary (Greene and Cross 2017).

The allocation of committee chairs follows a complex procedure (Whitaker 2011). First, corresponding to the share of MEPs, EPGs are assigned the committees to which they can nominate chairs. Next, at the EPG level, based on their delegation sizes, national parties select their preferred committees. Finally, national parties nominate one of their MEPs to the position of chair of a particular committee. This process mainly takes place behind closed doors, but the limited information that becomes publicly available betrays a climate of fierce competitiveness, in particular with regard to the nomination of chairs for the most powerful committees (see, e.g., Chiru 2020).[3] The few existing studies on committee chair allocation in the EP reveal that the decisive factors are seniority and loyalty to the EPG in form of voting behavior, general leadership skills, and personal relationships, rather than policy specialization (Bowler and Farrell 1995; Chiru 2020). While these studies provide some insight about the structural factors shaping who holds the committee chairs, they reveal little about their potentially gendered allocation.

As Figure 4.2 displays, women's access to these important positions in the EP is comparatively circumscribed. Fewer than 20% of committees were headed by women when the EP's first term began in 1979. While the proportion of women holding such positions has risen over time, the rate of increase was sluggish until the 2009–2014 term. Further progress toward parity was reached in the eighth term (2014–2019), during which a little more than 40% of the chairs were female MEPs. Similar patterns can be found in national parliaments in EU member states,

---

[2] Among MEPs, the position of committee chair is the most preferred according to survey results. When asked to choose their first preference from among the EP posts of group president, EP president, national delegation leader, or committee chair, more respondents opted for committee chair than any of the alternatives (McElroy 2006).

[3] Understanding powerful committees in terms of their legislative involvement and their influence over the EU budget, Chiru (2020) identified the following as powerful committees: AGRI (from 2009), BUDG, LIBE (from 2004), CULT (from 1994), ECON, EMPL (1989–2009), ENVI, ITRE, IMCO, INTA (from 2009), JURI, and TRAN (from 1989).

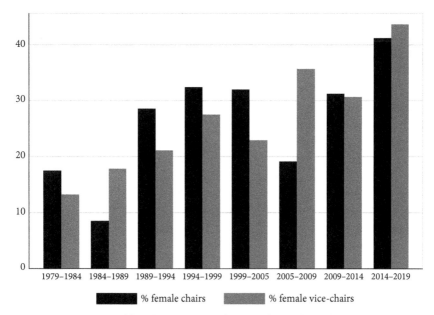

Fig. 4.2 Percentage of female committee chairs and vice-chairs by term

Source: Own calculation based on data retrieved from the automated database provided by Høyland et al. (2010). Only standing committees are included.

with women underrepresented in leadership positions.[4] Comparing the share of female chairs and vice-chairs, there is no consistent pattern of women disproportionately serving as vice-chairs, suggesting they have not faced higher hurdles than men to advance to the highest position overall. While during some terms (e.g., the second and sixth) the share of female vice-chairs clearly surpassed the share of female chairs, in others, we observe the opposite distribution (e.g., the third and fifth terms) or near parity (e.g., the seventh and eighth terms) between the positions.

Given that the nomination of chairs is in the hands of political parties, the literature has focused on examining the gendered patterns of nominations by gatekeepers. Explanations as to why party and institutional gatekeepers evaluate women's competence for leadership positions as less promising generally revolve around lingering gender stereotypes rather than institutional or supply-side factors. One set of studies conjectures that women are perceived to be less competent to fulfil leadership tasks based on traditional ideas about the role of men and women in a given society (see also Chapter 1 in this volume). Such stereotypes associate women with the domestic sphere and men with public life outside the home (Gatens 1991; Elshtain 1981; Landes 1998). Women are attributed character

---

[4] In the current Austrian Nationalrat, only around 20% of chairs and vice-chairs are female. In the 19th (2017–2021) German Bundestag, only around 35% of those positions were filled by women (mirroring their presence in the Bundestag as a whole).

traits such as being warm, sensitive, passionate, and compromising, while men are seen as strong, competitive, assertive, and aggressive (see Huddy and Terkildsen 1993 for an overview). These "masculine" traits are considered important for candidates when running for higher office (Huddy and Terkildsen 1993; Burrell 1994; Rosenwasser and Dean 1989).

A second set of explanations for women's limited access to leadership positions hinges on backlashes against women leaders once their role or status clashes with stereotypical expectations of what is appropriate for women, rather than on their perceived lesser competence (Rudman et al. 2012). Agentic women may be recognized as highly competent but risk prejudice and discrimination during selection processes for behaving counter-stereotypically. Female MEPs face such catch-22 situations. On the one hand, they must display agency to be perceived as qualified enough for leadership, yet on the other hand, they risk penalties if they show themselves as assertive.

Structural factors also account for some of the gatekeepers' incentives. For example, delegation size affects access to committee chairmanship (see Table 4.1). Women from larger national groups access committee chair positions more easily than those in smaller ones. Larger delegations (e.g., from Germany, the UK, and Italy) are allocated more leadership positions, which in turn increases the potential for women to participate. For example, 20% of all female chairs since the first election have been members of the German delegation and 17% have come from the UK. Only a few chairs or vice-chairs are drafted from younger member states and countries with small delegations such as Croatia, Estonia, and Slovenia. Women from these countries in turn face higher barriers to leadership positions, suggesting that the political parties of large member states have more influence not only over the composition of the EP but also on the gender balance of its positional leadership. Furthermore, gender equality within member states as well as the left–right dimension of political parties, which have been shown to influence positional leadership opportunities in national parliaments, may shape gatekeepers' nomination strategies across parties and countries (Goddard 2019; Krook and O'Brien 2012). Member countries are heterogeneous in terms of these factors, and it is difficult to disentangle which are more consequential for women.

Even if women overcome the hurdles and reach leadership positions, research demonstrates that unconscious and conscious bias continue to operate, resulting in women's appointment to "softer" and less powerful ministerial portfolios (Goddard 2019; Krook and O'Brien 2012). In the context of the EP, powerful committees can be identified by their legislative activity and influence over the EU budget (see Chiru 2020 for a discussion). The chairmanships of those with a high impact on legislative outcomes and policies may be assumed to be highly desirable to MEPs. Looking at the distribution of women's leadership over different types of committees shows that the allocation of powerful positions is gendered, almost thematically segregated, with the most influential committees disproportionally

Table 4.1 Share of MEPs, and share of female committee chairs and vice-chairs by country (1989–2014)

Country	Delegation Size MEP (%)	Chair Positions (%)	Female Chair (%)	Female Vice-chair (%)
Croatia	0.41	0.20	0.00	0.26
Malta	0.42	0.74	0.00	0.95
Cyprus	0.44	0.00	0.00	0.00
Estonia	0.44	0.20	0.00	0.26
Slovenia	0.52	0.20	0.00	0.26
Latvia	0.63	0.33	0.00	0.43
Lithuania	0.82	0.33	1.18	0.35
Slovakia	0.85	0.60	3.53	0.52
Luxembourg	1.01	1.00	2.35	0.95
Bulgaria	1.13	1.07	2.35	1.21
Czech Republic	1.49	2.01	0.00	2.34
Finland	1.52	1.74	1.18	2.16
Hungary	1.59	2.07	0.00	2.51
Austria	1.90	0.87	0.00	1.04
Sweden	2.01	2.34	4.71	2.25
Ireland	2.10	2.68	1.18	3.37
Romania	2.21	2.68	1.18	3.37
Denmark	2.34	2.74	0.00	3.46
Portugal	3.47	3.68	0.00	3.89
Poland	3.56	3.48	4.71	3.29
Belgium	3.78	2.95	1.18	2.94
Netherlands	3.99	4.42	7.06	4.07
Greece	4.13	4.28	2.35	4.76
Spain	8.34	7.10	5.88	6.40
United Kingdom	11.02	11.65	16.47	10.81
Italy	12.86	13.25	12.94	11.94
Germany	13.29	14.59	20	13.67
France	13.72	12.78	11.76	12.54
Total	100	100	100	100

Source: Own calculation based on data retrieved from the automated database provided by Høyland et al. (2010).

headed by men. As Figure 4.3 demonstrates, leadership of the powerful committees remains unequally distributed between men and women. In the eighth term, only about one-third of powerful committees were chaired or vice-chaired by women. While around 42% of the chairmanship positions were in the hands of women, only 36% of the powerful committees had a female chair. In contrast to the steady growth of the share of female MEPs we have witnessed, the share of women in influential committee chair positions has not grown significantly since the early 1990s. This is largely attributable to women's limited access to high-trust

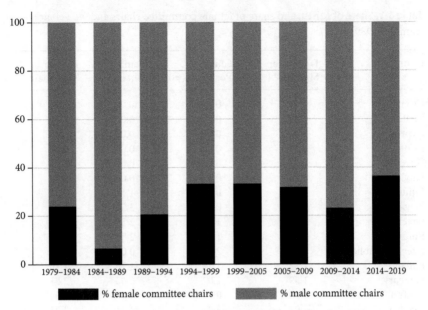

Fig. 4.3 Share of powerful committees headed by male and female MEPs

Source: Own calculation based on data retrieved from the automated database provided by Høyland et al. (2010). Only standing committees are included.

political networks—e.g., coteries that play pivotal roles in selecting group leaders before official votes (see Chapter 8 in this volume), who in turn exercise great sway in facilitating access to the most important, influential, and prestigious offices (Goddard 2019).

Gendered patterns of committee chair allocations are also discernable in committees' substantive focus. As illustrated in Figure 4.4, female MEPs are overrepresented in committees devoted to presumptively "feminine" policy areas—those that reflect stereotypical ideas about women's role in society. These include committees on women's rights, social welfare, and culture (see Krook and O'Brien 2012 for a detailed overview). In the last EP term, from 2014 to 2019, more than 80% of the "feminine" committees were headed by women, in comparison to around 40% of those depicted as "neutral" (e.g., environment) and 37% of those regarded as "masculine" (e.g., economy or finance). Women's promotion to leadership positions seems to hinge on committees' substantive scope and level of influence of committees, with men chairing the more powerful ones that deal with more "masculine" subjects.

These EP figures substantiate two broad lines of research on national parliaments. The first conjectures that gatekeepers holding unconscious and conscious bias against women attribute competence to women only in certain policy areas. A number of studies on national parliaments show that women in ministerial

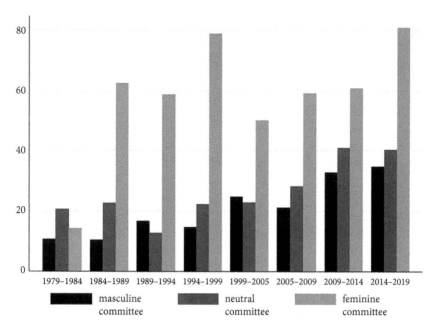

Fig. 4.4 Share of committees headed by women and type of committee

Source: Own calculation based on data retrieved from the automated database provided by Høyland et al. (2010). Categorization of masculine, neutral, and feminine committees based on Krook and O'Brien (2012). Only standing committees are included.

positions are appointed to a clearly defined "feminine" set of policy areas and are excluded from "masculine" fields (Krook and O'Brien 2012; O'Brien et al. 2015; Davis 1997; Pansardi and Vercesi 2017). The explanations for these patterns relate to the evaluation of men's and women's expertise in different policy domains, based on feminine stereotypes. Women are often—consciously or unconsciously—ascribed caretaker roles, involving the upbringing of children, taking care of the elderly, and organizing the household (Krook and O'Brien 2012; Goddard 2019). In addition to this role allocation, stereotypical assumptions about women's sensitivity and warmth translates into a more positive evaluation of their expertise in handling portfolios such as family, education, or health (Huddy and Terkildsen 1993). In turn, men's stereotypical role as organizers of the public sphere, as well as normative expectations about their assertiveness and aggression, underpin assumptions about their greater competence in dealing with "masculine" portfolios such as military, defense, and economic policy (Barnes and O'Brien 2017; Goddard 2019; Mackay 2008).

Beyond subjective assessments of women's ability to address certain issues better than others, several arguments have been advanced to explain women's assignment to more "feminine" committees. Some posit that they derive from gendered interests, priorities, and specializations and demonstrate that female officeholders promote traditional women's issues as revealed by analyses of women's parliamentary questions, speeches, bill sponsorship, and voting behavior. Others emphasize broader tendencies among women to regard certain committees as closer to their concerns (Studlar and Moncrief 1999; Davis 1997). The allocation of committee leadership positions may hence be a direct result not only of entrenched and informally gendered practices but also of the preferences and actual expertise of female members of parliament (Heath et al. 2005; Goddard 2019). While these arguments might be compelling in regard to national parliaments, a number of EP-related studies suggest that party groups have a strong influence in shaping the composition of committees (see Whitaker 2019 for an overview). The self-selection theory's explanatory power in this realm is questionable, as committee assignments are the result of a long and complicated bargaining process within and across parties. Researchers aiming to disentangle mechanisms leading to gendered patterns of committee leadership should not underestimate the partisan perspective. Whether gender differences in committee participation and leadership are driven by factors unfolding at the level of parties or at that of individual MEPs should be examined more closely (see Chapter 8 in this volume).

Even though women have had more success in winning seats in the European than in national parliaments, the distribution of prestigious positions in the EP has lagged behind the overall level of representation for many years. While systematic research on gendered committee chair appointments remains scant, this pattern does not support the perhaps naïve impression that the EP is a friendlier environment for women than national parliaments (Footitt 2002; Freedman 2002). It also suggests that the absence of entrenched male hegemony in the EP (Studlar and McAllister 1991; Studlar and Welch 1991) has been insufficient to provide women with uncomplicated access to power positions or increased opportunities for female candidates to succeed to the fullest after overcoming the hurdle of election. Once in office, female MEPs do not seem to benefit from contextual advantages compared to their colleagues in the lower houses of the member states. Despite having achieved a critical mass in the EP, women's access to the body's most influential and desirable positions has been limited and confined to specific policy fields.

Gendered differences in the allocation of committee leadership positions have profound consequences for the influence of women in policymaking but also for the visibility of female MEPs. The formal committee structure of the EP provides committee members with strategic advantages due to privileged access to information and opportunities to shape the plenary policy agenda and choices (Greene and Cross 2017). Committees' policy-specific expertise allows them to dominate or at least shape parliamentary decision-making. In turn, MEPs in committees concerned with salient and prestigious issues have a larger influence on the policy outcomes that are of most interest to the public. Even if women's presence in committees is not directly decisive for the degree to which political elites mirror female citizens' political preferences, as indicated by recent research at the national level (see Reher 2018; Bernauer et al. 2015; Dingler et al. 2019), women's absence from the most influential committees and positions limits their symbolic representation and evidences the obstacles that continue to restrict women's access to leadership positions (Phillips 1995; Mansbridge 1999; Rhode 2017).

4.5 Conclusion

This chapter underlines that the trajectory of women's representation in the EP deserves special attention. By contrast with what has taken place in many lower houses of individual member states, the course has been one of a smooth increase, with no visible setback to date. Yet, women's growing numerical strength has not yielded the same pattern of vertical mobility. Beyond the ostensibly advantageous access to legislative office the EP offers, the results presented here regarding leadership positions are much less optimistic than what the narrative of the EP as a success story for the representation of women seems to promise. So far, women's presence has not translated into gender-equal leadership opportunities, especially when it comes to the most influential positions. Even in the EP—role model of gender parity—women still do not have equal access to positional leadership and the pattern of the higher, the fewer persists.

Our observation that the EP is not as exceptional as assumed opens interesting avenues for future research. The degree to which the divergence in the pattern of women's overall empowerment from that of female MEPs' positional leadership is caused by factors intrinsic to the EP as an electoral arena versus a combination of mechanisms unfolding at the level of individual parties remains to be elucidated. The question of under what circumstances greater descriptive representation of women may also enhance vertical mobility within positional hierarchies remains unanswered. From a behavioral perspective, we know little about why a leadership imbalance in the EP exists even in cases where women are equally present in selection bodies and what the actual threshold is for a self-reinforcing process toward gender equality as proposed by critical mass theory (Dahlerup 1988). From an institutional perspective, future research could further investigate mechanisms that may increase women's ascension to top positions and whether the glass cliff theory, which proposes that women are set up to fail by more likely being appointed to power in times of crisis, is also applicable in the context of the EP (O'Neill et al. 2021; Ryan et al. 2010). Understanding such patterns will allow us to better trace spillover effects from one political arena to the other and the factors that continue to limit women's access to multiple hierarchies of positional leadership.

Aside from the factors that account for women's limited presence in powerful EP positions, we know little about the *consequences* of their relative absence from those positions. Women's numerical inferiority most likely affects both their substantive and symbolic representation in various ways. Case in point, women's limited visibility in powerful positions may well reinforce the already distal relation between the EP and its constituents.

References

Aldrich, Andrea S. 2020. "Party Organization and Gender in European Elections." *Party Politics* 26 (5): 675–688.

Barnes, Tiffany D. 2016. *Gendering Legislative Behavior*. New York: Cambridge University Press.

Barnes, Tiffany D., and Diana Z. O'Brien. 2017. "Defending the Realm: The Appointment of Female Defense Ministers Worldwide." *American Journal of Political Science* 62 (2): 355–368.

Bernauer, Julian, Nathalie Giger, and Jan Rosset. 2015. "Mind the Gap: Do Proportional Electoral Systems Foster a More Equal Representation of Women and Men, Poor and Rich?" *International Political Science Review* 36 (1): 78–98.

Bowler, Susan, and David Farrell. 1995. "The Organizing of the European Parliament: Committees, Specialization and Co-ordination." *British Journal of Political Science* 25 (2): 219–243.

Brescoll, Victoria L., Tyler G. Okimoto, and Andrea C. Vial. 2018. "You've Come a Long Way ... Maybe: How Moral Emotions Trigger Backlash against Women Leaders." *Journal of Social Issues* 74: 144–164.

Burrell, Barbara. 1994. *A Woman's Place Is in the House: Campaigning for Congress in the Feminist Era*. Ann Arbor, MI: University of Michigan Press.

Chiru, Mihail. 2020. "Loyal Soldiers or Seasoned Leaders? The Selection of Committee Chairs in the European Parliament." *Journal of European Public Policy* 27 (4): 612–629.

Cotter, David A., Joan M. Hermsen, Seth Ovadia, and Reeve Vanneman. 2001. "The Glass Ceiling Effect." *Social Forces* 80 (2): 655–681.

Dahlerup, Drude. 1988. "From a Small to a Large Minority: Women in Scandinavian Politics." *Scandinavian Political Studies* 11 (4): 275–298.

Davis, Rebecca Howard. 1997. *Women and Power in Parliamentary Democracies: Cabinet Appointments in Western Europe, 1968–1992*. Vol. 2. Lincoln, NE: University of Nebraska Press.

Dingler, Sarah C., Corinna Kroeber, and Jessica Fortin-Rittberger. 2019. "Do Parliaments Underrepresent Women's Policy Preferences? Exploring Gender Equality in Policy Congruence in 21 European Democracies." *Journal of European Public Policy* 26 (2): 302–321.

Elshtain, Jean Bethke. 1981. *Public Man, Private Woman*. Princeton, NJ: Princeton University Press.

Footitt, Hilary. 2002. *Women, Europe and the New Language of Politics*. New York: Continuum.

Fortin-Rittberger, Jessica, and Berthold Rittberger. 2014. "Do Electoral Rules Matter? Explaining National Differences in Women's Representation in the European Parliament." *European Union Politics* 15 (4): 496–520.

Fortin-Rittberger, Jessica, and Berthold Rittberger. 2015. "Nominating Women for EP Elections: Exploring the Role of Political Parties' Recruitment Procedures." *European Journal of Political Research* 54 (4): 767–783.

Freedman, Jane. 2002. "Women in the European Parliament." *Parliamentary Affairs* 55: 179–188.

Gatens, Moira. 1991. *Feminism and Philosophy*. Cambridge, UK: Polity.

Goddard, Dee. 2019. "Entering the Men's Domain? Gender and Portfolio Allocation in European Governments." *European Journal of Political Research* 58 (2): 631–655.

Greene, Derek, and James P. Cross. 2017. "Exploring the Political Agenda of the European Parliament Using a Dynamic Topic Modeling Approach." *Political Analysis* 25 (1): 77–94.

Heath, Roseanna Michelle, Leslie A. Schwindt-Bayer, and Michelle M. Taylor-Robinson. 2005. "Women on the Sidelines: Women's Representation on Committees in Latin American Legislatures." *American Journal of Political Science* 49 (2): 420–436.

Hix, Simon. 1999. *The Political System of the European Union: The European Union Series*. Basingstoke, UK: Macmillan.

Høyland, Bjørn, Indraneel Sircar, and Simon Hix. 2010. "An Automated Database of the European Parliament." *European Union Politics* 10 (1): 143–152.

Huddy, Leonie, and Nayda Terkildsen. 1993. "Gender Stereotypes and the Perception of Male and Female Candidates." *American Journal of Political Science* 37 (1): 119–147.

Hughes, Melanie M., and Pamela Paxton. 2019. "The Political Representation of Women over Time." In *The Palgrave Handbook of Women's Political Rights*, eds. Susan Franceschet, Mona Lena Krook, and Netina Tan, 33–51. London: Palgrave Macmillan.

Jalalzai, Farida. 2013. *Shattered, Cracked, or Firmly Intact? Women and the Executive Glass Ceiling Worldwide*. Oxford: Oxford University Press.

Kantola, Johanna. 2010. *Gender and the European Union*. London: Palgrave Macmillan.

Kjaer, Ulrik. 1999. "Saturation without Parity: The Stagnating Number of Female Councillors in Denmark." In *Elites, Parties and Democracy: Festschrift for Professor Mogens N. Pedersen*, ed. Erik Beukel, 149–168. Odense: Odense University Press.

Kroeber, Corinna, Vanessa Marent, Jessica Fortin-Rittberger, and Christina Eder. 2019. "Still a Glass Ceiling? Tracing the Limits to Women's Representation in Elected Office." *Comparative European Politics* 17 (1): 112–131.

Krook, Mona Lena. 2002. "'Europe for Women, Women for Europe': Strategies for Parity Democracy in the European Union." In *Democracy and Integration in an Enlarging Europe*, ed. John S. Micgiel, 67–86. New York: Institute for the Study of Europe.

Krook, Mona Lena, and Diana Z. O'Brien. 2012. "All the President's Men? The Appointment of Female Cabinet Ministers Worldwide." *Journal of Politics* 74 (3): 840–855.

Landes, Joan B. 1998. *Feminism, the Public, and the Private*. New York: Oxford University Press.

Leyenaar, Monique. 2013. "Netherlands: Gender Balance Here to Stay?" In *Breaking Male Dominance in Old Democracies*, eds. Drude Dahlerup and Monique Leyenaar, 172–196. Oxford: Oxford University Press.

Lühiste, Maarja. 2015. "Party Gatekeepers' Support for Viable Female Candidacy in PR-List Systems." *Politics & Gender* 11 (1): 89–116.

Lühiste, Maarja, and Meryl Kenny. 2016. "Pathways to Power: Women's Representation in the 2014 European Parliament Elections." *European Journal of Political Research* 55: 626–641.

McElroy, Gail. 2006. "Committee Representation in the European Parliament." *European Union Politics* 7 (1): 5–29.

Mackay, Fiona. 2008. "Thick Conceptions of Substantive Representation: Women, Gender, and Political Institutions." *Representation* 44 (2): 125–139.

Mansbridge, Jane. 1999. "Should Blacks Represent Blacks and Women Represent Women? A Contingent 'Yes.'" *Journal of Politics* 61 (3): 628–657.

Matland, Richard E. 1993. "Institutional Variables Affecting Female Representation in National Legislatures: The Case of Norway." *Journal of Politics* 55 (3): 737–755.

Norris, Pippa. 1997. "Conclusions: Comparing Passages to Power." In *Passages to Power: Legislative Recruitment in Advanced Democracies*, ed. Pippa Norris, 209–231. Cambridge: Cambridge University Press.

O'Brien, Diana Z. 2015. "Rising to the Top: Gender, Political Performance, and Party Leadership in Parliamentary Democracies." *American Journal of Political Science* 59 (4): 1022–1039.

O'Brien, Diana Z., Matthew Mendez, Jordan Carr Peterson, and Jihyun Shin. 2015. "Letting Down the Ladder or Shutting the Door: Female Prime Ministers, Party Leaders, and Cabinet Ministers." *Politics & Gender* 11 (4): 689–717.

O'Neill, Brenda, Scott Pruysers, and David K. Stewart. 2021. "Glass Cliffs or Partisan Pressure? Examining Gender and Party Leader Tenures and Exits." *Political Studies* 59 (2): 257–277.

Pansardi, Pamela, and Michelangelo Vercesi. 2017. "Party Gate-Keeping and Women's Appointment to Parliamentary Committees: Evidence from the Italian Case." *Parliamentary Affairs* 70 (1): 62–83.

Phillips, Anne. 1995. *The Politics of Presence*. Oxford: Oxford University Press.

Putnam, Robert D. 1976. *The Comparative Study of Political Elites*. Englewood Cliffs, NJ: Prentice Hall.

Reher, Stefanie. 2018. "Gender and Opinion-Policy Congruence in Europe." *European Political Science Review* 10 (4): 613–635.

Reynolds, Andrew. 1999. "Women in the Legislatures and Executives of the World: Knocking at the Highest Glass Ceiling." *World Politics* 51 (4): 547–572.

Rhode, Deborah L. 2017. *Women and Leadership*. Oxford: Oxford University Press.

Rosenwasser, Shirley Miller, and Norma G. Dean. 1989. "Gender Role and Political Office: Effects of Perceived Masculinity/Femininity of Candidate and Political Office." *Psychology of Women Quarterly* 13 (1): 77–85.

Rudman, Laurie A., Corinne A. Moss-Racusin, Julie E. Phelan, and Sanne Nauts. 2012. "Status Incongruity and Backlash Effects." *Journal of Experimental Social Psychology* 48 (1): 165–179.

Ryan, Michelle K., AS. Alexander Haslam, and Clara Kulich. 2010. "Politics and The Glass Cliff: Evidence That Women Are Preferentially Selected to Contest Hard-to-Win Seats." *Psychology of Women Quarterly* 34 (1): 56–64.

Salmond, Rob. 2006. "Proportional Representation and Female Parliamentarians." *Legislative Studies Quarterly* 31 (2): 175–204.

Stockemer, Daniel. 2008. "Women's Representation in Europe: A Comparison between the National Parliaments and the European Parliament." *Comparative European Politics* 6: 463–485.

Studlar, Donley T., and Ian McAllister. 1991. "Political Recruitment to the Australian Legislature: Toward an Explanation of Women's Electoral Disadvantages." *Western Political Quarterly* 44 (2): 467–485.

Studlar, Donley T., and Gary F. Moncrief. 1999. "Women's Work? The Distribution and Prestige of Portfolios in the Canadian Provinces." *Governance* 12 (4): 379–395.

Studlar, Donley T., and Susan Welch. 1991. "Does District Magnitude Matter? Women Candidates in London Local Elections." *Western Political Quarterly* 44 (2): 457–466.

Taagepera, Rein. 1994. "Beating the Law of Minority Attrition." In *Electoral Systems in Comparative Perspective: Their Impact on Women and Minorities*, eds. W. Rule and J. F. Zimmerman, 235–246. Westport, CT: Greenwood Press.

Thames, Frank C., and Margaret S. Williams. 2013. *Contagious Representation: Women's Political Representation in Democracies around the World*. New York: NYU Press.

Townsend-Bell, Erica. 2020. "Backlash as the Moment of Revelation." *Signs: Journal of Women in Culture and Society* 45 (2): 287–294.

Tremblay, Manon, and Réjean Pelletier. 2001. "More Women Constituency Party Presidents: A Strategy for Increasing the Number of Women Candidates in Canada." *Party Politics* 7 (2): 157–190.

Vallance, Elizabeth, and Elizabeth Davis. 1986. *Women of Europe*. Cambridge: Cambridge University Press.

Verge, Tània, and Maria de la Fuente. 2014. "Playing with Different Cards: Party Politics, Gender Quotas and Women's Empowerment." *International Political Science Review* 35 (1): 67–79.

Whitaker, Richard. 2011. *The European Parliament's Committees: National Party Influence and Legislative Empowerment*. London: Routledge.

Whitaker, Richard. 2014. "Tenure, Turnover and Careers in the European Parliament: MEPs as Policy-Seekers." *Journal of European Public Policy* 21 (10): 1509–1527.

Whitaker, Richard. 2019. "A Case of 'You Can Always Get What You Want'? Committee Assignments in the European Parliament." *Parliamentary Affairs* 72 (1): 162–181.

Wodak, Ruth. 2015. *The Politics of Fear: What Right-Wing Populist Discourses Mean*. London: Sage.

Wolbrecht, Christina, and David E. Campbell. 2007. "Leading by Example: Female Members of Parliament as Political Role Models." *American Journal of Political Science* 51 (4): 921–939.

Xydias, Christina. 2016. "Discrepancies in Women's Presence between European National Legislatures and the European Parliament: A Contextual Explanation." *Political Research Quarterly* 69 (4): 800–812.

PART III

EXERCISING POLITICAL LEADERSHIP

5

Women and Leadership across the EU Institutions

The Case of Viviane Reding

Michelle Cini

5.1 Introduction

Leadership is an attribute of individuals or groups, but it is also shaped by external factors. In research on leadership it is important, therefore, to integrate the personal, the institutional, and the situational. In other words, it is the interplay of agency and structure that determines a leader's success or failure. This perspective on leadership provides a point of departure for this chapter as it reviews the leadership of one woman, Viviane Reding. The choice of Reding as a subject for this research results from her having held positions in both the European Parliament (EP) and the European Commission. While not unique, this distinctive feature of Reding's career provides a focal point for the chapter.

Viviane Reding is one of Europe's most recognizable woman leaders. She began her adult life as a journalist and had a precocious career in national (Luxembourg) politics as a deputy representing the Christian Democratic, centrist, and pro-European Christian Social People's Party (CSV). She was subsequently a Member of the European Parliament (MEP) for two terms, then a member of the Commission, ultimately holding the office of vice-president in her third term, returning once again to the EP. She has devoted most of her career to political work within the European institutions.

The aim of this chapter is to investigate how the personal characteristics that shape an individual's "leadership style" facilitate or inhibit successful (or unsuccessful) leadership across different institutional settings. This aim is operationalized by means of an examination of Reding's leadership style and experience in the European institutions. The chapter addresses several questions: How might one characterize Reding's leadership style? Was Reding able to demonstrate successful leadership in the EP and the European Commission? How does Reding's leadership experience differ across the two institutions? Does Reding's leadership

Michelle Cini, *Women and Leadership across the EU Institutions: The Case of Viviane Reding*. In: *Women and Leadership in the European Union*. Edited by Henriette Müller and Ingeborg Tömmel, Oxford University Press.
© Oxford University Press (2022). DOI: 10.1093/oso/9780192896216.003.0006

style fit better with the EP or the Commission? How important is the institutional and situational setting in shaping a leader's success?

The chapter comprises a qualitative analysis of Viviane Reding's leadership style and experience, covering a period of almost 30 years. The analysis draws primarily on documentary sources, drawing from over 300 speeches she made during her time at the Commission and media commentary on her leadership. It also draws on interviews with Reding about her life and career. The chapter begins by setting out a conceptual framework that positions actor-centered leadership within an institutional/situational context. The empirical section offers an analysis first of Reding's leadership style and subsequently of her leadership experience in the EP and European Commission. The latter focuses on the institutional and situational setting within which her leadership was exhibited. The chapter concludes that while Reding's leadership style was better suited to the European Commission than to the EP, it was not so much the institutional or situational setting (in the EP or Commission) that determined her success, but the way in which the specific roles that she held in those institutions gave her a platform which she could use to pursue her agenda. It was the fit between certain key roles that she held and her leadership style that mattered most in determining her most high-profile leadership successes.

5.2 Framing Leadership

Leadership is a relatively new area of research for political scientists and even today this traditionally interdisciplinary concept may not always be taken seriously in academic circles. Political leadership therefore remains a contested concept without a general definition or theory (Müller 2020: 8, 17). While in the distant past, political leadership was associated with the "great man theory" of history, leadership studies now embrace greater nuance. Most contemporary studies focus on the way in which leaders and followers relate to each other to achieve goals. Political leadership suggests that the leaders in question will be politicians, the followers, citizens, and the type of goals to be achieved, those that impact the polity, economy, or society.

To assist with their analysis, scholars have found various ways of framing the concept of leadership. These frames are often presented as typologies or dichotomies. Thus, leadership might be considered transactional, relying on exchange relationships, or it might be transforming, producing outputs that lead to fundamental change (Burns 1978). It might be possible to distinguish between a positional form of leadership, deriving from offices and roles held, or a behavioral mode, which focuses on performance (see Chapter 1 in this volume). Leaders may be entrepreneurial or executive or they may be reactive or passive (Müller 2020: 25). Paradoxically, leaders may not even lead, or they may not lead well. While some leaders might be judged to be successful, others will fail in their leadership efforts.

Most important for this chapter is that leadership is a function of both agency and structure. Insofar as agency is concerned, an actor-centered leadership approach emphasizes the importance of the individual or group, and of their (personal) characteristics. Individual leaders possess characteristics or personal qualities that contribute to their style of leadership and which help to make their leadership more, or less, successful. Leaders might have a top-down, hierarchical leadership style (often thought of as a "masculine style" of leadership), or they might work in a more consensual (or "feminine") way. Successful leaders are likely to be able to visualize the future and to translate that vision into policy and strategy—in other words, to set agendas. They are likely to have (political) ambition coupled with resilience and focus. And as leaders cannot lead without followers, (political) reputation is also an important characteristic of leadership.

Actor-centered leadership does not take place within a vacuum, however. It is therefore important to consider institutional and situational settings in which leaders lead. The institutional setting (or "institutional structure") comprises institutional rules, norms, and procedures, as well as organizational resources and cultures (Müller 2020: 22). These institutional rules may include constitutional laws and operating guidelines; in a softer sense, they may also comprise ways of working that are embedded in the culture of the organization. Resources may be financial but can also relate to staffing, not only in terms of numbers but also quality of human resourcing. When judging the impact on leadership, therefore, the institutional setting might be thought of in terms of the institutional opportunities and constraints that facilitate and impede successful leadership.

The relevance of the situational setting for leadership is harder to pin down. It concerns the zeitgeist and the hard-hitting political realities of the moment. It can encompass momentous political, economic, technological, or social change and its impact on institutions, policies, and roles, but might also simply be about the vaguer notion of the "spirit of the times." The latter may determine the range of political possibilities at any moment (Müller 2020: 22).

This chapter focuses on the leadership style of an individual woman, and the institutional and situational setting that shaped her leadership experience. For the purposes of this chapter, it is assumed that leadership style remains constant over the course of one's career, whereas the institutional and situational setting changes and evolves. While the institutional setting can be about more than just the EP and Commission context, this chapter is especially interested in leadership across these two European institutions. Important, therefore, is how these two European institutions differ: in the roles that leaders may hold, the procedures that govern the day-to-day work of the institutions, and the resources at leaders' disposal. For example, in the EP it matters that the citizens of each member state are represented by a fixed number of MEPs, a number that is very roughly proportionate to population. While Germany currently has 96 MEPs, Luxembourg has only six; and while MEPs are important, only a small proportion of the now 705 MEPs in the Parliament will ever be able to hold leadership positions (for more detailed overviews, see Chapters 4 and 8 in this volume). However, in the EP, individual leadership may be difficult to deliver, as it is either a function of the more important roles, in "top-down" fashion, or it relies on a more collective form of group leadership. MEPs who do not hold senior positions in the institution have relatively little opportunity to demonstrate leadership.

The European Commission performs primarily executive functions. It has a political and an administrative wing. In the case of the former, the most important leadership roles are held by the now 27 members of the European Commission—the commissioners. The commissioners are led by the president of the European Commission, who is an important agenda setter and figurehead for the institution, even if formally a first among equals, as well as by a number of vice-presidents (currently eight). Commissioners are nominated by their national governments and are approved by the EP and European Council (in the case of the latter by a qualified majority vote). Commissioners are expected to act in the interests of the European Union and with their allocated policy portfolio in mind, rather than wear a national "hat." Leadership in the European Commission is also a function of the roles held by individuals. While there are fewer commissioners in the Commission than MEPs in the Parliament, there still exists a hierarchy of roles. Not only is the president more important than the vice-presidents, and the latter more important than regular commissioners, but the portfolios held by commissioners also carry, if only informally, unequal status. The most important are the "economic" and "external relations" portfolios, as well as those that have large budgets. Others may become more important because they raise issues "of the moment." Changes in the situational setting matter in this regard. Less influential are the portfolios in areas where EU competences are limited, such as social policy, education, and health, as well as the portfolios that have limited budgets and therefore limited scope to take action (see Hartlapp et al. 2014).

5.3 Leadership Style

Throughout her career, Viviane Reding has been highly ambitious. She has sought leadership positions in many organizations, expressing an interest in using the platforms to which she aspired to get things done. She has often expressed frustration in roles where she was unable to shape policy. Reding has always been looking for opportunities to take the initiative and to be innovative. She has been said "to have 'courage and a vision' and to like to 'pick her priorities and get things done'" (Laitner 2006a, quoted in Cini and Šuplata 2017: 148). She is someone who has achieved results and been unafraid to take responsibility (*European Voice* 2010a).

Over the course of her career, Reding has sought to take charge. This was something that she first pursued as a national politician. With reference to two early pieces of legislation she worked on: "The first time ... I let myself be pushed around a bit" (Reding 2015: 10). She went on to say that she learned her lesson and made sure it did not happen again. In the context of the Commission roles she has held, she has continued to value the importance of taking charge and being in control. This was very important to her:

> [W]ho is in charge of the Commissioner? Is the Commission's administration in charge of the Commissioner or is it the Commissioner in charge of him or herself? ... There are some Commissioners who leave matters to the Commission's administration. ... It all boils down to a Commissioner's personality, strength and vision. ... You have to be assertive. Oh yes. I had to assert myself.
>
> (Reding 2015: 23)

And again, on the role of commissioners: "If they want to be the governments' poodle, then they are free to do so. But this female politician always refused to do that, she always made her own proposals. ... [M]ost of the ideas that I brought to the table were 100% Viviane Reding" (Reding 2015: 22).

Especially as she entered her second term in the Commission, Reding developed a reputation for being tough and even "pugnacious" (Laitner 2007a). There are many examples of her forthrightness. She had an extremely heated argument with the French President, Nicolas Sarkozy, over French repatriation of Roma migrants in 2010 (discussed below) and a high-profile fight with Hungarian leader Viktor Orbán over the possible expulsion of his party, Fidesz, from the EPP (Gardner 2013). Even as a new commissioner, she became known as a straight talker. For example, in a speech on a controversial issue in sports policy, she tackled the subject of sports federations breaking the law by castigating "demagoguery and disinformation practices by the few" (Reding 2004a). She was not afraid to speak out against the most powerful individuals and organizations in Europe.

There is another element to Reding's leadership, which relates to the controversy that she seemed to court. She would often propose what some commentators considered to be outlandish proposals, then wait for the outcry and argue her corner, even as she was prepared to compromise. Ultimately, some would later say that she had "lost" the argument; others acknowledged that she never expected to get 100% of her proposal approved, and in the meantime was able to move the given policy along substantially (Laitner 2006b; 2007b). There are many such examples, including from the time of the Telecoms Package proposed by the Commission in 2007, where her proposals caused an outcry but were later modified and presented by Reding as a great success. One way of looking at Reding's leadership style is thus that it rested on outspoken assertiveness. This is not to say that Reding did not see the need to build coalitions and networks, but rather that "consensus-building" is not often a label attributed to her leadership style. Although she had a lot of support in the EP and her proposals were often appealing to the general public, on numerous occasions she alienated her colleagues in the Commission, as well as in the business community and national leaders across Europe. As she put it herself: "in the majority of cases, I made my proposals by myself and tried to persuade the Council afterwards" (Reding 2015: 22).

Prestige and reputation have been important to Reding. She has been very careful to mold her own image as a leader and to shape and defend her legacy. While in the Commission she was very attentive to public relations (PR), to the extent that media commentators called her publicity hungry (*European Voice* 2010b) or said she was "blowing her own trumpet" (Wyles 2012). One example was when she unashamedly declared that Barroso's first state of the union speech had picked up many of her own ideas. On another occasion she claimed to be "the voice of the EU" (Wyles 2012; *European Voice* 2011; see also *European Voice* 2012). In sum, Viviane Reding's leadership style was authoritative, agenda-setting, and strategic, a form of leadership sometimes characterized as "masculine." It was also a form of leadership that relied on a degree of public visibility, which is more associated with national than European politics. This did not always make her popular with her fellow commissioners or with national leaders, who seemed to view her approach as out of line with a European Union way of working which, in recent times, had been relatively low-key and behind the scenes.

5.4 Leadership Experience

Having introduced Reding's leadership style, the next section moves on to discuss the institutional structures, that is, the institutional constraints and opportunities that have shaped her leadership experience, with particular reference to successful and unsuccessful policy outcomes. To a lesser extent, it also considers the situational settings that provided the context in which Reding's leadership was exercised.

European Parliament

In 1989 Viviane Reding decided to launch a new phase in her career in the European institutions by standing for and winning election to the EP. She was reelected in 1994 for a second term. During this decade, Reding held several roles. On her initial appointment, she was elected as one of the (then) three members of the Luxembourg team in the EP and became leader of the Luxembourg delegation to the center-right European People's Party (EPP) and a member of the EPP Group's

Bureau. From 1988 to 1992, she was chairwoman of the Committee on Petitions and from 1992 to 1994 she was vice-chair of the Committee on Social Affairs, Employment, and the Working Environment. Between 1997 and 1999, she was also vice-chair of the Committee on Civil Liberties, Justice, and Home Affairs (European Parliament 2019a, 2019b, 2019c).

Although each had a leadership dimension, none of these roles were particularly high profile, though the chair of the Committee on Petitions was a relatively important position to be given to a new MEP. Reding does not claim any major successes from her time in the post, seeing it as an episode of political training, a "school of Europe" (Reding 2015: 15) in which she came to learn a great deal about the concerns of Europe's citizens, especially those living in cross-border regions. Likewise, as vice-chair of the Committee on Social Affairs and Employment, there was scant opportunity for her to make concrete policy contributions. Reding, normally quick to claim policy successes, professes none during this period. In fact, her experience as an MEP appears to have been a frustrating one as the roles she held lay in the social sphere, which, although of interest to her, was a policy domain in which the European Community/Union, let alone the EP, had little power.

Things were seemingly much the same during her time as vice-chair of the Committee on Civil Liberties and Justice. Once again, the lack of European-level competence in the area effectively prevented her from making an impact on policy. According to Reding, the Committee had "no say" (Reding 2015: 16) as there was no basis in the treaties for either a common security policy or for EU-level initiatives on citizenship at that time. Reding found the debates within the Committee interesting, however, and they laid the foundation for initiatives she would later advance in the European Commission as justice commissioner, after the Lisbon Treaty had introduced new powers in the field (Reding 2015: 16). Once again, even where she was unable to make a mark on policy, she grasped opportunities to educate herself, anticipating a time when she could put that education to good use.

It is not unusual for new MEPs to struggle to make a mark in the Parliament. There are hundreds of MEPs, many of whom are ambitious and vie for the key roles within the institution. Parliamentary seats are often held for long stretches, with political and social capital built up over several terms of office. New MEPs must usually serve a lengthy period before they can step up to the more important roles in the institution—it can take several parliamentary terms before an MEP is considered to have leadership potential (see Chapter 8 in this volume). Moreover, while personal characteristics are important in identifying MEPs who are potential future leaders, so too is political affiliation and nationality. The EPP is a large political group, which means that there is a great deal of competition for leadership roles. At the same time, Luxembourg is a very small country, which means that the country's representation in key roles in the EP is rarely considered the priority that it might be for the larger member states. It was not until her return to the

EP relatively late in her career that Reding's nationality would become especially relevant to her career prospects.

After her first two terms in the EP (1989–1999), Reding went on to spend three terms in the Commission between 1999 and 2014. She returned to the EP between 2014 and 2018. By this stage, Reding's status and prestige were extremely high. She had become one of the best-known European Union politicians. Her election as MEP in 2014 was far from unexpected as she had stood in each EP election since 1989. In 1999, 2004, and 2009, she had declined to take up her seat, preferring the European Commission to the Parliament (Taylor 2013). When she returned to the EP in 2014, she clearly came back with the intention of seeking high political office, putting her name up for the role of Parliament vice-president (Taylor 2016); any idea she may have had of standing as president of the EP (or the Commission for that matter) was quashed by Jean-Claude Juncker's appointment as Commission president (*European Voice* 2013a). The idea of Luxembourg nationals as both EP and Commission presidents was unthinkable.

Reding's leadership ambitions were checked, however; she ended up coming in last of six MEPs in the internal vote to select the EPP candidate for EP vice-president. She next put herself forward to chair the Committee on Legal Affairs. Once again, her ambitions were thwarted—while she was initially a front runner for the role, she seems to have lost that standing as the process went on (Taylor 2016). Instead she served her term in lower-profile roles, as a member of the EP's Committee on International Trade and serving on two EP intergroups, on Long-Term Investment and Reindustrialization and on the Digital Agenda. The Parliament itself had changed since her first terms as an MEP. After the Eastern Enlargement, there were many more MEPs and small countries with Members vying for a similar number of leadership positions.

There is very little evidence of Reding's impact during this period. This does not mean that she did not have influence, but her work was much more behind the scenes than it had been in the Commission. Even though she remained an important, high-profile figure within the Parliament, her influence and ability to launch new initiatives were diluted. It is hardly surprising that she left the EP in September 2018 to return to national (Luxembourg) politics without even completing one full term (Schumacher and Tasch 2018). This outcome had little to do with Reding's leadership style, but was more a product of the institutional and situational context in which she found herself, which—despite her level of ambition—made it difficult for her to perform a leadership role.

European Commission

Between her two careers in the EP, Reding spent three terms as a member of the European Commission, working first with Commission President Romano Prodi from 1999 to 2004 and then with José Manuel Barroso across his two terms as president. In the second Barroso Commission, her third term, Reding was elevated to one of the vice-presidential roles. In contrast to the EP, where it is not uncommon for politicians to remain as MEPs over many terms, in the Commission it is extremely rare for commissioners to see out three terms. This helped to reinforce her seniority.

In 1999 Reding was appointed as member of the Commission for Education, Culture, Youth, Media, and Sport. Although these policy areas are important, in a European context this was a low-profile portfolio, reflecting the fact that Reding lacked "ministerial or managerial experience" (*European Voice* 1999) and was very much a junior commissioner. Some of the frustrations of Reding's EP career thus continued into her first Commission term. The portfolio she held meant that her policy sphere covered a wide and rather disparate range of issues. In any given month, one might find Reding giving speeches on topics ranging from football (FIFA) and the music industry to educational exchanges and language diversity (e.g., Reding 2000a, 2000b, 2000c). These were all areas where the European Community had little competence. As she subsequently said: "I … needed a great deal of imagination to move forward" (Reding 2015: 17).

Reding certainly oversaw key policy developments within her portfolio during her first term in office. She worked on a new generation of educational exchanges (e.g., the Erasmus, Socrates, and Leonardo da Vinci programs) and, albeit beyond the framework of the European Union, pushed for the creation of a European Higher Education Area through the further development of the so-called Bologna process, which covered Europe-wide educational initiatives on quality assurance, the two-cycle system of bachelor's and master's degrees, and the recognition of qualifications and periods of study (Reding 2003a). She was also instrumental in carrying out a major reform of the Television without Frontiers Directive and strengthening the Culture 2000 and EU MEDIA programs (Reding 2004b). This work on new digital technologies would stand Reding in good stead in her second term as commissioner when she would become responsible for information-society issues. She also made some inroads into developing European cooperation in the area of sports policy, for example, by working with a sometimes resistant FIFA and UEFA on new legislation concerning youth transfer rights.

Reding's first term as commissioner was not unsuccessful, as evidence of the Bologna process demonstrates. Yet there were no outstanding achievements initiated by Reding herself. She appears to acknowledge this, albeit implicitly, when she points to her first Commission term as having helped to rebuild trust between the EP and the Commission following the Commission resignation crisis of 1999 (see Macmullan 1999): "I played a key role, not necessarily in my areas, which were soft power areas, but insofar as I was able to make a connection between the European Parliament and the Commission" (Reding 2015: 17). In this case, Reding plays down the importance of her portfolio, which did not allow her to get things done, focusing instead on achievements involving broader horizontal issues.

Reappointed to the Commission in 2004 for a second term, Reding took on a more important portfolio as Commissioner for Information Society and Media. During her second term, she became best known in the public sphere for her initiatives on telecommunications (Reding 2006). With this new portfolio, Reding was now able to push forward policies that could make a real impact on Europe's economy and society. The most high profile of these initiatives aimed to reduce and ultimately eliminate mobile roaming charges across the European Union.

Reding had been looking for a high-profile issue to focus her attention on, and mobile roaming charges met her needs. The initiative came from Reding herself, top-down, and not from the Commission services (Cini and Šuplata 2017: 148). She had become interested in the issue because of its connection with citizens' rights, and because the policy was relevant to both sections of the business community (cutting the costs of work travel) and ordinary people (doing the same for vacation travel). It seemed to tick lots of boxes. Some commentators were critical, however, and viewed her engagement with the policy initiative as little more than an example of Commission populism (Kubosova 2006). Moreover, there was substantial industry opposition to her initiative to cut mobile roaming charges, with intense lobbying by the large mobile operators against her proposals (Parker and Parker 2006).

With the backing of Commission President Barroso, Reding was able to contest the arguments of those "heavyweight colleagues in the European Commission" (Laitner 2008; see also Pignal 2009) who were more inclined to see the issue from the industry perspective and who at times briefed against her on the issue (Parker and Parker 2006). The fact that Reding was in the rare position of being praised in the media, and even sometimes in the Eurosceptic press, for supporting the consumer interest and taking the citizens' side, made it harder for her fellow commissioners to oppose her position. It did not, however, make her the most popular of commissioners among her peers.

Resistance to her proposals also came from national governments, defending what they still considered to be their "national champions." Pushing the mobile roaming agenda through the EU institutions, and the Council in particular, was thus no easy task. It helped her case that national governments were themselves divided on the question. By the time Reding moved on to a new portfolio at the end of her second Commission term, national government opposition had waned, and mobile roaming charges were on the way to being eliminated (Laitner 2006c), an outcome that won her "widespread praise" (Barber 2009). That said, it has been reported that Germany and Spain lobbied hard to ensure that Barroso would move her to a new portfolio in 2010 (Pignal 2009).

The review of the EU's telecommunications rules that began in 2006 did not quite have the same public profile as mobile roaming, but it was, from an industry and national government perspective, just as controversial (Middleton 2009). Its general aim was to create an EU internal market in telecoms by, for example, introducing the structural separation of network from service operations to promote competition and investment, developing policy on spectrum allocation, and improving the regulatory regime, whether by strengthening the Commission's role or establishing a new European agency based on a beefed-up version of the weak European Regulators Group (ERG) (Reding 2006, 2007; Laitner 2006c). Reding was criticized from various quarters during this period—for instance, it was claimed that her support of an open internet was mere lip service, given that she was advocating new online regulations to protect the film and music industries in Europe at the same time (Horten 2009). The strength of feeling to her proposals within the industry was such that in 2009 Reding was even named "internet villain of the year" (Middleton 2007).

Yet while Parliament and the Council balked at some of her ideas (Jones 2008), and some fellow commissioners expressed similar hostility, for example, in a leaked DG Competition report that labeled her proposals "superfluous and damaging" (Laitner 2007c; see also *European Voice* 2013b), others argued that Reding's previously described negotiating strategy—propose extreme initiatives, wait for the storm to abate, and then get what you really wanted all along (Simpson 2009)—was paying dividends. In the end, the Telecoms Package, including a more modest version of the new European regulator proposal, was agreed to in November 2009, in what Reding described as a "well-balanced compromise" (Reding 2010a; Warrell 2008).

In Barroso's second Commission (Reding's third term in the Commission), Reding returned as a vice-president, with responsibility for Justice, Fundamental Rights, and Citizenship, impressing the EP Committee at her nomination hearing (Brunsden 2010). Initially, oversight of the Commission's existing Directorate-General (DG) for Justice, Freedom, and Security was to be under the control of both Reding and Cecilia Malmström. Reding argued that the DG should be split, while Malmström and Barroso seemed content with the status quo. Reding ultimately won over Barroso (Taylor 2010), and the old department was divided into a new DG for Justice and another for Home Affairs, with Reding exclusively responsible for Justice as of July 2010. This has been referred to as a "power grab" (*European Voice* 2010b) on Reding's part and driven by personal not policy concerns—in other words, a turf war was seen as already developing between the two commissioners. That said, there was also a policy logic in separating work on the protection of basic freedoms from the focus on home affairs that had prevailed in the old DG (*European Voice* 2010b). In any case, Reding was satisfied with the organizational outcome.

During her third term in the Commission, Reding was responsible for introducing a new EU justice policy, based on the new provisions of the Lisbon Treaty. This had made the EU Charter of Fundamental Rights legally binding and promoted a new citizens' agenda that included the introduction of the European Citizens' Initiative. She sought to promote EU basic values, such as nondiscrimination and respect for and protection of minorities (Reding 2010b). Reding's most high-profile intervention on this issue came very early on in her term, in September 2010, when she caused a political storm over the repatriation of Roma migrants from France.

The Roma issue turned into a massive row between Reding and the French President, Nicolas Sarkozy. The argument originated with a French Ministry of the Interior circular that implied the country would pursue a policy of "collective deportation" of Roma (Hall and Chaffin 2010). Reding spoke out bluntly on the issue. She attacked France not only for its legal failings, but also for acting immorally in failing to protect the Roma stating, "Enough is enough," and drawing thinly veiled parallels between French policy and the deportation of Jewish people during the Second World War. The French president retorted that her attack was "an insult ... a wound ... a humiliation ... an outrage" (quoted in Rachman 2010). Reding's admittedly post hoc explanation for her strong language was that even after the Lisbon Treaty had come into force, member states were continuing to behave as though it was business as usual in the field of justice, values, and citizenship, not recognizing that the Commission had new powers and was entitled to propose new policies (Reding 2010a). While Barroso expressed support for Reding, he distanced himself from the manner in which she had made her attack on France (Hollinger et al. 2010), and ultimately France avoided any EU sanction in the matter (Pignal 2010). It did, however, dramatically raise the profile of the Roma issue in Europe.

As part of her portfolio, Reding became commissioner for women and made many speeches on relevant issues, such as violence toward women and female genital mutilation (Reding 2010c, 2010d, 2010e). Even before she held this portfolio, she had expressed an interest in gender equality issues and had spoken about her own experience as a woman leader in journalism and in politics (Reding 2003b). During her third term, however, she was particularly focused on the representation of women in Europe's company boardrooms. Reding made several speeches proposing a "Women on the Board Pledge for Europe" that would commit signatory companies to increase women's share of their boards to 30% by 2015 and 40% by 2020. Reding at first sought to encourage and cajole companies to sign on, recognizing that she had no policy tools other than the power of persuasion (Reding 2004c). However, only 24 companies signed on to the Pledge in 2011 and Reding became less patient, describing her efforts as one side of "a tug-of-war with two parties pulling and pushing at both ends" (Reding 2012). Opposition grew among both companies and some national governments resistant to increasing regulation. Ultimately, while Reding can take credit for raising the profile of this issue, her initiative had little concrete effect.

Over the course of her third term, there was speculation as to whether Reding might put herself forward for the post of Commission president (Euractiv.com 2012). However, once it was clear that fellow Luxembourger Jean-Claude Juncker, the country's former prime minister, was being promoted as a possible president, representing the same political group (EPP), it became evident that she had no chance at filling the most senior role in the Commission and she lined up behind Juncker's campaign (*European Voice* 2014). Despite her high profile in the Commission, and the fact that she would have been the first woman Commission president, she knew that she could not compete with Juncker, who had been a prime minister. While the roles she held and the competences attached to them were crucial in allowing Reding to use her leadership style to good effect, the institutional and situational setting of the Commission were thus also crucial in determining the boundaries within which she could act as a leader.

5.5 Discussion and Conclusion

Viviane Reding emerges from this review of her leadership style and experience as an ambitious and impressive political figure. She also emerges from it as an individual not afraid to court controversy. Reding's leadership style draws on publicity and her public profile. She realized that to get things done it is sometimes necessary to make extreme proposals. She did not wait to build consensus from the bottom up, but rather was prepared to state her maximalist position and work to a reasonable conclusion from that point. This is often what it takes to achieve results in the European Commission.

If her leadership style was at times abrasive, it also delivered results. While she did not achieve her goals in all the policies she pursued, she was most successful in areas where she had competence to act and where she was able to use her profile (and the publicity it generated) to good effect in marshalling support for her agendas. In those terms, Reding was most successful when working in the European Commission and least successful in the EP. This was in part due to the differences between the two institutions, most notably the part each plays in the decision-making process. An active commissioner can play ideas generator and agenda setter as well as brokering deals across the EP and Council/member states. The Commission sits at the hub of the EU system in a way that the EP does not. Power is more concentrated in the Commission than in the EP, and as the core executive in the EU system it serves as a quasi-government as much as it is the EU's administration. While the EP is an important actor within the policy process, one of the two co-legislators, its role is largely reactive, and power, though concentrated in the political groups, is more diffuse when it comes to the role of individual Members within the wider institutional structure. Within that institutional structure it is thus much harder (though admittedly not impossible) for MEPs—even those holding major roles—to perform a leadership function that is individual, as opposed to collective. In Reding's case, she held senior roles in the Commission but not in the EP. Even had she held such roles in the Parliament, however, the importance of the institutional and situational setting is such that it is likely that her leadership successes would still have been greater in the Commission than the Parliament.

Reding's leadership experience differed across the two institutions for other reasons as well. It seems from the evidence presented above that her assertive leadership style suited the European Commission more than it did the EP. There is clearly a big difference between serving as a member of the European Commission and as an MEP. As a commissioner, one is at the apex of a political and administrative organization that is designed to initiate and administer legislation. The commissioner is supported by a personal office (cabinet) of hardworking, motivated staff and supported by officials with both political and technical abilities. MEPs have assistants, and receive the support of the EP administration, but individual MEPs have much less backup than even the most junior of commissioners. Resources are important in delivering leadership success. Clearly commissioners are much better resourced than MEPs.

Most important of all, however, in this account of Reding's leadership success is what it tells us about the importance of roles, and the competences attached to them. It is not enough to say that Reding was more successful as a leader in the Commission than in the EP. While there is evidence to support that claim, it is more accurate to conclude by saying that Reding was most successful where the institutional and situational context were most conducive to her getting things done. In the case of telecoms policy, perhaps the most obvious example, it was the Commission's ability to legislate in the area, as well as the significance of its policy in the context of the fast-moving technological change then affecting Europe, that facilitated her successes. Reding's leadership style combined with the institutional resources on which she could draw and the situational setting that positioned the policy issue as timely were all important to her success.

References

Barber, Tony. 2009. "Election Set to Shake Up Commission." *Financial Times*, February 9.

Brunsden, Jim. 2010. "Reding Impresses for Third Commission Term." *European Voice*, November 12.

Burns, James MacGregor. 1978. *Leadership*. New York: Harper & Row.

Cini, Michelle, and Marián Šuplata. 2017. "Policy Leadership in the European Commission: The Regulation of EU Mobile Roaming Charges." *Journal of European Integration* 39 (2): 142–156.

Euractiv.com. 2012. "Reding Calls for Barroso Third Term." September 4.

European Parliament. 2019a. "Viviane Reding." http://www.europarl.europa.eu/meps/en/1185/VIVIANE_REDING/history/3#mep-card-content (first term).

European Parliament. 2019b. "Viviane Reding." http://www.europarl.europa.eu/meps/en/1185/VIVIANE_REDING/history/4#mep-card-content.

European Parliament. 2019c. "Viviane Reding." http://www.europarl.europa.eu/meps/en/1185/VIVIANE_REDING/history/5#mep-card-content.

European Voice. 1999. "The Make-up of Prodi's Team." July 14.

European Voice. 2010a. "Reding to the Rescue?" (Entre Nous). March 3.

European Voice. 2010b. "The Dangers of Too Many Commissioners." February 17.

European Voice. 2011. "Viviane's Taking over" (Entre Nous). February 2.

European Voice. 2012. "Shamefulness Quota Exceeded" (Entre Nous). November 21.

European Voice. 2013a. "Presidential Ambitions" (Entre Nous). June 26.

European Voice. 2013b. "The Digital Divide" (Entre Nous). September 18.

European Voice. 2014. "Reding Backs Juncker to Be Commission President." January 19.

Gardner, A. 2013. "Reding's Campaign on Hungary Angers EPP." *European Voice*, April 24.

Hall, Ben, and Joshua Chaffin. 2010. "Tensions over France's Gypsy Policy." *Financial Times*, August 25.

Hartlapp, Miriam, Julia Metz, and Christian Rauh. 2014. *Which Policy for Europe? Power and Conflict inside the European Commission*. Oxford: Oxford University Press.

Hollinger, Peggy, Nikki Tait, and Stanley Pignal. 2010. "Sarkozy Hits Back at Reding in Roma Row." *Financial Times*, September 15.

Horten, Monica. 2009. "Viviane Reding's Wake-up Call." IPtegrity, July 13, http://www.iptegrity.com/index.php/telecoms-package/2nd-reading/372-viviane-redings-wake-up-call.

Jones, Huw. 2008. "EU's Reding Agrees to Most Telecoms Package Changes." Reuters, October 23, https://www.reuters.com/article/eu-telecoms-reform/eus-reding-agrees-to-most-telecom-package-changes-idUSLN35685420081023?sp=true.

Kubosova, Lucia. 2006. "Brussels Clashes with UK and France on Mobile Phone Rates." *EU Observer*, December 11, https://euobserver.com/economic/23072.

Laitner, Sarah. 2006a. "The Brussels Bombshell Club" (Opinion). *Financial Times*, November 21.

Laitner, Sarah. 2006b. "Roaming: Put through Quickly" (Opinion). *Financial Times*, September 14.

Laitner, Sarah. 2006c. "Call for European Telecoms Super-regulator." *Financial Times*, November 16.

Laitner, Sarah. 2007a. "Brussels Seeks to Spur Telecoms Competition." *Financial Times*, August 27.

Laitner, Sarah. 2007b. "Zealous Reding Seeks to Mend Telecoms Fences." *Financial Times*, February 12.

Laitner, Sarah. 2007c. "Brussels Split over Telecoms." *Financial Times*, September 24.

Laitner, Sarah. 2008. "Hung up?" *Financial Times*, March 6.

Macmullen, Andrew. 1999. "Political Responsibility for the Administration of Europe: The Commission's Resignation March 1999." *Parliamentary Affairs* 52 (4): 703–718.

Middleton, James. 2007. "Reding Voted 'Internet Villain.'" Telecoms.com, February 20, https://telecoms.com/7825/reding-voted-internet-villain.

Middleton, James. 2009. "Viviane Reding, European Commissioner for the Information Society and Media." Telecoms.com, August 10, https://telecoms.com/13452/viviane-reding-european-commissioner-for-the-information-society-and-media.

Müller, Henriette. 2020. *Political Leadership and the European Commission Presidency.* Oxford: Oxford University Press.

Parker, George, and Andrew Parker. 2006. "EU Waters Down Plan to Cut Mobile Fees." *Financial Times*, July 10.

Pignal, Stanley. 2009. "EU Telecom Crusader's New Term in Doubt." *Financial Times*, July 7.

Pignal, Stanley. 2010. "France Avoids EU Discipline over Roma." *Financial Times*, September 29.

Rachman, Gideon. 2010. "Hysteria Will Not Help the Roma" (Opinion). *Financial Times*, September 20.

Reding, Viviane. 2000a. "Europe's Competitive Position in the Internet-Based Economy." Internet European Summit, Madrid, SPEECH-00-3_EN, January 11.

Reding, Viviane. 2000b. "Year 2001: European Year of Languages: Unity/Diversity." Multilingualism Conference, Brussels, SPEECH-00-35, February 10.

Reding, Viviane. 2000c. "The Community Vision of Sport." European Commission Meeting—Sport Federations, Brussels, SPEECH/00/148, April 17.

Reding, Viviane. 2003a. "We Need to Implement Wholeheartedly the Bologna Process." Berlin Conference on Higher Education, Berlin, SPEECH/03/418, September 18.

Reding, Viviane. 2003b. "Reinforcing Gender Equality: The Challenge for the EU Constitution." Gender Equality and Europe's Future Conference Closing Session, SPEECH/03/104, March 4.

Reding, Viviane. 2004a. "2004—A New Lease of Life for European Sport." Sportel-Monaco, SPEECH/03/411, September 16.

Reding, Viviane. 2004b. "The Future of European Audiovisual Policy." Westminster Media Forum, London, SPEECH/04/192, April 22.

Reding, Viviane. 2004c. "Investing in Tomorrow's Boardrooms." Meeting of European Business Schools and Executive Women on Boards, Brussels, SPEECH/11/04, September 26.

Reding, Viviane. 2006. "The 2006 Review of EU Telecoms Rules: Strengthening Competition and Completing the Internal Market." Annual Meeting of BITCOM, Bibliothèque Solvay, Brussels, SPEECH/06/22, June 27.

Reding, Viviane. 2007. "Towards a True Internal Market for Europe's Telecom Industry and Consumers: The Regulatory Challenge Ahead." 20th Plenary Meeting of the European Regulators Group, Brussels, SPEECH/07/86, February 15.

Reding, Viviane. 2010a. "A New Beginning for EU Telecoms Regulation: EU Telecoms Regulator Starts Work." First Meeting of the Board of Regulators of BEREC and the Management of the Office, Egmont Palace, Brussels, SPEECH/10/13, January 28.

Reding, Viviane. 2010b. "The Need for Convivencia: European Values and Non-discrimination at the Heart of Europe's Roma Strategy." Second European Roma Summit, Córdoba, SPEECH/10/147, April 8.

Reding, Viviane. 2010c. "Making Gender Equality a Reality Today: 'No' to Violence against Women and Female Genital Mutilation." UN High Level Conference on the Status of Women, New York, SPEECH/10/49, March 2.

Reding, Viviane. 2010d. "Stepping up a Gear to Eliminate Violence against Women in Europe." European Commission Conference on Violence against Women, SPEECH/10/694, 25 November.

Reding, Viviane. 2010e. "Women's Charter: Our Commitment to Gender Equality." Joint Press Conference with President Barroso, SPEECH/10/72, Brussels, March 5.

Reding, Viviane. 2012. "The Tug-of-War over the Women's Quota." DLDwomen, SPEECH/12/547, Munich, July 12.

Reding, Viviane. 2015. "Interview with Viviane Reding—Part 1" (Elena Danescu, interviewer). Sanem, CVCE, May 22, https://www.cvce.eu/en/histoire-orale/unit-content/-/unit/a403443d-a56e-4f96-81c2-d17ef3bc1443/927e53f0-7ba7-40ec-ad83-58e4b92c86c1.

Schumacher, Danielle, and Barbara Tasch. 2018. "CSV Announces Candidate Lists, Outlines Plan for Country's Future." 17 December, https://luxtimes.lu/luxembourg/33262-csv-announces-candidate-lists-outlines-plan-for-country-s-future.

Simpson Seamus. 2009. "Supranationalism through Institutionalization and Its Limits in European Telecommunications: The European Electronic Communications Market Authority Initiative." *Information, Communication and Society* 12 (8): 1224–1241.

Taylor, Simon. 2010. "A Departmental Split to End Turf Wars?" *European Voice*, June 9.

Taylor, Simon. 2013. "Commissioners Warned to Be Neutral before Parliamentary Elections." *European Voice*, December 18.

Taylor, Simon. 2016. "Reding to Miss Out on Chair of Legal Affairs Committee." *European Voice*, January 15.

Warrell, Helen. 2008. "EU Scales Back Telecoms Regulation Plan." *Financial Times*, November 7.

Wyles, John. 2012. "2012's Big Winners." *European Voice*, December 19.

6

Women on Mars

The Two Post-Lisbon High Representatives
and EU Foreign Policy on Libya

Maria Giulia Amadio Viceré and Giulia Tercovich

6.1 Introduction

This chapter examines women's leadership in EU foreign policy. Any women filling institutional posts in traditionally male-dominated policy sectors are bound to
face a series of difficulties (Lazarou and Braden 2019; Williams 2017). Frequently,
such difficulties are ascribed to the complexities of striking a balance between
family life and work as mothers and carers (European Commission 2018). In the
foreign policy sector, they are also often coupled with flawed cultural beliefs concerning women's alleged psychological and physical weaknesses (Gordon 2018;
Prasad 2019). To misquote John Gray (1992), one could say that, in the political
galaxy, Mars is still mainly inhabited by men. And yet, in the past decade two
women have been nominated and acted as chief of EU foreign policy. Ever since
the Lisbon Treaty's introduction of the new High Representative of the Union for
Foreign Affairs and Security Policy (HR, December 2009), in fact, Catherine Ashton and then Federica Mogherini have held the post.[1] Against this backdrop, two
main questions arise: How did Ashton and Mogherini access their positions? And
how have they performed their functions?

Addressing these questions not only provides crucial insights into women's
leadership in the foreign policy sector, it also contributes to the book's aim of
increasing our knowledge of women and leadership in the EU more broadly in
multiple ways. First, examining the nomination of the two post-Lisbon HRs sheds
light on the opportunities and obstacles faced by women seeking access to EU

---

[1] This chapter opts for the term "HR" to differentiate between the High Representative's activities as
chair of the Foreign Affairs Council and those as vice-president of the European Commission. It uses
the term "vice-president," and therefore the abbreviation "VP," only when referring to the HR's activities
in this latter capacity.

Maria Giulia Amadio Viceré and Giulia Tercovich, *Women on Mars: The Two Post-Lisbon High Representatives and EU Foreign Policy on Libya*. In: *Women and Leadership in the European Union*. Edited by Henriette Müller and Ingeborg Tömmel, Oxford University Press. © Oxford University Press (2022). DOI: 10.1093/oso/9780192896216.003.0007

leadership in such a traditionally male-dominated sector. As a matter of fact, the nomination of two women as chiefs of EU foreign policy for two mandates in a row constitutes a *unicum* for the EU. The first, pre-Lisbon HR was a man (Javier Solana), and female commissioners have routinely been allocated "soft" portfolios (see Chapter 3 in this volume).

Second, examining the HR nominations and tenures of two different women allows us to identify whether and to what extent their leadership—or lack thereof—was shaped by the EU institutional framework (Tömmel 2013). Foreign policy epitomizes the opportunities and challenges the EU institutional system poses to women's leadership (Tömmel 2017). The post-Lisbon HR was seen as a strategic actor in the enhancement of the coherence, and hence effectiveness, of the EU's position in the international arena (Amadio Viceré 2018). Nonetheless, the multiple separations of power characterizing the EU system of government (Fabbrini 2010) may set several constraints on the HR's leadership in EU foreign policy (Aggestam and Johansson 2017).

Third, and lastly, the mandates of Ashton and Mogherini were deeply affected by several foreign policy crises. These include the difficult political transition in the Northern African and Middle Eastern region, the ensuing migration emergency, the Ukrainian crisis in the Eastern neighborhood, and the terrorist attacks in Europe (Amadio Viceré et al. 2020). The fact that both HRs had to juggle challenging situational factors during their mandates (Tömmel 2013, 2020) allows us to capture differences in their leadership in a nuanced manner.

To ensure a comprehensive understanding of Ashton and Mogherini's leadership, we employ two complementary analytical approaches. We start by providing a comparative analysis of their nominations as HRs to examine their respective positional leadership and their behavioral leadership in facing the crisis in Libya (see Chapter 1 in this volume). Although Ashton and Mogherini both faced several political crises during their mandates, Libya represented a very complex policy dossier for both office holders. Ashton had to deal with the popular uprising and the civil war in Libya when she was in the process of establishing the new European External Action Service (EEAS; see Koops and Tercovich 2020). As for Mogherini, her tenure was characterized by the migration crisis related to the Libyan political transition and, following the terrorist attacks in Paris and Brussels, the need to find a balance between ensuring Europe's security and saving lives in the Mediterranean.

The contribution of our chapter is twofold. On a theoretical level, we employ the original and innovative analytical framework outlined in the introduction to this edited volume (see Chapter 1). By doing so, we participate in the effort to move research beyond the current state of the art. On an empirical level, we shed light on the access to and exercise of women's leadership in EU foreign policy, which has been largely uncharted territory. In particular, we conduct an empirical examination by triangulating primary and secondary sources, complementing the analysis of EU official documents with information gathered in academic and so-called gray literature.

The chapter is structured as follows: first, we outline the analytical framework and make a set of arguments on its basis; second, we examine the positional leadership of HR Ashton and HR Mogherini; third, we examine whether and how Mogherini and Ashton exercised behavioral leadership.

Our analysis shows that the appointments of Ashton and Mogherini can be explained by three equally important and interdependent factors: the situational, the institutional, and the structural settings. The different leadership performances of the two HRs in the management of the Libyan crisis, in turn, can be explained by the situational and the institutional setting.

6.2 Analytical Framework

Positional Leadership

Based on the analytical approach to positional leadership adopted in this volume (see Chapter 1) and on the Lisbon Treaty's provisions concerning nomination of the HR, we argue that Ashton and Mogherini's access to leadership was influenced by three equally important and interdependent factors: the situational, the institutional, and the structural setting. For each of these factors, we can develop a specific argument about the two HRs' positional leadership.

First, the *situational setting*. The situational setting in which Ashton's and Mogherini's nominations occurred might have had a significant influence on their respective selections for a leadership position (Tömmel 2020; Barber 1992). As foreign policy is one of member states' core state powers (Genschel and Jachten-fuchs 2014), national governments are generally resistant to handing over power to the Union and its actors in this field. In the post-Lisbon era, national governments would thus have been expected to seek to limit the HR's power and scope of responsibilities. The probability of member states' pressure in this regard could have limited the attractiveness of the post. The situational setting encompasses foreign policy crises as well. Over the past 10 years, the EU faced a series of crises both within and outside its borders. The attractiveness of the HR's portfolio to member states might also have been limited by the fear that anyone holding the office would face a volatile and increasingly hostile international arena.

Second, *the institutional setting*. Institutional settings may have significant implications for a person's access to a position of authority over other people (Tömmel 2013, 2017). These implications might be particularly evident in EU foreign policy governance, which is characterized by multiple separations of power. In principle, the HR is entitled to coordinate EU foreign policy's instruments

(Rüger 2011). Nevertheless, the functioning logic of EU foreign policy institutional construction allows the European Council to exert tight control over this institutional actor (Amadio Viceré 2020; Helwig 2017). Added to this, the HR's job risks being an impossible one due to the multiple tasks assigned to it (Laursen 2013). The nomination of two women as HRs can thus also be ascribed to the post's institutional features, which render it less influential than other high-level political positions within the EU.

Third, the *structural setting*. Women often encounter a "glass ceiling" in their career paths. Frequently, they do not manage to reach the highest political positions due to gender stereotypes and role expectations (Ridgeway 2001: 652). In the foreign policy sector, a "hard" and politically prestigious area, member states' representatives would have probably preferred to nominate male commissioners. In principle, since it is those representatives meeting within the European Council that nominate the HR, their preference in this regard could be of crucial importance. Nonetheless, the HR's appointment is confirmed only upon approval by the European Parliament (EP; see Art. 18 TEU). Notably, the EP has generally promoted gender balance in the allocation of high-level political positions within the EU. It is therefore likely that, when nominating the candidate for HR, member states took into consideration that the EP would presumably continue to support gender balance.

Behavioral Leadership

Considering the analytical approach to behavioral leadership adopted in this volume (see Chapter 1) and the Lisbon Treaty's provisions concerning the HR's main tasks, we argue that Ashton and Mogherini's leadership performances can be explained through two equally important and interdependent factors: the situational and the institutional setting. For each of these factors, we can again make a specific argument about Ashton and Mogherini's leadership performances.

First, *performing within the situational setting*. The situational setting in which the HR exerts her leadership can have relevant implications on her performance (Tömmel 2020). It can influence member states' and EU institutions' specific policy preferences. Due to the intergovernmental nature of EU foreign policy governance, when crises and conflicts have unequal costs among member states, the HR's activities may be severely constrained by policy stalemates within the European Council and the Foreign Affairs Council (FAC). On the contrary, in situations in which member states' preferences are aligned, the HR may be able to significantly influence EU foreign policy (Amadio Viceré 2020). Furthermore, the situational setting includes the attitude of member states' representatives and fellow commissioners toward the HR as an institutional actor. Since the post-Lisbon HR is placed at the crossroads of supranational and intergovernmental policymaking and execution, interinstitutional clashes are likely to occur that hinder the HR's leadership performance.

Second, *performing within the institutional setting*. As both chair of the FAC (Art. 27(1) TEU) and VP of the European Commission (Arts. 17(4 and 5) TEU), the post-Lisbon HR is at the nexus of the intergovernmental and supranational foreign policy sectors. Through her influence as chair of the FAC, the HR may activate a reciprocal process between herself and the foreign ministers via bilateral discussions. By using her agenda-setting prerogatives and, especially, by tempering divergences among member states' representatives (Puetter 2014: 61–65), she may mobilize and persuade foreign ministers toward specific policy directions. In parallel with her work within the FAC, the HR may establish a reciprocal process with the heads of state and government (heads, henceforth) by participating in the European Council's discussions when foreign policy issues are on the agenda (Art. 15(2) TEU). While doing so, she may promote alignment between the positions of the two intergovernmental forums (Amadio Viceré and Fabbrini 2017). Given the European Council's preeminence over the HR and EU foreign policy governance more broadly, the achievement of such alignment is particularly relevant to the success of her leadership performance (Arts. 15 and 22 TEU). At the same time, the HR may facilitate the pursuit of goals that she and member states' representatives mutually embrace, a crucial competence given the decentralized nature of EU foreign policy resources.

As VP of the European Commission, in turn, the HR may establish a reciprocal process with the External Relations Commissioners. By fostering the achievement of specific EU foreign policy goals among them, the HR may help ensure the consistency of EU activities on the supranational side of EU foreign policy (Art. 18(4) TEU). Furthermore, as VP, she may use the Commission's technical and material resources as leverage during the process of intergovernmental deliberation within the FAC and the European Council. By doing so, with the EEAS's support, she may influence the general direction of EU foreign policy and hence the pursuit of goals that she, member states' representatives, and the External Relations Commissioners aim to achieve through both supranational and intergovernmental instruments (Art. 21(3) TEU).

6.3 Positional Leadership

The First Post-Lisbon HR: Catherine Ashton

The accession to power in a highly male-dominated sector of a relatively unexperienced woman might have been facilitated by the complex and challenging nature of the situational setting in which the nomination occurred. Most likely, once appointed, the first post-Lisbon HR would have been constrained by member states' resistance to centralization of foreign policy powers. In particular, the French and British heads of state and government were determined to shape and control the new EU foreign policy structure. Furthermore, in the eyes of member states' representatives, the HR might have lost some of its attractiveness as a high-level portfolio due to the challenges stemming from the implementation of the Lisbon Treaty (Spence 2015). In fact, the first office holder would inevitably have to handle the implementation of the new treaty while dealing with representatives from the Commission and the Council. In particular, the HR would have to carry out a highly delicate task: the establishment of the EEAS, the diplomatic corps of a union of 28 member states (Blom and Vanhoonacker 2015; Spence and Bátora 2015).

As for the institutional setting, records show that the process that led to Ashton's selection was shaped by the institutional features of the post, which render it less influential than other high-level positions in the EU. Indeed, the biggest member states seemed to consider the HR as less "attractive" than other high-level EU positions. When the UK proposed its candidate, in fact, the HR was essentially the only high-level position still open. José Manuel Barroso had already been nominated again as president of the Commission. The then British Prime Minister and Labour Party leader, Gordon Brown, had just failed to obtain the appointment of Tony Blair as president of the European Council. Against this backdrop, Brown proposed a potential candidate as the first post-Lisbon HR only after former Belgian Prime Minister Herman van Rompuy was appointed to head the European Council and Michel Barnier of France had obtained the post of Internal Market Commissioner (Howorth 2011).

Lastly, concerning the structural setting, it would be inappropriate to consider Ashton's nomination as an example of a woman's breaking of the glass ceiling. When she was nominated as first post-Lisbon HR, Ashton faced several hurdles related to gender stereotypes and role expectations. While the criticism she faced was based especially on the comparison with her male predecessor (i.e., Javier Solana), her nomination especially disappointed those who would have preferred a male candidate, such as David Miliband, Carl Bildt, Olli Rehn, or Massimo D'Alema (Castle 2009). In this regard, it is relevant to note that the British choice was initially a man, UK Foreign Secretary Miliband. As Miliband was not interested in becoming HR, Brown suggested the names of two other men: former defense ministers Geoff Hoon and John Hutton. However, because of the "horse trading" logic underpinning the allocation of high-level political positions in the EU, the first post-Lisbon HR had necessarily to come from a big Northern member state; be affiliated with a center-left party; and ideally be a woman (Howorth 2011). After all, a man from a small Southern member state and the member of a center-right party had just been nominated president of the European Commission. Most importantly, nominating a woman would increase the chances of the EP giving a green light to the candidate, and hence to the entire Commission. Therefore, despite Brown's initial indications, the other heads chose Ashton for the role (Barber 2010).

After the European Council nominated Ashton as HR, the Members of the European Parliament (MEPs) gave their approval. Evidence suggests that their decision to do so can be mostly ascribed to the EP's interest in pursuing gender-balanced policies. In fact, MEPs were quite critical about Ashton's professional profile. In a nutshell, the candidate's foreign policy experience was considered insufficient (Koops and Tercovich 2020). This widespread opinion is clearly reflected in Ashton's first encounter with the EP in January 2010. On that occasion, several MEPs judged her performance as "uninspired and uninspiring," labeling her replies as "rich in subjunctives and poor on specifics" (Vogel 2009: 1).

The Second Post-Lisbon HR: Federica Mogherini

With regard to the situational setting, it is reasonable to argue that the attractiveness of the HR as a high-level, hard portfolio had not increased by the time of Mogherini's July 2014 nomination, even though it could be assumed that the new HR would benefit from the institutional initiatives undertaken by her predecessor, including the establishment of the EEAS, and have the opportunity to build on Ashton's successful work in areas such as the negotiations with Iran (Bassiri Tabrizi and Kienzle 2020) and the EU-brokered dialogue between Kosovo and Serbia (Amadio Viceré 2016). Nonetheless, the continuation of conflicts in Syria and Ukraine and the increasingly strained enlargement process in the Western Balkans underscored the challenging international context in which the new HR would have had to operate. Internally, meanwhile, the new office holder would have had to act in a situational context affected by the unfolding of the eurozone crisis and the ensuing decline in the EU's and member states' resources, as well as by the popular discontent triggered by migratory pressure on Europe. To sum up, both the international and the internal situational setting in which the second post-Lisbon HR was nominated reduced the attractiveness of the post.

As for the institutional setting, evidence suggests that Mogherini's selection as HR was influenced by the qualifying features of high-level institutional EU positions. Because of the distribution of such positions, after a member of the European People's Party (i.e., Jean-Claude Junker) was nominated president of the European Commission, it was accepted that the new HR should come from a social-democratic party. At the same time, the nomination had to respect a geographical equilibrium among the member states, according to which either Italy or Poland could present a candidate. It is in this context that the Italian social-democratic Prime Minister Matteo Renzi put forth Mogherini's candidacy as HR. Renzi strongly supported Mogherini, especially when some Central and Eastern European member states opposed her nomination on the basis of her alleged softness toward Russia (Vincenti 2014; Keating 2014). There are reasons to believe that Renzi's strong support was not entirely based on Mogherini's talents. Before nominating her, Renzi had rejected an offer from German Chancellor Angela Merkel and French President François Hollande to support his predecessor, Enrico Letta, for the position of president of the European Council (Valentino 2019). Renzi arguably saw that having his rival setting the agenda of the preeminent EU intergovernmental forum would put him in an uncomfortable position (Dempsey 2014). Unlike Letta, Mogherini was an ally of his. Hence, although the HR has less sway than the European Council's president, the Italian prime minister hoped to increase his personal influence in the EU through her appointment to the post (see Valentino 2019; Vincenti 2014).

Concerning the structural setting, in this case it would also be inappropriate to conceive Mogherini's nomination as a breaking of the glass ceiling. As with her predecessor, her nomination was colored by gender stereotypes and role expectations. In the first place, many were of the opinion that Mogherini was too young to be appointed as the second post-Lisbon HR (Gardner 2014; Tempest 2015). As it happened, though she had served only eight months as Italy's foreign minister, that still gave her more top-level foreign policy experience than Ashton had when the latter took office as HR (see Cameron cited in Dempsey 2014: 1). Regardless, there was speculation about the possible nomination of more senior male candidates, such as Radek Sikorski, Joschka Fischer, or Carl Bildt (Dempsey 2014). Additionally, powerful MEPs, such as Elmar Brok, expressed their disappointment with her nomination (Müller 2016) while using gendered stereotypes (Hansen 2016). Crucially, however, the EP had explicitly asked Juncker, the new Commission president, to reach a gender balance among his commissioners (Keating and King 2014), while suggesting the allocation of the HR post to a woman. Eventually, after a well-received performance at her EP hearings (Vincenti 2014), MEPs confirmed Mogherini's appointment as the second post-Lisbon HR.

6.4 Behavioral Leadership: Foreign Policy on Libya

The First Post-Lisbon HR: Catherine Ashton

In terms of situational setting, when civilian protests broke out in Libya in February 2011 and Colonel Muammar Gaddafi responded with a campaign of violent repression, member states' preferences over the management of the Libyan crisis clearly diverged. While France, Germany, and the Netherlands proposed the imposition of sanctions on Gaddafi's regime, Malta, Cyprus, and Italy opposed them. Many Southern European countries feared that such measures could hamper cooperation with Libya in the management of migration flows across the Mediterranean (Sutherlands 2011). Some European leaders, including Sarkozy in

France, Cameron in the UK, and Silvio Berlusconi in Italy, seemed ready to make clear to the first post-Lisbon HR that they still wanted to play a crucial role in the definition of EU foreign policy in Libya (Fabbrini 2014). In the immediate post-Lisbon period, institutional overlaps and tensions stemming from the fight for competences and resources and clashing organizational cultures characterized EU crisis management (Koenig 2016). The EEAS's establishment, in particular, took several months of interinstitutional negotiations. As the Libyan crisis escalated, the HR was busy trying to make her diplomatic service operational. In the words of Ashton, the situation could be likened to "trying to fly a plane while still bolting the wings on" (EEAS 2013: 1).

As for the institutional setting in which the HR performed her leadership, despite member states' diverging preferences over the Libyan crisis, she initially seemed to establish a reciprocal process between herself and the foreign ministers within the FAC. On February 20, 2011, Ashton expressed concerns regarding the situation in Libya and condemned Gaddafi's use of violence (High Representative 2011a). On the following day, under her chairmanship, the FAC requested the halt of violence as well (FAC 2011). However, the HR appeared unable to establish such a reciprocal process with the heads (Helwig and Rüger 2014). Ashton's inability to promote specific foreign policy goals among them emerged clearly during the extraordinary European Council held on March 11, 2011. On that occasion, the HR opposed the imposition of a no-fly zone, siding with Germany and those who believed that any action in Libya should take place under a UN mandate and with the support of the Arab countries (High Representative 2011b). France and the UK, for their part, called for a strong response to Gaddafi's violent repression of civilians (Traynor and Watt 2011; Koenig 2014). Sarkozy went as far as to accuse Ashton of being passive about Gaddafi's brutalities in Tripoli (Fabbrini 2014). In the end, the heads urged Gaddafi to step down and recognize the Benghazi-based Transitional National Council (TNC) as a "political interlocutor," without mentioning the no-fly zone (European Council 2011: 3).

One could adjudge the lack of reference to a no-fly zone in the European Council's statement as evidence that the HR had succeeded. The records, however, show that Ashton did not manage to foster a process of reciprocal coordination among the member states in the representation of the EU's position in the UN Security Council (UNSC), as per Art. 34 TEU and Art. 220(2) TFEU. Six days after the European Council took place, in fact, the UNSC (March 17, 2011) approved the imposition of no-fly zone over Libya (UNSC 2011). Notably, EU member states represented within the UNSC pursued the same national priorities they had supported within the European Council a few days beforehand. France and the UK voted in favor of UNSC Resolution 1973, which imposed the no-fly zone, while Germany abstained. It is reasonable to assume that the heads' agreement on recognizing the TNC in March 2011 was promoted by the French government rather than by Ashton. In fact, France had unilaterally recognized the TNC the day before the European Council took place, a move described by a French diplomat as "*diplomatie électrochoc*" (interview reported in Koenig 2012). As a consequence, several members of the EP openly questioned the HR's leadership and blamed her for not having provided a "proactive approach" on Libya (McMahon and Williss 2011).

Further evidence of Ashton's leadership performance within the EU institutional setting emerges from her management of the possible deployment of a military Common Security and Defence Policy (CSDP) operation in Libya. Certainly, the Council of the EU's decision on April 1, 2011 to deploy the European Union Military Operation in Libya (EUFOR Libya) seems to reflect the HR's advocacy of the EU's exercising "soft power with a hard edge" (High Representative 2011b: 1). In fact, EUFOR Libya's deployment was linked to the humanitarian activities of the UN Office for the Coordination of Humanitarian Affairs (UN-OCHA). Rather than to Ashton's leadership performance, however, this can be ascribed to member states' lack of agreement over a full-scale military operation (Gomes 2011; Euronews 2011). In addition, shortly after the European Council's decision, the Under-Secretary General for Humanitarian Affairs, Valerie Amos, made clear to Ashton that UNOCHA did not want to be associated with the EU military operation, fearing that its presence could put humanitarian workers in danger (Amos 2011). The planned operation was ultimately never deployed.

As for the supranational side of EU foreign policy, Ashton struggled to foster a process of reciprocal coordination between herself and the commissioners involved in EU external activities. The relationship between the EEAS's Crisis Platform and the European Commission's Directorate General for European Civil Protection and Humanitarian Aid Operations (DG ECHO) was especially marred by interinstitutional tensions. In principle, the HR's decision to establish an EU Crisis Platform, bringing together the EEAS and the Commission's relevant services, represented a significant attempt to promote consistency in the use of institutional instruments, and hence a comprehensive EU approach to external conflicts and crises. Yet this approach was mainly focused on maintaining interinstitutional stability, without identifying operationalizing methods and practical solutions to inconsistencies and overlapping (Amadio Viceré 2014). During the Libyan crisis, in particular, DG ECHO refused to be coordinated by the newly established EEAS Department of Crisis Response (interviews reported in Koenig 2016). Consequently, rather than Ashton, it was Kristalina Georgieva, the European Commissioner for International Cooperation, Humanitarian Aid and Crisis Response, who promoted and led the EU humanitarian response to the crisis.

The Second Post-Lisbon HR: Federica Mogherini

The situational setting within which Mogherini operated was more favorable than Ashton's situational setting. Political constellations were changing across

European national politics. In France, Sarkozy left the presidency to the socialist François Hollande. Cameron was increasingly focused on British national politics. As of February 2014, Renzi, who belonged to Mogherini's original social-democratic party, was leading Italy. In addition, from July to December 2014, Italy chaired the Council of the EU's rotating presidency and, together with Malta and Greece, was very vocal about irregular migration. Germany and France, meanwhile, were increasingly concerned about foreign fighters returning to Europe from Syria. All this provided fertile ground for an alignment of preferences among member states over the need to counter the influx of migrants from Libya, and hence for the HR to exercise her leadership in this regard. Furthermore, since the EEAS was fully operational when Mogherini took office, the second post-Lisbon HR could focus more than her predecessor on increasing interinstitutional coordination within EU foreign policy (Von Ondarza and Scheler 2017).

Concerning the institutional setting, evidence shows that the renegotiation of the mandate of the European Union Border Assistance Mission (EUBAM) in Libya represented an opportunity for the HR to exercise leadership as an agenda setter within EU intergovernmental forums. While foreign ministers were in favor of EU engagement in Libya (FAC 2014), Mogherini's priority was to address the humanitarian tragedy happening in the Mediterranean Sea. Mogherini used the EUBAM review to champion among the member states' representatives the change of focus that, she argued, was necessary to avoid a deterioration of the migration emergency (High Representative 2017). Consequently, following the FAC held on March 16, 2015, foreign ministers requested the HR to present a proposal on CSDP activities in Libya. They asked Mogherini to address their security concerns linked to migration even as they stressed their humanitarian concerns (FAC 2015a, 2015b). The interim EUBAM strategic review, released in April 2015, arguably reflected member states' appetite for a CSDP mission more centered on migration. It stated that, in case the civilian mission was relaunched, its main priority "would be on developing the Libyan naval coastguard's capacity and delivering a search and rescue concept" (EEAS 2015a: 1).

On April 19, 2015, around 900 migrants lost their lives in a shipwreck off the Libyan coast. The tragic event not only pushed the EU to launch a joint naval mission in the Mediterranean, it also helped Mogherini to successfully align the FAC's position with the European Council's. The day after the shipwreck, Mogherini presented to the FAC a 10-point plan addressing the issue of migrant traffickers (EEAS 2015a). A few days later, the Political and Security Committee (PSC), composed of member states' representatives at the ambassadorial level, invited the EEAS to present options to counter the smuggling of migrants in the Mediterranean (EEAS 2015a). The extraordinary European Council held on April 23, 2015 tasked the HR with the preparation of a naval operation to address irregular migration across the Mediterranean, while implicitly referencing the involvement of criminal networks in Libya (EEAS 2015b).

As events unfolded quickly, under the HR's direction, the EEAS had to come up with a Crisis Management Concept (CMC) for the mission. The CMC is normally based on the assessment presented in the Political Framework for a Crisis Approach (PFCA). As there was no PFCA on migration, however, nor time to prepare one, the EEAS employed the analysis contained in the PFCA on Libya. On Mogherini's indications, this document did not frame the EU support to Libya in terms of facilitating the transition from an autocratic regime to democracy (EEAS 2015b: 2). Instead, it listed the threats to the EU, including the increasing irregular migration flows, proliferation of foreign fighters, spread of weapon smuggling in the region, and risk to strategic economic sectors. Consequently, the EU focus on Libya shifted from the country's political transition to the migration emergency. It is in this context that EUNAFOR MED, the first-ever joint EU naval mission aimed at fighting human trafficking and arms smuggling, was agreed to on June 22, 2015. Notably, it took only two months to move from a political initiative to a full CSDP operation. With remarkable swiftness for an EU mission, consensus was built among EU member states, capabilities were identified, and the deployment started (Faleg and Blockmans 2015).

Mogherini was more effective than Ashton in exercising leadership on the supranational side of EU foreign policy. From the beginning of her mandate, she took advantage of her role as VP of the Commission (Von Ondarza and Scheler 2017). The second post-Lisbon HR gained the trust of her fellow commissioners in the Group of External Action. In particular, Mogherini established a reciprocal process with them by regularly reporting on the progress of her activities in Libya. Notably, she also organized several joint missions with her fellow commissioners (Blockmans and Montesano 2015). At the same time, she promoted a special relationship with the EP by regularly meeting with the EP Committee on Foreign Affairs to report on the status of the various policy dossiers, including Libya. This approach was not only welcomed by her fellow commissioners and the MEPs, it also reinforced Mogherini's status as the main interlocutor for issues related to EU foreign policy (Blockmans and Russack 2015).

6.5 Discussion and Conclusion

This chapter has offered an assessment of the positional and behavioral leadership of the first two post-Lisbon HRs in EU foreign policy. By shedding light on the processes that allowed Ashton and Mogherini to access the HR's office and by evaluating their leadership performance in facing the Libyan crisis, we offered an in-depth study of women's leadership in the EU. Concerning gender stereotypes and role expectations, we have shown that these were encountered by both Ashton and Mogherini when they became HRs. However, we found no evidence that they had a significant effect on the two HRs' exercise of their functions during the Libyan crisis.

As for positional leadership, based on the arguments presented in our analytical framework, we can draw some meaningful conclusions about the appointment of two women as HRs. The appointment of Ashton and Mogherini in what is traditionally considered a male-dominated portfolio is explained by three factors. First, in terms of situational setting, because of the growing instability of the geopolitical situation and the institutional uncertainties related to the Lisbon Treaty's implementation, the role of HR was considered an arduous and not very rewarding position. Hence, member states were less keen to seek a portfolio that could hamper the credibility and future prospects of their candidates. Second, in terms of institutional setting, among the top positions, the HR was considered less relevant than the president of the Commission, the president of the European Council, and even the Commissioner for Internal Market. Against this backdrop, the heads chose to leave the "less powerful" position to a woman. Third, and finally, the structural setting: the appointment of two women as HR should not be considered a success story in breaking the glass ceiling's constraints. In fact, despite the EP's growing pressure to maintain a good gender balance among the EU's high political positions, European leaders still tended to favor men.

Concerning the differences between the leadership performances of the two HRs, they are empirically evident in the management of the Libyan crisis. At the intergovernmental level, Ashton focused on finding a common denominator among the member states' positions. Yet she often had to leave the leading role to other actors, such as the heads of state and government, the president of the European Commission, the president of the European Council, or the EP. Overall, we can conclude that in the case of Libya she could exercise leadership neither in the intergovernmental settings nor in the supranational EU forums. She was sidelined, attacked and—at best—ignored by member states' representatives. At the supranational level, Ashton could not efficiently coordinate the EU's external actions. Her attempts to foster coordination were often interpreted by other commissioners as ways to impose her—and the EEAS's—leadership on them. On the contrary, Mogherini benefitted from the changing situational setting to set a new agenda for EU actions in the Mediterranean and to reshape the EU approach on Libya. Overall, she was successful in interpreting member states' preferences and in adjusting her narrative to gain support from her different audiences. Her active involvement in the EU supranational forums reinforced her position in the intergovernmental debates as well.

To conclude, even if both HR Ashton and HR Mogherini faced similar challenges in accessing their leadership positions, they represent two quite different models for how women may operate in a complex, male-dominated institutional system such as the domain of EU foreign policy.

References

Aggestam, Lisbeth, and Markus Johansson. 2017. "The Leadership Paradox in EU Foreign Policy." *Journal of Common Market Studies* 55 (6): 1203–1220.

Amadio Viceré, Maria Giulia. 2014. "Review Article: Strategic Formalism or Formalised Strategy? Features and Limits of the New EU 'Process-Oriented Comprehensive Approach' to External Conflicts and Crises." *Conflict, Security & Development* 14 (5): 651–663.

Amadio Viceré, Maria Giulia. 2016. "The Roles of the President of the European Council and the High Representative in Leading EU Foreign Policy on Kosovo." *Journal of European Integration* 38 (5): 557–570.

Amadio Viceré, Maria Giulia. 2018. *The High Representative and EU Foreign Policy Integration: A Comparative Study of Kosovo and Ukraine*. Basingstoke, UK: Palgrave Macmillan.

Amadio Viceré, Maria Giulia. 2020. "Looking towards the East: The High Representative's Role in EU Foreign Policy on Kosovo and Ukraine." *European Security* 29 (3): 337–358.

Amadio Viceré, Maria Giulia, and Sergio Fabbrini. 2017. "Assessing the High Representative's Role in Egypt during the Arab Spring." *International Spectator* 52 (3): 64–82.

Amadio Viceré, Maria Giulia, Giulia Tercovich, and Caterina Carta. 2020. "Assessing the Post-Lisbon High Representatives: From Treaty Provisions to Europe's Multiple Crises." *European Security* 29 (3): 337–358.

Amos, Valerie. 2011. "Statement to the Security Council on Libya." May 9, UN Security Council, New York.

Barber, James D. 1992. *The Presidential Character: Predicting Performance in the White House*. 4th ed. Englewood Cliffs, NJ: Prentice Hall.

Barber, Tony. 2010. "The Appointments of Herman van Rompuy and Catherine Ashton." *Journal of Common Market Studies* 48: 55–67.

Bassiri Tabrizi, Aniseh, and Ben Kienzle. 2020. "The High Representative and Directories in European Foreign Policy: The Case of the Nuclear Negotiations with Iran." *European Security* 29 (3): 320–336.

Blockmans, Steven, and Francesco Saverio Montesano. 2015. *Mogherini's First 100 Days: Not the Quiet Diplomat*. Brussels: Centre for European Policy Studies (CEPS).

Blockmans, Steven, and Sophia Russack. 2015. *The Commissioners' Group on External Action: Key Political Facilitator*. Brussels: Centre for European Policy Studies (CEPS).

Blom, Tannelie, and Sophie Vanhoonacker. 2015. "The European External Action Service (EEAS), the New Kid on the Block." In *The Palgrave Handbook of the European Administrative System*, eds. Michael W. Bauer and Jarle Trondal, 208–223. Basingstoke, UK: Palgrave Macmillan.

Castle, Stephen. 2009. "E.U. President Takes Tough Line on Filling Top Jobs." *New York Times*, November 11.

Dempsey, Judy. 2014. *Judy Asks: Is Renzi's Italy Back in the EU Game*. Brussels: Carnegie Europe.

EEAS. 2013. *EEAS Review* (cited September 4, 2020). Available from https://www.statewatch.org/media/documents/news/2013/jul/eu-eeas-review.pdf.

EEAS. 2015a. *Interim Strategic Review of EUBAM Libya*. Working document 7886/15, Brussels, April 13 (cited September 4, 2020). Available from https://www.statewatch. org/news/2015/jun/eu-eeas-interim-report-UBAM-7886-15.pdf.

EEAS. 2015b. *Crisis Management Concept. Working document of the European External Action Service* (cited September 4, 2020). Available from www.statewatch.org/news/ 2015/may/eu-med-military-op.pdf.

Euronews. 2011. "Ashton Defends EU Unity over Libya." March 22.

European Commission. 2018. *Report on Equality between Women and Men in the EU* (cited September 4, 2020). Available from https://ec.europa.eu/newsroom/just/ document.cfm?doc_id=50074.

European Council. 2011. *Declaration Extraordinary European Council* (cited September 4, 2020). Available from https://www.consilium.europa.eu/uedocs/cms_data/ docs/pressdata/en/ec/119780.pdf.

Fabbrini, Sergio. 2010. *Compound Democracies: Why the United States and Europe Are Becoming Similar*. Oxford: Oxford University Press.

Fabbrini, Sergio. 2014. "The European Union and the Libyan Crisis." *International Politics* 51 (2): 177–195.

FAC. 2011. *3069th Council Meeting, Foreign Affairs, Brussels, 21 February* (cited September 4, 2020). Available from https://ec.europa.eu/commission/presscorner/ detail/en/PRES_11_32.

FAC. 2014. *Council Conclusions on Libya*. Foreign Affairs Council meeting, Luxembourg, October 20.

FAC. 2015a. *Council Conclusions on Libya*. Foreign Affairs Council meeting, Brussels, 16 March. (cited September 4, 2020). Available from https://www.consilium.europa. eu/en/meetings/fac/2015/03/16.

FAC. 2015b. *Special Meeting of the European Council: Statement. Foreign Affairs and Home Affairs Council meeting*. Brussels, April 23 (cited September 4, 2020). Available from https://www.consilium.europa.eu/en/press/press-releases/2015/04/ 23/special-euco-statement.

Faleg, Giovanni, and Steven Blockmans. 2015. *EU Naval Force EUNAVFOR MED Sets Sail in Troubled Waters*. Brussels: Centre for European Policy Studies (CEPS).

Gardner, Andrew. 2014. "Federica Mogherini: The Promotion of Inexperience." Politico, September 3.

Genschel, Philipp, and Markus Jachtenfuchs, eds. 2014. *Beyond the Regulatory Polity? The European Integration of Core State Powers*. Oxford: Oxford University Press.

Gomes, Ana. 2011. "Was Eufor Libya an April Fool's Joke?" *EUobserver*, July 13.

Gordon, Eleanor. 2018. "Gender and Defence Sector Reform: Problematising the Place of Women in Conflict-Affected Environments." *Journal of Intervention and Statebuilding* 13 (1): 75–94.

Gray, John. 1992. *Men Are from Mars, Women Are from Venus: The Classic Guide to Understanding the Opposite Sex*. London: HarperCollins.

Hansen, Suzy. 2016. "E.U. Foreign-Policy and Security Chief Federica Mogherini Is Often the Only Woman in the Room." *Vogue*, February 29.

Helwig, Niklas. 2017. "Agent Interaction as a Source of Discretion for the EU High Representative." In *The Principal Agent Model and the European Union*, eds. Tom Delreux and Johan Adriaensen, 105–129. London: Palgrave Macmillan.

Helwig, Niklas, and Carolin Rüger. 2014. "In Search of a Role for the High Representative: The Legacy of Catherine Ashton." *International Spectator* 49 (4): 1–17.

High Representative [of the Union for Foreign Affairs and Security Policy]. 2011a. "Declaration by the High Representative, Catherine Ashton, on behalf of the European Union on Events in Libya" (cited September 4, 2020). Available from: https://www.consilium.europa.eu/uedocs/cms_data/docs/pressdata/en/cfsp/119397.pdf.

High Representative [of the Union for Foreign Affairs and Security Policy]. 2011b. "A World Built on Co-operation, Sovereignty, Democracy and Stability" (cited September 4, 2020). Available from: https://ec.europa.eu/commission/presscorner/detail/en/SPEECH_11_126.

High Representative [of the Union for Foreign Affairs and Security Policy]. 2017. "Speech by the High Representative/Vice-President Federica Mogherini at the High-Level Conference on Migration Management at the European Parliament" (cited September 4, 2020). Available from https://eeas.europa.eu/headquarters/headquarters-homepage/29047/node/29047_en.

Howorth, Jolyon. 2011. "The 'New Faces' of Lisbon: Assessing the Performance of Catherine Ashton and Herman van Rompuy on the Global Stage." *European Foreign Affairs Review* 16 (3): 303–323.

Keating, Dave. 2014. "Italy Officially Nominates Mogherini for Commission." *Politico*, August 1.

Keating, Dave, and Tim King. 2014. "Women Commissioners: Juncker Struggles to Reach Eight." *Politico*, August 27.

Koenig, Nicole. 2012. "The EU and the Libyan Crisis in Quest of Coherence?" *International Spectator* 46 (4): 11–30.

Koenig, Nicole. 2014. "Between Conflict Management and Role Conflict: The EU in the Libyan Crisis." *European Security* 23 (3): 250–269.

Koenig, Nicole. 2016. *EU Security Policy and Crisis Management: A Quest for Coherence*. Abingdon, UK: Routledge.

Koops, Joachim A., and Giulia Tercovich. 2020. "Shaping the European External Action Service and Its Post-Lisbon Crisis Management Structures: An Assessment of the EU High Representatives' Political Leadership." *European Security* 29 (3): 275–300.

Laursen, Finn, ed. 2013. *The EU's Lisbon Treaty: Institutional Choices and Implementation*. Farnham, UK: Ashgate.

Lazarou, Elena, and Francesca Braden. 2019. *Women in Foreign Affairs and International Security: Contours of a Timely Debate*. Brussels: European Parliamentary Research Service.

McMahon, Meabh, and Andrew Willis. 2011. "Member States Responsible for EU 'Single Voice.'" *EUobserver*, May 16.

Müller, Peter. 2016. "Federica Mogherini Is Hope of European Social Democrats." *Spiegel International*, May 24.

Prasad, Ritu. 2019. "Are Voters Biased against Women Candidates?" *BBC News*, September 11.

Puetter, Uwe. 2014. *The European Council and the Council: New Intergovernmentalism and Institutional Change*. Oxford: Oxford University Press.

Ridgeway, Cecilia L. 2001. "Gender, Status, and Leadership." *Journal of Social Issues* 57 (4): 637–655.

Rüger, Caroline. 2011. "A Position under Construction: Future Prospects of the High Representative after the Treaty of Lisbon." In *The High Representative for the EU Foreign and Security Policy: Review and Prospects*, eds. Gisela Müller-Brandeck-Bocquet and Carolin Rüger, 201–234. Baden-Baden: Nomos.

Spence, David. 2015. "The EEAS and Its Epistemic Communities: The Challenges of Diplomatic Hybridism." In *The European External Action Service: European Diplomacy Post-Westphalia*, eds. David Spence and Jozef Bátora, 43–64. London: Palgrave Macmillan.

Spence, David, and Jozef Bátora, eds. 2015. *The European External Action Service: European Diplomacy Post-Westphalia*. London: Palgrave Macmillan.

Sutherlands, Peter. 2011. "Europe's Test in North Africa." *European Voice*, June 5.

Tempest, Matthew. 2015. "Mogherini Defends Herself against Age Jibes." *Euractive*, November 4.

Tömmel, Ingeborg. 2013. "The Presidents of the European Commission: Transactional or Transforming Leaders." *Journal of Common Market Studies* 51 (4): 789–805.

Tömmel, Ingeborg. 2017. "The Standing President of the European Council: Intergovernmental or Supranational Leadership?" *Journal of European Integration* 39 (2): 175–189.

Tömmel, Ingeborg. 2020. "Political Leadership in Times of Crisis: The Commission Presidency of Jean-Claude Juncker." *West European Politics* 43 (5): 1141–1162.

Traynor, Ian, and Nicholas Watt. 2011. "Libya No-Fly Zone Plan Rejected by EU Leaders." *Guardian*, March 11.

UNSC. 2011. "Security Council Approves 'No-Fly Zone' over Libya, Authorizing 'All Necessary Measures' to Protect Civilians, by Vote of 10 in Favour with 5 Abstentions." 6498th Meeting (Night), March 17. Available from https://www.un.org/press/en/2011/sc10200.doc.htm.

Valentino, Paolo. 2019. "Renzi 'pentito' della scelta Mogherini." *Corriere della Sera*, February 17.

Vincenti, Daniela. 2014. "Profile: Federica Mogherini, the Next EU Foreign Affairs Chief." *Euractiv*, August 31.

Vogel, Toby. 2009. "Ashton Gives Underwhelming Performance." *Politico*, January 11.

Von Ondarza, Nicolai, and Ronja Scheler. 2017. "The High Representative's 'Double Hat': How Mogherini and Ashton Have Differed in Their Links with the Commission." London School of Economics (blog), March 16, https://blogs.lse.ac.uk/europpblog/2017/03/16/high-representative-mogherini-ashton.

Williams, Kristen P. 2017. "Feminism in Foreign Policy." *Oxford Research Encyclopedia of Politics*. DOI: 10.1093/acrefore/9780190228637.013.368.

7

Rhetoric and Leadership

A Comparison of Female Vice-Presidents of the European Commission (1999–2019)

Henriette Müller and Pamela Pansardi

7.1 Introduction

The backdrop to Ursula von der Leyen's successful campaign to substantially increase the number of female commissioners in 2019 is the acute lack of women in leadership positions in the European Commission throughout the institution's history. This lack is best illustrated by contrasting the list of female vice-presidents with the overall number of presidents and vice-presidents that have so far headed the Commission. Of 89 presidents and vice-presidents between 1958 and 2019, only seven were women, including the two female High Representatives for Foreign Affairs and Security Policy who served ex officio as Commission vice-presidents.

This chapter focuses on six of the seven female vice-presidents of the European Commission between 1999 and 2019: Loyola de Palacio (1999–2004), Margot Wallström (2004–2009), Viviane Reding (2009–2014), Neelie Kroes (2009–2014), Catherine Ashton (2010–2014), and Kristalina Georgieva (2014–2016).[1] We study the leadership performance of these vice-presidents by systematically comparing their speeches' rhetorical characteristics throughout their tenures. In this context, we understand political language and public speech-making as "essential means of enacting leadership" (Baxter 2010: 7). Language is part of performing leadership; it is process and result at the same time, indivisibly intertwined with the exercise of leadership.

Empirically, the chapter applies an explorative approach. It evaluates to what extent EU female leaders make use of charismatic rhetoric in their speeches, if their speeches differ in this regard from those of men, and if there were any relevant

---

[1] Federica Mogherini, vice-president of the European Commission in 2014–2019, was excluded from this study due to lack of data availability.

Henriette Müller and Pamela Pansardi, *Rhetoric and Leadership: A Comparison of Female Vice-Presidents of the European Commission (1999–2019)*. In: *Women and Leadership in the European Union*. Edited by Henriette Müller and Ingeborg Tömmel, Oxford University Press. © Oxford University Press (2022). DOI: 10.1093/oso/9780192896216.003.0008

trends between 1999 and 2019. Our investigation is based on software-assisted text analysis (Diction 7) of the entire corpus of speeches of the respective female vice-presidents as well as all other European Commission members in the period under study, i.e., female commissioners and male commissioners, vice-presidents, and presidents (N = 8,945). Since we study the rhetoric of women and men, it is important to note that we distinguish between individuals' self-identification as "female" or "male," "woman" or "man" (usually, but not always, because of biological characteristics), and the social and cultural construction of gender that assigns conventional and stereotyped designations of "masculinity" and "femininity" to the performances of men and women.

7.2 Women's Public Speeches in the European Context

While in theory the exercise of all kinds of leadership roles and their linguistic expressions is available to both sexes, in contemporary Western societies the practice often remains characterized by "both prejudice and internalized anxiety about the female voice in public contexts" (Cameron 2006: 4). The binary oppositions of male/female and public/private are still often considered as defining distinct and salient spheres of activity, with masculinity assigned to the former and femininity to the latter (Bean 2006). Hence, when we study the exercise of leadership in the context of speech-making, we have to take into account the widespread and enduring patterns of structural and ideological resistance to the equal participation of women in the public sphere. This is particularly important in the political domain, since in hardly any other arena of society does the successful exercise of leadership depend "so strongly upon an individual's ability to speak effectively in public and often adversarial contexts" (Shaw 2006: 81).

In general, language constitutes behavior, intent, and creates and reproduces social constructs; it is more than a simple tool of communication or reflection of a state of mind (Baxter 2017). In the context of gender and leadership, language has the capacity to both inhibit women's access to and performance of leadership as well as provide "a powerful set of resources for accomplishing leadership successfully" (Baxter 2017: 113). This means that if we speak of women's voices in public contexts, we identify, on the one hand, "women's language" as a symbolic category and, on the other, "the language used by women" as an empirical category (Litosseliti 2006: 44). This chapter will focus on the latter.

When we think of sociolinguistic differences between women's and men's speech-making, one major social construct and gender stereotype about women's public voices becomes apparent—the idea of the female voice as an "emotional" one. "Research on stereotypes has shown emotionality to be one of the general dimensions of sex stereotypes: women are said to be more expressive, excitable and easily hurt than men" (Fischer 1993: 303). In Western societies, rationality and productive labor have become associated with notions of masculinity and thus men, whereas the household and emotional labor, such as caring for family members, were long considered feminine in nature, thus fitting ideals of femininity (Fischer 1993).

Although many features of femininity have been redefined and socially deconstructed and reconstructed, especially since the 1960s, the idea that women's language is particularly emotional somehow sticks and is still considered an important characteristic of culturally nurtured feminine traits. It is important to note that while men and women in principle are equally disposed to experience and express a variety of emotions, men have tended to be culturally punished for expressing emotions in public, especially fear or sadness (Fischer 1993). Research into gender differences in the recognition of vocalized emotions has shown that women have a consistent advantage in decoding and encoding verbal emotional expressions (Lausen and Schacht 2018). As this advantage is considered to be related to processes of socialization rather than biology, "[t]he general claim that women are more emotional than men tells us more about our cultural stereotypes than about actual sex differences in emotions" (Fischer 1993: 312).

The idea of the "emotional" voice exemplifies the expressive double bind that women face: "that is, if they speak and sound overly 'masculine,' they are characterized by colleagues as aggressive, and if they speak and sound overly 'feminine,' they are characterized as tentative, hesitant, or weak" (Baxter 2017: 116; see also Chapter 1 in this volume). In other words, women have been socially expected to avoid tough language and overtly confrontational tones. This yields the paradox that characteristics often associated with women leaders' rhetoric—e.g., being relational and socially oriented—are considered necessary leadership qualities, while at the same time these "very relational skills … have acted as barriers to [women's] career progression" (Baxter 2017: 119).

Thus, if women use these skill sets, they kind of blend in with the mass, whereas if men use these same skill sets combined with "their" competitiveness and assertiveness, "they are seen as versatile and socially skilled leaders" (Baxter 2017: 119). To be more precise, research has shown that "[i]n contexts where the primary function of talk is interpersonal or social, women tend to contribute more. When the primary function of talk is referential and focused on information, men often talk more" (Holmes 1992: 132). These findings reinvigorate the idea of women being emotional in a negative fashion and as a self-perpetuating cycle of self-devaluation and other-valuation.

Challenging this stereotype and social construction in the context of gender and language, sociolinguist Judith Baxter found that skillful leaders "deploy linguistic strategies that range along the feminine–masculine continuum according to topic, purpose, the degree of 'publicness' of the meeting, and the norms of the professional community they belong" (2017: 121). Women's language and rhetoric are more likely to be affected by contradictory socially and culturally constructed expectations and institutional constraints as compared to their male counterparts (Baxter 2010; Cameron 2006; Shaw 2006). This means that there is, of course, no "female linguistic deficiency" or lack of "proper" communication skills. In contrast, "[s]enior women are often highly skilled and astute communicators with a sophisticated awareness of the effect of their words on others" (Baxter 2010: 3). The point is thus not women's capacities as public speakers but the gendered discourses surrounding women's speech-making.

According to Baxter's comparative analysis of women managers, successful "female leaders use a style of language that is a more proscribed and self-regulated version of men's, because they need to use special linguistic strategies in order to preempt negative evaluation in a business [or else political] world that continues to be male-dominated" (2010: 169). This means that while women certainly do not use a totally different style of rhetoric from men, they often have to engage—more than men—in complex forms of so-called impression management "in an effort to ensure they are neither dismissed as insufficiently authoritative nor derided as aggressive 'battleaxes'" (Cameron and Shaw 2016: 11, 134). This double bind in the context of speech-making impels women managers and executives to become "highly skilled, linguistically expert, [applying] diverse and nuanced version[s] [of rhetoric], finely-tuned to colleagues and context" (Baxter 2010: 169).

The difference thus lies not in sex but in gender stereotypes and social constructions thereof as well as men's still overwhelming dominance in political speech-making in modern democracies and the European Union, specifically. By means of unequal representation, "[m]en speak more frequently and for longer than women; they more often take leadership roles in formal settings, and are more likely to be the speakers whose contributions are most influential, in the sense that others take them up and refer to them in subsequent discussion" (Cameron and Shaw 2016: 8). The European Commission with its long-standing underrepresentation of women in leadership positions until very recently (see Chapter 3 in this volume) can be considered such a constraining context to women's speech-making. Thus, it provides for an interesting case to systematically study the extent as to which women's rhetoric differs from that of their male counterparts. The office of vice-president of the European Commission is the highest position that women were able to obtain until 2019. Though the post does not entail special responsibilities,[2] we can assume that it increases officeholders' prestige and public exposure. In this context, we want to know: (1) What characterizes EU women leaders' rhetoric; (2) to what extent their rhetoric changed over time (1999–2019); and, finally, (3) to what extent their rhetoric differs from that of their male counterparts.

---

[2] Exceptions concern the first vice-president (position introduced by Barroso in 2004) and the executive vice-president (position introduced by von der Leyen in 2019).

Summing up, women's performances in the context of public speeches do not necessarily differ from those of men, but social expectations based on assumptions and stereotypes about gender often expose women leaders to a double bind in the context of speech-making and rhetoric that can lead to differing performances and different evaluations thereof—often negatively impacting women's exercise of leadership. Sociolinguistic research indicates, however, that women leaders also often emerge as highly skilled and trained public rhetors due to the constraints they encounter on their pathways to and exercise of leadership.

7.3 The Nexus between Gender, Rhetoric, and Charisma

One way of studying the oratorical abilities of leaders in a systematic, comparative fashion is through the concept of charisma and, more precisely, charismatic rhetoric. In essence, charisma is inherently personal and refers to agency; it is not a characteristic of office or institutional structure. While the majority of leaders in world history considered charismatic have been male, both normative and empirical examinations of the phenomenon of charisma have been surprisingly gender-blind. In fact, core characteristics of what constitutes a charismatic leader essentially incorporate both nominally masculine and feminine traits (Antonakis et al. 2016).

Charisma in leaders is considered an ability to "show action, confidence and to influence followers," not by means of transactional rewards but rather by building a strong relationship between leaders and followers (Olsson and Hammargård 2016: 553; see also Shamir et al. 1994). Charismatic leaders "increase the appeal of collective goals by clearly linking core aspects of the leader's vision to core aspects of followers' self-concepts" (Bligh et al. 2010: 829). To achieve that linkage successfully, a leader's communicative strategy and rhetoric are considered vital components for exercising and evaluating charismatic leadership (Rosenberg and Hirschberg 2009; Bligh et al. 2004; Shamir et al. 1994). Furthermore, we follow the argument of Antonakis et al. that "charisma is values-based, symbolic, and emotion-laden leader signaling" and thus in essence a highly "skilled performance" (2016: 304, 296). In other words, rather than evaluating the legitimacy of charismatic leadership as such, we use charisma as a proxy to study a leader's skillfulness.

To link *vision* and *collective goals* means that charismatic leaders embrace the stereotypes of both the "masculine" leader, considered to be agentic, dominant, determined, and self-oriented, and the "feminine" leader, considered to be emotional, caring, empathetic, and other-oriented (Chapter 1 in this volume). In the words of Bligh et al., "charismatic leadership uniquely straddles or transcends the double-bind of gender stereotypes" (2010: 828). According to research at the intersection of language and charisma, the exercise of seven characteristics are deemed essential to rendering a leader's speech-making charismatic (Bligh et al. 2010; Shamir et al. 1994).[3]

These oratorical characteristics do indeed combine nominally feminine and masculine—as well as purportedly gender-neutral—leadership attributes: Three of the seven rhetorical features (*collective focus, followers' worth*, and *similarity to followers*) are seen as appealing to community and collectivity, whereas two characteristics (*action* and *adversity*) are seen as indicating task-orientation and authoritativeness. The two additional markers of charismatic rhetoric (*temporal orientation, [in-]tangibility*) are considered to be gender-neutral (Bligh et al. 2010; Shamir et al. 1994; Antonakis et al. 2016; Bligh et al. 2004). In sum, a charismatic leader is a competent leader who employs skilled rhetoric, embracing both stereotypically masculine and feminine (as well as gender-neutral) rhetorical strategies.

To address the collective focus and build consensus, a collective identity, and trust with and among their constituencies, charismatic leaders use collective language (e.g., "we," "us," "our"). A useful tool in this context is to compare how often a leader uses the aforementioned signifiers in contrast to self-referential signifiers, such as "I" and "my" or "me" (Bligh et al. 2010; Seyranian and Bligh 2008). Moreover, to emphasize their similarity to their followers and the latter's worth, charismatic leaders express more strongly positive affirmations with their constituencies, embracing and sharing moments of joy and triumph as well as focusing their language on rhetorical familiarity and human interest (Bligh et al. 2010; Choi 2006; Seyranian and Bligh 2008; Shamir et al. 1994). In addressing these collective needs through the usage of collective language, charismatic leaders create a sense of empathy and belonging, "displaying sensitivity to their followers' needs and emotions" (Choi 2006: 27).

In contrast, action and authoritativeness in the context of charismatic leadership involves providing "a bold, purposeful vision and a sense of confidence in attaining that vision" (Bligh et al. 2010: 831; see also Choi 2006). For example, a charismatic leader is proactive rather than reactive in his or her agenda-setting, using action-related language (e.g., emphasizing task completion) (Seyranian and Bligh 2008). This technique suggests authoritativeness, which contributes to creating a "sense of excitement and adventure" among the constituency to follow that lead (Bligh et al. 2010: 831). In employing this technique, leaders express their readiness to compete, capacity to be agentic, and possession of the will to succeed. Of course, the envisioned action should not be random; rather, the leader describes the context in which the action will take place in terms of adversity, clearly articulating "why action is necessary and in some cases inevitable" (Bligh et al. 2010: 831).

---

[3] The literature mentions an eighth construct, *value and moral justification*. However, this characteristic cannot be studied directly via Diction 7 and has thus been excluded from this analysis. Diction 7 studies references to values and evaluation by means of other variables, especially *followers' worth* and *adversity* (Olsson and Hammargård 2016; Tortola and Pansardi 2019).

These characteristics of charismatic rhetoric can be studied by evaluating the extent to which leaders' speeches invoke blame and hardship concerning the current political situation. The charismatic leader, in sum, creates support for his or her agenda by addressing the deficiency of the current situation and the willingness to overcome it (Bligh et al. 2010).

Charisma in rhetoric is also expressed through a temporal dimension in which leaders frequently express continuity between past, present, and future, connecting an often glorious past with a promising future to build on a collective history and traditions (Shamir et al. 1994). Scholars have argued, as well, that charismatic leaders tend to embrace greater intangibility when it comes to future outcomes, meaning they tend to be more vague and less concrete, addressing distant goals and painting the future in flowery, grandiose terms (Bligh et al. 2010; Shamir et al. 1994). This suggests the relative prevalence of general and abstract terms in their speech-making versus a more concrete, down-to-earth vocabulary.

Conclusively, being evaluated as a charismatic leader with regard to the usage of rhetoric means one is a highly skilled speaker and a linguistic expert who is capable of nuanced and diverse speech-making (Baxter 2010). Hence, we understand charismatic rhetoric as a proxy for the skillfulness of women rhetors (with higher levels of charisma indicating higher rhetorical skillfulness). In addition, the focus on charisma in the context of language and leadership means going beyond long-held gender biases in the leadership context, since charismatic leaders embrace attributes of leadership performance stereotypically considered both masculine and feminine, as well as those considered gender-neutral. While women and men are in principle equally disposed to provide charismatic leadership, the question is whether the sociostructural context of women's underrepresentation in the political domain along with societal gender biases contribute to women leaders engaging—more strongly than men—in the exercise of charismatic leadership.

7.4 Method and Empirical Analysis

Our empirical investigation concentrates on the study of charismatic rhetoric of the aforementioned six female vice-presidents (henceforth, female VPs) through the analysis of their official speeches. To investigate the characteristic traits of the female VPs' speech-making vis-à-vis that of other Commission members, including other male and female commissioners, male VPs, and the presidents of the Commission, we collected all speeches delivered by Commission members between 1999 and 2019, a total of 8,945 speeches.[4] Our corpus covers

---

[4] Speeches were downloaded between January and October 2019 from the European Commission Press Release Database: http://europa.eu/rapid/search.htm. Since November 1, 2019, the Commission repository has migrated to https://ec.europa.eu/commission/presscorner/home/en.

four different Commissions and three different Commission presidents—Romano Prodi (1999–2004), José Manuel Durão Barroso (2004–2014), and Jean-Claude Juncker (2014–2019)—with the speeches comprising 564 by female VPs, 1,698 by female commissioners, 4,183 by male commissioners, 1,145 by male VPs, and 1,355 by the Commission presidents.[5] For female VPs, our data collection ends in 2016, when Kristalina Georgieva resigned from her role as VP in the Juncker Commission; no female VPs were subsequently appointed under Juncker.

To analyze the language and tone of the speeches we relied on the software Diction 7 (Hart 2001). Specifically created to analyze the tone of political discourse in written texts, Diction codes text according to 31 predefined variables using built-in dictionaries (word lists). For each variable, Diction automatically assigns each text raw scores that are subsequently standardized on the basis of a built-in corpus of 50,000 texts to ensure generalizability of the results. This means that the scores for each text are defined on a single scale and immediately ready for comparison, and that comparative analysis is not affected by the N-size. The built-in corpus was last updated in 2015, when the latest version, Diction 7, was released. Approximately 25% of the included texts—which range from political speeches to poetry—are authored by women. Whereas a more gender-balanced corpus would better ensure the gender neutrality of the software analysis, Diction's capacity to place the results for all analyzed texts on a single scale partly overcomes its drawbacks, allowing us to compare female and male commissioners' speeches in light of a well-defined and systematized set of variables.

To analyze the commissioners' charismatic rhetoric, we followed previous studies (Bligh et al. 2004; Bligh and Robinson 2010; Davis and Gardner 2012; Olsson and Hammargård 2016; Tortola and Pansardi 2019) and combined Diction variables into seven composite constructs, based on the linguistic characteristics of charisma listed in the previous section. Table 7.1 summarizes the seven constructs and the corresponding formulas of Diction variables, along with sample words for each variable and its gender connotation.

The charismatic constructs presented in Table 7.1 are also aggregated in a single indicator of charismatic rhetoric—which we label *charisma*—by subtracting the value of *tangibility* from the sum of the six remaining constructs (Bligh et al. 2004; Tortola and Pansardi 2019).

Figure 7.1 presents an overview of the charismatic content of the corpus under study by plotting the year-by-year mean value of the speeches' aggregate index of charisma and showing the use of charismatic rhetoric by the Commission as a whole, by all female members of the Commission, and by female VPs.

---

[5] Speeches delivered exclusively or prevalently in languages other than English were manually excluded, as were written press statements not orally delivered. We are aware that European Commission members' speeches are usually written in part or entirely by speechwriters. However, we do not consider this problematic for our analysis, since by approving and adopting a speech, the speaker acquires "ownership" of its content and language (Tortola and Pansardi 2019: 114).

Table 7.1 The seven charismatic constructs and operationalization in Diction 7

Construct	Diction 7 Variables	Sample Terms	Stereotypical Gender Connotation
Collective Focus: charismatic leaders show a collective orientation and describe their actions and goals as directed toward common achievements and interests.	Collectives + People references − Self-reference	assembly, cabinet, humanity, mankind, nation crowd, residents, constituencies, majority, citizenry, population crowd, residents, constituencies, majority, citizenry, population	Feminine
Followers' Worth: charismatic leaders highlight the positive aspects of the followers and reinforce their sense of awareness vis-à-vis the achievement of collective goals (collective self-efficacy).	Praise + Inspiration + Satisfaction	admirable, brave, delightful, intelligent, kind, lovely, respected ambition, devotion, ideals, leadership, merit, optimism, promise, reassurance comfort, cherish, delight, fascinate, gratify, laugh, love, pleasure, rejoice	Feminine
Similarity to Followers: charismatic leaders highlight their own similarity to followers by describing themselves as "one of them."	Levelling + Familiarity + Human interest	anybody, everybody, fully, obvious, permanent, totally, unquestionably about, between, for, on, past, than, who, with children, family, friends, parents, relatives, widows, yours, charity, blessing, eternal, faith, hope, mercy	Feminine
Action: charismatic leaders use an action-oriented language to mobilize followers and describe themselves as "proactive."	Aggression + Accomplishment − Passivity − Ambivalence	attack, challenge, combat, dominate, furious, hurt, kill, oppose, preempt achieve, aspire, create, finish, motivate, pursuit, resolution, succeed accept, acquiesce, complacent, disinterested, hesitate, lackadaisical blur, confound, hesitate, puzzle, quandary, vacillate, wonder	Masculine

Continued

Table 7.1 *Continued*

Construct	Diction 7 Variables	Sample Terms	Stereotypical Gender Connotation
Adversity: charismatic leaders describe the situation as intolerable with the aim of supporting the proposed alternative "visionary future" and moving to action.	Blame + Hardship + Denial	contemptible, desperate, guilty, incompetent, mediocre, rash, senile conflict, crisis, death, fear, insecurity, loss, outrage, sorrow, tension didn't, hadn't, never, wasn't, wouldn't	Masculine
Temporal Orientation: charismatic leaders use more temporal references and tend to highlight continuity between the past and the present.	Present concern + Past concern	become, care, desire, make, need, request, take became, cared, desired, made, needed, requested, took, wanted want	Gender-neutral
Tangibility: charismatic leaders devote less attention to concrete and short-term goals, and are more prone to discuss their expectations and goals in abstract and general terms.	Concreteness + Insistence − Variety	animal, cancer, factory, household, movie, school, silk, sugar score calculated on the basis of repetition of key terms score calculated by dividing the number of different words in a passage by the total words	Gender-neutral

Source: Adapted from Tortola and Pansardi (2019), table 1, 105–106.

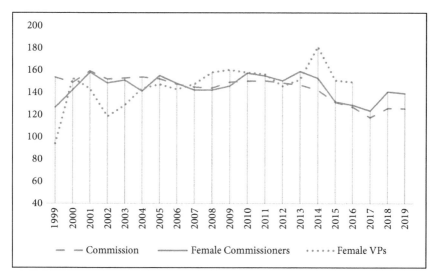

Fig. 7.1 Charismatic rhetoric of the Commission, of female commissioners, and of female VPs (1999–2019)

An initial visual inspection reveals that while the charismatic rhetoric of the Commission overall decreases over the years, that of female Commission members rose in 2010 and since that year has consistently been greater than the Commission average (except in 2015, when they were roughly equal).

To test whether gender has an actual effect on the charismatic rhetoric of Commission members, we perform a univariate analysis of covariance (ANCOVA), a technique for testing the significance of mean differences in a dependent variable of interest (in our case, *charisma*) across groups, while controlling for other variables (covariates) that might affect that variable. In the absence of statistical significance, the null hypothesis that differences across groups are due to sheer chance cannot be discarded. A first test is accordingly performed by using *charisma* as dependent variable, the two groups—female and male members of the Commission, including VPs and presidents—as a fixed factor, and the number of words per speech as a covariate. Table 7.2 presents in its first row the results of the ANCOVA, which confirms the existence of a significant difference ($p < 0.05$) in the use of charismatic rhetoric in relation to the Commission members' gender, where female members overall use more charismatic rhetoric than their male counterparts.

To allow for a more detailed interpretation, we perform a multivariate analysis of covariance (MANCOVA) to investigate variations among the seven constructs that compose our formulation of charismatic language, which are all included as

Table 7.2 The commissioners' charismatic rhetoric by gender. Results for the aggregated index of charisma and for single constructs

	Male Commrs Mean	Standard Error	Female Commrs Mean	Standard Error	Univariate F (2, 8942)	Partial eta squared	Observed Power
Charisma	146.654	0.467	148.630	0.803	4.524*	0.001	0.566
Single Constructs:							
Collective focus	2.571	0.078	0.827	0.134	125.865***	0.014	1.000
Temporal orientation	14.093	0.064	15.201	0.111	74.614***	0.008	1.000
Followers' worth	17.177	0.105	17.225	0.180	.054ns	0.000	0.056
Similarity to followers	158.922	0.239	160.836	0.411	16.202***	0.002	0.981
Tangibility	61.918	0.356	61.144	0.612	1.197ns	0.000	0.194
Action	8.429	0.134	7.769	0.231	6.089**	0.001	0.694
Adversity	7.381	0.056	7.917	0.096	23.069***	0.003	0.998

Notes: Estimated marginal means adjusted for the covariate *total words analyzed*. Male Commission members N = 6,683; female Commission members N = 2,262. ***p < 0.001, **p < 0.01, *p < 0.05, ns = nonsignificant.

dependent variables. The MANCOVA results again confirm a significant difference between male and female Commission members: Wilks's lambda = 0.978, F (7, 8936) = 28.899, p < 0.001. Table 7.2 reports the estimated marginal means and univariate results for the two groups in light of the seven constructs. The analysis of the single charisma constructs highlights significantly more frequent references to *temporal orientation*, *similarity to followers*, and *adversity* by female members of the Commission, while *collective focus* and *action* are invoked with significantly greater frequency by male members.

Concerning the charismatic rhetoric of female VPs, Figure 7.1 describes a pattern similar to the one of female Commission members overall. Starting in 2007, and with the sole exceptions of 2012 and 2013, the use of charismatic rhetoric by female VPs is consistently higher than that of the Commission as a whole. Additionally, again since 2007, and with the same exceptions of 2012 and 2013, the rhetoric of female VPs is consistently more charismatic than that of female commissioners overall (in 2010 and 2011, they are roughly equal). To test for an actual effect of gender and role in the Commission on charismatic rhetoric among female VPs, we perform a univariate analysis of covariance (ANCOVA). Table 7.3

Table 7.3 The Commission's charismatic rhetoric by group. Results for the aggregated index of charisma and for single constructs

		Mean	SD	Univariate F (4, 8939)
Charisma	Female VPs	151.317	38.117	14.176***
	Female commissioners	147.627	38.383	
	Male commissioners	149.228	37.424	
	Presidents	144.865	41.840	
	Male VPs	139.53	37.163	
Single Constructs:				
Collective focus	Female VPs	1.125	6.627	39.790***
	Female commissioners	.731	6.806	
	Male commissioners	2.310	6.216	
	Presidents	2.559	6.714	
	Male VPs	3.535	5.765	
Temporal orientation	Female VPs	16.468	5.778	32.443***
	Female commissioners	14.775	5.529	
	Male commissioners	14.256	5.164	
	Presidents	13.872	4.963	
	Male VPs	13.768	5.255	
Followers' worth	Female VPs	17.532	8.251	59.462***
	Female commissioners	17.141	9.911	
	Male commissioners	16.541	7.928	
	Presidents	20.383	9.389	
	Male VPs	15.677	6.923	
Similarity to followers	Female VPs	161.998	18.703	21.963***
	Female commissioners	160.430	15.916	
	Male commissioners	158.710	19.519	
	Presidents	162.155	23.248	
	Male VPs	155.895	19.718	
Tangibility	Female VPs	59.981	29.647	18.415***
	Female commissioners	61.626	29.373	
	Male commissioners	59.908	28.601	
	Presidents	67.159	32.487	
	Male VPs	65.468	27.874	
Action	Female VPs	6.124	8.267	32.062***
	Female commissioners	8.315	9.915	
	Male commissioners	9.231	10.835	
	Presidents	5.771	11.681	
	Male VPs	8.641	12.716	
Adversity	Female VPs	8.051	5.018	6.714***
	Female commissioners	7.861	5.092	
	Male commissioners	7.388	4.411	
	Presidents	7.285	4.560	
	Male VPs	7.483	4.390	

Notes: Female VPs N = 564, Female commissioners N = 1,698, Male commissioners N = 4,183, Male VPs N = 1,145; Commission presidents N = 1,355. ***p < 0.001.

reports the results of the comparisons between female VPs and female commissioners, male commissioners, presidents of the Commission, and, finally, male VPs. It shows that, in relation to the different comparison groups, female VPs' rhetoric has been more charismatic in a statistically significant way.

To offer a more detailed interpretation of these findings, we run a MANCOVA to further investigate the differences among the five different groups of Commission members (our independent variables) in relation to the seven charismatic constructs (our dependent variables)—still using the total words in the speeches as covariate. The MANCOVA confirms the presence of a significant difference (Wilks's lambda = 0.916, $F_{(28, 32,210)}$ = 28.174, $p < 0.001$) between female VPs, female commissioners, male commissioners, male VPs, and the presidents of the Commission. Table 7.3 presents the mean and standard deviation for the five different groups for single charismatic constructs, as well as the univariate F.

According to our analysis, female VPs are on average the most charismatic group among Commission members. Their speeches are characterized by high scores on all seven charismatic constructs. In particular, on *temporal orientation* and *adversity* they present higher mean values than those of all the other three groups, while on *similarity to followers* and *followers' worth* they present the second highest mean values, following only the values of Commission presidents; on *tangibility*, moreover, they present the second lowest mean value—as expected by the definition of charismatic language as characterized by the use of abstract concepts and general terms—following only, and by a few decimal points, that of the commissioners.

Moving to the individual level of analysis, we find differences between single female VPs in terms of their reliance on charismatic rhetoric (Table 7.4). According to our ANCOVA analysis, Georgieva is the most charismatic speaker overall, although she delivered a very small number of speeches (N = 13). De Palacio and Reding, by contrast, are the least charismatic.

By looking at the seven constructs, we confirm a significant difference among female VPs (MANCOVA results: Wilks's lambda = 0.469, $F_{(35, 2320)}$ = 13.088, $p < 0.001$) in terms of charismatic rhetoric. Table 7.4 presents descriptive statistics for the individual VPs, as well as the univariate F for single construct. According to our findings, no specific pattern in the use of language pertaining to the seven charismatic constructs can be detected among female VPs; their charismatic language relies on different constructs. For example, Georgieva scores the highest mean value for *similarity to followers*, de Palacio scores the highest mean value for *collective focus* and *action*, and Kroes scores the highest value on *similarity to followers* and the lowest on *tangibility*.

Table 7.4 Female VPs' charismatic rhetoric. Results for the aggregated index of charisma and for single constructs

		Mean	SD	Univariate F (6, 557)
Charisma	Ashton	160.611	38.976	16.918***
	Georgieva	168.762	33.812	
	Kroes	161.202	33.238	
	de Palacio	134.991	37.428	
	Reding	130.914	41.991	
	Wallström	151.476	30.759	
Single Constructs:				
Collective focus	Ashton	1.402	8.122	4.476**
	Georgieva	2.100	4.665	
	Kroes	−0.528	7.143	
	de Palacio	2.300	4.656	
	Reding	0.839	5.884	
	Wallström	2.834	5.072	
Temporal orientation	Ashton	14.771	5.615	25.370***
	Georgieva	14.778	5.249	
	Kroes	19.742	6.328	
	de Palacio	12.501	3.741	
	Reding	15.847	4.164	
	Wallström	16.458	4.759	
Followers' worth	Ashton	18.339	9.972	4.622***
	Georgieva	14.213	4.171	
	Kroes	17.637	7.887	
	de Palacio	14.448	4.714	
	Reding	20.032	8.836	
	Wallström	16.500	7.413	
Similarity to followers	Ashton	169.679	22.317	12.352***
	Georgieva	169.980	15.047	
	Kroes	155.587	16.983	
	de Palacio	155.079	18.258	
	Reding	164.204	16.047	
	Wallström	164.656	14.803	
Tangibility	Ashton	56.332	26.116	33.247***
	Georgieva	52.055	21.458	
	Kroes	45.575	22.097	
	de Palacio	64.750	29.838	
	Reding	86.056	34.976	
	Wallström	61.362	22.466	

Continued

Table 7.4 *Continued*

		Mean	SD	Univariate F (6, 557)
Action	Ashton	6.698	7.819	3.908**
	Georgieva	5.950	5.814	
	Kroes	5.136	9.003	
	de Palacio	9.603	7.359	
	Reding	6.750	7.596	
	Wallström	4.332	8.306	
Adversity	Ashton	6.055	3.976	13.665***
	Georgieva	13.796	6.570	
	Kroes	9.204	4.721	
	de Palacio	5.810	3.108	
	Reding	9.297	6.547	
	Wallström	8.058	4.217	

Notes: Ashton N = 120, Georgieva N = 13, Kroes N = 166, de Palacio N = 65, Reding N = 95, Wallström N = 105. ***p < 0.001. **p < 0.01.

While studying the role of gender in the language of Commission members in general and of female VPs in particular, we are also interested in isolating the effect of appointment to an institutional leadership role—that of Commission vice-president—on female commissioners' rhetoric. Out of the six female VPs, five were commissioners in the previous Commission (Reding was a commissioner in two previous Commissions: Prodi and Barroso I). It is thus possible to identify changes in their use of charismatic rhetoric due to their appointment to a more exposed leadership position. We performed five different ANCOVAs testing for the presence of statistically significant differences in the charismatic rhetoric of female VPs before and after appointment to the post. Table 7.5 presents the results for the five VPs who also served as commissioners.

Only one female VP (Kroes) significantly increased her charisma after taking up the VP role; for three others, the results were not statistically significant (Ashton, Georgieva, Wallström), and in one case charisma significantly decreased (Reding). Accordingly, we cannot claim that appointment to the role of Commission vice-president has any direct "charisma" effect. To the contrary, the data offers contradictory or null evidence of such an effect.

Table 7.5 The effect of VPs' role on charismatic rhetoric. Results for the aggregated index of charisma

Charisma	Commissioner Mean	Standard Error	VP Mean	Standard Error	F	Partial eta squared	Observed Power
Ashton (1)	152.260	9.669	160.753	3.637	$F (2, 134)$ 0.676 ns	0.005	0.129
Georgieva (2)	172.741	4.467	168.905	9.605	$F (2, 70)$ 0.131 ns	0.002	0.065
Kroes (3)	130.988	2.986	164.254	3.133	$F (2, 345)$ 56.518***	0.141	1.000
Reding (4)	145.591	3.090	131.191	3.885	$F (2, 240)$ 8.158**	0.033	0.812
Wallström (5)	160.841	3.915	151.219	3.193	$F (2, 173)$ 3.485 ns	0.020	0.459

Notes: Estimated marginal means adjusted for the covariate *total words analyzed*. Ashton (1): Commissioner N = 17, VP N=120; Georgieva (2): Commissioner N = 60, VP N = 13. Kroes (3): Commissioner N=182, VP N=166; Reding (4): Commissioner N = 148, VP N = 95; Wallström (5): Commissioner N = 71, VP N=105. ***p < 0.001, **p < 0.01, * p < 0.05, ns = not significant.

7.5 Discussion and Conclusion

Our empirical analysis of the female vice-presidents' rhetoric provides core results that may be groundbreaking not only within the context of the European Commission but concerning the relationship between gender, leadership, and charismatic speech-making in public contexts more broadly. There are five major points to consider, following the results of the empirical investigation.

First, using charismatic rhetoric as a proxy to evaluate the skillfulness of female leaders in their public speech-making, our analysis corroborates what sociolinguist Judith Baxter has already observed in the managerial context. Female political leaders seem to be highly skilled, linguistic experts who provide a combination of both authoritativeness and relatability (2010; Cameron and Shaw 2016). Both groups, female VPs and female commissioners, show consistently higher levels of charisma in their rhetoric than do Commission members as a whole. Moreover, while there is a general decrease of charisma in the Commission's public speeches over time (1999–2019), the speeches of these two groups (female commissioners and VPs) become more charismatic, meaning that they lift the overall level of the Commission's charisma.

Second, the foregoing indicates a significant difference between male and female speech-making, which our analysis of male and female commissioners (irrespective of position) confirms. Indeed, female commissioners are consistently more charismatic in their public speeches than their male counterparts. While we reject the idea that this gap could be based on biological differences, we understand it as corroboration that women speakers are indeed more affected by contradictory socially and culturally constructed expectations and institutional constraints; within that context, women more than men are obliged to engage in complex forms of impression management in which they combine both so-called masculine and feminine rhetorical norms, which are then expressed in higher levels of rhetorical skillfulness. In our analysis, this is expressed through higher levels of charismatic rhetoric.

Third, we have argued that the phenomenon of charisma transcends gender binaries, and our study of the individual constructs of charisma used by male and female commissioners confirms this assumption. Whereas female commissioners show overall higher levels of charisma, both male and female commissioners make use of nominally feminine, masculine, and gender-neutral features of rhetorical charisma. In fact, female commissioners lean strongly toward *temporal orientation*, which is considered gender-neutral, *similarity to followers*, which involves relatability and is considered feminine, and *adversity*, which shows assertiveness and is considered a masculine feature of charisma. In contrast, the male commissioners lean strongly toward *collective focus*, which is considered feminine, and *action*, which shows authoritativeness and is considered masculine. This also confirms that, at least in the context of the European Commission, women incorporate and apply more diverse features of charismatic rhetoric than do men.

Fourth, zooming in on the female VPs in comparison to all other groups in the European Commission, a dual picture emerges. On the one hand, the female VPs are the most charismatic group in the European Commission. This is confirmed by comparing them to the group of female commissioners, the Commission as a whole (excluding female VPs), the group of male VPs, and, in particular, the group of presidents. On the other hand, there is no clear pattern in how the female VPs make use of the individual features of charismatic rhetoric. Each woman has her own preferred approach to the use of those features in her speeches. This supports the idea that charisma is inherently personal, making it a highly distinguishable capacity from one politician to the next. It also confirms that gender is not an all-determining feature but that apart from it and individuality, other social categories—e.g., age, class, race, ethnicity, cultural background, education, and professional status—also contribute to differences among speakers (Baxter 2017). Gender is but one social category among many, and narrowing leadership performance down to only this one actually contributes to gender demarcation rather than to overcoming it in the leadership context (Chapter 1 in this volume).

Finally, our analysis has rejected the idea that there is a significant institutional effect in moving from the position of commissioner to that of vice-president. While the office of VP does not entail a substantial shift in political responsibilities, it still involves a higher level of public exposure. Nonetheless, no clear pattern—at least rhetorically—has been found and the results of our analysis point again to individuality and individual factors in the shaping of rhetorical approaches. This again suggests that charisma is a highly individualistic category and implies either that career progression cannot be studied meaningfully through charisma analysis or that, much like charisma, career progression is a highly individualistic process for which no clear patterns can be found.

No doubt, our exploratory empirical analysis has its methodological shortcomings. While we focused on speeches and rhetorical skillfulness, future research at the intersection of gender, rhetoric, and leadership should look more closely at contextual factors to study how women leaders accommodate and address different environments and groups of followers in their speeches. As for the example of the European Commission, it is also important to investigate whether and to what extent different portfolios and topics, as well as national or transnational constituencies, make a difference in speech-making and how women may or may not differ in this regard from their male counterparts. And, crucially, the European Commission is a multilingual institution. Future investigations into the nexus of language and leadership at the European level should include a cross-lingual perspective as well, particularly for speakers whose native language is not English.

In conclusion, this research has shown that while women and men are in principle equally disposed to provide charismatic leadership, the sociostructural context of women's underrepresentation in the political domain along with gender stereotypes seem to contribute to demands that women leaders—more so than men— engage in highly skilled forms of speech-making. Female VPs and commissioners have shown consistently higher levels of charisma than their male counterparts over the past 20 years. At the same time, our research has confirmed that speech-making and rhetoric are highly individual forms of exercising leadership without clear patterns among individual politicians. In addition, while our research shows a decline in charismatic rhetoric, especially since 2010, the new president, Ursula von der Leyen, and her College of Commissioners—gender-equal since 2020—have the potential to raise the charismatic quality of Commission rhetoric.

References

Antonakis, John, Nicolas Bastardoz, Philippe Jacquart, and Boas Shamir. 2016. "Charisma: An Ill-Defined and Ill-Measured Gift." *Annual Review of Organizational Psychology and Organizational Behavior* 3: 293–319.

Baxter, Judith. 2010. *The Language of Female Leadership*. New York: Palgrave Macmillan.

Baxter, Judith. 2017. "Sociolinguistic Approaches to Gender and Leadership Theory." In *Handbook of Research on Gender and Leadership*, ed. Susan R. Madsen, 113–126. Cheltenham, UK: Edward Elgar.

Bean, Judith Mattson. 2006. "Gaining a Public Voice: A Historical Perspective on American Women's Public Speaking." In *Speaking Out: The Female Voice in Public Context*, ed. Judith Baxter, 21–39. Basingstoke, UK: Palgrave Macmillan.

Bligh, Michelle, Jeffrey C. Kohles, and James R. Meindl. 2004. "Charisma under Crisis: Presidential Leadership, Rhetoric, and Media Responses before and after the September 11th Terrorist Attacks." *Leadership Quarterly* 15: 211–239.

Bligh, Michelle, Jennifer Merolla, Jean Reith Schroedel, and Randall Gonzalez. 2010. "Finding Her Voice: Hillary Clinton's Rhetoric in the 2008 Presidential Campaign." *Women's Studies* 39 (8): 823–850.

Bligh, Michelle, and Jill L. Robinson. 2010. "Was Gandhi 'Charismatic'? Exploring the Rhetorical Leadership of Mahatma Gandhi." *Leadership Quarterly* 21 (5): 844–855.

Cameron, Deborah. 2006. "Theorising the Female Voice in Public Contexts." In *Speaking Out: The Female Voice in Public Context*, ed. Judith Baxter, 3–20. Basingstoke, UK: Palgrave Macmillan.

Cameron, Deborah, and Sylvia Shaw. 2016. *Gender, Power and Political Speech: Women and Language in the 2015 UK General Election*. London: Palgrave Macmillan.

Choi, Jaepil. 2006. "A Motivational Theory of Charismatic Leadership: Envisioning, Empathy, and Empowerment." *Journal of Leadership and Organizational Studies* 13 (1): 24–43.

Davis, Kelly M., and William L. Gardner. 2012. "Charisma under Crisis Revisited: Presidential Leadership, Perceived Leader Effectiveness and Contextual Influences." *Leadership Quarterly* 23 (5): 918–933.

Fischer, Agneta H. 1993. "Sex Differences in Emotionality: Fact or Stereotype?" *Feminism & Psychology* 3 (3): 303–318.

Hart, Roderick P. 2001. "Redeveloping Diction: Theoretical Considerations." In *Theory, Method and Practice of Computer Content Analysis*, ed. Mark D. West, 43–60. New York: Ablex.

Holmes, Janet. 1992. "Women's Talk in Public Contexts." *Discourse & Society* 3 (2): 131–150.

Lausen, Adi, and Annekathrin Schacht. 2018. "Gender Differences in the Recognition of Vocal Emotions." *Frontiers in Psychology* 9 (822): 1–22.

Litosseliti, Lia. 2006. "Constructing Gender in Public Arguments: The Female Voice as Emotional Voice." In *Speaking Out: The Female Voice in Public Context*, ed. J. Baxter, 40–60. Basingstoke, UK: Palgrave Macmillan.

Olsson, Eva-Karin, and Kajsa Hammargård. 2016. "The Rhetoric of the President of the European Commission: Charismatic Leader or Neutral Mediator?" *Journal of European Public Policy* 23 (4): 550–570.

Rosenberg, Andrew, and Julia Hirschberg. 2009. "Charisma Perception from Text and Speech." *Speech Communication* 51: 640–655.

Seyranian, Viviane, and Michelle C. Bligh. 2008. "Presidential Charismatic Leadership: Exploring the Rhetoric of Social Change." *Leadership Quarterly* 19: 54–76.

Shamir, Boas, Michael B. Arthur, and Robert J. House. 1994. "The Rhetoric of Charismatic Leadership: A Theoretical Extension, a Case Study, and Implications for Research." *Leadership Quarterly* 5 (1): 25–42.

Shaw, Sylvia. 2006. "Governed by the Rules?: The Female Voice in Parliamentary Debates." In *Speaking Out: The Female Voice in Public Context*, ed. Judith Baxter, 81–102. Basingstoke, UK: Palgrave Macmillan.

Tortola, Piero D., and Pamela Pansardi. 2019. "The Charismatic Leadership of the European Central Bank Presidency: A Language-Based Analysis." *European Journal of Political Research* 58: 96–116.

8

Gendered Leadership in the European Parliament's Political Groups

Johanna Kantola and Cherry Miller

The 2019 European parliamentary elections saw a historical increase in women's political representation to 40%. While not constituting full parity, it is considered a threshold for a gender-balanced institution in many European countries. The European Parliament (EP) has been considered a highly gender-equal actor in comparison to other EU institutions. It has historically been more amenable to claims to equal representation and the Parliament has succeeded in pushing for progressive gender-equality policies (Ahrens and Rolandsen Agustín 2019; Kantola 2010). In recent years, scholars have begun to question this image of the EP as an unequivocally gender-friendly actor. Gender equality as a norm and a policy question has been shown to be highly politicized, contested, and polarized in the Parliament. The EP's political groups are highly divided in their support for and promotion of gender equality (Kantola 2022; Kantola and Rolandsen Agustín 2016, 2019). The share of radical-right populists has increased to one-quarter and they voice strong opposition to gender-equality norms in the plenary debates both directly and indirectly (Kantola and Lombardo 2020).

In this chapter, we contribute to these debates by analyzing how leadership continues to be gendered in the EP, failing to provide a level playing field for MEPs. We do this by focusing on the leadership positions provided by the political groups of the Parliament. Political groups have grown in importance alongside the institutional development of the EP (Ahrens et al. 2022; Kreppel 2004). Political group leadership positions include political, policy, and administrative leadership. This chapter analyzes *political leadership* in terms of political group leaders and national party delegation leaders; *policy leadership* in terms of nominations to the key positions of committee chairs and coordinators; and *administrative leadership* in terms of political groups' secretaries general (SGs).

Funding statement: This research received funding from the European Research Council (ERC) under the European Union's Horizon 2020 research and innovation programme grant number 771676.

Johanna Kantola and Cherry Miller, *Gendered Leadership in the European Parliament's Political Groups*. In: *Women and Leadership in the European Union*. Edited by Henriette Müller and Ingeborg Tömmel, Oxford University Press.
© Oxford University Press (2022). DOI: 10.1093/oso/9780192896216.003.0009

Theoretically, we draw on the concepts of positional leadership (see Chapter 1 in this volume) and gendered norms and practices, which shape the conditions of leadership in the Parliament. We use extensive interview material (n = 123), which covers MEPs and staff and includes responses to questions about political, policy, and administrative leadership within the political groups in the 8th (2014–2019) and 9th legislatures (2019–2024). Key findings show how men continue to dominate political leadership despite the gender-equal reputation of the EP (see Chapter 4 in this volume). A particular hidden gendered structure is the leadership of national party delegations (NPDs), where women are significantly in the minority. Policy leadership, in contrast, is the most gender-balanced area, though the conservative European People's Party (EPP)—the biggest political group—is a notable exception in this regard. Finally, women are underrepresented in administrative leadership of the political groups. Gendered norms and practices continue to shape the scope of action within these leadership positions and underpin the challenges involved in making the EP a gender-equal arena.

8.1 Studying Gendered Leadership in the European Parliament: Background, Concepts, and Research Material

Focusing on leadership in the EP provides important insights into how gender works within the institution. The concept of *positional leadership* captures the dynamics around women's access to power (Chapter 1 in this volume) and helps us answer questions raised by the "women and politics approach" (Kantola and Lombardo 2017): where are the women leaders and what factors contribute alternately to their underrepresentation in politics or to gender parity? Open, transparent, and democratic selection norms and processes enhance women's opportunities to enter political leadership positions. Gender-equality guarantees, such as gender quotas or comparable rules in party or parliamentary statutes, can enable women's access to power.

Studies of women's leadership in the EP are rare and most scholarly efforts have been directed at studying women MEPs' political representation and pathways to power (Fortin-Rittberger and Rittberger 2015; Kantola 2010; Kenny and Luhiste 2016). Women's representation has increased steadily in the EP, now providing a strong pool of women candidates for parliamentary leadership positions (see the Appendix to this volume; Ahrens and Rolandsen Agustín 2019). This representation, however, varies greatly by political groups. In the 9th legislature (2019–2024), women constituted a majority in the Greens/EFA; achieved near parity with at least 40% representation in the left and liberal S&D, GUE/NGL, and Renew Europe groups, as well as in the radical-right populist ID; and were underrepresented in the conservative EPP and the radical-right populist ECR, with just above 30% of the groups' MEPs (see Ahrens and Rolandsen Agustín 2019; Kantola and Rolandsen Agustín 2019).

There have been several studies looking at women's positional leadership in the EP beyond the MEP level. These studies show that women have historically been underrepresented within EP leadership structures. Chapter 4 in this volume gives an overview of the underrepresentation. Beauvallet and Michon (2010) suggest that in 2004, during the 6th legislature, only 14% of the political group leaders, 19% of committee chairs, and 22.5% of vice-chairs were women (see Chapter 4 in this volume). This was partially explained by seniority, a key factor in MEPs' obtaining the highest leadership positions in the EP, especially the presidencies of the Parliament and the political groups (Beauvallet and Michon 2010). Committee vice-presidents, rapporteurs, and shadow rapporteurs, in contrast, are policy-related positions that on occasion go to relatively new MEPs (Beauvallet and Michon 2010: 158).

It seems then vital to provide an updated analysis of women's positional leadership within the EP structures. The EP offers a wide spectrum of leadership positions at the parliamentary level including the presidency (only once held by a woman—see the Appendix to this volume), Conference of Presidents, Bureau, questors, and SGs. Instead of analyzing the entire Parliament, we focus on the *political group* level. In addition to providing a novel empirical perspective, we demonstrate differences in women MEPs' representation that suggest gendered leadership may vary considerably by political group. Understanding this diversity allows us to analyze gendered leadership in a more nuanced way.

We identify and analyze three key leadership position types in political groups: political, policy, and administrative. First, *political leadership* is exercised by political group leaders and national party delegation leaders. Political group leaders represent the groups both within the Parliament and outside of it. While there is a public and academic debate about how well known they are outside the Brussels bubble, their roles and powers are wide-ranging. Group leaders participate in setting the agendas of parliamentary politics in the EP's Conference of Presidents as well as when preparing group meetings and chairing them. They play a central role in coalition-building within the groups and work to ensure their discipline and cohesion (Bressanelli 2014). The group leaders sit in the front row in the plenary and are often called first to speak. They also exercise power in relation to appointments to the EP's permanent committees. Their leadership is complemented, but also challenged, by the heads of NPDs. On the one hand, heads of delegations (HoDs) complement the group leader because they can exert discipline more readily (Corbett et al. 2016: 139–140). These leaders chair their national party delegation meetings, provide a link with national parties, can influence party electoral lists in member states, and can also informally control the distribution of leadership positions within the EP hierarchy and the committees (Kreppel 2004: 217). On the other hand, they can challenge group leadership by joining forces with other national party delegation leaders on votes.

Second, *policy leadership* takes place in the EP's committees. Committees elect their chairs and up to four vice-chairs on the basis of proportional allocation between political groups and bargaining between the party leaders and national delegations. The chairs are in a powerful position, leading the committees' meetings and determining their policy agendas (Whitaker 2019; Chiru 2020). In addition to chairs, coordinators are important policy leadership positions. The political groups also select committee coordinators, who act as the groups' representatives within the committees. The coordinators are responsible for allocating committee reports (legislative and own-initiative) in the political groups and are chosen on the basis of incumbency in the committee system and professional background (Daniel and Thierse 2018).

Third, *administrative leadership* in political groups is represented by SGs. They are often professionals who have worked in transnational environments and are familiar with the EU institutions. The SGs are heads of the Secretariat of the political groups, the permanently staffed administrative body. They are responsible for staffing both in a representation and expertise sense. In the representation sense, when a group is formed, the SGs and their deputies need to ensure that national delegations are represented, so they may simultaneously have to fire and engage staff. In the expertise sense, they ensure that the MEPs receive effective expertise from advisors. Crucially, the SGs prepare the agenda for the Conference of Presidents, the organ charged with the EP's legislative planning. Overall, SGs perform a gatekeeping role by shielding the group president from everyday problems, allowing the president to focus on the most critical matters.

Questions about positional leadership address but one aspect of gendered leadership. For example, Müller and Tömmel (Chapter 1 in this volume) suggest focusing on behavioral leadership to inquire how women lead and what gender differences there might be. In this chapter, we combine an analysis of positional leadership with a focus on *gendered norms and practices*, which shape the ways in which positional leadership is exercised in political groups. In short, gendered norms and practices constitute different forms of gender bias that influence women's and men's leadership opportunities. For example, women carry the burden of doubt about their competences and may face different forms of surveillance when they enter leadership positions. If they don't conform to gendered norms, they may face sanctions and their leadership ambitions may be thwarted (see Kenny 2013; Verge and de la Fuente 2014). Men, in contrast, may benefit from having more access to informal networks where political decisions are taken—not least on leadership positions (Bjarnegård 2013).

Gendered norms and practices are institutionalized in the ways that parliaments and political groups work, which makes changing them difficult. This is evidenced by the persistence of horizontal segregation: women are delegated to those committee and working-group positions deemed feminine, while men's expertise in areas such as economics, finance, and foreign and security policy is more easily recognized (Kantola and Rolandsen Agustín 2019). Appointments to committees in national parliaments likewise show how this gendered division of labor is intimately connected to prestige, with men holding the key positions in most prestigious committees (Goodwin et al. 2020; Pansardi and Vercesi 2016; Krook and O'Brien 2012; O'Brien 2012).

As a transnational parliament, the EP provides a specific context for gendered norms and practices. The culture of long working hours in Brussels makes it difficult to combine care responsibilities with the representative role, affecting both women and men MEPs but particularly amplifying the difficulties that younger women MEPs face in the Parliament (Kantola and Rolandsen Agustín 2019). Young mothers suffer from the difficulties of combining a career in Brussels and Strasbourg with a family and the lack of political will in the EP to address these issues (Kantola and Rolandsen Agustín 2019). The EP has also been shown to be a site of significant sexual harassment and attempts to remedy the situation have faced resistance (Berthet and Kantola 2020). At the political group level, a familiar left–right distinction emerges, with gender equality a recognized political goal for left, liberal, and green groups, while unequal gendered norms hold sway in the conservative and right groups (Kantola 2022; Kantola and Rolandsen Agustín 2019; Kantola and Lombardo 2020).

In order to explore both positional leadership and the gendered norms and practices that shape it in the political groups, we draw on interviews conducted with 123 MEPs and staff during the 8th and 9th legislatures. We used an in-depth qualitative approach, speaking with different actors involved in different aspects of the political groups, including both women and men. The interviewees came from all of the existing political groups. The category of staff included the powerful secretary and deputy SGs, whom we interviewed from six political groups. The transcribed interviews were coded by the research group using Atlas.ti. While we have read the interviews in their entirety, we have selected the citations under the codes "Leadership" and "Secretary General: role and function" for closer scrutiny. In addition, we analyzed all of the secretary and deputy secretary general interviews in detail. We also used group statutes as primary documents to analyze some of the political groups' formal practices.

8.2 Political Leadership: Political Group and National Party Delegation Leaders

In this section, we explore political group leaders and national party delegation leaders as key agents of political leadership. We first explore positional leadership and then the gendered norms and practices through which leaders are selected and enact leadership. As discussed above, up through the 6th legislature the position of group leader was very male dominated (Beauvallet and Michon 2010). This has since improved to an extent. Table 8.1 shows that three out of 14 (21%) group chairs were women in the 8th legislature and three out of 11 (27%) were women in the 9th legislature, when the number of political groups fell from eight to seven. While the progress between the last two legislatures may seem remarkable, the number of women leaders in fact stayed the same. Two female chairs served in these two Parliaments as absolute chairs, Iratxe Garcia Perez (S&D) and Gabi Zimmer (GUE/NGL), the remaining three—Marine Le Pen (ENF), Ska Keller (Greens/EFA), and Manon Aubrey (GUE/NGL)—as cochairs. The second largest group, the S&D, selected its third female leader in 2019, which left the EPP as the only one of the three mainstream groups never to have had a female leader (Table 8.1).

The group leaders are chosen via elections whose procedures are set out in the groups' statutes (e.g. ALDE 2009: 4, 5; EPP 2013: 27) and that take place every two and a half years. Group leaders are selected through voting by the respective groups' MEPs. A number of our interviewees described the practices around the election of the political group leaders as democratic, which should support women's chances of winning these positions. Yet, after making statements about "straightforward elections" (ECR MEP F 210219, ALDE MEP F 210219),

Table 8.1 Political group leaders in the 8th and 9th European legislatures

	8th European Legislature	*9th European Legislature*
EPP	Manfred Weber (M, DE)	Manfred Weber (M, DE)
S&D	Gianni Pitella (M, IT) Udo Bullman (M, DE)	Iratxe Garcia Perez (F, ES)
ECR	Syed Kamall (M, UK) Ryszard Legutko (M, PL) (from 2017)	Raffaele Fitto (M, IT) Ryszard Legutko (M, PL)
ALDE/Renew Europe	Guy Verhofstadt (M, BE)	Dacian Ciolios (M, RO) Stéphane Séjourné (M, FR)
Greens/EFA	Phillipe Lamberts (M, BE) Ska Keller (F, DE)	Phillipe Lamberts (M, BE) Ska Keller (F, DE)
GUE/NGL	Gabi Zimmer (F, DE)	Martin Schwirdewan (M, DE) Manon Aubrey (F, FR)
EFDD	Nigel Farage (M, UK) David Borrelli (M, IT) (until 2017)	N/A
ENF/ID	Nicolas Bay (M, FR) Marine Le Pen (F, FR) (until 2017) Marcel de Graaff (M, NL)	Marco Zanni (M, IT)

the interviewees gave quite different descriptions of the politics surrounding the leadership contests. Despite formal democracy and open voting, nominations are agreed to in advance by a small group and "settled at the very high level" (ALDE MEP F 210219). One male MEP from the ECR said that sometimes "they can be very hotly fought elections" and "different delegations want different things and different deals are done." He said that leadership elections can also be used as a "tactic" to get other things (ECR MEP M 051218). MEPs from other populist right groups said that the political group leader "sort of emerged" and "appeared" out of negotiations between the national delegations (EFDD MEP M 290119_3; EFDD Group Staff M 070219). Women's positional leadership can be weakened in situations where other concerns and priorities, such as national representation, dominate and gender-equality norms are pushed aside.

Beneath the group leadership, NPDs are key players within the groups at the start of each new legislature, when agreements over leadership positions are brokered. NPDs vary widely in size from single-person delegations to ones of around 30 MEPs in the two most recent Parliaments. One of our findings—missing from all previous literature—is that the leadership of the largest NPDs remains heavily dominated by men (see Table 8.2). These are powerful leadership positions as HoDs are often called to speak first in group meetings; they also meet in HoD meetings to discuss pressing matters and broker intra-group compromises.

Table 8.2 shows that, in the 9th legislature, all of the biggest NPDs in the EP are headed by men. In fact, the leaders of all five of the largest NPDs within the S&D, ID, and ECR groups are male as are four out of the five largest EPP delegations. Renew, Greens/EFA, and GUE/NGL each have two or three female leaders among their five largest NPDs. In the words of one MEP, becoming an HoD involves a gendered "hidden structure," particularly in the larger political groups (S&D M MEP 060320; S&D F MEP 060320). One male HoD said:

> [W]e have a lot of women leaders, not just Iratxe, at all levels in the group. But I can say that all the biggest delegations that count for most of the MEPs are led by men. So there is not real equality in terms of the heads of delegation, which are the stakeholders of the group. In the end, the heads of delegation are the ones that are in fact after the group leader, to some extent even more than the group vice-presidents, the ones that are giving the political impulse and are the ones that are the leadership behind the group leader. So if you look at our heads of delegation, only the smallest delegations they have women leading. The bigger ones, all men. So this is not totally balanced.
>
> (S&D M MEP, 060320)

The way that HoDs are selected also varies. Some NPD leaders are elected by the members of their delegations, while, in other cases, those who head the domestic

Table 8.2 Leaders of the five largest national party delegations in the 8th and 9th European legislatures

8th European Legislature				9th European Legislature			
Delegation	Group	Leader	Size	Delegation	Group	Leader	Size
PD (IT)	S&D	Patrizia Toia (F)	31	**Lega (IT)**	ID	Marco Campo (M)	29
CDU (DE)	EPP	Herbert Reul (M)	29	**PiD (PL)**	ECR	Ryzard Legutko (M)	27
SPD (DE)	S&D	Udo Bullman (M)	27	**Bündnis 90/Die Grünen (or some shorter version) (DE)**	Greens/ EFA	Sven Giegold (M)	25
UKIP (UK)	EFDD	Roger Helmer (M)	24	**CDU (DE)**	EPP	Daniel Caspary (M)	23
FN (FR)	ENF	Édouard Ferrand (M)	23	**En Marche (FR)**	Renew	Stéphane Séjourné (M)	23

party list are supposed to become HoDs, though this is not always a certainty (S&D MEP F 060320):

> [W]e have delegations where the leader of the delegation is decided by the leader of the party, so there is no vote in the delegation on who becomes a leader, but they're told, this is your leader, full stop. I mean in this kind of culture then it depends on who is, who's vice-president, who's president, I mean you could see certain elements and see some cultural differences there as regards to the way certain things are dealt with.
>
> (S&D Group Staff M 040320)

Discussing persistent gender inequalities and gendered norms and practices was difficult for the interviewees on the political right. An ECR MEP said that she had never felt "any bias": "where we have women contest, they win. So, I think it's very good, freedom" (ECR MEP F 210219). Another spoke to us about the "great desire to see more women in these positions. So we would have voted for a woman if there was one willing to stand" (ECR MEP F 21021). Typical of right-wing gender-equality discourse, according to such interviewees it remained the personal choice of women to come forward—and a personal failure if gender parity was not achieved. This perspective appears to turn a blind eye to the gendered structures that potential women candidates may face when putting themselves forward for leadership positions. At the same time, it must be noted that the ECR was the only group to have a Muslim leader and some interviewees recognized the significance of a right populist group being the only one in the EP to elect a leader with a BAME (Black, Asian, and minority ethnic) background (ECR Staff M 200219).

Members of other radical-right populist groups saw gender as irrelevant to political leadership of the groups. Either it did not and should not matter at all, according to the interviewees, or they saw women everywhere. An ENF interviewee said: "I have to disappoint you on all your questions that are related to gender balance for instance. We, no one mentions this in our group. And as you say we don't need to do so because we have some very strong women" (ENF Staff M 260419). Yet the share of women MEPs in the ENF was the lowest of all political groups in the Parliament (about 30%), similar to that of the EPP and EFDD. The interviewee went on to argue that gender-equality measures—especially quotas—would be offensive to the group's women MEPs (ENF Staff M 260419), and indeed there were no equality provisions in the ENF statutes (ENF 2015, modified 2018).

Interviewees from other political groups, in contrast, discussed how leadership might be based on gendered norms and practices. A female interviewee from the ALDE, formerly a group vice-president, explained her lack of power and the way that power was concentrated in the group leader:

> I was part of that presidency and we met once a week or something. We never dealt with political questions, we dealt with some practical issues. Then me and also some others, we complained, sometimes that we should discuss policy. But no, it is … . In our group it is the group leader. And nobody wants to quarrel. That's why those who don't agree, they are quiet.
>
> (ALDE MEP, F 210219)

This observation illustrates the relatively weak position of the vice and deputy political group leaders. In the well-established S&D, too, some of our interviewees suggested that, as one put it, the group is "both formally and informally, tightly controlled by a very small group of people, in a very undemocratic, unaccountable way. And it's very hierarchical, it's, everything goes up to there and it characterizes everything, I think" (S&D MEP M 161018).

This masculine leadership style was perpetuated through *favoring seniority* in the selection process for key positions. While ensuring that leaders had valuable experience of the way that the group and the Parliament work and maintaining continuity, some of our interviewees were also critical about the way in which this reproduced the institutions—often based on the norms of whiteness and maleness.

As one interviewee commented on the election of Udo Bullman as chair of the S&D group:

R : You mean a middle-aged white man, and a German?
I : Yeah, well, I think that's true. The alternative was a Belgian woman who would
    have been better, I think. But I don't really think it makes that much difference,
    because the shape of the institution is very fixed, and you'd have to have a leader
    who is resolutely determined to do even quite modest reform.

(S&D MEP M 161018)

The interviewee also stated that many politicians have broader ambitions than reforming their political groups: "But the problem with that is that the institution
never gets reformed, and it gets increasingly run in the image of invisible people
behind the scenes, their interests as well as their image" (S&D MEP M 161018).
This argument implies that it doesn't matter whether a group leader is an insider
woman or a man—either is likely to maintain existing practices and focus on policy issues rather than reforming internal group practices and making them more
democratic.

To summarize the position of women in group leadership, while women remain
underrepresented among sole group leaders, a more significant gap exists in the
underrepresentation of women—or rather the overrepresentation of men—at the
head of delegation level in the largest delegations.

8.3 Policy Leadership: Committee Chairs and Coordinators

In this section, we look at EP committee chairs and coordinators. More specifically,
we present the positional leadership of committee chairs and coordinators in terms
of female and male officeholders (for horizontal segregation in committees, see
Chapter 4 in this volume). We then consider the structures, norms, and practices
that affect how these actors perform leadership.

In the 8th legislature, 12 committee chairs were men and eight were women.
The women came from the S&D, ECR, and ALDE (see Table 8.3). In the 9th Parliament, 10 were men and 11 were women, pointing to a stepwise progression toward
gender balance. Women are now well represented as committee chairs in relation
to their total presence in the Parliament. The EPP, in particular, saw a major improvement, with women's share of committee chairs held by the group growing
from 15% to 43% between the two legislatures.

In terms of the total share of coordinators, the gender composition of the 8th and
9th Parliaments was exactly the same: 56% men and 44% women (see Table 8.4).
The EPP had a significantly poorer share of female coordinators in both the 8th
and 9th legislatures than other groups, an issue explored in more detail below. The

Table 8.3 Committee chairs by gender and political group

	8th Legislature	8th Midterm Legislature	9th Legislature
EPP	7	7	7
	1 F (14%)	2 F (29%)	3 F (43%)
	6 M (86%)	5 M (71%)	4 M (57%)
S&D	7	7	5
	3 F (43%)	3 F (43%)	3 F (60%)
	4 M (57%)	4 M (57%)	2 M (40%)
ECR	2	2	2
	2 F (100%)	2 F (100%)	1 F (50%)
			1 M (50%)
ALDE/Renew	3	3	4
	2 F (67%)	2 F (67%)	2 F (50%)
	1 M (33%)	1 M (33%)	2 M (50%)
GREENS/EFA	1	1	2
	1 M (100%)	1 F (100%)	2 F (100%)
GUE/NGL	1	1	1
	1 M (100%)	1 M (100%)	1 M (100%)
EFDD	0	0	0
ENF/ID	0	0	0

Table 8.4 Committee coordinators in the 8th and 9th European legislatures

	8th Legislature F	8th Legislature M	9th Legislature F	9th Legislature M
EPP	4 (19%)	18 (81%)	3 (18%)	14 (82%)
S&D	14 (64%)	8 (36%)	13 (57%)	10 (43%)
ECR	7 (35%)	13 (65%)	6 (29%)	15 (71%)
ALDE/Renew	9 (39%)	14 (61%)	11 (52%)	10 (48%)
Greens/EFA	13 (59%)	9 (41%)	12 (52%)	11 (48%)
GUE/NGL	13 (59%)	9 (41%)	10 (53%)	9 (47%)
EFDD	8 (35%)	15 (65%)	NA	NA
ENF/ID	7 (33%)	14 (67%)	10 (45%)	12 (55%)

S&D and GUE/NGL have more female coordinators than male. The ID group now has 45% female coordinators.

Given this imbalance, let us turn to coordinator selection to see whether there are gendered norms. The ALDE, S&D, and EPP have statutory rules to achieve more equal gender representation. An ALDE statute makes it the responsibility of the bureau to "confirm the election of all the Coordinators in order to guarantee a fair representation" (ALDE 2009: 11). The EPP and S&D mention women and sex composition explicitly but make only general references to parliamentary bodies and posts. The S&D uses a formulation of "balanced representation": "The bureau should also seek to bring about balanced representation of women in all parliamentary bodies" (S&D 2014: 14.4). The EPP sets the goal at one-third women: "The Chairman should ensure that, as the result of elections, the overall representation of members holding posts within the Group are composed of at least one third of members belonging to another sex than the majority of members" (EPP 2013: 19.6). This has not been achieved among EPP coordinators, but there has been a clear improvement in committee chair positions as noted above.

The practical means by which the groups select coordinators vary. An ECR member said that she had served under two different selection procedures; originally, she was nominated by her leader and then in the second half, she was voted unanimously (ECR MEP F 060219, also in ECR MEP M 310119). If there is a disagreement in the grouping, then this is resolved at bureau level (ECR M Staff 180319). In the EFDD, one female MEP said that nomination was based on national delegations (EFDD MEP F 290119_1). According to another EFDD member, there was little transparency in how coordinators were chosen, they just "sort of appeared"; this paralleled interviewees' responses about the selection of EFDD leaders more generally (EFDD MEP M 290119_3, see also EFDD 2014). Again, "appearing" and "emerging" point to a lack of open procedures, and a lack of political will about implementing democratic decision-making structures. Yet there was no deep discontent among the EFDD interviewees regarding this matter. A staff member from the EFDD compared the process to the "usual channels" in the UK Parliament and as overseen by the secretary general of the group (EFDD staff member, M). In the EPP, in contrast, coordinators were selected by a "simple election" where candidates campaign for the position and lobby their colleagues (EPP MEP F 210219). In both the ENF and ID groups, the Committee on Women's Rights and Gender Equality, hereafter FEMM, coordinators were also coordinators for PETI and CULT committees respectively in the 8th and 9th Parliaments. This practice suggests that FEMM may be devalued when allocating coordinators because responsibility is combined with another committee, the FEMM work does not occupy the sole focus of the coordinator (cf. Krook and O'Brien 2012).

Looking at Table 8.5, we can assess the gendered results such processes bring. The EPP's selection procedure (despite the stipulation of gender balance in its rules) brings only 19% female coordinators. ECR had dropped to under 30% in the 9th Parliament. The EFDD had 36% women coordinators in the 8th Parliament. As noted above, over 50% of coordinators in the left–green–liberal groups were women.

The position of the EPP is interesting from a gender perspective considering the norms, practices, and structures in the EP and the relationships between political groups. Structurally, it is the biggest and most powerful group and so highly significant for gender relations in the EP and yet it is the farthest from gender balance, especially among coordinators. Gender, age, and policy issues produce hierarchies in the EPP. For example, the EPP's Economic and Monetary Affairs, hereafter ECON, committee group was called "the most conservative," a point underscored by one interviewee:

> [I]n the very beginning of my work there, I applied for every report, but I noticed I didn't get any report at all. Up until the moment where I started applying for just opinions. So I do think a certain informal hierarchy plays a role. I do think the age/experience within the EPP ECON family definitely plays a role as well. Because now I have ended up being the rapporteur of the semester file, but I'm 100 percent sure I would never have been able to do that in 2015. Because of a certain trust-building with the coordinator, that's you might have known, who definitely had a very carrying voice there as well. You can see that there needs to be trust-building relationship or a trust-relationship that needs to be built up. And that definitely plays a role. There is a very interesting element there, and that is the element of the group assistants, so the people who work, who support the coordinator.
>
> (EPP MEP M 220319)

The EPP thus appears to be a hierarchical group, where the hierarchy, according to the interviewee, is built from norms based on age, experience, and obtained "trust." The established, largely informal procedures for the selection of committee leaders, such as coordinators, are not immediately comprehensible to new MEPs, who have to learn the rules of the game. Specifically, previous research supports the conclusion that the ECON Committee—and thus the direction of economic policy—appears to be especially conservative, closed off, and strongly dominated by men and a masculine leadership style (see Kantola and Rolandsen Agustín 2019).

One of the women MEPs interviewed from the EPP put the focus on gendered structures within the group. Asked whether women get the support they need and have a real chance of winning or not, she suggested that a practice exists where if women agree not to run for top positions they may be rewarded with deputy posts, resulting in women occupying "vice vice vice this and that." Women and men competing for top leadership positions are framed in gendered ways, as well: "if a man campaigns, 'Good for you. It was a fine campaign. We have to raise you because you did your best,' and if a woman stands and stands, 'Oh but she's a difficult one,' and then, 'Do not pick her because she's the difficult one.' It's always incentivized to be a mediocre good girl" (EPP MEP F 291118). The MEP suggests that leadership norms are gendered and tough, ambitious women are not tolerated. By her account, the price of testing these boundaries is being sidelined in the group (EPP MEP F 291118).

To summarize the position of women in policy leadership, women have at an aggregate level been overrepresented in policy leadership in relation to their overall numbers in the Parliament. However, this varies significantly by group, with the EPP having a smaller share of women in policy leadership positions at both committee chair and coordinator level.

8.4 Administrative Leadership: Secretaries General of Political Groups

In this final section, we turn our focus to the SGs of the political groups, powerful administrative leadership positions. The SGs have been underresearched in general and from a gender perspective in particular. In terms of positional leadership, in the 8th legislature, there were three women (37.5%) and five men SGs (62.5%). The three women came from Greens/EFA, GUE/NGL, and EFDD. In the 9th legislature, two women SGs from Greens/EFA and GUE/NGL continued in their positions and the EFDD group ceased to exist, making the positions more male dominated (29% women, 71% men).

Table 8.5 makes it evident that the SGs ensure continuity for the political groups, tending to stay in their positions from one parliamentary term to another. They take part in the formation of the political group after EP elections, sitting in talks with national party delegation leaders. Both the ALDE and ENF, which respectively transformed into the new political groups Renew Europe and ID, changed political group leadership but maintained their same SGs and most deputies (Table 8.5).

From a positional leadership perspective, the ECR and ENF SGs and deputies were all men. The GUE/NGL has more women than men in these positions and other groups have about one-third women.

In some groups, the SGs and their deputies are elected by all the MEPs (Greens/EFA Group Statutes 2010: 3.4); in others, they are proposed by the group president and appointed by the group bureau (S&D, EPP Group Statutes, Article 27, ENF, GUE/NGL). The S&D group is committed to gender balance in the nomination of their top management, including secretary and deputy SGs (S&D Staff F 050320). The ECR and the ENF give no formal consideration to equality in staffing. In the words of one male staffer, this was "not a concern….We just go from the principle that we take the best person. And whether that person is a man or a woman, it's not relevant to me really." He described the recruitment rules as "objective," with professional experience and education taking precedence (ENF Staff

Table 8.5 Secretaries general and their deputies in the 8th and 9th legislatures

	8th Legislature	*9th Legislature*
EPP	SG: Martin Kamp (M, DE) Deputy: Natacha Scriban-Cuvelier (F, FR) Joanna Jarecka-Gomez (F, PL)	SG: Martin Kamp (M, DE) until March 01 2020 Simon Busuttil (M, MT) March 01 2020 Deputy: Juan Salafranca (M, ES) Natacha Scriban-Cuvelier (F, FR)
S&D	SG: Javier Moreno Sanchez (M, ES) Deputy: Annabel Garnier (F, FR) Michael Hoppe (M, DE)	SG: Michael Hoppe (M, DE) Deputy: Annabel Garnier (F, FR) Annalisa Gliubizzi (F, IT) Fraser Clarke (M, UK) Antony Beumer (M, NE)
ECR	SG: Frank Barrett (M, IE) Deputy: Gabriel Beszlej (M, PL) Stephen Woodard (M, UK)	SG: Gabriel Beszlej (M, PL) Deputy: Oumar Doumbouya (M, FI) Stephen Woodard (M, UK)
ALDE/Renew Europe	SG: Alexander Beels (M, NL) Deputy: François Pauli (M, FR) Marieta Colera (F, IT)	SG: Alexander Beels (M, NL) Anders Rasmussen (M) DK from Jan 2020 Deputy: François Pauli (M, FR) Marieta Colera (F, IT) (until 2019) Philip Drauz (M, DE)
Greens/EFA	SG: Vula Tsetsi (F, EL) Deputy: José-Luis Linazasoro (M. ES) Jan-Paul Brouwer (M, NL)	SG: Vula Tsetsi (F, EL) Deputy: José-Luis Linazasoro (M, ES) Jan-Paul Brouwer (M, NL)
GUE/NGL	SG: Sanna Lepola (F, FI) Deputy: Francisco Orozco Dopico (M, ES) Soultana Pantazidou (F, EL) Mireia Rovira (F, ES)	SG: Sanna Lepola (F, FI) Deputy: Francisco Orozco Dopico (M, ES) Stelios Christodoulou (M, CY) Panayota Maniou (F, EL)
EFDD	SG: Aurélie Laloux (F, FR) Deputy: Tobias Teuscher (M, DE) Dovile Rucyte (F, LI)	N/A

Continued

Table 8.5 *Continued*

	8th Legislature	*9th Legislature*
ENF/ID	SG:	SG:
	Philip Claeys (M, BE)	Philip Claeys (M, BE)
	Deputy:	Deputy:
	Dietmar Holzfeind (M, AT)	Sergio Garuzzo (M, IT)
	Marco Campomenosi (M, IT)	Tobias Teuscher (M, DE)
		Dietmar Holzfeind (M, AT)
		Thibaut Francois (M, FR)

Member M 260419). In the 9th Parliament, the appointment of the EPP SG was described as a "mystery" and a "total surprise" by one of our interviewees, who said she had "read about it in the newspaper" and then later the group meeting was "informed that he had been selected" (EPP MEP F 100320). What happened prompted members of the group to raise questions about the selection process.

The administrative leadership is nested alongside a political leadership structure. A practice is that SGs have moved from PG administrative to political leadership posts and vice versa. SGs and deputy SGs have also moved from administrative group leadership to the parliamentary administration (ALDE Staff M 050419). A staff member said, "the previous secretary-general, he was more focused in his political career in the future than in the wellbeing of the secretariat … we have more trust for [the new secretary general] in terms of how he's going to, support our work, and value our work" (S&D Staff, F 060220), while another participant observed that the newly appointed EPP secretary general in the 9th legislature was "an outsider (with political allies actually)" (EPP Staff F 060320). The literature on national party leadership tells us that back office party political experience can confer gendered resources for political actors (Verge and Claveria 2018). The SG and DSG positions then may be important stepping stones to other political and administrative positions in the Parliament. Because more men have historically been SGs and DSGs, this matters for gendered movement at the very top of the EP. Examples include Klaus Welle (EPP–ED SG to EP SG), Javier Moreno Sanchez (S&D MEP to S&D SG to S&D MEP), Bo Manderup Jensen (ELDR SG to the EP president's cabinet), and Marco Campomenosi (ENF Deputy SG to MEP).

Group secretariats, mirroring the political organs (Bressanelli 2014) are both vertically and horizontally differentiated through departments and subunits. Each department and subunit is managed. For secretary and deputy SGs who have come through the group career structures, the norm is that they and managers have often served as political advisors to committees (ALDE Staff M 050419). According to one participant, this means that managers may not have had adequate management training: "we have managers that don't really care about management" (S&D Staff F 060220, see also Renew Staff F 240320). This is important since, as mentioned above, SGs and DSGs are in charge of considerable recruitment and redundancy processes after the European elections.

To summarize the position of women in administrative leadership, the Greens/EFA group and GUE/NGL group have women represented at the very top of their administrative structures. The secretary and deputy SGs are key positions to examine in terms of movement from and into other leadership positions in the Parliament.

8.5 Conclusion

Looking at the gender composition of a range of leadership positions in the EP's political groups illustrates how gender continues to matter. Although the share of women MEPs has increased rapidly to reach a gender balance of around 40% in the 9th EP, these numbers are not matched at the level of political group leaders. The leadership of NPDs within groups and the power of the largest national delegation leaders is built on a hidden gender structure and these positions remained heavily dominated by men in all but three groups (Renew, Greens/EFA, and GUE/NGL).

Policy leadership in committees has been more gender balanced. Women were even slightly overrepresented in committee coordinator posts relative to the total number of women in the Parliament. While women's share of committee chairs also increased between the 8th and 9th Parliaments, positional leadership varies numerically and qualitatively for different political groups, with the EPP having an especially low share of female coordinators. In administrative leadership, the position of secretary general continued to be male dominated. Selection procedures vis-à-vis all of these political and administrative leadership positions tended to be clear on paper (for example in political group statutes), with nominally democratic voting within the groups, yet power politics, the influence of trust networks, and the prioritization of seniority were rife, routinely trumping gender concerns.

Political, policy, and administrative leadership are thus organized through gendered norms and practices. Political group leadership is shaped in some groups through norms such as seniority in the EPP. Stepping-stone structures also exist between administrative leadership and the political leadership and the Parliament; therefore, analyzing positional leadership through a gendered lens matters.

It is evident that the political groups fare differently in relation to women's positional leadership. The Greens/EFA and GUE/NGL are most systematically gender equal and show a strong commitment to gender equality in relation to political, policy, and administrative leadership. In the ALDE/Renew and S&D, gender equality and leadership is more negotiated—a commitment to gender equality is not always evident and gaps remain, for the S&D especially in relation to national party delegation leadership. Renew, certainly at the level of committee leadership and coordinators, is very gender equal and it is only the top group leadership positions that are not equally shared between women and men. The EPP, ECR, EFDD, and ENF/ID are at the bottom when it comes to gender-equal leadership, barely reaching the 30% threshold in many cases. (There are exceptions: for example, the ECR has put forward women committee chairs and coordinators and the ID women coordinators.) These are the most gender-conservative groups in the interview data too. This can be expected from the radical-right populist groups on the basis of what we know of their hostile or indifferent stances toward gender equality. The role of the EPP is, however, most decisive for the fate of gender-equal leadership in the EP. As the largest political group, it exerts the most power in leadership selection and the loudest voice in democratic representation and participation. And, as ever, gender-equal representation does not automatically translate into gender-equal leadership. Maintaining focus on the substance of policies as well as broader gendered norms and structures thus remains vital.

References

Ahrens, Petra, and Lise Rolandsen Agustín, eds. 2019. *Gendering the European Parliament*. London: Rowman & Littlefield.

Ahrens, Petra, Anna Elomäki, and Johanna Kantola. eds. 2022. *European Parliament's Political Groups in Turbulent Times*. Basingstoke, UK: Palgrave, forthcoming.

ALDE. 2009. "Alliance of Liberals and Democrats for Europe: Rules of Procedure" (04/02/09), internal document.

Beauvallet, Willy, and Sébastien Michon. 2010. "Professionalization and Socialization of the Members of the European Parliament." *French Politics* 8 (2): 145–165.

Berthet, Valentine, and Johanna Kantola. 2020. "Gender, Violence and Political Institutions: Struggles over Sexual Harassment in the European Parliament." *Social Politics* 28 (1): 143–167.

Bjarnegård, Elin. 2013. *Gender, Informal Institutions and Political Recruitment: Explaining Male Dominance in Parliamentary Representation*. Basingstoke, UK: Palgrave Macmillan.

Bressanelli, Edoardo. 2014. "Necessary Deepening: How Political Groups in the EP Adapt to Enlargement." *Journal of European Public Policy* 21 (5): 776–792.

Chiru, Mihail. 2020. "Loyal Soldiers or Seasoned Leaders? The Selection of Committee Chairs in the European Parliament." *Journal of European Public Policy* 27 (4): 612–629.

Corbett, Richard, Francis Jacobs, and Darren Neville. 2016. *The European Parliament*. 9th ed. London: John Harper.

Daniel, William T., and Stefan Thierse. 2018. "Individual Determinants for the Selection of Group Coordinators in the E.P." *Journal of Common Market Studies* 56 (4): 939–954.

EFDD. 2014. *Statutes of the Europe of Freedom and Direct Democracy Group*, 14/06/14, available at EFDD-Statute.pdf (retrieved July 13, 2020).

EPP. 2013. *Rules of Procedure of the Group of the European People's Party (Christian Democrats) in the European Parliament* (October 2013), available at www.eppgroup.eu/sites/default/files/download/rules-of-procedure/en.pdf (retrieved 13/07/20).

European Parliament. 2019. *Rules of Procedure, 9th Parliamentary Term—July 2019, 2019–2024*, available at www.europarl.europa.eu/doceo/document/RULES-9-2019-07-02_EN.pdf (retrieved July 13, 2020).

Fortin-Rittberger, Jessica, and Berthold Rittberger. 2015. "Nominating Women for Europe: Exploring the Role of Political Parties' Recruitment Procedures for European Parliament Elections." *European Journal for Political Research* 54 (4): 767–783.

Goodwin, Mark, Stephen Holden Bates, and Stephen Mckay. 2020. "Electing to Do Women's Work? Gendered Divisions of Labor in UK Select Committees, 1979–2016." *Politics and Gender.* DOI: https://doi.org/10.1017/S1743923X19000874.

Greens/ EFA. 2010. "Statutes of the Greens/EFA Group," updated 10/04/10, available at www.greens-efa.eu/en/article/document/statutes-of-the-greens-efa-group.

Kantola, Johanna. 2010. *Gender and the European Union.* Basingstoke, UK: Palgrave Macmillan.

Kantola, Johanna and Emanuela Lombardo. 2017. *Gender and Political Analysis.* Basingstoke: Palgrave.

Kantola, Johanna, and Lise Rolandsen Agustín. 2019. "Gendering the Representative Work of the European Parliament: A Political Analysis of Women MEPs' Perceptions of Gender Equality in Party Groups." *Journal of Common Market Studies* 57 (4): 768–786.

Kantola, Johanna, and Emanuela Lombardo. 2020. "Opposition Strategies of Right Populists against Gender Equality in a Polarized European Parliament." *International Political Science Review.* Online first. DOI: https://doi.org/10.1177/0192512120963953

Kantola, Johanna. 2022. "Parliamentary Politics and Polarisation around Gender: Tackling Inequalities in Political Groups in the European Parliament." In Petra Ahrens, Anna Elomäki, and Johanna Kantola, eds. *European Parliament's Political Groups in Turbulent Times.* Basingstoke: Palgrave, forthcoming.

Kenny, Meryl. 2013. *Gender and Political Recruitment: Theorizing Institutional Change.* Basingstoke, UK: Palgrave Macmillan.

Kreppel, Amie. 2004. *The European Parliament and Supranational Party System: A Study in Institutional Development.* Cambridge, UK: Cambridge University Press.

Krook, Mona Lena, and Diana O'Brien. 2012. "All the President's Men? The Appointment of Female Cabinet Ministers Worldwide." *Journal of Politics* 74 (3): 840–855.

Luhiste, Maarja, and Meryl Kenny. 2016. "Pathways to Power: Women's Representation in the 2014 European Parliament Elections." *European Journal of Political Research* 55 (3): 626–641.

O'Brien, Diana Z. 2012. "Gender and Select Committee Elections in the British House of Commons." *Politics and Gender* 8 (2): 178–204.

Pansardi, Pamela, and Michelangelo Vercesi. 2016. "Party Gate-Keeping and Women's Appointment to Parliamentary Committees: Evidence from the Italian Case." *Parliamentary Affairs* 70 (1): 62–83.

S&D (2014) Rules of Procedure. Adopted 15 October 2014.

Verge, Tania, and Sara Claveria. 2018. "Gendered Political Resources: The Case of Party Office." *Party Politics* 24 (5): 536–548.

Verge, Tania, and Maria de la Fuente. 2014. "Playing with Different Cards: Party Politics, Gender Quotas and Women's Empowerment." *International Political Science Review* 35 (1): 67–79.

Whitaker, Richard. 2019. "A Case of 'You Can Always Get What You Want'? Committee Assignments in the European Parliament." *Parliamentary Affairs* 72 (1): 162–181.

PART IV
NATIONAL LEADERS IN EUROPEAN ARENAS

9

Becoming Prime Minister

Women and Executive Power in EU Member States

Karen Beckwith

9.1 Introduction

Few women have governed nations.[1] Worldwide, no woman served as prime minister of any country until 1960; no woman served as president of any country until 1974. The first female prime minister and the first female president did not govern in Europe.

Few women have held political executive leadership positions in European politics. Of the two most powerful governing positions, only 28 women have served as prime minister[2] and only 13 as presidential heads of state. Among European Union member states, fewer women still have held such offices; 23, women have served as prime minister and 11 have been heads of state.[3] Italy has never had a female prime minister or president; the Netherlands, Spain, and Sweden[4] have never had a female prime minister, and France, Poland, and Portugal have never had a female president. At this writing, only three women serve as prime ministers in EU member states,[5] and only three as presidential heads of state.[6] No European country has had a female president fully empowered as head of government.

Among EU member countries, female prime ministers are rare and recent. Focusing specifically on prime ministerships, from the date of a country's admission

---

[1] Many thanks to Professor Henriette Müller and Professor Ingeborg Tömmel, and to my CWRU colleague Professor Elliot Posner, whose expert advice on European Union institutions has greatly improved this chapter. I also thank CWRU undergraduate research assistants Katherine Dabkowski and Maximus Ross for their work in data collection for this chapter.

[2] This includes two women who came into power during transitions to democracy (Milka Planinc in Yugoslavia and Maria de Lourdes Ruivo da Silva de Matos in Portugal). It excludes Irene Degutiené, who was Acting Prime Minister of Yugoslavia twice, for very brief periods, in 1999.

[3] This includes cases where the country joined the EU after the woman served as prime minister (Croatia, Lithuania, Poland, and Portugal).

[4] See, however, "Sweden moves closer to getting first woman prime minister", Reuters, November 4, 2021 (https://www.reuters.com/world/sweden-moves-closer-naming-first-woman-prime-minister-2021-22-04/).

[5] Mette Frederiksen (Denmark), Sanna Marin (Finland), and Angela Merkel (Germany).

[6] Kersti Kaljulaid (Estonia), Katerina Sakellaropoulou (Greece), and Zuzana Čaputová (Slovakia).

Karen Beckwith, *Becoming Prime Minister: Women and Executive Power in EU Member States*. In: *Women and Leadership in the European Union*. Edited by Henriette Müller and Ingeborg Tömmel, Oxford University Press.
© Oxford University Press (2022). DOI: 10.1093/oso/9780192896216.003.0010

to EU membership, only 17 women have become prime ministers; of these, 15 became prime minister in the twenty-first century (2000–2020). Of the 14 female prime ministers in office from 2010 to 2020, 13 entered office for the first time.[7] Of the 27 EU member states, since membership, women have been prime ministers in only 12 countries, fewer than half; only four EU member states have had more than one female prime minister; no country has had more than two. Of the 17 women who became prime minister after their country joined the EU, 11 were the first in their country's history to do so.

The number of women serving as prime ministers in EU member countries (following the year of admission), although still small, has increased in the last decade. Until 2010, no two women served concurrently as prime ministers of EU member states (see Figure 9.1).

Those numbers increased substantially, however modest the overall figures, from 2010 to 2014, with seven female prime ministers serving in the same half-decade; this number increased to eight in 2015–2019. There was, however, no substantial increase in the number of governments headed by female prime ministers; only UK Prime Minister Theresa May led two governments in the half-decade between 2015 and 2019.

The conventional path to the prime ministership in parliamentary systems has two components: (1) becoming party leader; (2) of the party holding a majority

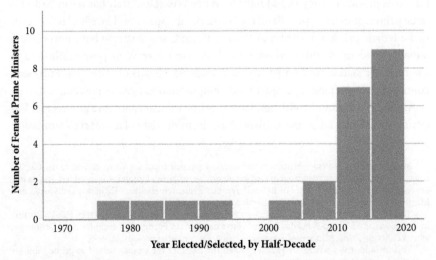

Fig. 9.1 Number of female prime ministers in EU member states, by year elected/selected, five-year intervals

---

[7] Angela Merkel (Germany) first became chancellor of Germany in 2005; reelected three times, she is currently in office and anticipates standing down in 2021 (https://www.economist.com/europe/2018/11/03/angela-merkel-will-step-down-as-cdu-party-leader-in-december).

of seats in parliament. Party leaders may assume the prime ministership by leading their party to electoral victory, by achieving a majority of seats, or by winning a proportion of parliamentary seats sufficient to enable the leader to construct a coalition of parties that, combined, constitute a parliamentary majority. Alternatively, party leaders may ascend to the prime ministership as "heir" prime ministers, replacing a "predecessor between two parliamentary elections" (Müller-Rommel et al. 2020: 241). In either case, the general voting electorate has little impact on the selection of the prime minister who, as party leader, has been selected by a subset of the party's elite (Cross and Blais 2012). As a result, analyses of women's access to the position of prime minister need to consider the party leader contest and to recognize that women lose, as well as win, such contests (O'Brien and Reyes-Housholder 2020).

9.2 Research Questions

How do women rise to political executive leadership of European Union member states? Are there gendered pathways in EU countries that advance women to positions of executive power? Using 17 cases in 12 countries, the chapter examines the pathway(s) that led women to prime ministerships in EU countries. Finally, the chapter asks about subsequent career pathways, as women leave the prime ministership. When a woman ends her tenure as prime minister, what does her subsequent career path entail? More specifically, for the purposes of this volume, does she move from the national arena to a supranational post in the EU?

The chapter rehearses several hypotheses concerning women's political executive access, considering the political factors related to women's access to prime ministerships. Working in reverse from the descriptive data, the chapter then turns to an examination of the political context within which women contest for the party leader position, analyzing two cases from the United Kingdom of women's strategic behavior within specific political openings in their party's leadership (Beckwith 2015). The chapter concludes with a consideration of the connections between women's prime ministerial leadership and women's post-prime-ministerial political experience in EU institutions.

9.3 Data and Methods

An original quantitative dataset was constructed of the universe of women who have served as prime minister in an EU member state. The unit of analysis is female prime minister by term. Four women who became prime minister before their country joined the EU are excluded from the dataset; female prime ministers of non-EU member states are also excluded, as are "caretaker" prime ministers.[8] The dataset neatly comprises four decades of female prime ministers in EU member states (1979–2019; see Table 9.1).

Table 9.1 Female prime ministers in EU member states

	Country		Prime Minister	Years in Office	Party
1	Austria	1	Brigitte Bierlein	2019–2020	independent
2	Belgium	2	Sophie Wilmès	2019–2020	Mouvement Réformateur (right)
3	Denmark	3	Mette Frederiksen	2019–present	Social Democratic (left)
		4	Helle Thorning-Schmidt	2011–2015	Social Democratic (left)
4	Finland	5	Sanna Marin	2019–present	Social Democratic (left)
		6	Mari Kiviniemi	2010–2011	Centre (right)
		7	Anneli Jäätteenmäki	April 2003–June 2003	Centre (right)
5	France	8	Edith Cresson	1991–1992	Parti Socialiste (left)
6	Germany	9	Angela Merkel	2005–2009, 2009–2013, 2013–2017, 2017–present	Christian Democratic Union (center)
7	Latvia	10	Laimdota Straujuma	2014–2016	New Unity (right)
8	Poland	11	Beata Szydło	2015–2017	Law and Justice (right)
		12	Ewa Kopacz	2014–2015	Civic Platform (right)
9	Romania	13	Viorica Dăncilă	2018–2019	Social Democratic (left)
10	Slovakia	14	Iveta Radičová	2010–2012	Civic Democracy SKDU (right)
11	Slovenia	15	Alenka Bratušek	2013–2014	Positive Slovenia (left)
12	United Kingdom	16	Theresa May	2016–2017, 2017–2019	Conservative (right)
		17	Margaret Thatcher	1979–1983, 1983–1987, 1987–1990	Conservative (right)

---

[8] "Caretaker" prime ministers are those who serve only a short period of time, and are generally seen as holding the position while political parties negotiate for leadership. For example, Vassiliki Thanou-Christopholou, who served as Greek prime minister for 25 days in 2015, is excluded as a "caretaker" prime minister.

Becoming party leader is the conventional penultimate step toward becoming prime minister in parliamentary systems. Two comparative cases were selected for further qualitative analysis, providing a comparative case focus on women's political strategizing for party leadership in specific contexts: the UK Conservative and Labour parties' 2016 leadership contests. Finally, a dataset was constructed of those who have held positions of political executive authority within European Union institutions to identify female prime ministers whose post-ministerial career led them to such supranational positions.

This research design involves a combination of methodological strengths and limitations. An obvious strength of the methodology is the universe of cases. In two analytical foci of this chapter, the universe of cases is considered: female prime ministers of EU member countries and female former prime ministers in leadership positions in EU institutions. Only two cases concerning women's strategic positioning for party leadership are analyzed, involving cases in a single country (UK); hence, these cases may not be representative (see, however, Müller-Rommel and Vercesi 2017; Beckwith 2015). Finally, the chapter does not provide comparative data for men who contend for leadership.[9]

9.4 Female Prime Ministers: Region, Newness, and Party

Research on female prime ministers identifies several factors that shape favorable political opportunity contexts for women's accession to executive power: European region, "newness" of country or regime, and political party type. These factors may serve to explain or predict in which locations female prime ministers are likely to emerge in EU member states.

Regional Explanation

Region is not easily theorized in regard to gender and party leadership or prime ministerships.[10] Moreover, variation in region, an artifact of EU formation and the late(r) EU entry of Central and Eastern European countries, is further complicated by the relative regime "newness" of many of these countries. In descriptive terms, there is little variation in numbers of female prime ministers when countries are categorized by region, with the exception of Southern Europe. Since becoming

---

[9] See Müller-Rommel and Vercesi (2017) and Beckwith (2015), for consideration of male party leader contestants; see also Pilet and Cross (2014: 235–237).

[10] I classify "region" as the following: Belgium, Denmark, Finland, France, Germany, Latvia, and the United Kingdom as "Northern Europe" (n = 7); Austria, Poland, Romania, and Slovakia are classified as "Central and Eastern Europe" (n = 4); Slovenia is classified as "Southern Europe." Classifying Germany as "Central Europe" would not change the conclusions about the relationship between region and female prime ministers.

members of the European Union, Croatia, Greece, Italy, Portugal, and Spain have never advanced a woman to the prime ministership.[11] Among EU member countries in Southern Europe, only Slovenia has had a female prime minister after joining the EU.

Although Müller-Rommel and Vercesi found that "the absolute number of female prime ministers is higher in Central–Eastern Europe than in Western Europe" (2017: 254), this is no longer the case. 11 women served as prime ministers in seven Northern European countries and five women were prime minister in four countries classified as Central/Eastern European; moreover, Northern European female prime ministers have headed more governments (17) than have their Central/Eastern European sisters (5). No woman served as prime minister in a Central or Eastern European EU member country until 2010. In sum, among EU member states, more women have emerged as prime ministers in Northern than in Central and Eastern countries, and substantially more than in Southern Europe. Again, region is a location, not an explanation for women's access to prime ministerships.

"Newness" Explanation

Another explanation of women's access to prime ministerships compares "new" and "established" states, with the expectation that newly formed states may offer opportunities to activists to craft new institutions more favorable to women and may expand office-holding opportunities to all contenders in the absence of entrenched incumbents (Mackay 2014; Mackay and Waylen 2014; Sikk 2011). Moreover, to the extent that countries with new regimes have more women elected to new parliaments, they will have more women from whom to draw for potential party leaders and prime ministers. As a result, women may emerge more frequently as prime ministers in new regimes. Conversely, to the extent that entrenched incumbents in established political systems are men, women will find entry to party leader and prime minister positions blocked.

New countries are identified as those EU member countries that have had a complete regime change following the end of the Cold War. This subset includes Bulgaria, Croatia, the Czech Republic, Estonia, Hungary, Latvia, Lithuania, Poland, Romania, Slovakia, and Slovenia. Women were selected as prime ministers six times in five new countries; no female prime minister led more than one government, and six new countries (54.5%) have not yet had a female prime minister. In eight of the 17 established EU member countries, women have been selected

---

[11] Croatia's only female prime minister was Jadranka Kosor (2009–2011), who held office before Croatia joined the EU in 2013. Maria de Lourdes Ruivo da Silva de Matos, Portugal's only female prime minister, was appointed to the post during the transition from military dictatorship to democracy in 1979, well before Portugal joined the EU in 1986.

as prime minister in 17 instances; nine established countries have yet to be led by a female prime minister (52.9%). Among all cases, only in Germany (Angela Merkel) and the UK (Margaret Thatcher, Theresa May) have women led more than one government (see Table 9.1). In sum, newness of country appears to make little difference in the numbers of female prime ministers or in the number of terms they have served.

Party Explanation

Finally, are women in left-wing parties more likely to emerge as prime ministers than their counterparts in right-wing parties? Answering this question poses a challenge, given the difficulty of classifying parties in the newly established countries, with new party systems that do not easily fit within Western Europe's immediate post–World War II ideological spectrum (Mair 1990; Sikk 2011). Nonetheless, bluntly categorized (see Table 9.1), center parties have advanced women to prime ministerships in six instances (27.3%), as have left-wing parties (27.3%); right-wing parties have advanced women to 10 terms as prime minister (45.4%).[12]

However, the instances of center party female prime ministers are heavily weighted by Angela Merkel's four terms as German chancellor, as are those of right-wing parties by Margaret Thatcher's three terms and Theresa May's two terms as UK prime minister. Assessing party ideology and its influence on numbers of female prime ministers (rather than numbers of terms of female prime ministers), left-wing parties have advanced six individual women in five EU member countries, a ratio of 1.2:1 female prime ministers to country (Denmark, Finland, France, Romania, and Slovenia); center parties have advanced one individual woman in one country, a 1:1 ratio (Germany); and right-wing parties have supported nine women as prime minister in six countries, a 1.5:1 ratio (Belgium, Finland, Latvia, Poland, Slovakia, and the UK). In terms of numbers of individual women advanced as prime ministers, left-wing and right-wing parties perform better than do center parties in terms of numbers of female prime ministers; in terms of ratios of female prime ministers to countries, there is little difference across different parties in success in promoting women as prime ministers, and no support for claims that left-wing parties do better than other parties on these grounds.[13]

---

[12] These data exclude Brigitte Bierlein (Austria, 2019), who is an independent.

[13] Differences by type of party are not statistically significant. Some of these findings are inconsistent with findings by Müller-Rommel et al. (2017), the result, in part, of different operationalizations, case inclusions, and time frames. Since 2015, an additional nine women have served as prime minister—three from left-wing parties, four from right-wing parties, one from a center party, one independent, only two of them in Central/Eastern Europe.

9.5 Becoming Party Leader

How do women rise to the position of party leader? Are there particular gendered routes to the party leader position in parliamentary systems? Aspiring party leaders must compete for the leader position in contests that are shaped by: (1) party selection rules; (2) the conditions that established the contest itself; (3) the resulting political opportunity structure; and (4) the range of leader candidates. Each of these factors has gendered consequences.

Most women in EU member states who have become prime minister have done so by replacing a sitting prime minister of their own party, entering office without a national electoral mandate. For those women who became prime minister after their country joined the EU, nine (56.25%) have done so in this way, entering office without an electoral mandate.[14] Seven women (43.75%) have come into the post first by becoming leader of an opposition party and subsequently becoming prime minister by winning an election.[15]

A single country serves as an exemplary case (rather than a full test) of the extent to which party leader contests are gendered and how women navigate the path to party leadership and the prime ministership. In the United Kingdom, two major political parties had party leader contests in 2016: the Conservatives and Labour. One contest produced a female party leader and hence a prime minister; the other contest confirmed male party leadership.

Party Leader Contests in the United Kingdom, 2016

The Conservative Party leadership contest
Conservative Party rules for leadership selection, instituted in 1998, authorize Conservative Party MPs to nominate leader candidates. "For the 2016 leadership election, an MP needed to be nominated by two colleagues" (Johnston 2018: 5). Upon nomination, potential candidates submit their names for a vote to the Conservative Party parliamentary members. In the case of three or more contenders, a series of nominating ballots among the MPs eliminates the candidates with the fewest votes, until two contenders remain. Once two candidates are identified, the wider party membership votes by postal ballot to elect the leader by majority vote

[14] Sophie Wilmès (Belgium, 2019), Mari Kiviniemi (Finland, 2010), Sanna Marin (Finland, 2019), Edith Cresson (France, 1991), Ewa Kopacz (Poland, 2014), Beata Szydło (Poland, 2015), Viorica Dăncilă (Romania, 2018), Alenka Bratušek (Slovenia, 2013), and Theresa May (UK, 2016). Brigitte Bierlein (Austria, 2019) has no party affiliation and is not included in these data; she replaced a sitting prime minister.
[15] These include Margaret Thatcher, following the 1979 UK parliamentary elections; Angela Merkel, following the 2005 German parliamentary elections; and Helle Thorning-Schmidt (Denmark, 2011), Mette Frederiksen (Denmark, 2019), Anneli Jäätteenmäki (Finland, 2003), Laimdota Straujuma (Latvia, 2014), and Iveta Radičová (Slovakia, 2010).

(Johnston 2018: Appendix 3). In the case of only one nominee, that candidate is declared the winner without a membership vote.

The political opportunity structure for Conservative Party leadership candidates opened early. In March 2015, prior to the May 2015 parliamentary elections, Prime Minister David Cameron announced that he would not stand for a third term, signaling that the likely time frame for the next leadership contest would be 2020.[16] Moreover, Cameron identified (hence authorizing) three potential candidates to succeed him as party leader: Chancellor of the Exchequer George Osborne, former Mayor of London Boris Johnson, and Home Secretary Theresa May.

Following the 2015 parliamentary elections, the Conservative Party held a strong position in the Commons, having won a 12-seat majority, and no longer needed to govern in coalition. Hence, the opportunity was not only open but was particularly attractive for aspiring party leaders. Knowing that Cameron would not be a future contestant for the leader position allowed those with party leader aspirations to prepare for the opportunity in 2020.

Given clear signals, May and Johnson[17] had begun to position themselves for the prospective party leadership contest.[18] Sooner than anticipated, however, Cameron resigned as leader, following Britain's 2016 national referendum on EU membership. In his resignation speech, Cameron indicated that he would "remain in place for the short term and ... then hand over to a new prime minister by the time of the Conservative conference in October."[19] Cameron's resignation shifted the political opportunity structure for an internal leadership change: the successful leader candidate would not have to lead the party into a general election, and could govern with a Commons majority for at least four years.

With the new time frame, May and Johnson advanced their candidacies. Two additional candidates announced: Stephen Crabb and Liam Fox; they were subsequently joined by Michael Gove. Gove, who had been a supporter of Johnson's candidacy, rescinded his endorsement when he declared his own candidacy. Johnson, recognizing he would lose the leadership contest, withdrew.[20] Faced with Theresa May as the likely victor, pro-Brexit Tories moved quickly to recruit Andrea

---

[16] Stephen Castle, "David Cameron Rules Out Third Term as Prime Minister," *New York Times*, March 24, 2015, https://www.nytimes.com/2015/03/25/world/europe/david-cameron-rules-out-third-term-as-prime-minister-of-britain.html.

[17] Johnson resigned as Mayor of London in May 2016 to take a seat in the House of Commons, making him eligible to run as a party leader candidate.

[18] George Osborne never declared himself a candidate, anticipating that he lacked the necessary support. See Nicola Slawson, "George Osborne Will Not Contest Tory Leadership Race," *Guardian*, June 28, 2016, https://www.theguardian.com/politics/2016/jun/28/george-osborne-will-not-contest-tory-leadership.

[19] "Brexit: David Cameron to Quit after UK Votes to Leave EU," *BBC News*, June 24, 2016, https://www.bbc.com/news/uk-politics-36615028.

[20] Jessica Elgot and Peter Walker, "Michael Gove to Stand for Conservative Party Leadership," *Guardian*, June 30, 2016, https://www.theguardian.com/politics/2016/jun/30/michael-gove-to-stand-for-conservative-party-leadership. Space constraints preclude a detailed discussion of the politics around Gove's entry into the leadership race and Johnson's withdrawal; see Quinn (2019).

Leadsom, who was endorsed by Johnson and others. Thus recruited, Leadsom entered the party leader race.

How was the 2016 Conservative Party leadership contest gendered? First, the leadership race was gendered by the presence of four male contenders. The most prominent was Boris Johnson, who, like May, had been preparing to become party leader. All four male candidates had self-recruited; two, Crabb and Fox, had little support from the outset and the first ballot brought both of their campaigns to an end.[21]

Second, the leadership contest was gendered by the presence of two female contenders: Theresa May, home secretary, and Andrea Leadsom, energy minister. The 2016 Conservative Party leader contest unfolded within the history of near-exclusive male dominance of leader candidacies and party leaders. Until May 2016, only one woman had ever contested for party leadership in the UK Conservative Party: Margaret Thatcher in 1975. "Between Margaret Thatcher's resignation in 1990 and David Cameron coming to power in 2005, the Conservatives had seen six leadership elections featuring 14 candidates, with not a single woman to be found on the ballot."[22]

Third, the leadership contest shifted to May's advantage with the implosion of the Johnson candidacy. As her strongest opponent, Johnson was ambitious and concerted in his pursuit of the UK prime ministership, which the 2016 Conservative leadership contest provided. His continued candidacy might have forced a second round of balloting, with unpredictable consequences. With Johnson's withdrawal, May won a majority of nominating votes on the first ballot and a supermajority of over 60% on the second ballot, leaving Leadsom as her only opponent; Leadsom thereafter withdrew her candidacy. This left May as the sole remaining candidate and, by Conservative Party rules, the new leader and new prime minister (see Table 9.2).

The Labour Party Leadership Contest

In 2015, new Labour Party leadership selection rules were introduced, making the contest more open to participation by Labour Party members and supporters. Leadership candidates were nominated by endorsement of 15% of members of the Parliamentary Labour Party (PLP; in 2015, at least 35 MPs). The new voting electorate included all party members and registered and affiliated supporters, with one vote per member and all votes weighted equally.

[21] Fox placed last and was thus eliminated in the first round of voting; Crabb withdrew from further competition after the first round.

[22] Eve Livingston, "Don't Confuse the Conservatives' Embrace of Female Leaders with Feminism," *Guardian*, July 8, 2016, https://www.theguardian.com/commentisfree/2016/jul/08/conservatives-female-leaders-feminism-margaret-thatcher-theresa-may-andrea-leadsom.

Access to the nominating ballot is more difficult in the Labour Party than for the Conservatives, since a larger number of endorsements is required. Once nominees are identified, the selection decision is sent to the wider membership to be determined by the alternative vote system.[23] Under the new rules, however, tens of thousands of new members and supporters had paid the modest fee to join the party, introducing substantial unpredictability into the leadership contest. The decision to open the leadership selection vote to "anyone prepared to pay £3 to vote for the leader, significantly weakened the influence of the party's MPs but empowered activists and supporters. In this way, Labour has made itself vulnerable to possible outside manipulation by those who wish it ill, as well as 'entryism' from the extra-parliamentary left."[24] This also contributed to the defeat of two female candidates who had been strongly endorsed by the PLP.

Understanding the 2016 Labour Party leadership contest begins with recalling the previous leadership race in 2015. The 2015 contest resulted from a challenge to sitting leader Jeremy Corbyn. Corbyn had been selected as leader following Labour's defeat in the 2015 parliamentary elections and Ed Miliband's resignation as party leader. The 2015 leadership contest was marked by several factors that suggested the existence of a gendered political opportunity structure closed to female leader candidates.

Two women competed in the 2015 contest, both of whom were highly qualified: Yvette Cooper, shadow home secretary, and Liz Kendall, shadow minister for care and older people. Of the two, Cooper, first elected to parliament in 1997, was the more experienced candidate. She had served in two sub-ministerial positions in Labour Prime Minister Gordon Brown's government, and had been Labour's shadow foreign secretary; she had been mentioned as a possible party leader as early as 2010. Former UK Prime Minister Gordon Brown endorsed Cooper's 2015 leadership candidacy, as did the *New Statesman*[25] and the *Guardian*.[26] Kendall, elected to Parliament in 2010, was appointed junior shadow minister for health and, shortly thereafter, shadow minister for care and older people. Her candidacy was endorsed by the *Sun*.[27]

With 59.5% of the vote, Corbyn won the leadership election by a landslide on the first ballot, defeating both women and a third candidate, Andy Burnham

---

[23] Ray Collins, *Building a One Nation Labour Party: The Collins Review into Labour Party Reform*, February 2014, https://action.labour.org.uk/page/-/Collins_Report_Party_Reform.pdf.

[24] "The NS Leader: The Choice before Labour," *New Statesman*, August 19, 2015, https://www.newstatesman.com/politics/2015/08/ns-leader-choice-labour.

[25] "The NS Leader: The Choice before Labour," *New Statesman*, August 19, 2015, https://www.newstatesman.com/politics/2015/08/ns-leader-choice-labour.

[26] "The Guardian's View on Labour's Choice: Corbyn Has Shaped the Campaign But Cooper Can Shape the Future," August 13, 2015, https://www.theguardian.com/commentisfree/2015/aug/13/guardian-view-labour-leadership-choice-yvette-cooper-jeremy-corbyn.

[27] Jon Stone, "The *Sun* Newspaper Endorses Liz Kendall as Its Choice for Next Labour Leader," *Independent*, June 19, 2015, https://www.independent.co.uk/news/uk/politics/sun-newspaper-endorses-liz-kendall-its-choice-next-labour-leader-10329121.html.

(Quinn 2016). Despite their superior experience, their loyalty to Labour, and a greater number of endorsements for their nominations, both Cooper and Kendall were defeated by a man with no cabinet or shadow cabinet experience, who had defied the direction of his party by "breaking the whip 534 times since 1997."[28] The outcome of the 2015 Labour leadership election would not have been encouraging to women in the party considering a future leadership bid.

Although half of the candidates in Labour's 2015 leadership contest were women, only one woman contested for leader in 2016. First, the 2016 leadership race was the result of a challenge to a sitting leader. Shadow Foreign Minister Hilary Benn, along with other members of Corbyn's shadow cabinet, had lost confidence in Corbyn. As a result, Corbyn removed Benn from his post; thereafter, 20 shadow cabinet ministers resigned or were fired. Twelve of these were women, reducing their number in the Shadow Cabinet from 22 to 10.[29]

Following these resignations, the PLP held a vote of no confidence in Corbyn, which Corbyn lost (172:40). Nonetheless, Corbyn declined to resign,[30] and he was then faced with a formal leadership challenge. Because Corbyn's potential opponents strategized to minimize the number of candidates to strengthen the odds of removing him, only two challengers—Angela Eagle and Owen Smith—prepared to compete for the Labour leadership.

Eagle was a highly qualified candidate. First elected to Parliament in 1992, she had been minister of state for work and pensions, exchequer secretary for the treasury minister, and parliamentary secretary of the home office across the Blair and Brown Labour governments. She was shadow chief secretary to the Treasury as Labour entered opposition in 2010. Her rival, Smith, had been an MP only since 2010, had no cabinet experience, and had been shadow secretary for work and pensions only since 2015. Nonetheless, despite her early challenge to Corbyn and a large number of PLP endorsements, within days Eagle removed herself from contention, under pressure to step aside for Smith. Corbyn defeated Smith in a landslide, with a slightly greater percentage of the vote than he had won in 2015.

How was the 2016 Labour leadership contest gendered? Unlike the Conservative Party, the British Labour Party has had several women stand for party leader. This history, however, has not mitigated the exclusive male dominance of successful leadership candidacies and male party leaders. This historic exclusion of women from Labour Party leadership signaled the disadvantageous context of the 2016

---

[28] "The NS Leader: The Choice before Labour," *New Statesman*, August 19, 2015, https://www.newstatesman.com/politics/2015/08/ns-leader-choice-labour.

[29] Rajeev Syal, Frances Perraudin, and Nicola Slawson, "Shadow Cabinet Resignations: Who Has Gone and Who Is Staying," *Guardian*, 27 June 2016, https://www.theguardian.com/politics/2016/jun/26/labour-shadow-cabinet-resignations-jeremy-corbyn-who-has-gone.

[30] Labour Party rules did not provide for a leadership vote of no confidence. Corbyn was not formally required to resign following the vote, and he did not do so, although "[l]eaders in this position are usually presumed to have forfeited all authority and are compelled to resign" (Quinn 2018: 479).

race. Only one woman, among the many who had been Labour shadow ministers, was willing to compete.[31] As a consequence, the 2016 Labour leadership race drew attention to the party's gendered political opportunity structure. Multiple media reports and editorials excoriated the Labour Party for its "terrible record"[32] of failing to support women in its leadership, and Conservative commentators were happy to join in. Finally, the party itself engaged in negative recruitment, encouraging the sole female contender to step aside for a male candidate, leaving two men to contest for party leadership (see Table 9.2).

Table 9.2 Leader candidates for UK Conservative and Labour parties, 2016

Factors	Conservatives	Labour
Leader Candidates	Stephen Crabb Liam Fox Michael Gove Boris Johnson Andrea Leadsom Theresa May	Jeremy Corbyn Angela Eagle Owen Smith
Political opportunity structure	Opportunity for leader contest announced in advance; leader resigns earlier than anticipated	Opportunity for leader contest created by formal leadership challenge, following no-confidence vote in Corbyn
Likelihood of success for female candidate	High likelihood for May; little likelihood for other women	Little for any women; Eagle withdrew
Recruitment of female candidates	May self-recruited; Leadsom recruited by opponents of May	Eagle self-recruited and recruited by others, also the target of negative recruitment; no other women were willing to compete
Recruitment of male candidates	Johnson, Gove, Crabb, and Fox self-recruited	Corbyn and Smith self-recruited
Gendered nature of political opportunity structure	Positive for women and men	Closed to women

[31] Harriet Harman, Deputy Labour Party Leader (2007–2010) and Deputy Labour Opposition Leader (2010–2015), declined to run in leadership elections in 2010 and 2015.

[32] Anne Perkins, "Angela Eagle Was Never Going to Be Labour Leader," *Guardian*, July 19, 2016, https://www.theguardian.com/commentisfree/2016/jul/19/angela-eagle-labour-leader-gender-party-patriarchy; Deborah Orr, "Labour: A Party Meant to Help Women But Run by Men," *Guardian*, July 8, 2016, https://www.theguardian.com/commentisfree/2016/jul/08/labour-party-women-run-by-men; Sophie Ridge, "The Embarrassing Truth about Labour's Record on Women Has Been Exposed," *Telegraph*, July 5, 2016, https://www.telegraph.co.uk/women/politics/the-tory-leadership-race-has-exposed-the-embarrassing-truth-abou/; Julia Rampden, "We're Still Waiting for a Female Labour Leader; It's Getting Embarrassing," *New Statesman*, July 7, 2016, https://www.newstatesman.com/politics/staggers/2016/07/were-still-waiting-female-labour-leader-its-getting-embarrassing.

Conclusion

What do the UK cases suggest about women's access to party leadership and hence to the prime ministership in EU member countries? First, party selection rules that make the nature of the competition and its likely outcome relatively predictable provide a visible path for all party leader candidates, including women. For the Conservatives, a limited, confined leadership electorate, with relatively easy nomination rules, clarified for potential competitors how they should prepare for a leadership contest and when that contest would likely occur. Changes in Labour Party rules, and the unpredictability introduced by them, favored those who were prepared for a leadership contest in 2016 and who could mobilize large numbers of new members; those who had not anticipated a leadership contest and/or did not have a new and substantial base of members for support were disadvantaged. This was the case for Labour Party women, of whom only one was willing to compete in 2016. Clarity and visibility of formal party rules, where the path to the position of leader is known and predictable, facilitates candidacies for all potential contenders, including women.

Second, the conditions that led to the contests in each major party were unanticipated and created uncertainty; the unexpected nature of both leadership contests should have been disadvantageous for all potential contenders, particularly women. Prepared candidates, however, having long anticipated a future challenge for party leadership, were advantaged in the leadership contest in each party, although "unprepared" candidates nonetheless competed. Labour Party candidates competed for party leader under conditions of combined unpredictability of the impact of new rules and the uncertainty of the contest itself, making the resulting political opportunity structure unfavorable to women; the unexpected leader contest for the Conservatives favored ambitious, prepared candidates like Boris Johnson and Theresa May, but disadvantaged other candidates who had not expected a leadership contest to occur so soon after the 2015 parliamentary elections.

The political opportunity structure in each party influenced the range of leadership candidates. It is not clear that Theresa May would have prevailed in the 2016 Tory leadership race had Boris Johnson not withdrawn his candidacy. In the Labour Party, despite multiple candidates across time, no woman has won a leadership contest and, in the 2016 leadership contest, a highly qualified and experienced woman was convinced by the party elite to withdraw her candidacy. The quality and preparation of female leadership candidates, combined with a political opportunity structure where potentially competitive male candidates have not contended or have withdrawn, facilitates women's access to the position of party leader and hence to the possibility of becoming prime minister.[33] Additional case

---

[33] See also Beckwith (2015); Müller-Rommel et al. (2020).

studies of women's access to party leadership, including those where the leader does not become prime minister, will be necessary to test this claim.

9.6 Beyond Prime Minister?

Women who became prime minister after their country joined the EU have had relatively short tenures in office;[34] those who came to the prime ministership without contesting an election had statistically significant shorter tenures in office[35] than those who first led their party into a parliamentary election.[36] Aside from Margaret Thatcher (UK) and Angela Merkel (Germany), only Helle Thorning-Schmidt (Denmark) completed a full term as a female prime minister who first came to office following an election. Theresa May (UK) is the only woman in an EU member state who, becoming prime minister by replacing her party's leader, was able to lead her party into a subsequent parliamentary election and continue thereafter as prime minister.

With relatively short tenures, former prime ministers are left to contemplate their next career steps (Theakston and de Vries 2012). Moreover, the average age of exit from office of the 13 former female prime ministers of EU member countries is 55.62 years, with a median of 55.00 years; 69.2% of female former prime ministers were younger than 60 at the time they left office. Relatively young, female former prime ministers could anticipate a future of several years of continued public service. Given the EU's commitment to gender equality, it would be reasonable to hypothesize that women, once concluding their tenures as prime minister, might move to leadership positions in the EU. Do former female prime ministers in fact seek positions in European Union institutions?[37]

EU member countries include many old, well-established democratic political systems (Dahlerup and Leyenaar 2013), and all member countries are bound by EU rules concerning gender equity, "a fundamental principle of the European Union" (Galligan and Buckley 2010: 337). This commitment to gender equality and "gender balance in political life" (Galligan and Buckley 2010: 337)

---

[34] The mean number of months as prime minister for women in EU member states, excluding the current term in office, is 26.42, less than a full term of office; the median is 25.

[35] The mean number of months as prime minister for women who replaced a sitting prime minister of their own party is 20.5, or 1.71 years. The cases exclude the current term of prime ministers still in office.

[36] The mean number of months as prime minister for women who led their parties to electoral victory is 69.4, or 5.78 years; the mode and median are 48 months. Again, these cases exclude the current term of a prime minister still in office. These values are heavily weighted by the multiple terms in office of Margaret Thatcher (137 months) and Angela Merkel (144 months, excluding her most recent term as chancellor). When these two cases are removed, the mean number of months in office for those who first became prime minister following an election is 22, or 1.83 years.

[37] A full discussion of female prime ministers' post-prime-ministerial careers is beyond the scope of this chapter. See Theakston and de Vries (2012).

may make EU institutions particularly amenable to female political executives as post-prime-ministerial career steps.

Although much has been written about women in European Union member countries (Avdeyeva 2015; Freedman 2002; Galligan 2015; Roth 2005; Xydias 2016) and in the European Parliament (EP) (Stockemer and Sundstrøm 2019; Lěhiste and Kenny 2016), there is scant scholarship on women's leadership in the EU institutions (see, however, Kantola 2010). So few women have assumed EU leadership positions that Galligan and Buckley (2010) do not provide a separate table for them. Given the rarity and relative recency of female prime ministers, we should expect few women to have forged post-prime-ministerial careers in the European Union.

Two EU institutions, in theory, offer leadership opportunities for former prime ministers: the European Council and the European Commission. Neither, however, has been an actual option for former prime ministers, male or female (Theakston and de Vries 2012). The pattern of (lack of) appointment of women to positions in these institutions speaks to the additional decreased likelihood that female ex-prime ministers will find post-career homes therein.

First, European Council membership is limited to "the heads of state or government of the … EU member states, the European Council President and the President of the European Commission";[38] the president is elected by European Council members. Until 2009, presidents of the European Council were sitting prime ministers or presidents; regular European Council membership is not available to former prime ministers.[39] With so few female prime ministers in EU member states, women have always constituted a minority in the European Council. Since 2009, the permanent presidents of the European Council have been former prime ministers; none have been women.[40]

Second, the European Commission consists of one commissioner from each EU member country, who serves in the "College" for five-year terms.[41] The Commission president is nominated by the European Council and elected by the European Parliament.[42] Elected in 2019, Ursula von der Leyen is the current president of the European Commission, the first woman to hold the position (see Chapter 16 in this volume). Of the three current Commission executive vice-presidents, one is female; of the four Commission vice-presidents, two are women; the lone High

---

[38] https://www.consilium.europa.eu/en/european-council/, accessed 26 October 2020.
[39] As of this writing, three current female prime ministers (Denmark, Finland, and Germany) are Council members (https://www.consilium.europa.eu/en/european-council/members (accessed October 27, 2020); Ursula von der Leyen, European Commission President, also sits as a Council member.
[40] See https://www.europarl.europa.eu/factsheets/en/sheet/5/the-treaty-of-lisbon. The three permanent presidents have been former prime ministers of Belgium (Herman van Rompuy [2009–2014] and Charles Michel [2019–present]) and Poland (Donald Tusk [2014–2019]).
[41] https://ec.europa.eu/info/about-european-commission/organisational-structure/how-commission-organised_en.
[42] Thanks to Ingeborg Tömmel for the wording that clarifies this procedure.

Representative, also a Commission vice-president, is a man. Of the 18 remaining commissioners, nine are women.[43] The current secretary general of the Commission is a woman (Ilze Juhansone), as is one of the two deputy secretaries general (Céline Gauer) (see Chapter 3 in this volume).[44] None of the persons in these positions, however, is a former prime minister, and the European Commission appears not to offer a post-prime-ministerial career path to female former prime ministers.

There are some additional, minor connections between the European Union and women who have served as prime minister. The EP may offer a post-prime-ministerial career path, although with more than 700 members, it provides former prime ministers with considerably less power and influence as MEPs than they had as their country's head of government. Two former Polish prime ministers, Ewa Kopacz and Beata Szydło, were elected as MEPs in 2019; Kopacz serves as an EP vice-president. Following her tenure as prime minister of Finland, Anneli Tuulikki Jäätteenmäki was thrice elected as an MEP (2004–2019).

As Kantola (2010: 74) concludes, because the "number of women in national governments varies … and women are concentrated in particular ministerial posts," women's representation in the European Council and the Council of the European Union is low. It continues to be the case that the structure of the EU institutions and their membership criteria effectively preclude former prime ministers from continuing their careers in EU institutions.[45]

9.7 Conclusion

In the more than 60 years since the founding of the European Union, and even as EU membership has greatly expanded, only 17 women have become prime ministers in EU member states. Only 12 EU member countries—fewer than half—have had even one female prime minister since admission. This underscores the precarious and time-bound history of women as heads of government in postwar Europe, confirming a pattern of "recent and rare" regarding female prime ministers in EU member states. With few exceptions, female prime ministers do not serve a full term of office, and they leave office at a relatively young age. EU institutions have not been inviting destinations for post-prime-ministerial careers for the few women who have served as prime minister in EU member states. These data also confirm that EU member states have been less than exemplary in advancing women as national political executives (see Jalalzai 2013).

Is there a unique path to the prime ministership for women in EU member states? In terms of political party and newness of country, there appears to be no

---

[43] https://ec.europa.eu/commission/commissioners/2019-2024_en.
[44] https://ec.europa.eu/info/departments/secretariat-general_en.
[45] Former prime ministers, of course, may choose not to pursue a career in the EU, given other options. See, e.g., Paterson (2012).

distinctively gendered path. Women with prime ministerial ambitions in "new" EU member countries are not more advantaged (or less disadvantaged) than are their sisters in established democracies. Furthermore, for the universe of female prime ministers in EU member states, the evidence does not support claims that women in left-wing parties are more successful in becoming prime ministers than are women in right-wing parties. Even considering only the most recent decade (2010–2020), the pattern of no differences among female prime ministers, in regard to left-wing and right-wing parties, persists. Although there is substantial evidence that left-wing parties in EU member states advance more women to national parliaments (Beckwith 2014) and appoint more women to governing cabinets (Annesley et al. 2019), left-wing and right-wing parties have similarly bleak records of producing female prime ministers. Whatever paths there may be to the prime ministership in EU member countries, only a few women have been able to find and follow them.

Is there a female route to power in EU institutions? If such a route exists, it is not open to former prime ministers. The distinctive membership of the European Council, which includes the prime ministers of all member states sitting as delegates of their countries, will encompass few women so long as few women are prime ministers. Overall, EU institutions and positions of leadership and power appear to be closed to female former prime ministers. Future research is necessary to map the routes that have brought an increasing—if still small—number of women into EU institutional leadership positions.

Regardless of the routes to power, increasing the number of women in national political office would increase the likelihood of more women holding positions of supranational leadership in European Union institutions. More women as prime ministers will mean more women sitting as European Council members. Changes in rules and practices may increase the likelihood of another woman becoming European Commission president. Until then, women in positions of high political power, nationally and supranationally in the EU, are likely to continue to be few in number and of short duration.

References

Annesley, Claire, Karen Beckwith, and Susan Franceschet. 2019. *Cabinets, Ministers, and Gender*. Oxford: Oxford University Press.

Avdeyeva, Olga A. 2015. *Defending Women's Rights in Europe: Gender Equality and EU Enlargement*. Albany, NY: SUNY Press.

Beckwith, Karen. 2014. "Women, Gender, and Conservative Parties in the 21st Century." Paper presented at the Research Conference on Women, Gender, and Conservative Parties in the 21st Century, Case Western Reserve University, Cleveland, Ohio, October 9–11.

Beckwith, Karen. 2015. "Before Prime Minister: Margaret Thatcher, Angela Merkel, and Gendered Leadership Contests." *Politics & Gender* 11 (4): 718–745.

Cross, William, and André Blais. 2012. "Who Selects the Party Leader?" *Party Politics* 18 (2): 127–150.

Dahlerup, Drude, and Monique Leyenaar. 2013. *Breaking Male Dominance in Old Democracies*. Oxford: Oxford University Press.

Freedman, Jane. 2002. "Women in the European Parliament." *Parliamentary Affairs* 55 (1): 179–189.

Galligan, Yvonne, ed. 2015. *States of Democracy: Gender and Politics in the European Union*. Abingdon, UK: Routledge.

Galligan, Yvonne, and Fiona Buckley. 2010. "Women and Political Leadership in the European Union." In *Gender and Women's Leadership: A Reference Handbook*, ed. Karen O'Connor, 331–344. Thousand Oaks, CA: SAGE.

Jalalzai, Farida. 2013. *Shattered, Cracked, or Firmly Intact? Women and the Executive Glass Ceiling Worldwide*. Oxford: Oxford University Press.

Johnston, Neil. 2018. *Leadership Elections: Conservative Party*. House of Commons Library: Briefing Paper 01366, December 13.

Kantola, Johanna. 2010. *Gender and the European Union*. New York: Macmillan.

Lёhiste, Maarja, and Meryl Kenny. 2016. "Pathways to Power: Women's Representation in the 2014 European Parliament Elections." *European Journal of Political Research* 55 (3): 626–641.

Mackay, Fiona. 2014. "Nested Newness, Institutional Innovation, and the Gendered Limits of Change." *Politics & Gender* 10 (4): 549–571.

Mackay, Fiona, and Georgina Waylen. 2014. "Introduction: Gendering 'New' Institutions." *Politics & Gender* 10 (4): 489–494.

Mair, Peter. 1990. "Continuity, Change, and the Vulnerability of Party." In *Understanding Party System Change in Western Europe*, eds. Peter Mair and Gordon Smith, 169–187. London: Frank Cass.

Müller-Rommel, Ferdinand, and Michelangelo Vercesi. 2017. "Prime Ministerial Careers in the European Union: Does Gender Make a Difference?" *European Politics and Society* 18 (2): 245–262.

Müller-Rommel, Ferdinand, Corinna Kroeber, and Michelangelo Vercesi. 2020. "Political Careers of Ministers and Prime Ministers." In *The Oxford Handbook of Political Executives*, eds. Rudy B. Andeweg, Robert Elgie, Ludger Helms, Juliet Kaarbo, and Ferdinand Müller-Rommel, 229–250. Oxford: Oxford University Press.

O'Brien, Diana Z., and Catherine Reyes-Housholder. 2020. "Women and Executive Politics." In *The Oxford Handbook of Political Executives*, eds. Rudy B. Andeweg, Robert Elgie, Ludger Helms, Juliet Kaarbo, and Ferdinand Müller-Rommel, 251–272. Oxford: Oxford University Press.

Paterson, William. 2012. "The Political Afterlives of German Chancellors." In *Former Leaders in Modern Democracies: Political Sunsets*, ed. Kevin Theakston and Jouke de Vries, 103–123. Basingstoke, UK: Palgrave.

Pilet, Jean-Benoit, and William P. Cross. 2014. "The Selection of Party Leaders in Comparative Perspective." In *The Selection of Political Party Leaders in Contemporary Parliamentary Democracies*, eds. Jean-Benoit Pilet and William P. Cross, 222–239. New York: Routledge.

Quinn, Thomas. 2019. "The Conservative Party's leadership election of 2016: choosing a leader in government." *British Politics* 14: 63–85.

Quinn, Thomas. 2016. "The British Labour Party's Leadership Election of 2015." *British Journal of Politics and International Relations* 18 (4): 759–778.

Quinn, Tom. 2018. "From Wembley Conference to the 'McDonnell Amendment': Labour's Leadership Nomination Rules." *The Political Quarterly* 89 (3): 474–481.

Roth, Silke. 2005. *Gender Politics in the Expanding European Union: Mobilization, Inclusion, Exclusion.* New York: Berghahn Books.

Sikk, Allan. 2011. "Newness as a Winning Formula for New Political Parties." *Party Politics* 18 (4): 465–486.

Stockemer, Daniel, and Askel Sundstrøm 2019. "Women's Representation across Different Generations: A Longitudinal Analysis of the European Parliament." *Journal of Common Market Studies* 57 (4): 823–837.

Theakston, Kevin, and Jouke de Vries. 2012. *Former Leaders in Modern Democracies: Political Sunsets.* Basingstoke, UK: Palgrave.

Xydias, Christina. 2016. "Discrepancies in Women's Presence between European National Legislatures and the European Parliament." *Political Research Quarterly* 69 (4): 800–812.

10

Winning by Spending Leadership Capital?

Angela Merkel's Approach to the Refugee and COVID-19 Crises

Femke A. W. J. van Esch and Christoph Erasmy

10.1 Introduction

According to the literature, in times of crisis national political leaders are expected to lead from the front, and their actions can have a profound impact on their political fate ('t Hart 2014). We know much less about what type of leadership is successful in EU crisis management and whether this also affects the fate of leaders. Faced with an international security crisis, citizens often rally around the flag, and national leaders may rise to states(wo)man status in the public eye. However, EU affairs were long seen as "second order" politics with no real bearing on national leaders' political fortunes. Nowadays, EU governance significantly affects the daily lives of the European people, which complicates the role of national political leaders. In the multilevel EU system, national leaders are responsible for the welfare of their national constituents, but also provide pan-European leadership for the European people and their fellow leaders in the European Council (Van Esch 2017). This makes balancing key political values like legitimacy, sovereignty, and solidarity a challenging task.

So, what does constitute successful EU crisis management, and to what extent is the way national leaders handle European crises consequential for their domestic political fate? German Chancellor Angela Merkel's 16 years of crisis-ridden chancellorship provides an excellent case through which to explore these questions. A previous study of her first 10 years in office showed that she maintained a steady and strong level of leadership capital even in the face of the eurozone crisis (Helms and Van Esch 2017). However, the authors suggest that the reason for this is that the chancellor never spent any leadership capital. Five years and two EU crises later, we put this hypothesis to the test and explore how Chancellor Merkel managed the European refugee and COVID-19 [coronavirus disease 2019] crises, to

Femke A. W. J. van Esch and Christoph Erasmy, *Winning by Spending Leadership Capital? Angela Merkel's Approach to the Refugee and COVID-19 Crises*. In: *Women and Leadership in the European Union*. Edited by Henriette Müller and Ingeborg Tömmel, Oxford University Press. © Oxford University Press (2022). DOI: 10.1093/oso/9780192896216.003.0011

what extent she *expended* leadership capital in these efforts, and to what extent this affected her *repository* of leadership capital.

To answer the chapter's central questions, we employ the Leadership Capital Index (LCI) as an analytical tool (Bennister et al. 2015, 2017). The LCI consists of 10 indicators outlining leaders' skills, relations, and reputations, the sum of these scores providing a snapshot of a leader's authority. Using the LCI allows scholars to establish the extent to which leaders have consolidated or lost authority over time and how this relates to their leadership behavior. It also allows us to draw plausible comparisons between Merkel's leadership during the European refugee crisis and the COVID-19 crisis.

10.2 Chancellor Merkel as EU Crisis Manager

In their LCI study of Merkel's leadership trajectory from 2005 to 2015, Helms and Van Esch (2017) conclude that the German chancellor qualifies as a "rock solid leader" with high LCI scores (score over 31) for eight years since 2007 (cf. 't Hart 2014). Rock-solid leaders are able to carry out their functions over the course of years while maintaining their authority. This finding is especially interesting because during much of this period, Merkel had to manage the eurozone crisis, one of the worst crises in the history of the EU. Moreover, Chancellor Merkel experienced only a minor and temporary decline in leadership capital at the start (score of 31 in 2010), and eventually gained leadership capital during the eurozone crisis reaching a score of 39 in the years 2012–2014.

Helms and Van Esch explain this remarkable finding by arguing that Merkel retained her leadership capital simply by not spending it, that is, by refraining from unpopular decisions and policies. It was only after the Greek referendum in 2015 that she went against the wishes of several powerful German actors, like the minister of finance and the president of the Bundesbank, and sided with those advocating to keep Greece in the EU (Van Esch 2017). This conclusion raises the question of how Chancellor Merkel's authority would fare in cases where she did spend political capital, like in the European refugee and COVID-19 crises.

To answer this question, this chapter employs the LCI. The LCI consists of 10 indicators that provide insights into leaders' vision and communication, their popularity with constituents and their party, and their ability to influence party policy and parliamentary effectiveness (Bennister et al. 2015, 2017). Depending on the nature of the indicator, a combination of quantitative and qualitative data is used to determine a leader's score, from a minimum of one to a maximum of five per indicator. The sum of these scores provides a snapshot of a leader's capital during a given period. According to Bennister et al. (2017: 16), a total score of between 20 and 30 denotes a medium level of leadership capital, between 30 and 40 a high level, and above 40 an exceptional level. Analyzing a leader's performance over time shows whether they were able to consolidate or increase capital over time—or lost it. Analyzing this development in context may also provide an indication of whether particular crisis management behavior affected a leader's political capital. In order to ensure comparability of the results, this chapter uses an approach similar to that of Helms and Van Esch (2017). Although a certain amount of interpretation is involved in determining the scores, the LCI offers scholars a useful and structured framework to identify and compare leaders' political capital over time (Bennister et al. 2017).

The refugee and COVID-19 crises were selected because in both cases Merkel spent political capital. During the refugee crisis, she decided to divert from EU policy by opening the German border to thousands of refugees. During the COVID-19 crisis, she sacrificed the sacred German "black zero" budget rule and agreed to the mutualization of European debt, a policy Germany had fiercely resisted during the eurozone crisis. Following the hypothesis raised by Helms and Van Esch (2017), we would thus expect to see her LCI decline in both cases.

As EU leaders represent multiple and transnational audiences, it would also be worthwhile to explore how Merkel's standing in the European arena was affected during these crises. However, Merkel's crisis leadership was received very differently internationally than domestically and data for a transnational LCI (polling data in particular) is hard to find. In any event, as national leaders' political fate ultimately relies on winning domestic elections, this chapter focuses on Merkel's domestic LCI.

10.3 Refugee Crisis

In 2015, with the influx of over a million refugees into the EU, the member states went into crisis mode (Benedikter and Karolewski 2016). While Hungary and Bulgaria erected barriers and fences along their borders, in August 2015, German Chancellor Merkel declared that Germany's border would stay open (Mushaben 2017). Proclaiming her now famous phrase "Wir schaffen das" ("We can manage this"), the German chancellor "singlehandedly reset EU immigration and refugee policy, and ... unilaterally suspended ... the Dublin Convention" that determines that asylum requests should be processed in the first country of arrival (Benedikter and Karolewski 2016: 424). While she received praise from the international community, her decision was controversial. In addition to being criticized by other member states, she faced fierce domestic criticism, especially from within her own alliance (*Der Spiegel* 2015). Over the following two years, Merkel was frequently at odds with contingents of the CDU/CSU [Christian Democratic Union of Germany/Christian Social Union in Bavaria], and the CSU even threatened to break with its sister party unless a cap on immigration was made alliance policy (Benedikter and Karolewski 2016). Given these intra-alliance controversies,

historically bad federal election results in 2017, and Merkel's subsequent decision to give up party leadership (BBC 2018), "Wir schaffen das" was clearly an
expenditure of political capital.

To analyze the effects of her management of the refugee crisis on Merkel's leadership trajectory, we look at four successive periods. Functioning as a base index,
the first period encompasses the months leading up to August 2015 (T_0). The next
period extends from August 2015 to April 2016 (T_1) and includes the events in
Cologne on New Year's Eve at the end of 2015 when men of mainly migratory
backgrounds sexually assaulted dozens of women, which led to a significant increase in anti-refugee hate crime (Frey 2020). This contributed to considerable
losses for the CDU and gains for the far-right Alternative für Deutschland (AfD)
in the spring elections (Mushaben 2017). Within the European context, this period is marked by the negotiations on the Turkey refugee deal in early March 2016
(Cremer 2017). The second phase of the crisis extends from April 2016 to January
2017 (T_2), during which several Islamic terror attacks shook Europe and Germany.
The final period ends in October 2017 (T_3), just after the federal election. While
about 15,000 refugees were still coming to Germany every month, the situation
was beginning to stabilize.

Vision and Communication

In the run-up to the refugee crisis (T_0), Merkel generally refrained from staking
out strong policy positions, as she had been doing throughout much of her career. Her strong stance in the refugee crisis thus constituted a "unique break with
her style" (Helms and Van Esch 2017: 30; Jäger 2016). Acting as a "conviction
leader," Merkel went against her pragmatic inclinations and stuck to her controversial position for an extended period despite considerable opposition (Helms
et al. 2019). Despite the criticism from within her own party, Merkel rearticulated
and defended her stance on refugees and the open-door policy throughout the first
phase of the crisis (T_1; Lange 2017). During the later stages of the crisis, however,
it became increasingly obvious that she lacked a clear vision of how to manage the
domestic problems stemming from her policies. Eventually, in September 2016,
the chancellor conceded that her famous phrase had become almost "an empty
formula" (*Süddeutsche Zeitung* 2016: 1). Moreover, while she took a straightforward consistent stance on the upper limit of immigration, the chancellor avoided
taking a position on the issue of family reunification (Dernback 2017).

In the European context, Merkel's vision was clearer. Even before her decision
to open the borders (T_0), she emphasized that EU states shared responsibility for
the crisis and solidarity between the member states was imperative (Merkel 2015).
Throughout the fall of 2015, the chancellor criticized those member states who
reinstated border controls, arguing that such efforts lead to a displacement of the
problem, and called for an effective refugee distribution system and mandatory

relocation quota (Helms et al. 2018). In addition, she played a pivotal role in brokering an EU deal with Turkey and in both autumn 2015 and spring 2016 she approached Turkish President Erdoğan to start a dialogue (Alexander et al. 2016). Considering the domestic and EU context, for the "vision" indicator, Merkel receives a score of three for T_0, T_2, and T_3 and a score of four for T_1 (see Table 10.1).

Merkel was never an inspiring speaker (Kohler 2016). Rather, she stands out for her calmness in discussions, her persuasiveness, and her ability to avoid communicative faux pas (Helms and Van Esch 2017). Before the crisis, questions of asylum were usually framed in terms of national economic interest and Merkel argued that immigration would counterbalance the negative economic impact of the aging of Germany's population (Laubenthal 2019; score of three for T_0). While the chancellor's communicative style remained largely the same over the course of the crisis, her factual and nuanced communication style response to emotionally charged arguments backfired (Kohler 2016). In July 2015, for example, Merkel's explanation of why not all migrants could remain in Germany left a young refugee girl crying on national TV. T_1 starts with Merkel's now historic opening of the German borders. The way she delivered her famous statement was calm and factual; her performance did not reflect the bold, triumphant move it was later framed to be (Phoenix 2016). It was only later that the chancellor's public declarations started to evoke more pathos. In September 2015, for instance, she stated that "we were quick to save the banks; we can act immediately to help communities save human beings" (Mushaben 2017); at a press conference later that month, she added, "if we had not shown a friendly face, that's not my country" (Alexander 2020). During this period, Merkel was very active in public communications, giving numerous interviews on the radio and in newspapers, as well as speaking out against hate speech. Her appeals, however, were less well received after the New Year's Eve events in Cologne.

In the latter two stages of the crisis, Merkel became less communicative. In a speech to the Bundestag, she stood by her decision to open Germany's borders as well as the Turkey deal. While conceding that a lot must still be done to integrate the refugees, she asserted that "Germany will still be Germany, with all that is precious to us" (Bundeskanzlerin 2016). In 2017, the chancellor largely fell silent on the topic, addressing it only in international venues, where she repeatedly called for more European solidarity and reform of the European asylum system (Bundeskanzlerin 2017). Overall, Merkel's communicative performance remained average throughout the crisis, leading to a score of three across all four periods.

Polls and Party Leadership

Over the course of the European refugee crisis, the satisfaction of Germans with Merkel's performance fluctuated. Whereas an average of 69% of Germans were content with Merkel in the period before the crisis (T_0), following her announcements in August 2015, her approval rating dropped to an average of 56% and 53% in T_1 and T_2, respectively (Infratest dimap). By the time she was reelected in October 2017, Merkel's public approval rating was restored to an average of 62 for T_3. Accordingly, Merkel scores a four in T_0 and T_3 and a three for T_1 and T_2 for the "public trust in leader" indicator.

Comparing Merkel's personal polling with that of her main contenders shows that the European refugee crisis had a particular negative effect for the chancellor. While prior to the opening of the borders, Merkel trailed Foreign Minister Frank-Walter Steinmeier by 3% on average (T_0, score of three), in T_1 and T_2 her approval rating declined while Steinmeier grew more popular. This led to an average polling difference between Merkel and her main contender of 14% and 21% in the periods T_1 and T_2 (Infratest dimap; scores of two and one). By early 2017, the effects of her controversial stance in the crisis slowly disappeared and the difference between her and Steinmeier returned to 3% in T_3 (score of three).

The overall polling of the CDU/CSU showed a similar trend: Prior to August 2015, 41% of people on average indicated they would vote for the alliance, only 0.5% less than the performance of the CDU/CSU in the previous federal election. After the New Year's Eve sexual assaults, this dropped almost 4%, yielding a score of two for the "party polling" indicator in T_1. The alliance continued to poll poorly between 2016 and January 2017, with an average support of 34% in T_2 (minus 8%, score of two). In T_3, poll numbers fluctuated significantly and ultimately the CDU/CSU received only 32.9% of the vote in the September 2017 elections (Infratest dimap; score of two).

Having been at the helm of German politics for almost 10 years when the refugee crisis started, Merkel receives a score of five across all periods for longevity ("time in office"). With regard to party leadership, her scores decline over time. Following her reelection in 2014 with a stunning 96.7% of the vote (score of five for T_0 and T_1), at the party convention of 2016 the chancellor received only 89.5% (*Welt* 2016). Compared to the outcome of CDU leadership elections and the fact that the party counts abstentions as invalid votes, this is a small margin for party leadership (score of two for T_2 and T_3).

While Helms and Van Esch (2017) projected a very low chance of a credible challenge to Merkel's leadership in the years leading up to the European refugee crisis (score of five for T_0), this changed significantly after "Wir schaffen das," for which she was heavily criticized by fellow Christian Democrats and members of the CDU/CSU leadership. Within two months, German newspapers asked whether Schäuble, one of Merkel's most vocal critics, would be taking over (Ulrich 2015). The regional elections in spring 2016 showed, however, that CDU state politicians who distanced themselves from Merkel did not fare well and that the chancellor continued to be the dominant reason voters cast ballots for the CDU/CSU (Turner 2016). The likelihood of a leadership challenge was thus moderate in T_1

(score of three). While there was speculation regarding a possible reshuffle of CDU/CSU leadership (Strauß 2016), however, getting a consensus on replacing her as chancellor in the run-up to new elections was unlikely (score of five for T_2). Despite the historically bad election result, poll numbers in October showed that 94% of CDU/CSU voters preferred that Merkel remain chancellor (Infratest dimap). A leadership challenge thus remained highly unlikely in T_3 (score of five).

Policy Influence and Parliamentary Effectiveness

Throughout her time as chancellor, Merkel had shown a strong sensitivity to the different sentiments in the CDU and never alienated large segments of the party with her policy proposals (Clemens 2011; score of five for T_0). With the worsening of the refugee crisis, the chancellor lost the ability to control the CDU/CSU's policy platform and was forced to compromise with different factions within the CDU and CSU. For instance, in October 2015 Merkel made a U-turn on the transit zones and found herself defending a policy she previously described as "simply not useful" (NDR 2015). Similarly, in the summer and fall of 2016, policies regarding dual citizenship, deportation, and caps on yearly immigration were proposed that were at odds with her positions. Although many of these proposals were not adopted by the CDU, Merkel was unable to swing the vote on important issues such as dual citizenship (Fischer and Weiland 2016). Then, in December 2016, just days after the party convention, a terrorist attack occurred in Berlin that reignited the debate on internal security and immigration policy, prompting several CDU/CSU members to promote their own ideas. Even though Merkel defied the CSU on, for instance, an immigration cap, she had plainly lost some of her influence over the alliance's policy platform. At the European level, Merkel also faced considerable opposition and was unable to sway opinions, particularly in regard to refugee relocation. In late 2015, several Eastern European countries voted against the proposal by the Council for mandatory relocation (Sabic 2017). In the following months, Slovakia and Hungary challenged the policy at the European Court of Justice (Zalan 2016). Considering the domestic and European context, Merkel receives a score of three on the "shape party policy" indicator for T_1, T_2, and T_3.

Merkel had always been very effective in getting her preferred policies approved in parliament (Helms and Van Esch 2017; score of four for T_0). However, as her sway over her own party decreased in the second half of 2015 (Arnett et al. 2016), she receives a score of only three for T_1. In contrast Merkel's policies in the early phase of the refugee crisis did not arouse deep dissent from within the CDU/CSU parliamentary party groups (Deutscher Bundestag ND). On bills concerning asylum, the party alliance voted in unison, with only one MP—accidentally—voting against the second asylum package. Even though 40 CDU/CSU parliamentarians criticized Merkel's refugee policy in an open letter in January 2016 (Schuler

2016), this opposition was not reflected in executive–parliamentary relations. Significantly, in terms of policy Merkel had moved away from her initial welcoming posture and the actual measures she proposed were primarily restrictive (Mushaben 2017). As the dissenting votes of the SPD did not hamper the super-majority coalition government, Merkel receives a score of four for parliamentary effectiveness for T_2 and T_3.

In conclusion, with her welcoming attitude and unilateral suspension of the Dublin Convention, Angela Merkel engaged in daring spending of her political capital. In the months after her bold statement, the consequences of her position, the Cologne events, and the ensuing rise in domestic and European resistance to the German open-door policy forced the chancellor to accept many policies she personally opposed. The analysis shows that her leadership capital during the crisis clearly took a hit. In the period after "Wir schaffen das," her overall score declined seven points from 40 to 33 and dropped again to 31 after the Cologne events (see Table 10.1). Giving in to public and political pressure to adopt more restrictive measures did not lead to a significant restoration of her LCI; in the last stage of the crisis, although her LCI started to improve, the rehabilitation was only partial.

Zooming in on the details, her initial welcoming stance toward refugees had a strong negative impact on her personal polling rates and those of her party as well as her ability to lead the CDU and determine its platform. The Cologne events caused a further drop in her scores and ultimately led to her resignation as party leader. Overall, this analysis thus supports the thesis of Helms and Van Esch, that even the "rock-solid" leadership of Angela Merkel was subject to the simple rule

Table 10.1 Chancellor Merkel's leadership capital during the refugee crisis

Time Indicator	T_0 11–14/7–15	T_1 8–15/4–16	T_2 5–16/1–17	T_3 2–17/10–17
01 Political vision	3	4	3	3
02 Communicative performance	3	3	3	3
03 Personal polls vs. opposition	3	2	1	3
04 Time in office	5	5	5	5
05 Reelection margin for party leadership	5	5	2	2
06 Party polling	3	2	2	2
07 Public trust in leader	4	3	3	4
08 Leadership challenge	5	3	5	5
09 Shape party policy	5	3	3	3
10 Parliamentary effectiveness	4	3	4	4
Total	40	33	31	34

that spending political capital leads to its reduction. In comparison to Merkel's LCI in the early years of her chancellorship as well as the LCI norms, however, the total scores of 31 to 34 indicate that she still maintained a medium level of leadership capital (Helms and Van Esch 2017; Bennister et al. 2017).

10.4 COVID-19 Crisis

Germany was swift to respond to the COVID-19 crisis. Only five days after the first German case of COVID-19 was confirmed, 124 Germans were evacuated from Wuhan and quarantined. On February 12, with 16 confirmed cases, the government apportioned €23 million to fighting the virus (Marcus 2020a). In this first phase of the crisis, Health Minister Jens Spahn was in the lead, conducting the EU negotiations and managing the federal response. However, health policy and many lockdown measures fell within the mandate of the German *Länder* (states). To enable more efficient crisis management, on March 25, the Bundestag passed the Infection Protection Act, increasing Spahn's powers (Robinet-Borgomano 2020). That month, as well, the European Council laid out its EU crisis management priorities (European Council and Council of Ministers 2020).

In early April, crisis measures started to take effect and the chancellor professed to being "cautiously hopeful," while emphasizing that following the distancing and lockdown rules discipline was still important (Marcus 2020a). From mid-April onward, COVID-19 restrictions were gradually eased, starting with the reopening of shops and schools. In May, the initiative by Merkel and French President Emmanuel Macron to set up an EU recovery fund of €500 billion gave high-level political impetus to the Union's crisis response (Bundeskanzlerin 2020). Remarkably, the proposal implied a huge incurrence of debt as well as its European mutualization, each of which Germany and its chancellor had adamantly rejected for years. Over the next few months, the situation within the country stabilized: despite local outbreaks, the infection rates remained low and Germany and Merkel were widely praised for their effective crisis management (Henley 2020).

At the end of June, the number of infections began to rise again. Despite warnings from the Robert Koch Institute and a steady rise in infection rates throughout August and September, the German political response was tepid (Marcus 2020a). Under the lead of the German presidency of the European Council and the Commission president, the EU made more progress: on September 11, for instance, the Council agreed to a €6.2 billion budget increase to fight the pandemic. In October, a coordinated approach to travel restrictions, quarantine regulations, cross-border contact tracing, and testing was established (European Council and Council of the European Union).[1] Domestically, it took until October 28 for

---

[1] For measures taken under the lead of Commission President von der Leyen, see Chapter 16 in this volume.

Merkel to convince her peers to pursue more decisive action. This time schools remained open, but restaurants, hotels, and cultural venues were closed and travel restricted (*Deutsche Welle* 2020a). The measures, which met with fierce public and political opposition, turned out—as the chancellor predicted—to be insufficient. At the end of November, more severe measures were announced and eventually extended over Christmas.

To trace Merkel's leadership capital during the COVID-19 crisis, the analysis covers four phases between May 2019 and January 2021: the six months before the crisis, from the EP elections in May until December 2019 (T_0); the first wave of the crisis until April 2020 (T_1); the period of relative calm from April to August 2020, which also included Merkel's U-turn on the mutual EU debt issue (T_2); and the outbreak of the second wave from August to January 2021 (T_3).

Vision and Communication

Chancellor Merkel, never a visionary leader, returned to her trademark pragmatism after the refugee crisis (score of three for T_0). Initially, the outbreak of the COVID-19 crisis did not change this. During the first phase of the crisis, Merkel hardly spoke publicly about it. Once she did, she showed herself to be concerned, even somewhat fatalistic, and predicted that 60%–70% of Germans would become infected (Marcus 2020b). From March 2020 onward, Merkel demonstrated a consistent stance and warned against ending the lockdown too soon. Her response was also of a piece with her views on European integration: in contrast to other leaders, she stressed the transnational nature of the pandemic, advocated the need for a collective EU response, and rejected closing the borders between member states (Solms-Laubach et al. 2020; cf. Nykänen 2016; score of three for T_1).

By the start of T_2, Merkel had thus established a clear vision of the crisis. Moreover, her speeches during this period showed a keen awareness of how the elderly, the cultural sector, and social cohesion were affected by the lockdown (Merkel 2020a; 2020b). In her view, however, the main challenge was curtailing infection rates down and not overburdening the healthcare system. Consistent with her initial response to the crisis, Merkel advocated further EU cooperation and solidarity. Most notable in this regard was her joint initiative with French President Macron for an EU rescue fund—a plan involving a departure from the sacred German black zero budget rule and an acceptance of European debt mutualization (Merkel 2020b; Van Esch 2014). Despite this exceptional deviation from her long-held positions, her clear vision, calm guidance, and show of empathy justifies a vision score of four for T_2.

From July onward, Merkel issued warnings about the increasing infection rates but again refrained from speaking publicly. When in October she started pushing for another light lockdown, she met with public and political resistance (Merkel 2020c). She was vindicated by a surge of new infections in early November; on November 26, she defended the new lockdown in a powerful speech to the Bundestag. As infection rates continued to increase, on December 9, she pleaded in an unprecedentedly emotional manner for Germans to comply with the rules, stating she was sorry "from the bottom of my heart" for the hard lockdown, "but if the price we [otherwise] pay is 590 deaths a day, then that is unacceptable in my view" (Merkel 2020d; *Deutsche Welle* 2020b). Merkel thus remained consistent in her vision in T_3 and by November succeeded in persuasively conveying her views (score of five; see Table 10.2).

With regard to Merkel's communication, the period before the crisis saw no significant changes to her usual style (score of three for T_0). With the outbreak of the crisis, her communicative performance at first declined: The chancellor remained eerily silent for months and when in March she did address the nation, her tone was negative, fatalistic, offering Germans no reassurance or a credible path forward. Although her performance gradually improved, her communicative efforts during T_1 were obviously below par (score of two).

At the end of March, Merkel started communicating publicly on a regular basis. She held regular press conferences updating citizens about her crisis meetings with the *Länder*, and on April 23 she spoke at length about the crisis in the Bundestag. True to her style, her communication during this period was factual, consistent, calm, and lucid, but also emphatic. During an April 16 press conference, she explained the danger of exponential growth in the infection rate in a scientific but accessible manner. A video of her remarks went viral and she was widely applauded for her clarity and persuasiveness (*Guardian* 2020). Merkel also led by example, conducting her work online. Her starkly improved communication performance in T_2 earns the chancellor a score of five.

Despite her own warnings, the subsequent decline in infection rates and holiday season brought Merkel back to her natural wait-and-see style. Although aware of the risks, she gave no national public speeches between July and October. Behind the scenes, she continued to voice her vision, but with little result. When on September 29 she warned fellow party members that, without further measures, infections would reach 20,000 a day by Christmas, she was deemed overly alarmist, ridiculed by the media and members of her own party, and booed by dissenting parliamentarians in the Bundestag (Weinl 2020; Merkel 2020c). In November, the steep rise in infection rates restored her credibility, allowing her to reach agreement with the heads of the *Länder* on new lockdown measures. Defending her decisions before the Bundestag in early December, Merkel gave one of the best and most emotional communicative performances of her career (*Deutsche Welle* 2020b). However, given her insufficient and ineffective communication at the start of phase three, she receives a score of four.

Polls and Party Leadership

The year 2019 was a difficult one for the chancellor and her party.[2] After she stepped down as party leader, many now saw Merkel as a lame-duck chancellor. However, during T_0 Merkel still polled on average 5.9 points higher than any opposition leader (score of four for "personal polls vs. oppositions"). The onset of the crisis further raised her popularity, and her lead over SPD leader Scholz, roughly seven points in T_1 and T_2, grew to 13 points in T_3 (Infratest dimap; all scores of four).

With regard to longevity, by late 2019, the German chancellor had been in office for 14 years, giving her a "time in office" score of five for all periods. In contrast, her scores on the "reelection margin for party leadership" indicator are low. However, after her successor stepped down in February 2020, calls emerged for her return (Fabian 2020; Schuler 2020); if she had been interested, she actually might have had a chance to win back the position (score of one in T_0 and two throughout the crisis).[3]

In the federal elections of 2017, the CDU/CSU obtained 32.9% of the vote. In T_0 the alliance polls fell to an average of 26%, marking a decline of 7% (Infratest dimap). This figure improved by just one point during T_1, resulting in a score of two for both periods. However, in periods T_2 and T_3, the CDU/CSU rose steadily in the polls, reaching averages of 37% and 36%, respectively (3%–4% increase, score of four). A similar boom occurred in the level of public trust in Merkel. In periods T_0 and T_1, 53% of Germans saw her as trustworthy (score of three). This climbed to 68% and 72% in T_2 and T_3 (score of four).

A German chancellor can be removed from office only by a so-called constructive vote of no confidence implying that an alternative candidate needs the support of a majority in the Bundestag. The likelihood of a credible challenge to Merkel's chancellorship has thus always been low. However, given her public approval rate and the lack of any sort of agreement on her successor, it was even less likely during T_0 (score of five). In February 2020, the media briefly voiced doubts about her ability and willingness to stay on until the end of her fourth term, reducing her score to four. In April, however, her successful management of the crisis prompted calls for the chancellor to stay on for a fifth term (Schuler 2020; Schuler and Uhlenbroich 2020). As similar calls were heard throughout the crisis (Bild plus 2020a; Fabian 2020), a leadership threat soon became extremely unlikely once again (score of five for T_2 and T_3).

---

[2] No polls are available for June 2020.
[3] CSU leadership elections were postponed until 2021.

Policy Influence and Parliamentary Effectiveness

As she was no longer party leader in 2019, Merkel's ability to shape the CDU's policy positions was lower than in her heyday. Moreover since in the early days of the crisis, her ministers took the lead—she receives a score of three for T_0 and T_1. From the end of March onward, however, the chancellor firmly took back the reins (Schuler 2020). Despite opposition from high-level party members, she extended the lockdown over Easter, sacrificed the zero-budget rule, agreed to a huge European rescue fund, and solidified agreement on the German COVID-19 rescue fund. This warrants a score of four for T_2. Subsequently, neither the CDU leadership nor its state prime ministers supported her calls for harsher measures until the end of October (Weinl 2020; Bild plus 2020b). As the chancellor was again securely in control by the end of November, however, overall her influence on party policy warrants a score of four for T_3.

Merkel's parliamentary effectiveness has always been strong and this remained the case during the months before the crisis (Deutscher Bundestag n.d.; Helms and Van Esch 2017; score of four). During the crisis, a total of only four governmental bills—most with no relation to the crisis—drew some opposition (Deutscher Bundestag n.d.). More importantly, in T_1 the Bundestag passed the Infection Protection Act and agreed to a €156 billion support package by an overwhelming majority (Deutscher Bundestag 2020a). In T_2, more contentious measures were on the agenda—the bill on the protection against a national epidemic and the provision of crisis support through the European Stability Mechanism—yet both passed with large majorities (Deutscher Bundestag 2020b, 2020c). While the Merkel–Macron initiative proved surprisingly uncontroversial domestically, at the EU level the "Frugal Four" (Austria, Denmark, the Netherlands, and Sweden) fiercely objected to it (Mallet et al. 2020). After several intense debates and personal talks between Merkel and Dutch Prime Minister Mark Rutte, in June 2020 a compromise was reached, upholding the key elements of the plan. In T_3, the strengthening of the national epidemic law drew eight dissenting votes, but together with the third crisis support package was adopted by another large majority in the Bundestag (Deutscher Bundestag 2020d). At the EU level, the COVID-19 support package was briefly jeopardized by a Polish–Hungarian veto, but the issue was solved through Merkel's intervention. Overall, a score of five is thus warranted throughout the crisis.

In conclusion, it is clear that, during the COVID-19 crisis, Angela Merkel was again spending political capital. Most remarkably, in May she joined French President Macron in calling for a European COVID-19 support fund. This constituted a complete U-turn, as for years—and reportedly until the beginning of May—the chancellor had fiercely advocated very different policies (Mallet et al. 2020). However, the decision had no negative effect on her leadership capital. In fact, in subsequent months, we see her LCI skyrocket from 33 to 42 points, an exceptional

Table 10.2 Chancellor Merkel's leadership capital during the COVID-19 crisis

Time Indicator	T_0 5–19/12–19	T_1 1–20/3–20	T_2 4–20/7–20	T_3 8–20/11–20
01 Political vision	3	3	4	5
02 Communicative performance	3	2	5	4
03 Personal polls vs. opposition	4	4	4	4
04 Time in office	5	5	5	5
05 Reelection margin for party leadership	1	2	2	2
06 Party polling	2	2	4	4
07 Public trust in leader	3	3	4	4
08 Leadership challenge	5	4	5	5
09 Shape party policy	3	3	4	4
10 Parliamentary effectiveness	4	5	5	5
Total	33	33	42	42

level of leadership capital and the highest of her entire career (see Table 10.2). To a lesser but still considerable degree, Merkel also spent political capital by sticking to her restrictive stance and appealing for the extension (T_1) and reinstitution (T_3) of the lockdown. This caused only small and short-term declines in her LCI. Overall and even more than the eurozone crisis, the COVID-19 crisis added to the chancellor's capital.

Zooming in on the finer details also reveals the weaknesses in Merkel's crisis management. Her wait-and-see attitude at the start of the first and second waves temporarily reduced her LCI, especially with regard to vision and communication. However, at the heights of the crisis, her performance in these areas improved, culminating in the extraordinary speech of December 9. The crisis also shows the chancellor's strengths: her effectiveness in building consensus both in the Bundestag and at the EU level, her personal popularity, her standing as the head of the country, and her calm and steadfast stance on the crisis all contributed to the rise in her leadership capital, more than reversing the negative long-term effects of the refugee crisis.

10.5 Conclusions

This chapter analyzes Chancellor Merkel's management of two EU crises, the refugee crisis of 2015–2017 and the COVID-19 crisis that began in early 2020. More specifically, it tests whether the secret behind Merkel's longevity in the face of the EU's multiple crises is her tendency to lead from behind and not spend any political capital. Our findings with regard to this thesis are mixed.

First, in contrast to the eurozone crisis, the chapter shows that Merkel spent considerable political capital in the refugee and COVID-19 crises. The LCI analyses show that while this had a long-term depletive effect on her leadership capital in the case of the refugee crisis, it actually helped foster her authority in the COVID-19 crisis. Thus, while Merkel's management of the refugee crisis supports the thesis that spending capital depletes capital, the COVID-19 case shows that sometimes leaders can win capital by spending it.

So, what explains the difference? Without further research, we can only speculate. But comparing the refugee, COVID-19, and eurozone crises reveals that the refugee crisis and Merkel's management thereof deviates in four ways from the other cases: First, more than in the other crises, her expenditure of leadership capital centered on identity politics. As post-functionalists suggest, identity politics may be more consequential for public opinion than economic politics (Hooghe and Marks 2009). Second, although in all cases Merkel came down on the side of solidarity, in the refugee case she defined the concept globally, while in the COVID-19 crisis her policies implied solidarity with other Europeans (Gerhards et al. 2018). As European solidarity is more widely supported in Germany, this may partly explain some of the difference in the level of support for Merkel's crisis management. Third, for similar reasons, the decision to deepen European (financial) cooperation during the COVID-19 crisis may have sat better with the German public than her decision to proceed unilaterally during the refugee crisis. Finally, while the repercussions of Merkel's decision to open the borders to refugees were direct and immediate, the repercussions of backing the eurozone and COVID-19 support funds are abstract and long-term, making them less contentious.

Although these lessons may not apply to other European political cultures or systems to the same extent, this chapter's findings suggest that it is possible for national leaders to show European solidarity *and* put their money where their mouth is without jeopardizing their political fate. In fact, recent research shows public support for European solidarity across the EU is much higher than is often assumed (Gerhards et al. 2018). Moreover, our analysis also suggests that opting for greater European cooperation is potentially a more rewarding strategy than acting unilaterally, and that rejecting European solidarity and adopting uniformly nationalistic positions may jeopardize national leaders' leadership capital.

In any case, while this chapter may not have revealed all the secrets behind the enigma of Merkel's "rock-solid" leadership, it has indicated that her particular, nontraditional leadership style and tendency to choose cooperation and solidarity in the face of multiple EU crises may have won, rather than lost, her leadership capital.

References

Alexander, Robin. 2020. "Die Geschehnisse des Septembers 2015." *Bundeszentrale für politische Bildung*, July 17. Available from https://www.bpb.de/apuz/312828/sprachkaempfe-um-die-fluechtlingskrise.

Alexander, Robin, Manuel Bewarder, C. Schiltz, Daniel Friedrich Sturm, and Deniz Yücel. 2016. "Wie Merkel und Erdogan den Türkei-Deal einfädelten." *Welt*, March 13. Available from https://www.welt.de/politik/deutschland/article153234567/Wie-Merkel-und-Erdogan-den-Tuerkei-Deal-einfaedelten.html.

Arnett, George, Diego Caponera, Marcel Pauly, and Anne Gathmann. 2016. "Abnicker oder Rebell—Wer ist was im Bundestag." *Welt*, January 27. Available from https://www.welt.de/politik/deutschland/article151296429/Abnicker-oder-Rebell-Wer-ist-was-im-Bundestag.html.

BBC. 2018. "Angela Merkel to Quit as CDU Party Leader." October 29. Available from https://www.bbc.com/news/world-europe-46016377.

Benedikter, Roland, and Ireneusz Pawl Karolewski. 2016. "'We Can Handle This': How the Refugee and Migration Crisis Is Changing the German Political Landscape." *Israel Journal of Foreign Affairs* 10 (3): 423–435.

Bennister, Mark, Paul 't Hart, and Ben Worthy. 2015. "Assessing the Authority of Political Office-Holders: The Leadership Capital Index." *West European Politics* 38 (3): 417–440.

Bennister, Mark, Paul 't Hart, and Ben Worthy. 2017. *The Leadership Capital Index: A New Perspective on Political Leadership*. Oxford: Oxford University Press.

Bild plus. 2020a. "BILD-Wahlcheck; Wie Merkel die Umfragewerte der Union beeinflusst." June 8. Available from https://www.bild.de/wa/ll/bild-de/unangemeldet-42925516.bild.html.

Bild plus. 2020b. "Am Mittwoch diskutieren Merkel und die Länderchefs über einen Lockdown; Ist die Corona-Lage wirklich so schlimm?" October 26. Available from https://www.bild.de/bild-plus/politik/inland/politik-inland/corona-diskussion-ueber-neuen-lockdown-ist-die-lage-wirklich-so-schlimm-73609214.html.

Bundeskanzlerin. 2016. "Germany Will Still Be Germany." Bundeskanzlerin.de. Available from https://www.bundeskanzlerin.de/bkin-en/news/-germany-will-still-be-germany-393594.

Bundeskanzlerin. 2017. "Angela Merkel Calls for an Open and Strong Europe." Bundeskanzlerin.de. Available from https://www.bundeskanzlerin.de/bkin-en/news/angela-merkel-calls-for-an-open-and-strong-europe-479460.

Bundeskanzlerin. 2020. "Gestärkt aus der Krise kommen." Bundeskanzlerin.de, May 18. Available from https://www.bundeskanzlerin.de/bkin-de/aktuelles/dt-franz-initiative-1753644.

Clemens, Clay. 2011. "Explaining Merkel's Autonomy in the Grand Coalition: Personalisation or Party Organisation?" *German Politics* 20 (4): 469–485.

Cremer, Hendrik. 2017. "Das Flüchtlingsabkommen zwischen der Europäischen Union und der Türkei." *Bundeszentrale für politische Bildung*, March 6. Available from https://www.bpb.de/gesellschaft/migration/laenderprofile/243222/fluechtlingsabkommen-eu-tuerkei.

Der Spiegel. 2015. "Merkel's Refugee Policy Divides Europe." September 21. Available from http://www.spiegel.de/international/germany/refugee-policy-of-chancellor-merkel-divides-europe-a-1053603.html.

Dernbach, Angela. 2017. "Flucht als Wahlkampfthema." *Der Tagesspiegel*, September 3. Available from https://www.tagesspiegel.de/politik/bundestagswahl-2017-flucht-als-wahlkampfthema/20276958.html.

Deutscher Bundestag.   2020a.   *Fraktionen   befürworten   MilliardenPaket   im Kampf   gegen   Corona-Pandemie.*   Available   from   https://www.bundestag.de/dokumente/textarchiv/2020/kw13-de-corona-generalaussprache-688948.

Deutscher Bundestag. 2020b. *Streit über Strategien in der Gesundheitspolitik.* Available from https://www.bundestag.de/dokumente/textarchiv/2020/kw20-de-schutz-der-bevoelkerung-695070.

Deutscher Bundestag. 2020c. *Bundestag stimmt europäischen Corona-Finanzhilfen zu.* Available from https://www.bundestag.de/dokumente/textarchiv/2020/kw20-de-kreditlinie-eccl-esm-695092.

Deutscher Bundestag. 2020d. *Drittes Anti-Corona-Paket.* Available from https://www.bundestag.de/presse/hib/804038-804038.

Deutscher Bundestag. n.d. *Namentliche Abstimmungen* (cited July 6, 2017; December 2, 2020). Available from https://www.bundestag.de/abstimmung.

Deutsche Welle. 2020a. "Coronavirus: Germany to Impose One-Month Partial Lockdown." October 28. Available from https://www.dw.com/en/coronavirus-germany-to-impose-one-month-partial-lockdown/a-55421241.

Deutsche Welle. 2020b. "Opinion: Angela Merkel Rocks Bundestag with Pandemic Speech." December 9. Available from https://www.dw.com/en/opinion-angela-merkel-rocks-bundestag-with-pandemic-speech/a-55889232.

European Council, Council of the European Union. 2020. "Timeline—Council Actions on CORONA." Available from https://www.consilium.europa.eu/nl/policies/coronavirus/timeline.

Fabian, Philipp. 2020. "CDU-Machtkampf; Warum Merkel wieder die (heimliche) Parteichefin ist." Bild Plus, October 27.

Fischer, Sebastian, and Severin Weiland. 2016. "Terror lässt Schwesterstreit wieder aufflammen." *Spiegel Online*, December 22. Available from http://www.spiegel.de/politik/deutschland/nach-anschlag-in-berlin-csu-chef-seehofer-streitet-wieder-mit-cdu-a-1127061.html.

Frey, Arun. 2020. "'Cologne Changed Everything'—The Effect of Threatening Events on the Frequency and Distribution of Intergroup Conflict in Germany." *European Sociological Review* 36 (5): 684–699.

Gerhards, Jürgen, Holger Lengfeld, Zsófia S. Ignácz, Florian K. Kley, and Maximilian Priem. 2018. "How Strong Is European Solidarity?" *Berlin Studies on the Sociology of Europe (BSSE)* 37.

Guardian. 2020. "Angela Merkel Uses Science Background in Coronavirus Explainer." April 16. Available from https://youtu.be/22SQVZ4CeXA.

Helms, Ludger, and Femke A. W. J. van Esch. 2017. "Turning Structural Weakness into Personal Strength: Angela Merkel and the Politics of Leadership Capital in Germany." In *The Leadership Capital Index: A New Perspective on Political Leadership*, eds. Mark Bennister, Paul 't Hart, and Ben Worthy, 27–45. Oxford: Oxford University Press.

Helms, Ludger, Femke A. W. J. van Esch, and Beverly Crawford. 2019. "Merkel III: From Committed Pragmatist to 'Conviction Leader'?" *German Politics* 28 (3): 350–370.

Henley, Jon. 2020. "Female-Led Countries Handled Coronavirus Better, Study Suggests." *Guardian*, August 18, 2020. Available from https://www.theguardian.com/world/2020/aug/18/female-led-countries-handled-coronavirus-better-study-jacinda-ardern-angela-merkel.

Hooghe, Liesbet, and Gary Marks. 2009. "A Postfunctionalist Theory of European Integration: From Permissive Consensus to Constraining." *British Journal of Political Science* 39 (1): 1–23.

Infratest dimap. n.d. "ARD-DeutschlandTREND." Available from http://www.infratest-dimap.de (cited July 1, 2017; December 6, 2020).

Jäger, Thomas. 2016. "Warum Merkel die Flüchtlingskrise zum 'deutschen Problem' machte." *Focus Online*, January 27. Available from http://www.focus.de/politik/experten/jaeger/die-motive-der-kanzlerin-warum-merkel-die-fluechtlingskrise-zum-deutschen-problem-machte_id_5018945.html.

Kohler, Berthold. 2016. "Merkels Manhatten-Projekt." *Frankfurter Allgemeine Zeitung*, 30 August. Available from http://www.faz.net/aktuell/politik/ein-jahr-fluechtlingskrise-angela-merkels-fluechtlingspolitik-14413171.html.

Lange, Nico. 2017. "5 Reasons Why Angela Merkel Won't Change on Migration." *Politico*, March 18. Available from http://www.politico.eu/article/3-reasons-why-angela-merkel-wont-change-on-migration-afd-germany.

Laubenthal, Barbara. 2019. "Refugees Welcome? Reforms of German Asylum Policies between 2013 and 2017 and Germany's Transformation into an Immigration Country." *German Politics* 28 (3): 412–425.

Mallet, Victor, Guy Chazan, and Sam Fleming. 2020. "The Chain of Events That Led to Germany's Change over Europe's Recovery Fund." *FT.com*, May 22.

Marcus, Imanuel. 2020a. "Germany and the COVID-19 Pandemic: Chronology 2020." *Berlin Spectator*. Available from https://berlinspectator.com/2020/11/22/chronology-germany-and-the-coronavirus-7.

Marcus, Imanuel. 2020b. "Merkel on Coronavirus: 'We Need to Pass the Test.'" *Berlin Spectator*. Available from https://berlinspectator.com/2020/03/11/merkel-on-coronavirus-we-need-to-pass-the-test.

Merkel, Angela. 2015. "Regierungserklärung von Bundeskanzlerin Merkel." June 18. Available from https://www.bundeskanzlerin.de/bkin-de/aktuelles/regierungserkl aerung-von-bundeskanzlerin-merkel-798908.

Merkel, Angela. 2020a. "Chancellor's Statement Following the Meeting of the 'Corona Cabinet.'" April 20. Available from https://www.bundesregierung.de/breg-de/themen/coronavirus/meeting-of-the-corona-cabinet-1746070.

Merkel, Angela. 2020b. "Government Statement by the Federal Chancellor: 'Let's Not Squander What We Have Achieved.'" April 23. Available from https://www.bundesregierung.de/breg-de/themen/coronavirus/coronavirus-covid/regierungserklaerung-merkel-1746838.

Merkel, Angela. 2020c. "Regierungserklärung von Bundeskanzlerin Merkel." October 29. Available from https://www.bundeskanzlerin.de/bkin-de/aktuelles/regierungserklaerung-von-bundeskanzlerin-merkel-1807160.

Merkel, Angela. 2020d. "Regierungserklärung von Bundeskanzlerin Merkel." November 26. Available from https://www.bundeskanzlerin.de/bkin-de/aktuelles/regierungserklaerung-von-bundeskanzlerin-merkel-1807160.

Mushaben, Joyce Marie. 2017. "Angela Merkel's Leadership in the Refugee Crisis." *Current History* 116 (788): 95–100.

NDR Panorama 3. 2015. "Merkel und die Transitzonen—Kehrtwende oder Taktik." *ARD*, October 13. Available from http://www.ardmediathek.de/tv/Panorama-3/Merkel-und-die-Transitzonen-Kehrtwende/NDR-Fernsehen/Video?bcastId=1404 9184&documentId=31087632.

Nykänen, Anne. 2016. *Operational Code Analysis of Continuity and Change in German Federal Chancellor Angela Merkel's Foreign and European Policy*. Tampere: Tampere University Press.

Phoenix. 2016. "Flüchtlingspolitik: 'Wir schaffen das'—Statement von Angela Merkel am 31.08.2015." YouTube. Available from https://youtu.be/kDQki0MMFh4.

Robinet-Borgomano, Alexandre. 2020. "Europe versus Coronavirus—Germany, a Resilient Model." Institut Montaigne Blog. Available from https://www.institut montaigne.org/en/blog/states-facing-coronavirus-crisis-germany-resilient-model.

Sabic, Selo. 2017. *The Relocation of Refugees in the European Union—Implementation of Solidarity and Fear*. Zagreb: Friedrich Ebert Stiftung.

Schuler, Katharina. 2016. "CDU—Abgeordnete auf Anti-Merkel-Kurs." *Zeit Online*, January 13. Available from http://www.zeit.de/politik/deutschland/2016-01/angela-merke-cdu-fluechtlinge-streit/komplettansicht.

Schuler, Ralf. 2020. "Bundeskanzlerin Angela Merkel; 5. Amtszeit wegen Corona?" Bild plus, April 3.

Schuler, Ralf, and Burkhard Uhlenbroich. 2020. "Innenminister im Interview; Seehofer spricht über 5. Amtszeit für Merkel." Bild plus, May 3.

Solms-Laubach, Franz, Filipp Piatov, and Ralf Schuler. 2020. "Während sich Nachbarn abschotten; Merkel blockiert harte Grenzkontrollen." Bild plus, March 13.

Strauß, Hagen. 2016. "Kanzlerkandidat der Union 2017: Merkel, Seehofer—oder wer?" *Westdeutsche Zeitung*, 11 September. Available from http://www.wz.de/home/politik/inland/kanzlerkandidat-der-union-2017-merkel-seehofer-oder-wer-1.2272148.

Süddeutsche Zeitung. 2016. "Merkel räumt Fehler bei Flüchtlingspolitik ein—beharrt aber auf ihrem Kurs." September 19. Available from http://www.sueddeutsche.de/politik/reaktionen-auf-berlin-wahl-merkel-raeumt-fehler-bei-fluechtlingspolitik-ein-beharrt-aber-auf-ihrem-kurs-1.3168732.

't Hart, Paul. 2014. *Understanding Political Leadership*. London: Palgrave.

Turner, Ed. 2016. "Germany's State Elections: The Rise of the AfD and the Vicious Circle of Grand Coalition Politics." LSE European Politics and Policy (EUROPP) Blog.

Ulrich, Bernd. 2015. "Does He Want to Be Chancellor?" *Zeit Online*, trans. George Frederick Takis, October 31. Available from http://www.zeit.de/politik/deutschland/2015-10/wolfgang-schaeuble-chancellor-candidate-angela-merkel (cited July 4, 2017).

Van Esch, Femke A. W. J. 2014. "Exploring the Keynesian–Ordoliberal Divide. Flexibility and Convergence in French and German Leaders' Economic Ideas during the Euro-Crisis." *Journal of Contemporary European Studies* 22 (3): 288–302.

Van Esch, Femke A. W. J. 2017. "The Paradoxes of Legitimate EU leadership. An Analysis of the Multi-level Leadership of Angela Merkel and Alexis Tsipras during the Euro Crisis." *Journal of European Integration* 39 (2): 223–237.

Weinl, Volker. 2020. "19.200 Infektionen pro Tag; Wie kommt Angela Merkel auf diese Schockzahl? Bild plus, September 29.

Welt. 2016. "Schlechtestes Ergebnis während Merkels Kanzlerschaft." December 6. Available from https://www.welt.de/politik/deutschland/article160041837/Schlechtestes-Ergebnis-waehrend-Merkels-Kanzlerschaft.html.

Zalan, Eszter. 2016. "The Rise and Shine of Visegrad." *EUObserver*, December 30. Available from https://euobserver.com/europe-in-review/136044.

11

Theresa May's Leadership in Brexit Negotiations

Self-Representation and Media Evaluations

Sandra Eckert and Charlotte Galpin

11.1 Introduction

Theresa May entered the scene as prime minister (PM) at a moment of multiple crises. In June 2016, a narrow majority of UK voters opted to leave the EU in a referendum, and soon thereafter Prime Minister David Cameron announced his resignation. May rose to power thanks to her low profile during the referendum campaign, her success in presenting herself as a unity candidate, and her reputation as a competent politician, a "safe pair of hands" (Allen 2018: 108). Her task was to implement the Brexit agenda after the outcome of the UK's referendum on EU membership, while at the same time facing deep divisions in her party and a political crisis in her country. Having lost the Conservative Party's majority in the snap general election she called in June 2017, her success in Parliament was dependent on support from the strongly pro-Brexit Northern Irish Democratic Unionist Party (DUP) and the European Research Group (ERG), the hard-right and staunchly pro-Brexit wing of her party. She failed to achieve parliamentary support for her Brexit deal—the Withdrawal Agreement—negotiated with the EU, and her proposals for amendments were met with sharp criticism and rejection from EU leaders and domestic opponents. Following pressure from within her party, she eventually announced she would step down as PM and party leader.

Theresa May's tenure (July 13, 2016–July 24, 2019) offers the opportunity to explore women's leadership at times of crisis for the EU. One could easily jump to the conclusion that May's leadership in the Brexit process is a story of outright failure. This contribution takes a more nuanced view, drawing on gender and leadership studies. We seek to shed light on the type of leadership adopted by May in the Brexit negotiations as well as the ways in which her performance has been assessed

Sandra Eckert and Charlotte Galpin, *Theresa May's Leadership in Brexit Negotiations: Self-Representation and Media Evaluations*. In: *Women and Leadership in the European Union*. Edited by Henriette Müller and Ingeborg Tömmel, Oxford University Press. © Oxford University Press (2022). DOI: 10.1093/oso/9780192896216.003.0012

by addressing the following research questions: First, *how did Theresa May position herself as a leader?* And second, *how was her leadership portrayed and evaluated?*

To address these research questions, we conduct computer-assisted analysis of two sets of material: a corpus composed of Theresa May's speeches on Brexit, and a corpus of media coverage of May in the UK and Germany during her time in office. The chapter is structured as follows: We first develop a conceptual framework discussing concepts in gender and leadership studies to analyze May's role as a government leader during the Brexit negotiations, and explain how we operationalize these concepts when conducting the empirical analysis. We then address the first research question by looking at her official statements on Brexit during her premiership. The evaluation of her leadership is discussed based on our findings from the media corpus, which includes both quality newspapers and tabloids published in the UK and Germany. We argue that gender provides a crucial lens for understanding the ways in which Theresa May constructed her leadership and how her leadership performance was evaluated.

11.2　Women and Leadership: Type of Position and Gendered Evaluations

Women in power face two major challenges. First, women tend to occupy less promising leadership positions than their male counterparts, often taking over at times of crisis when there are fewer opportunities for success (Ryan and Haslam 2005). Second, the leadership of women is evaluated differently and less positively than that of men when they hold the same type of leadership position (Eagly et al. 1992). We first revisit the discussion about the type of leadership positions women tend to hold in politics, paying particular attention to the "glass cliff" metaphor. We then discuss how women holding political leadership positions are evaluated.

Think Crisis, Think Female? Facing the Glass Cliff

The metaphor of the glass cliff was coined by Ryan and Haslam (2005), who found that women were more likely to be appointed to head failing rather than successful companies. The authors' choice of metaphor for such precarious positions intentionally resonated with the already established terms "glass ceiling" and "glass escalator." While the glass cliff framing was developed for the corporate world, it can also be usefully applied to political leadership (Ryan et al. 2010). The glass cliff phenomenon emerges from particular gendered ideas about leadership that rest on traits associated with hegemonic masculinity (Connell 2005).

Generally speaking, evidence suggests that the uncertainty which prevails in moments of crisis leads organizations to assume new risks and try new things

(Boin and Hart 2003), as well as to signal that they are "undertaking change" (Ryan et al. 2016: 450). Lending power to women may thus become an option, also because some of the attributed feminine characteristics are thought to be assets in such a context (Eagly and Carli 2003). Ryan et al. (2011) have described this as the "think crisis–think female association," in contrast with the established "think manager–think male" association. Leadership in normal times, they find, is associated with traditionally masculine stereotypes. Here we identify two traditionally masculine types of leadership. Scholarship in international relations has drawn our attention to militarism as a leadership type, which celebrates traditionally masculine traits such as "heterosexuality, strength, power, autonomy, resilience, and competence" (Achilleos-Sarll and Martill 2019: 23). In this context, political leadership during Brexit is associated with militaristic notions of war and aggression (Achilleos-Sarll and Martill 2019: 23). Alternatively, masculine leadership is associated with "deal-making," suited to the neoliberal "business*man*'s world" in which "tough-talking business attitudes" and values such as individualism, rationality, and autonomy are prioritized (Achilleos-Sarll and Martill 2019: 21; Hooper 2000: 35).

Leadership during moments of crisis or failure, by contrast, has been associated with traditionally feminine traits such as understanding, modesty, and avoidance of controversy, but only in those cases where leaders were expected to manage a company through a crisis, stay in the background, or take responsibility for failure, rather than to act with agency and determination in making improvements (Ryan et al. 2011: 479). In short, women are expected to act "communally" and remain passive, while men are perceived and expected to have agency, pursue their interests, and behave confidently and dominantly (Hoyt and Murphy 2016: 388). In comparison to dealmaking and militarism, the expectations made of women imply a leadership style based on cooperation and responsiveness in which leaders demonstrate "feminine" traits such as behaving collectively and demonstrating understanding and strong communication skills (Ryan et al. 2011: 477). In view of such diverse images of leadership and expectations, the question is why women take on leadership positions during crises and how they present that leadership to others. Addressing the first part of that question, as Beckwith (2015) shows in her comparative analysis of female government leaders, women are particularly likely to accept leadership positions during crises due to the lack of opportunity to reach those positions during normal times.

As Henriette Müller highlights, political leaders also have to perform their leadership for the public (2020). Rhetoric is an important element of such self-representation, as Müller and Pamela Pansardi illustrate (see Chapter 7 in this volume). Women leaders are aware of the stereotypes they face and need to find ways to navigate them in how they behave and represent themselves—for example, in thinking about how much and what kind of emotion they can display without being penalized (Brescoll 2016: 420). As Brescoll notes, women in high-level leadership positions are aware they may be subject to greater scrutiny than men in similar positions and women in lower-level positions (2016: 421). Such scrutiny and the awareness of the existence of stereotypes may contribute to women leaders experiencing "stereotype threat," which may have particular consequences for how they behave in office. Hoyt and Murphy, for example, argue that women may try to separate their gender identity from their professional one or engage in reactive behavior such as consciously adopting a more masculine style (2016: 391). Such a process may contribute to the reconstruction of those very same gender stereotypes, but also result in women becoming particularly skilled leaders. As Müller and Pansardi find, women leaders are adept at "charismatic" leadership styles, which combine masculine, feminine, and gender-neutral traits. Our aim here is to contribute to the literature on women political leaders during crisis by seeking to understand how they themselves construct their leadership. Our second question addresses the issue of gendered evaluations of women leaders. Women in high-level political leadership roles not only tend to be subjected to unusually high levels of scrutiny, but the performance evaluations that result are likely to be based on gendered stereotypes.

Facing Gendered Discourse and Biased Evaluations

Exploring gendered discourse and biased evaluations of women in leadership positions can help us to understand why women often fail shortly after assuming such positions. Political leadership is "mediatized," in this case, through politicization in European public spheres (Müller 2020: 185). Scrutiny of women leaders during crises is likely to be particularly severe because, as Ryan et al. argue, "the co-occurrence of two relatively rare events—a crisis and the appointment of a female leader—may motivate observers with particular identity concerns to hone in on the correlation between the two" (2016: 447). It is with respect to these "illusory correlations" (Hamilton and Gifford 1976) that the type of position (research question 1) and biased evaluations (research question 2) connect.

Media coverage plays a crucial role in the gendered representation of women in leadership (Elliott and Stead 2017). Gender bias in coverage of women candidates is driven not just by the political institutional context but also by a media logic (Lühiste and Banducci 2016). Women leaders are subject to gendered stereotypes, negative reporting of their performance, and even misogynistic abuse. The perception of women in leadership positions tends to draw on specific stereotypes that depart from typical masculine attributes of leadership. Carole Elliott and Valerie Stead identify three stereotypes that are commonly applied to women leaders in media coverage: "queen bee," "iron maiden," and "selfless heroine" (2017: 351–352). The "queen bee" metaphor is used for women in senior positions who do not help or support their female colleagues. The "iron maiden" metaphor labels a woman in a leadership position who takes on masculine character traits. Former UK Prime Minister Margaret Thatcher is frequently portrayed as the incarnation of this type of leader. The "selfless heroine" draws on the stereotype of women as self-sacrificing and duty bound, associated with motherhood. Their effectiveness is perceived to be lower than that of men (Eagly et al. 1992). Moreover, women as non-prototypical leaders are more likely to be punished for mistakes (Brescoll et al. 2010). Women not only face harsh criticism; they are often taken less seriously and diminished on the grounds of their gender. News coverage, for instance, tends to focus on their appearance and attractiveness (Baxter 2017: 11). Byerly and Ross argue that there is a "patriarchal ideology" underpinning media coverage of women that results in women politicians often being undermined as serious actors by an excessive focus on their appearance (2006: 45). Mavin et al. (2018) argue that women political leaders are "tied to their bodies," which are then commodified, with the dual effect of making their bodies more visible but their leadership invisible.

Finally, there is the "differential treatment" of women and men in similar political roles, where men's decisions tend to be evaluated positively and women's negatively (Byerly and Ross 2006: 45). Feminist scholars note that women leaders often face a "double bind" in perceptions of their leadership (Brescoll 2016: 421; Hoyt and Murphy 2016: 388): on the one hand, they are judged on their ability to demonstrate masculine traits such as behaving dominantly or instrumentally; on the other hand, they then experience "backlash effects" as a result of demonstrating these very traits and for not conforming with societal gender norms associated with women, such as acting tactfully or humbly or for the benefit of all. Identical behavior by men and women leaders is evaluated more negatively for women because of the perception that they allow their emotions to influence their decisions, in contrast to men, who are presumed to be more rational (Brescoll 2016: 416–417). At the same time, women leaders who do not show emotion are often described as "cold" or calculating. Brescoll argues, however, that it is not the absence of emotion that is expected from leaders, but rather control over what kinds of emotions they show to ensure they are (perceived as) appropriate to the leadership context. Men, for example, are permitted to express emotions such as pride or anger, which demonstrate dominance, rather than sadness or fearfulness, which imply weakness (Brescoll 2016: 420). Such manifestations of differential treatment link back to the earlier discussion of the glass cliff. Ryan et al. found that there was a preference for women leaders only in those times of crisis when a scapegoat or a leader who would simply manage or "endure" the crisis was sought, while men were routinely preferred for leadership positions seen as needing more active, agentic qualities (2011: 479). This suggests that, when women leaders behave in proactive ways and show agency, they are likely to face a penalty in how they are evaluated.

Case Selection, Data Collection, Operationalization, and Method

The EU has faced a number of crises over the last decade, which provides an opportunity to investigate women's leadership at such moments. The case of Theresa May is a particularly intriguing one of a national leader facing both a domestic and an external crisis. Our case study covers aspects of May's self-representation, as well as media coverage of her leadership. This case selection is motivated by the fact that May's term in office coincided with an unprecedented political and constitutional crisis in the UK (Glencross 2016). The Brexit vote produced a political vacuum after the referendum as key (male) figures who had been involved in the campaign stepped back. May's subsequent assumption of the prime ministerial office in July 2016 has been described as exemplifying the glass cliff phenomenon (Hozić and True 2017). The shock of the Brexit referendum result, the installation of the UK's second woman PM, and her central role in the typically male-dominated domains of economic and foreign policy meant that she would be confronted with a particularly high level of scrutiny.

Our analysis of Theresa May's self-representation and evaluation draws on a corpus composed of 26 speeches she delivered on Brexit during her time in office, and a corpus of media coverage that comprises 256 news items. For the latter, we included four UK-based outlets including both tabloids and quality newspapers and Leave- and Remain-supporting outlets. We also included two German newspapers to understand how far and in what way gendered discourse was a phenomenon specific to the UK-based Brexit debate. While the UK press is known for its sexualized coverage of women politicians (Baxter 2017: 11), Angela Merkel has also been subject to gendered representations in the German press, most notoriously the label of "Mutti" (Mummy) (Mushaben 2017: 35). We extracted the news items via LexisNexis using the search terms "Theresa May" and "Brexit" with a minimum of four hits. For the UK, we analyzed *The Sun* (tabloid, Leave), *The Telegraph* (quality, Leave), *Daily Mirror* (tabloid, Remain), and *The Guardian* (quality, Remain). For Germany, we looked at *Bild* (largest-circulation tabloid) and *Süddeutsche Zeitung* (largest-circulation quality newspaper) (see Table 11.1).

We used the qualitative analysis software MAXQDA to conduct the corpus analysis. We established a coding scheme consisting of three parent codes, for leadership, performance evaluation, and gendered discourse (see Table 11.2). The subcodes for leadership integrate various ways to approach leadership. More specifically, we have coded whether May's leadership was discussed (by herself or in the media) as a means of providing a public service, capturing the expectation that women leaders serve the interests of the community; whether her leadership style was portrayed as cooperative and responsive, thus capturing expectations that women listen carefully and act collectively; and whether her exercise of leadership was associated with masculine leadership traits—again, either in the PM's self-representation or in media discourse—differentiating between the categories of

Table 11.1 Media corpus of UK and German newspapers

Country	Tabloids		Quality Newspapers	
UK	**Remain**	**Leave**	**Remain**	**Leave**
	Daily Mirror: 47	*The Sun*: 50	*The Guardian*: 45	*The Telegraph*: 67
Germany	*Bild*: 22		*Süddeutsche*: 25	
Sum	**119**		**137**	

Table 11.2 Coding scheme for leadership performance analysis

Leadership	Performance Evaluation	Gendered Discourse
Public service	Steady/Stubborn	Woman
Cooperative	Adaptation/Vicissitude	Daughter
Uncooperative	Control/Cold	Wife
Dealmaking	Empathy/Emotional	Motherhood
Militarism	Pride/Arrogance	Comparing women
	Modesty/Shame	Appearance
	Success/Failure	Chauvinism/Sexism

dealmaking and militarism. In our analysis of how leadership performance is eval-uated during glass cliff scenarios, we want to interrogate the "double bind" faced by women in such leadership positions who may be judged negatively regardless of whether they adopt so-called masculine or feminine leadership styles. To do this, we develop a set of evaluation subcodes that relate to particularly gendered leadership characteristics, such as rationality, dynamism, or pride (more likely to be associated with masculine leadership traits), and empathy, modesty, or stabil-ity (more likely to be associated with feminine leadership traits). Each of these characteristics can be framed in a positive (e.g., "steady") or negative way (e.g., "stubborn"), analysis of which may reveal particularly gendered forms of evalu-ation. We also want to understand when and under what circumstances overall performance is evaluated as either a success or a failure. Finally, the category on gendered discourse seeks to capture instances where a woman in a leadership po-sition is mainly portrayed in relation to her gender and her body, be it as a woman, a daughter, a wife, or a mother; in comparison to other women; or in relation to her appearance or sexuality.

11.3 Theresa May's Self-Representation as a Leader

Theresa May's premiership was dominated by the Brexit saga. We will focus on how the PM portrayed her leadership and to some extent include the ways in which she evaluated her leadership. Details of the coding results are reported in the appendices at the end of this chapter. We find that May framed her leadership as embodying both "masculine" and "feminine" attributes, specifically dealmaking and public service. In her self-representation, the PM mostly evaluated her performance and leadership style positively, describing herself as giving steady guidance and being in control of events, while also being able to adapt. Toward the end of her tenure, however, we will also see instances where she acknowledged her failure and expressed regret.

The Dealmaking Discourse

> That is why this government has a Plan for Britain. One that gets us the right deal abroad but also ensures we get a better deal for ordinary working people at home.
>
> (January 17, 2017)

Theresa May strongly engaged with one of the masculinity framings identified by Achilleos-Sarll and Martill (2019: 16). We find the dealmaking discourse in more than 70% of the speech corpus. Getting the "right deal" and the "best deal" (November 14, 2019, January 17, 2017) was the PM's key objective from the outset. Early on—during the first, pre-negotiation phase of her tenure—she showed her determination to choose, if necessary, no deal over a "bad deal for Britain" (November 21, 2017). This effort to demonstrate her compliance with the masculine norms of the businessman's world was arguably her biggest failure, insofar as it put the potentially catastrophic no-deal option on the table. Yet, in the course of negotiations, May was trying to deliver the deal that Brexit supporters had asked for. Metaphors of dealmaking and securing economic benefits for the UK are ubiquitous in her public speeches, reaching almost 80% during the second phase of her tenure, covering the period of substantive negotiations. May addressed the theme of Brexit's economic benefits throughout the process, referring to the generation of wealth and growth on numerous occasions. Her emphasis on the economic benefits to be gained from the UK's departure from the EU resonated with the legacy of the British attitude toward membership—one expressed mainly in terms of a cost–benefit analysis (Achilleos-Sarll and Martill 2019: 25; George 2000). In the third and final phase of her tenure, when she was seeking support for the Withdrawal Agreement, May insisted that she had reached "the best deal possible" as well as the "only deal on the table" (January 14, 2019) and the "very best deal" (March 8, 2019). She thus stood firm and sought to defend her deal as a choice without alternatives. It is in this respect that she frequently adjudged her own performance positively for providing steady leadership and being in control (steadiness in around 40% and control in around 20% of the speech corpus—see Appendix 11.1).

This assertiveness would be expected to invite mobilization of the "iron maiden" stereotype in media coverage (Elliott and Stead 2017: 351–352). By contrast, however, there was only one incident where May adopted a militaristic metaphor to address the Brexit process, when she deplored a political culture where "rigorous debate between political opponents is becoming more like a confrontation between enemies" (October 3, 2018). By eschewing the more adversarial language of much Brexit discourse and instead emphasizing her public duty throughout the three phases, May attempts to evade the double bind, trying to avoid criticism for being "too dominant" for her gender.

A Sense of Duty: Serving the Public

> Today, I want to talk about how—by working together—we can seize
> that opportunity and deliver the change that people want.
> (November 21, 2016)

While dealmaking features prominently in most of Theresa May's speeches, the public service frame is omnipresent, appearing in 89% to 100% of her speeches in each phase of her tenure. Moreover, she presents her leadership style predominantly as being cooperative and responsive, a point she emphasizes as frequently as her public duty (above 90%). In line with the emphasis May had put on delivering Brexit, she framed her major duty in her "job" as PM to "respond" to public and policy demands. This sense of duty links to the stereotype of the selfless heroine discussed earlier, but it was also often put into a biographical perspective in relation to her upbringing as a vicar's daughter. This construction of duty manifested in her commitment to deliver Brexit as the "democratic will of the British people" (October 9, 2017) and to implement the "changes people voted for" (March 8, 2019), stressing that the public "want us to get on with it" (January 17, 2017). Here she presented her task as PM in terms of the public duty to follow through with the referendum decision, as she also declared to the Conservative Party conference: "Leadership is doing what you believe to be right and having the courage and determination to see it through. That is the approach I have taken on Brexit" (October 3, 2018). Toward the end of her tenure, when she was struggling to achieve the necessary support in Parliament for her deal, she warned that if MPs failed to back it they would be "betraying the vote of the British people" (January 14, 2019). As noted above, women in glass cliff situations are often expected to simply see through a crisis while staying in the background rather than acting with agency, and indeed May constructed the necessity of delivering Brexit as part of her broader public and democratic duty in office.

Women in leadership positions are also expected to act communally, and often penalized when perceived as acting in their own interests. May constructed an especially wide sense of public duty—as she put it in her final speech, "the unique privilege of this office is to use this platform to give a voice to the voiceless, to fight the burning injustices that still scar our society" (July 24, 2019). In particular, she attached her leadership to the left-behind narrative of the referendum and the duty to ensure the country's future prosperity, stressing, for example that there is a "need to do more to respond to the concerns of those who feel that the modern world has left them behind" (January 19, 2017). She presented herself in something of a motherly or nurturing role, referring often to providing leadership and positive results for the "country's children and grandchildren" (January 17, 2017). She also stressed a protective element to her responsibility as leader, such as in the domain of security: "ensuring the safety and security of our people" (July 8, 2019). She spoke about her leadership mainly with reference to "the government I lead" or with reference to a group ("we," "the party," etc.; see, e.g., October 3, 2018); directly addressing the British public, for instance, she asserted, "we will do everything we can to give you more control over your lives" (July 13, 2016). In line with the glass cliff scenario of women leaders needing to bring people together, but also surely aware of the need to overcome the divisions in her party, May often emphasized her desire to unify, to "help our country move beyond the division of the referendum and into a better future" (May 21, 2019). Finally, near the end of her tenure, she presented her efforts to secure support for her deal as "selfless," stressing, for example, that "I sought the changes MPs demanded. I offered to give up the job I love earlier than I would like" (May 21, 2019). It is also with respect to her sense of duty that May, in her last speech as PM, expressed "deep regret" that she did not deliver a Brexit deal (July 24, 2019) and thus evaluated her own performance negatively.

In conclusion, our analysis of the speech corpus illustrates the PM's efforts to stand firm and provide leadership in a setting that reflects the so-called glass cliff phenomenon (Hozić and True 2017). Overall, we find that Theresa May adopted traditionally "feminine" leadership attributes, especially in her emphasis on public duty and cooperation. Additionally, she employed the neoliberal masculine "dealmaking" discourse identified by Achilleos-Sarll and Martil, framing her leadership within the context of business deals. At the same time, however, we find that she mostly avoided the militaristic framing utilized by many of her male party colleagues.

11.4 Leadership, Gendered Discourse, and Performance Evaluation in Media Coverage

The composition of the media corpus allowed us to check for patterns of variation. We could not detect clear differences between the tabloids and quality newspapers in terms of gendered discourse, proving our initial assumptions wrong. We find that the tabloids evaluated Theresa May's performance more negatively than did the quality newspapers, but the difference is again not particularly great. We do, however, find other differences: first, between Remain and Leave newspapers in the UK; second, between UK and German newspapers. In what follows, we first discuss the leadership and performance evaluation parent codes, and then move on to gendered discourse.

Images of Leadership and Its Evaluation

We find that media coverage of Theresa May's leadership portrayed her role in the UK government as a prime example of a glass cliff moment, for instance in the *Süddeutsche Zeitung* (15 October 2018), where it was argued that no matter what kind of Brexit deal she managed to strike, she would have a hard time getting Parliament to accept it. Similarly, it was argued in *The Guardian* (February 7, 2018) that May faced an almost impossible task in her effort to act as "an honest neutral" between Remain and Leave supporters. In accordance with glass cliff expectations, our findings indicate that Theresa May was subject to harsh scrutiny, as negative evaluations prevail in several dimensions, "shame" and "failure" in particular.

Media coverage frequently referred to Theresa May's duty to deliver on the Brexit vote, and thus framed her leadership in terms of public service. This code, alongside militarism, was most frequent across the newspaper corpus. It is important to note, however, that this framing could appear either in the form of an acknowledgment that May was making every effort to deliver Brexit—here the code links to positive evaluation codes such as "steady," "control," and "success"—or an assessment that she was failing to do so, thus linking to the negative analogues of those evaluation codes. The mixed assessment of her leadership is most apparent when we consider the results for the cooperative versus uncooperative subcodes. While the latter is more frequent, especially in the Remain and German news coverage, there is also recognition that the PM had made an effort to seek consensus. The two facets of masculinity discourse are most pronounced in the Leave newspapers, yet all of the analyzed newspapers depict May's leadership in terms of dealmaking and militarism to a significant extent. For instance, we find the militarism discourse in the *Süddeutsche Zeitung*, with the headline "Retreat of the Troops" over a report about the Tories' in-fighting (June 21, 2018). This framing, however, was mainly drawn from press coverage in the UK tabloids on which the article reports, suggesting a transnational dimension to gendered leadership evaluation. Another example is the reference made to Johnson's comment on May's Brexit negotiations in the *Mail on Sunday* where he argued that with her Brexit plan Theresa May had "wrapped a suicide vest" around the British constitution and "handed the detonator" to Brussels, on which the *Süddeutsche* reported (September 11, 2018). The UK tabloids, in particular, used clearly militaristic metaphors, for instance when a columnist for *The Sun* opined that "a hasty execution would trigger a leadership bloodbath and likely defeat in a consequent election" (June 12, 2017).

Finally, the aspect of the PM's last statement at No. 10 Downing Street that attracted the most attention was her tears as she spoke her final line, referencing her decision to leave office: "I do so with no ill will, but with enormous and enduring gratitude to have had the opportunity to serve the country I love" (July 24, 2019). Rather than engaging substantively with the departing leader's account of her premiership, the tabloids took issue with her display of emotion. Parallels were drawn with her female predecessor—Margaret Thatcher—who had also been tearful when leaving No. 10. Moreover, the prime minister's husband, Philip May, was depicted as having played a crucial role in her decision to step down, as a headline in the free weekly newspaper *Metro* insinuated: "Just Tell Her Phil" (May 24, 2019). In his *Guardian* commentary on the media echo around May's final speech, Stefan Stern observed: "This image of the apparently broken, tearful female prime minister seemed to be demanded by the macho Westminster village, and now it has been granted" (May 25, 2019). Similarly, Sarah Shaffy, in her weblog *The Stylist*, wondered, "How many column inches and internet think pieces will be devoted to that show of emotion at the expense of the other things she said? And how much of that coverage will contain thinly veiled sexist attitudes about a woman crying at work?" (May 24, 2019). Theresa May had mastered her emotions throughout her tenure—reflected by the extent to which she was portrayed as "cold" in a negative sense (see subcode "cold" in Appendix 11.2)—yet she will also be remembered for this last, tearful moment.

Gendered Discourse

We find that Theresa May's leadership is discussed in gendered terms, but there are clear differences between the Remain, Leave, and German newspapers. We find few instances of outright chauvinism involving sexualization of May (and most of those are from the German newspapers), but many of subtle forms of sexism that draw attention to her gender. While Remain newspapers used gendered discourse in just under one-quarter of their articles, more than 50% of the Leave newspapers' items engaged in such discourse. Of the gendered codes in the Remain sample, over half involved comparing her with other women, mostly Margaret Thatcher. The obvious comparison of May with her lone female predecessor is a quintessential example of gendered reporting. *The Guardian* columnist Hadley Freeman commented on this tendency: "women are such rare creatures that they can only be understood through the prism of one another, like unicorns or sporting triumphs by the England football team" (May 23, 2016). The comparison often related to Thatcher's demise at the hands of her party or was used to contrast with and criticize May's supposed vicissitude: "Mrs May Has Done a U-Turn Mrs Thatcher Would Have Despised" (*Daily Mirror*, April 19, 2019). The comparison with Thatcher is particularly appealing as it facilitates deployment of the "iron maiden" stereotype. Sharing his views about various Conservative leadership candidates with former cabinet minister Malcolm Rifkin on Sky News, Tory grandee Ken Clarke referred to May as "a bloody difficult woman, but you and I both worked for Margaret Thatcher!" (August 31, 2016). Just under one-quarter of our media items drew direct attention to the PM as a woman, at times in derogatory terms, such as an item in the *Daily Mirror* that proclaimed, "It seems this woman just cannot stop telling lies" (September 4, 2017).

In the Leave sample, one-third of the gendered codes involved making May's gender explicit by focusing on her as a woman—for example, contrasting her with her male colleagues, the "boys," who had not been willing to face the double challenge of a disunited party and Brexit. One-fifth involved comparisons with other women, often Thatcher, but also Angela Merkel. Another one-fifth drew attention to her appearance by describing her clothing. The way in which *The Sun* and *The Telegraph* reported about Theresa May's appointment as PM is revealing in several respects. Their choice of pictures, specifically of the new PM's leopard-print shoes, is emblematic of their focus on her attire and appearance. Some articles simply described her passion for fancy shoes or her outfits, while others used her clothing to build metaphors—"Theresa May Scraped Home by the Skin of her Leopard-Print Heels" (*The Sun*, September 3, 2017)—compare her clothes with those of other women leaders, such as Merkel (*The Telegraph*, April 11, 2019), or mock her movements, such as with the infamous video of her dancing in Africa (*The Telegraph*, May 25, 2019). The most striking example of sexualization occurred when the *Daily Mail* in March 2017 published the headline "Never Mind Brexit, Who Won Legs-it!" The headline compared Scotland's First Minister, Nicola Sturgeon, and May, sexualizing and infantilizing them through a focus on their bodies in relation to each other (Mavin et al. 2018). This disturbing emphasis on the appearance of two women in power triggered strong reactions in social media and was referred to throughout our corpus. The focus on appearance and attire is a classic trope in the media coverage of women leaders (Elliott and Stead 2017: 349), and is not specific to the UK press. We also found that German newspapers used gendered discourse, most commonly—comprising almost one-third of the codes—by mentioning her appearance. Most of these references were in *Bild* and mention her shoes or clothing, while several overlap with the chauvinism subcode in which she was sexualized by reference to her legs (two articles mention the *Daily Mail* "Legs-it" article). Overall, while explicitly sexualized representations of May were relatively rare, we nevertheless find that she was portrayed in a variety of gendered and negative—albeit more subtle—ways.

11.5 Conclusions

Theresa May is likely to be remembered as PM for at least three reasons: first, for being the UK's second woman PM; second, as one of the shortest-serving government leaders; and, third, as the leader who failed to deliver Brexit. We have approached this particularly intriguing case of a woman holding a leadership position at a time of crisis from a gender perspective, examining May's self-representation and media evaluations of her leadership. We find that May preempted gendered expectations of her, through a focus in her public discourse on her steady leadership, her commitment to public duty, and her stated desire to overcome divisions. Yet, while eschewing the sometimes militaristic discourse of the referendum campaign, she also constructed her leadership in masculine terms, using the language of business-world dealmaking to assert her toughness in the Brexit negotiations. In so doing, May tried to square the circle in order to be seen as playing a caring and communal role while at the same time displaying strong leadership in masculine terms.

Such balancing acts by women leaders have been associated with successful leadership (see Chapter 7 in this volume). For May, however, it did not save her from gendered evaluations in the media, nor help her to achieve her primary objective of delivering Brexit. As the glass cliff concept suggests, women leaders tend to come to power when opportunities for success are low. In many respects, Brexit was an impossible task, with incompatible promises made by both sides during the referendum campaign resulting in ambiguity over its meaning. The polarized and adversarial state of Parliament and the deeply divided Conservative Party further cemented a context antithetical to the building of consensus (McConnell and Tormey 2020).

Despite this context, the failure to deliver Brexit during May's tenure has been described by many as a personal failure of her leadership. She is charged with having taken "risky" decisions such as calling a general election, adopting a "hardline" interpretation of Brexit, and succumbing to a strategic misunderstanding of the EU (McConnell and Tormey 2020). We argue, however, that May's failure cannot be fully understood without consideration of the gendered nature of the evaluations of her leadership. In fact, we might question whether similar decisions by a male leader would have been described in similar ways. Our analysis of media evaluations demonstrates this crucial gender dimension. Though May herself largely avoided militaristic language in discussing the Brexit negotiations, the newspapers did not, with her leadership frequently described in the language of war and defeat. While she was, at least for a time, evaluated in the Leave-supporting press as "steady" and "in control," elsewhere she was depicted as "unreliable" and "cold." Reflecting the double bind facing women leaders, she was criticized both as too weak and timid, and as too stubborn and inflexible. While explicitly chauvinist language was uncommon in the press, attention was frequently drawn to her appearance and she was often compared to other women leaders, not least Margaret Thatcher and Angela Merkel. While no firm conclusions can be made about the gendered evaluation of women leaders across the EU, our German data indicates that gendered discourse and evaluations emerge in media coverage of women leaders outside the UK as well. Overall, we find that May's leadership was constructed both by her and in the media in gendered terms, and that this contributed to the perception of her failure in the glass cliff moment.

References

Achilleos-Sarll, Columba, and Benjamin Martill. 2019. "Toxic Masculinity: Militarism, Deal-Making and the Performance of Brexit." In *Gender and Queer Perspectives on Brexit*, eds. Moira Dustin, Nuno Ferreira, and Susan Millns, 15–44. Cham: Palgrave Macmillan.

Allen, Nicholas. 2018. "'Brexit Means Brexit': Theresa May and Post-Referendum British Politics." *British Politics* 13 (1): 105–120.

Baxter, Judith. 2017. *Women Leaders and Gender Stereotyping in the UK Press: A Poststructuralist Approach* [online version]. Cham: Palgrave Macmillan.

Beckwith, Karen. 2015. "Before Prime Minister: Margaret Thatcher, Angela Merkel, and Gendered Party Leadership Contests." *Politics & Gender* 11 (4): 718–745.

Boin, Arjen, and Paul 't Hart. 2003. "Public Leadership in Times of Crisis: Mission Impossible?" *Public Administration Review* 63 (5): 544–553.

Brescoll, Victoria L. 2016. "Leading with Their Hearts? How Gender Stereotypes of Emotion Lead to Biased Evaluations of Female Leaders." *Leadership Quarterly* 27 (3): 415–428.

Brescoll, Victoria L., Erica Dawson, and Eric Luis Uhlmann. 2010. "Hard Won and Easily Lost: The Fragile Status of Leaders in Gender-Stereotype-Incongruent Occupations." *Psychological Science* 21 (11): 1640–1642.

Byerly, Carolyn M., and Karen Ross. 2006. *Women and Media: A Critical Introduction*. London: Blackwell.

Connell, R. W. 2005. *Masculinities*. 2nd ed. Cambridge, UK: Polity.

Eagly, Alice H., and Linda L. Carli. 2003. "The Female Leadership Advantage: An Evaluation of the Evidence." *Leadership Quarterly* 14 (6): 807–834.

Eagly, Alice H., Mona G. Makhijani, and Bruce G. Klonsky. 1992. "Gender and the Evaluation of Leaders: A Meta-Analysis." *Psychological Bulletin* 111 (1): 3–22.

Elliott, Carole, and Valerie Stead. 2017. "The Effect of Media on Women and Leadership." In *Handbook of Research on Gender and Leadership*, ed. Susan Madsen, 344–358. Cheltenham, UK: Edward Elgar Publishing.

George, Stephen. 2000. "Britain: Anatomy of a Eurosceptic State." *Journal of European Integration* 22 (1): 15–33.

Glencross, Andrew. 2016. *Why the UK Voted for Brexit*. London: Palgrave Macmillan.

Hamilton, David L., and Robert K. Gifford. 1976. "Illusory Correlation in Interpersonal Perception: A Cognitive Basis of Stereotypic Judgments." *Journal of Experimental Social Psychology* 12 (4): 392–407.

Hooper, Charlotte. 2000. "Disembodiment, Embodiment and the Construction of Hegemonic Masculinity." In *Political Economy, Power and the Body: Global Perspectives*, ed. Gillian Youngs, 31–51. Basingstoke, UK: Macmillan.

Hoyt, Crystal L., and Susan E. Murphy. 2016. "Managing to Clear the Air: Stereotype Threat, Women, and Leadership." *Leadership Quarterly* 27 (3): 387–399.

Hozić, Aida A., and Jacqui True. 2017. "Brexit as a Scandal: Gender and Global Trumpism." *Review of International Political Economy* 24 (2): 270–287.

Lühiste, Maarja, and Susan Banducci. 2016. "Invisible Women? Comparing Candidates' News Coverage in Europe." *Politics & Gender* 12: 223–253.

McConnell, Allan, and Simon Tormey. 2020. "Explanations for the Brexit Policy Fiasco: Near-Impossible Challenge, Leadership Failure or Westminster Pathology?" *Journal of European Public Policy* 27 (5): 685–702.

Mavin, Sharon, Carole Elliott, Valerie Stead, and Jannine Williams. 2018. "Economies of Visibility as a Moderator of Feminism: 'Never Mind Brexit. Who Won Legs-it!'" *Gender, Work & Organization* 26 (8): 1156–1175.

Müller, Henriette. 2020. *Political Leadership and the European Commission Presidency*. Oxford: Oxford University Press.

Mushaben, Joyce Marie. 2017. *Becoming Madam Chancellor: Angela Merkel and the Berlin Republic*. Cambridge, UK: Cambridge University Press.

Ryan, Michelle K., and S. Alexander Haslam. 2005. "The Glass Cliff: Evidence That Women Are Over-Represented in Precarious Leadership Positions." *British Journal of Management* 16 (2): 81–90.

Ryan, Michelle K., S. Alexander Haslam, Mette D. Hersby, and Renata Bongiorno. 2011. "Think Crisis–Think Female: The Glass Cliff and Contextual Variation in the Think Manager–Think Male Stereotype." *Journal of Applied Psychology* 96 (3): 470–484.

Ryan, Michelle K., S. Alexander Haslam, and Clara Kulich. 2010. "Politics and the Glass Cliff: Evidence That Women Are Preferentially Selected to Contest Hard-to-Win Seats." *Psychology of Women Quarterly* 34 (1): 56–64.

Ryan, Michelle K., S. Alexander Haslam, Thekla Morgenroth, Floor Rink, Janka Stoker, and Kim Peters. 2016. "Getting on Top of the Glass Cliff: Reviewing a Decade of Evidence, Explanations, and Impact." *Leadership Quarterly* 27 (3): 446–455.

Coding Results of the Speech Corpus

Code	Subcode	Dimension	no. [%] I	no. [%] II	no. [%] III	∑ [%]
Leadership						
	Public service		6 [100]	8 [88.9]	10 [90.9]	**24 [92.3]**
	Cooperative		6 [100]	9 [100]	9 [81.8]	**24 [92.3]**
	Uncooperative		1 [16.7]	0	1 [9.1]	**2 [7.7]**
	Dealmaking		4 [66.7]	7 [77.8]	8 [72.7]	**19 [73.1]**
	Militarism		0	1 [11.1]	0	**1 [3.8]**
Performance evaluation						
	Steady/Stubborn					
		positive	0	4 [44.4]	6 [54.5]	**10 [38.5]**
		negative	0	0	0	**0**
	Adaptation/Vicissitude					
		positive	1 [16.7]	0	2 [18.2]	**3 [11.5]**
		negative	0	0	0	**0**
	Control/Cold					
		positive	1 [16.7]	5 [55.6]	0	**6 [23.1]**
		negative	0	0	0	**0**
	Empathy/Emotional					
		positive	0	0	1 [9.1]	**1 [3.8]**
		negative	0	0	0	**0**
	Pride/Arrogance					
		positive	0	2 [22.2]	2 [18.2]	**4 [15.4]**
		negative	0	0	0	**0**
	Modesty/Shame					
		positive	0	0	2 [18.2]	**2 [7.7]**
		negative	0	0	1 [9.1]	**1 [3.8]**
	Success/Failure					
		positive	0	0	0	**0**
		negative	0	0	1 [9.1]	**1 [3.8]**
∑ documents [%]			6 [100]	9 [100]	11 [100]	26 [100]

Phase I: July 13, 2016 (May takes office) through June 18, 2017 (eve of Brexit negotiations); phase II: June 19, 2017–November 13, 2018 (negotiations); phase III: November 14, 2018 (Brexit withdrawal agreement) through July 24, 2019 (May steps down); note that the codes have been counted once per document; the figures in square brackets reflect the relative importance of the code as a percentage of the speeches in each respective phase.

Coding Results
of the Media Coverage Corpus

Code	Subcode	Dimension	no. [%] Remain	no. [%] Leave	no. [%] German	no [%] ∑
Leadership						
	Public service		16 [17.4]	46 [39.3]	7 [14.9]	**69 [27]**
	Cooperative		7 [8.7]	15 [12.8]	10 [21.3]	**33 [12.9]**
	Uncooperative		24 [26.1]	14 [12.0]	9 [19.1]	**47 [18.4]**
	Dealmaking		10 [10.9]	25 [21.4]	15 [31.9]	**50 [19.5]**
	Militarism		16 [17.4]	44 [37.6]	9 [19.1]	**69 [27]**
Performance evaluation						
	Steady/Stubborn					
		positive	5 [5.4]	32 [27.4]	4 [8.5]	**41 [16]**
		negative	20 [21.7]	31 [26.5]	14 [29.8]	**65 [25.4]**
	Adaptation/Vicissitude					
		positive	5 [5.4]	13 [11.1]	2 [4.3]	**20 [7.8]**
		negative	23 [25]	49 [4.9]	12 [25.5]	**84 [32.8]**
	Control/Cold					
		positive	4 [4.3]	11 [9.4]	4 [8.5]	**18 [7.4]**
		negative	11 [12]	16 [13.7]	5 [10.6]	**31 [12.5]**
	Empathy/Emotional					
		positive	0	6 [5.1]	2 [4.3]	**8 [3.1]**
		negative	8 [8.7]	9 [7.7]	2 [4.3]	**19 [7.4]**
	Pride/Arrogance					
		positive	1 [1.1]	11 [9.4]	1 [2.1]	**13 [5.1]**
		negative	14 [15.2]	15 [12.8]	5 [10.6]	**34 [13.3]**
	Modesty/Shame					
		positive	0	3 [2.6]	15 [31.9]	**3 [1.2]**
		negative	46 [50]	51 [43.6]	0	**112 [43.8]**
	Success/Failure					
		positive	2 [2.2]	21 [71.9]	2 [4.3]	**25 [9.8]**
		negative	47 [51.1]	51 [43.6]	26 [55.3]	**124 [48.4]**
Gendered discourse						
	Woman		5 [5.4]	20 [17.1]	3 [6.4]	**28 [10.9]**
	Daughter		0	5 [4.3]	2 [4.3]	**7 [2.7]**
	Wife		3 [3.3]	9 [7.7]	3 [6.4]	**15 [5.8]**
	Motherhood		1 [1.1]	1 [0.9]	1 [2.1]	**3 [1.2]**
	Comparing women		12 [13.04]	12 [10.3]	5 [10.6]	**29 [11.3]**
	Appearance		0	13 [11.1]	7 [14.9]	**20 [7.8]**
	Chauvinism/Sexism		1 [1.1]	1 [0.9]	3 [6.4]	**5 [2]**
	∑ gendered discourse		22 [23.9]	61 [52]	24 [51]	**107 [41.8]**
∑ documents [%]			**92**	**117**	**47**	**256 [100]**

Note that the codes have been counted once per document; the figures in square brackets reflect the relative importance of the code as a percentage of the articles in each group.

PART V
EXERCISING ADMINISTRATIVE LEADERSHIP

12

A Tightrope Walk?

Catherine Day and the Interplay of Political and Administrative Leadership in the European Commission

Ingeborg Tömmel

12.1 Introduction

In 2005, after a swift rise within the Brussels civil service, Catherine Day took office as secretary general of the European Commission. She was the first woman to hold this highest position in the Commission bureaucracy and, by all accounts, she excelled in it. Nicknamed "Catherine Night and Day," she innovated decision-making procedures, enhanced policy coordination, defined priorities and work programs, collaborated closely with the president, and built consensus across the Commission and beyond. In short, she engaged in managing the services, shaping the agenda, and mediating in different institutional settings.

Research on Day's performance as chief civil servant and leading figure in Commission policymaking is largely lacking. In contrast to the abundant studies on the European Commission, its civil service has hardly attracted attention. Yet recently, a number of detailed analyses have yielded valuable insights into the structure, procedures of decision-making, preference formation, performance, self-perception, and "mission" of the Commission's bureaucracy (Ellinas and Suleiman 2012; Hartlapp et al. 2014; Kassim et al. 2013; Hooghe 2001, 2012; Trondal 2010; Wille 2013). Further scholarship has focused on the reorganization of the Commission after the Santer resignation in 1999, the so-called Kinnock reforms (Kassim 2004, 2008; Stevens and Stevens 2006; Bauer 2007; Peterson 2008; Schön-Quinlivan 2011; Kassim et al. 2013).

Despite this rich literature, systematic research into the leadership of high-level administrators in the EU and especially their cooperation with political leaders remains scarce (yet see Smeets and Beach 2020). Female administrative leaders in the Union, in particular, have largely been ignored in scholarly research. This focuses attention on Catherine Day, a pioneer in women's leadership at the EU's administrative top.

Ingeborg Tömmel, *A Tightrope Walk? Catherine Day and the Interplay of Political and Administrative Leadership in the European Commission*. In: *Women and Leadership in the European Union*. Edited by Henriette Müller and Ingeborg Tömmel, Oxford University Press. © Oxford University Press (2022). DOI: 10.1093/oso/9780192896216.003.0013

Day's tenure as secretary general largely coincided with José Manuel Barroso's ten-year-long Commission presidency. Barroso, though generally considered a weak president (Dinan 2010; Müller 2020), managed to 'presidentialize' the office, particularly by "convert[ing] the Secretariat General into a personal office of the Presidency" (Kassim et al. 2016: 660; see also Kassim et al. 2013: 176–179; Peterson 2008). While Kassim and his coauthors ascribe this and related achievements to Barroso, this chapter raises the question, first, of whether it was instead Catherine Day who converted the Secretariat General (SecGen) into such an office. Second and more broadly, it examines how and to what extent Day provided leadership in the high-profile administrative and political functions of her office.

The chapter is organized as follows: Drawing on leadership theory, it elaborates a conceptual framework for analyzing the leadership of the Commission's chief administrator. The empirical part first provides an overview of Day's career path and her ascendance to positional leadership. It then analyzes Day's behavioral leadership in three steps: first, her strategies in managing and reforming the Commission's civil service; second, her role in shaping the Commission agenda and her relationship with the president; and, third, her performance as mediator in intra- and interinstitutional settings. The chapter concludes that Day skillfully performed the three functions of her office and succeeded in centralizing leadership at the heart of the Commission.

The study is based on qualitative research methods, drawing mainly on primary sources and a series of semi-structured expert interviews with Catherine Day (Interviews Day 1–4) and EU officials (Interviews EU 1–4). In addition, it draws on interviews held with Commission officials by Henriette Müller in her research on President Barroso (Interviews EC 3, 9, and 11; Müller 2020: Appendix 2) and two publicly available interviews with Day (Interviews Euractiv and Elvert) (for a list of all interviews see Appendix 12.1 to this chapter).

12.2 Leadership of the Commission's Secretary General

Leadership is generally conceptualized as a relationship between leaders and followers. According to Burns (1978: 18), leadership is exercised "when persons with certain motives and purposes mobilize ... institutional, political, psychological, and other resources so as to arouse, engage, and satisfy the motives of followers." Similarly, Nye (2008: 19) defines leadership as "the power to orient and mobilize others for a purpose." Hence, leadership is a reciprocal process between leaders and followers (Chapter 1 in this volume).

Leadership in administrative organizations has, in principle, the same characteristics as political leadership, and "leadership skills truly do matter in improving the performance of public sector organizations" (Orazi et al. 2013: 487). This is especially the case in modern political systems, as the roles of political leaders and administrators are converging, "reflecting ... a 'politicization' of bureau-cracies and a 'bureaucratization' of politics" (Aberbach et al. 1981: 49). Indeed, "elected officials and administrators join together in the common pursuit of sound governance" (Svara 2001: 179).

Yet certain differences are also at play. In a public administration context, lead-ers "coexist collectively" and leadership is always exercised in collaboration with others, that is, "different leaders interact in complementarity at different lev-els" (Lemay 2009: 1). Furthermore, administrators and politicians complement each other in their actions. Such "complementarity entails ongoing interaction, reciprocal influence, and mutual deference between elected officials and admin-istrators" (Svara 2001: 180). The responsibilities of political and administrative leaders are reciprocal, as "one needs the other to function, especially strategi-cally" (Lemay 2009: 2). Acting strategically implies that administrative leaders perform political functions to an extent, albeit always in collaboration with polit-ical leaders (e.g., Peters 2001). Yet administrative leaders do not and should not perform as entrepreneurial leaders, as they are not democratically accountable (Terry 1998).

Scholars generally agree that leaders act within a framework of institutional as well as situational opportunities or resources and constraints (e.g., Blondel 1987; Elgie 1995). Accordingly, they theorize that the interplay between the institutional setting, situational factors, and the personal capacities of officeholders determines their performance as leaders (for the EU, see Endo 1999; Tömmel 2013, 2020; Müller 2020).

The European Commission is an organization where political and administra-tive functions are exercised in a highly conflated way. More than do the analogous branches of national governments, the Commission's political representatives (the president, the commissioners, and their cabinets) and its civil service (the SecGen and the DGs) engage in both these functions. This Janus face of the Commission is closely linked to its core responsibility in the EU system: its nearly exclusive right to propose legislation and act as motor of integration. Fulfilling this responsibility requires making political choices, yet not in the sense of partisan politics (Tömmel 2020). Rather, such choices "result" from a continuous process of deliberation on and mediation between different views and options, in pursuit of the common good of the Union as a whole (Bauer and Ege 2013; Ellinas and Suleiman 2012; Hartlapp et al. 2014; Nugent and Rhinard 2019; Trondal 2010). The Commission administration is not only closely involved in this process of priority setting, strate-gic planning, and policy formulation, but often initiates these activities and thus plays a crucial political role.

The Secretariat General is a unique institution at the interface between the po-litical and administrative levels of the Commission. "It provides administrative support to the College, offers a channel for two-way communication between the Commissioners and the services, and oversees interdepartmental coordination"

(Kassim 2006: 75). Furthermore, it may advocate Commission proposals in the other EU institutions.

The secretary general, as the head of the SecGen, is "the Commission's most senior official" and, hence, "the captain on the ship" (Hooghe and Rauh 2016: 196). The incumbent performs three substantial functions, which roughly correspond to the leadership functions of Commission presidents (Kassim et al. 2013: 164; Müller 2020): managing the services, shaping the Commission agenda, and mediating conflicting views and positions.[1] Managing the services involves structuring and guiding intra- and interinstitutional decision-making. Shaping the Commission agenda encompasses launching policy proposals and providing advice across the Commission's administrative and political levels. Mediating conflicting views refers to the Commission's internal decision-making and, less directly, that of the legislative bodies. In view of this multifaceted role, the officeholder is positioned to exercise leadership, yet not as policy entrepreneur, but rather by strategically collaborating with all parties involved "in pursuit of sound governance" (Svara 2001: 179).

The most important institutional resources of the secretary general stem from its position at the interface between the political and administrative levels of the Commission, providing opportunities to leverage the strengths of both these levels. Major institutional constraints follow from the mismatch between a surfeit of heterogeneous tasks and the limited size of the SecGen as a support structure.

A preeminent situational opportunity for Day's tenure was Barroso's ten-year presidency, providing continuity in the relationship with the president and the Commission's political level. The situational constraints of her office were manifold: first, after enlargement, a much bigger and more heterogeneous College of Commissioners and, consequently, more fragmented portfolios (Hooghe and Rauh 2016); second, in the wake of the Kinnock reforms, a completely overhauled and frustrated Commission administration (Bauer 2007; Kassim 2004, 2008; Schön-Quinlivan 2011); third, following the Lisbon Treaty, a more powerful European Council and a more assertive European Parliament (EP); and, fourth, particularly during the financial crisis, the assumption of proactive leadership by the European Council at the Commission's expense (Bickerton et al. 2015).

The personal capacities or resources of a secretary general, besides those of any leader, should include working experience in high-level offices, a deep understanding of European policies and governance, and clear views regarding the Commission's function in the EU. The officeholder's leadership style should be authoritative but also cooperative and collaborative. Major constraints may follow from these clashing requirements of the office. Female incumbents may face particular constraints resulting from contradictory expectations: of a "masculine"

---

[1] The Commission has also a supervising function in policy implementation that is not at issue here.

leadership style in view of the position, of a "feminine" one in view of their sex (see Chapter 1 in this volume).

12.3 Catherine Day: Ascending to Positional Leadership

Catherine Day has spent most of her career in the Commission, in both political and administrative positions (Interviews Day 1 and Elvert). After having earned in 1974 a master's in international economics and trade, she held professional affiliations in Ireland for a few years. In 1979, she joined the Commission as an officer in DG III (now DG MARKT). From 1982 to 1996, she served successively in the cabinets of Richard Burke, Peter Sutherland, and Sir Leon Brittan; in her last year with Brittan, she was deputy head of cabinet. From 1996 to 2005, she moved to the positions first of director, then deputy director general, and finally director general in DGs External Relations and Environment, respectively. In sum, she served in high-level political and administrative Commission offices and accumulated a wealth of experience across policy areas and sectors.

Day's career evolved through a process of path dependency, as promotions to higher positions followed prior qualifications and merits. For her first job with the Commission, her degree in international economics was important. It was also an asset for her move to Burke's cabinet, where she was the only economist. Her work there on state aid and infringement procedures recommended her for a position in the cabinet of Sutherland, then commissioner for competition. Subsequently Brittan, as commissioner for competition and then trade, needed an expert in competition matters; he also involved her in the preparations for Eastern enlargement. This latter area then constituted a stepping stone for her ascent, in 1996, to the position of director in DG External Relations, first, for the non-accession states of Europe, then for enlargement and pre-accession. In 2000, Chris Patten, Commissioner for External Relations, nominated Day as deputy director general, responsible for the non-accession states. Finally, her success in high-level offices qualified Day for the move to Wallström's DG Environment as director general (2002). Remarkably, except for her initial affiliations, Day has been promoted by her superiors to higher offices, often against her expectations (Interview Elvert). Remarkably, too, most of Day's responsibilities were in positions and policy areas that are generally considered "masculine" preserves.

Yet Day's seemingly straightforward career also involved deep changes. Experiencing these changes was pivotal for the evolution of her leadership qualities in substantial and managerial terms. Switching between administrative and political positions was instructive. In the cabinets of commissioners, "you see the political and technical coming together, what kind of briefing they need, and how to advise them." Her moves between policy areas exposed her both to ones with exclusive Commission competences and to others lacking such powers and operating under severe budget restrictions. Day appreciated the latter as "a completely new experience" and "a good training for later." Working in External Relations and Environment led her to build closer relationships with national governments and civil society representatives. Finally, Day experienced the profound transformation in the Commission's performance under President Delors: "that was like an electric shock; the bar we had to jump over was suddenly much higher" (all citations Interview Day 1).

During her career, Day developed specific leadership qualities suitable for holding high-level office in the Commission. Particularly, her political views and visions evolved. Before entering the Commission, she had a general interest in international affairs and, specifically, the debates around Ireland's accession to the Community. As an official in the organization, her political views became more focused, but not partisan; she was never a member of a party. "I came to understand what the Commission could be and should be: I did learn to compromise, how to balance the purity of the law with the reality of where you can get to." She understood "the importance of the Commission in Europe's modern life," as it can adopt a long-term perspective. With long-term projects, the Commission "is at its best" (all citations Interview Day 1). She also experienced clashes between the basic political ideologies of liberalism and state centrism, represented respectively by Sutherland and Delors. In sum, during her career, Day developed a clear understanding of the Commission's political function in the EU and its wider "mission" in Europe (Ellinas and Suleiman 2012).

When Barroso in 2005 offered her the position of secretary general, Day thus plainly possessed the capacities for the office. "Very few [had] a broad policy background like that" (Interview Day 1). Clearly, Barroso nominated her for merit, that is, "competence and efficiency. You need a strong personality; it is a difficult job; the most difficult in the Commission" (Interview EU 1). Yet he had to persuade Day to accept the post; she finally agreed, as she "could share his agenda" and recognized the offer as "a once in a lifetime opportunity" (Interview Day 1).

To conclude, Catherine Day's nomination to the position of secretary general formed the apex of a straightforward career in high-level Commission offices, based on the meritorious performance of managerial and policy functions. This career enabled her to develop leadership qualities for highest office: thorough knowledge of multifaceted policy sectors, vast experience in both political and administrative functions, and a deep understanding of the Commission's political role in the EU and beyond.

12.4 Catherine Day: Exercising Behavioral Leadership

Day's agency as secretary general involved performing the three functions of her office: (1) managing the services, (2) shaping the Commission's agenda, and

(3) mediating conflicting views and positions. To successfully exercise leadership in these functions, she had to navigate the manifold tensions and contradictions inherent to her position as well as the challenges emanating from the institutional and situational contexts.

Managing the Services

Just prior to Day's entering office as secretary general, the Commission had gone through major changes—the enlargement of the Union and the Kinnock reforms. The enlargements increased the College to an unmanageable size and reduced its coherence (Kassim et al. 2013), while the reforms were "not a masterpiece at all" (Interview EU 1) and their implementation had turned into a protracted process (Kurpas et al. 2008). The combination of these changes formed a challenging situational context for managing the services, yet they also provided opportunities for proactive leadership.

Day, who wanted "to work closely to the president and the College, but also the DGs," analyzed the situation in the Commission as "undisciplined" and characterized by "a lot of cacophony," with "different commissioners announcing things" and DGs "having their own policies." In view of this situation, she saw the need for "a stronger sense that we are one organization; a sense of what are the main priorities" (all citations Interview Day 2; see also Interview EU 3). Accordingly, she put priority setting and policy coordination across the Commission high on the agenda and fundamentally reformed the procedures of decision-making.

Two procedural innovations stand out in this context: first, the Strategic Planning and Programming (SPP) cycle; second, the introduction of obligatory Impact Assessments (IAs) for every legislative initiative (Tholoniat 2009). Both these procedural innovations were part of the Better Regulation Agenda (BRA), already formulated under the Prodi presidency; Day advanced these innovations through tangible reforms and brought them "to fruition" (Kurpas et al. 2008: 43; see also Kassim et al. 2016). While SPP enhances the Commission's overall capacity to systematically define its priorities, IAs focus more narrowly on improving the quality of legislative proposals.

The SPP cycle consists of five stages (Kurpas et al. 2008: 43–44; Tholoniat 2009: 229): First, the Commission defines political priorities and key initiatives in an Annual Policy Strategy. Second, on this basis it elaborates an Annual Legislative and Work Programme. Third, each DG develops an Annual Management Plan that defines its contribution to the Commission priorities. Fourth, the DGs have to report on their achievements in Annual Activity Reports (AARs). Fifth, and finally, the Commission summarizes these achievements in a Synthesis Report and presents it to the Council and the EP for deliberation. Under Day's leadership, the SecGen acted as the primary manager of the process throughout the five stages.

It organized priority setting as a two-way interaction and mediation endeavor between the Commission's political and administrative levels (stage 1 and 2). It supervised the DGs "to make sure that the priorities get delivered" (Interview Day 2) (stage 3 and 4), and it summarized the results for deliberation in the Council and the EP (stage 5). On the whole, "planning and programming has put the [Sec-Gen] in a key position for the priority-setting of the Commission and has granted it a supervising role in a process that has become more centralised and coordinated" (Kurpas et al. 2008: 44).

Like SPP, IAs had already been introduced under the Prodi Commission, yet their quality had varied widely and was often low. Under Barroso's and especially Day's leadership, they became a priority, "strongly linked to the [Commission's] work programme" (Interview Day 2). Day issued and regularly reviewed guidelines laying down common standards for the assessments (Kurpas et al. 2008: 45, see also Golberg 2018: 19; Radaelli and Meuwese 2010). In 2006, she established an Impact Assessment Board, chaired by the deputy secretary general and consisting of directors of relevant DGs (those responsible for economic, employment, and environmental issues; Kurpas et al. 2008: 45). The board issued opinions on all IAs and oversaw due implementation (Schön-Quinlivan 2011: 128; Radaelli and Meuwese 2010: 147). It rejected incomplete or insufficient assessments, gave advice on how to improve them, and offered training to DG officials responsible for IAs (Interview EU 4). The DGs initially did not welcome the new procedure; yet, over time, they were "smart enough" to understand that their proposals were more easily accepted with a "proper evaluation" (Interview Day 3). In sum, "the practice of IA has … increased the control of the Secretariat General on the overall process of policy formulation" (Radaelli and Meuwese 2010: 148) and "strengthens the Commission in negotiations" (Golberg 2018: 4). Member states welcomed the assessments, while preferring that they be performed by an external agency under their control. Day strictly rejected that idea, as the procedure referred to legislative proposals, not adopted laws. "It was a long battle," but she finally won it (Interview Day 2). The IAs remained an internal Commission procedure. In the longer run, both the Council and the EP appreciated the Commission's assessments as a benefit to their decision-making (Interview EU 1; Golberg 2018).

Another concern for Day was reforming the service she headed, the SecGen, so that it could fulfill an expanded role. Implementing the Kinnock reforms meant "to lead by example" (Schön-Quinlivan 2011: 132–136). "The SecGen was keen to demonstrate by its own actions the usefulness of the reforms and how they could be extended and developed" (Schön-Quinlivan 2011: 143). More importantly, Day reorganized the SecGen according to the new priorities. In the beginning, she introduced only slight changes: "a briefing unit for the president, a unit for surveying the member states, and a unit for stronger coordination with the different DGs" (Interview Day 3). She also put the Better Regulation Agenda at the heart of the SecGen by assigning not fewer than four (out of eight) directorates to various aspects of it (Schön-Quinlivan 2011: 125; Radaelli and Meuwese 2010: 146). Over a longer span, she fundamentally reorganized the SecGen by focusing "on policies instead of procedures" and nominating "thematic directors" (Interview EU 3). Day thus succeeded in changing the culture of the SecGen, as "the analytical skills were [now] valued more than the procedural skills" (Interview EU 3) and the SecGen "became a solution provider with an enhanced role in networking among the services" (Schön-Quinlivan 2011: 143). In sum, Day transformed the SecGen "into a policy-steering entity" (Interview EU 3).

However, the most important innovation regarding the SecGen consisted in transforming it into the personal office of the president, thus fundamentally changing its 'mission.' The general idea behind this step was Barroso's. When nominating Day to the position of secretary general, he expressed the wish to have a personal office, comparable to that of a prime minister, "a service more focused on his role as President" (Interview Day 3). Day turned this idea into a workable reality, overcoming some resistance on the part of the staff. The SecGen had traditionally defined itself as "the service at the service of the services"; Day reconceived it as "the service of the President and of the College of Commissioners" (Interview Day 3). In contrast to her predecessor, O'Sullivan, who had "a rather technical vision of the SecGen's role, … Day made the clear decision to … advance its political analysis capacity" (Schön-Quinlivan 2011: 143). She thus transformed the primarily administrative function of the SecGen into a more political role. This allowed her to centralize power in the SecGen (Kurpas et al. 2008) and put a strong imprint on Commission decision-making.

In sum, in the wake of the Kinnock reforms and the Commission's significant expansion, Day's commitment to improving the procedures and practices of decision-making across the organization resulted in sophisticated priority setting, more systematic planning and programming, and thorough assessing of legislative proposals. In addition, she succeeded in raising the profile of the SecGen and in transforming its 'mission' into a more pronounced political one. Together, these innovations paved the way for Day's performance in the second function of her office: shaping the Commission agenda.

Shaping the Commission Agenda

Of course, Day or the SecGen could not act as the Commission's agenda setter, a prerogative of the president and the College. However, Day developed a clear strategy to shape the Commission agenda: by prioritizing policy above procedures, laying down guiding principles, giving guidance to decision-making across the Commission, and closely collaborating with the president. She thus succeeded in shaping Commission agenda-setting as a collaborative and interactive endeavor of all parties involved. Her personal qualities and her leadership style further facilitated her proactive role.

The institutional and situational context during Day's tenure was not particularly favorable for agenda-shaping. In addition to the factors mentioned above, affecting the Commission's internal working, the Lisbon Treaty amplified the power of the European Council and the financial crisis further enhanced its activism; at the same time, the EP became more assertive (e.g., Bickerton et al. 2015).

In contrast to her predecessors, Day as secretary general explicitly prioritized policy above procedures. "I wanted not just procedures, but policies," and "my real drive was to get the Secretariat General from procedural issues to an interest in policy" (Interviews Day 2 and 4; see also Kassim et al. 2013: 187–197). The challenge then was "how you develop the policy; to deliver it in the right way" (Interview Day 4). Of course, this implied both mastering the procedures as well as the policy choices, but "a slave to procedures will never catch the imagination" of policies (Interview Day 4). Day hence saw her role as shaping policy choices. Her broad policy experiences and her political views about what was necessary and feasible facilitated her performance in this role. "She could talk to DGs about policy" and "had a tremendous capacity to master her files" (Interview EU 3). In many cases, the SecGen itself took on dossiers (Kurpas et al. 2008: 32–33).

Early on in her tenure, Day laid down basic principles for guiding Commission agenda-setting and her own agency therein:

- working with a long-term perspective;
- raising the quality of legislative proposals;
- focusing on a limited set of priorities; and
- elaborating integrated packages instead of individual regulations.

Day saw working with a long-term perspective as both a necessity and a unique opportunity that only the Commission commands: "for me, one of the strengths of the Commission has been, and will be in the future, our ability to think about 15–20 years' framework" (Interview Euractiv). Raising the quality of legislative proposals and limiting the number of priorities appeared a political must in the face of growing Euro-skepticism and an increasing reluctance of governments against further integration steps: "if you have 100 items on your agenda, nobody is listening to you" (Interview Day 2). Elaborating integrated packages "superintended by the Secretariat General" (Kassim et al. 2016: 664) implies mediating ex ante between contradicting interests and raising the quality of legislative proposals. In DG Environment, "I understood that you do not get things through if you do not speak with Energy" (Interview Day 2). Throughout Day's tenure, these principles formed the basis for her shaping of the Commission's agenda.

Translating these principles into practice was not always easy. DGs often advocated 'their' policy proposals, regardless of the overall agenda. Furthermore, they did not appreciate integrated packages, which they saw as encroaching on their autonomy. Sometimes even Barroso chose things to do "at the edge of defined priorities" (Interview Day 3). Obviously, this did not please Day, but she accepted it. "I knew he is the boss and had to take wider political concerns into account" (Interview Day 3). The EP attempted to expand the Commission's agenda by pressuring Barroso. When in 2009 he needed a vote of consent for his second term (Dinan 2010), the EP claimed the right to include its preferred agenda items in the Commission's work program. Day wanted to avoid diluting the agenda, and the Commission successfully resisted the claim (Interview Day 2).

In the process of agenda-setting, Day gave guidance to the decision-making of the political and administrative levels, simultaneously working with both sides (Interview Day 3). Regarding the services, she filtered their policy proposals to a limited selection; regarding the political level, she provided advice and engaged in building consensus for the adoption of priorities and policy proposals.

The filtering of DG proposals followed previously agreed-upon priorities and additional criteria: for some it was not the right time, others appeared less salient or had no chance of being adopted by the Council and EP (Interviews Day 2 and 4). The IAs, too, worked as a filter, since the SecGen "could use the procedure to hold back initiatives" (Kassim et al. 2016: 664). IAs gave the SecGen "a considerable gate-keeper function for the College" (Kurpas et al. 2008: 45). Privileging legislative packages constituted an additional filter. "Over the years, the Secretariat General introduced a much more centralized coordination of policies" (Interview EU 1) and played "an increasingly important monitoring role throughout the whole internal coordination" (Hartlapp et al. 2014: 250). In sum, Day succeeded in focusing the Commission agenda on policy initiatives of major significance and broad application.

Her work as adviser to the president and the College had two primary dimensions: technical–administrative and political. In technical terms, Day was keen to provide swift and sound information to the president and the College on all relevant matters. For example, when she or SecGen staff participated in meetings of other EU institutions, she always arranged briefings on what had been learned about the other party's thoughts, positions, and preferences the following day (AARs of the SecGen, 2005–2015). In political terms, Day bundled the proposals of the DGs into a consistent concept-agenda and promoted it via various channels. For the "bigger priorities, you organize meetings with the Chefs de Cabinet and the Directors General" (Interview Day 3). As chair of these meetings, she often could already at this level mold a common position on the agenda and annual work programs (Interview Day 3). Yet she also participated at the highest level in the meetings of the College to advocate basic principles and policy proposals. In sum, in all arenas at the political level, "she very much advised and she had a huge influence; … in that [her advice] she was also explicit"

(Interview EU 2). This indicates that her advice was not just advice; to a far-reaching extent, it shaped decisions at the political level.

However, the most important asset for shaping the Commission's agenda was Day's close collaboration with the president. This put her in the position to tighten priority setting, in contrast to Barroso's rather broad and diluted agenda (Müller 2020). Day's relationship with Barroso was characterized by mutual respect and trust. She was "fair to Barroso and always loyal to him, in view of his difficult job"; "she tried to make the best of him" and "there was no tension between them" (Interview EU 1). She spoke of "a good working relationship" with Barroso (Interview Day 3) and her respect, esteem, and admiration for him (Interview Elvert: 20–21). Barroso for his part "appreciated her" as well (Interview EU 1). This is best expressed by the fact that he included her in frequent meetings of his cabinet as well as the weekly management meetings with representatives of the services (Kassim et al. 2016: 662). In addition, she had individual meetings with him, and also with an inner circle of high-level political and administrative office holders: "I saw him several times a week" (Interview Day 3). In all these settings, Day acted as policy adviser to the president (Interview EC 11); he in turn very much relied on her. For example, she always prepared written summaries and conclusions of the College of Commissioners meetings for him in advance, which he presented at the end of the meetings (Interview EC 11). Regarding the Commission's work program, an interviewee observed: "I believe ... that he [Barroso] finally looks at it, ... but it is very much made by the Secretariat General in connection with the Chefs de Cabinet" (Interview EC 3). According to Kassim et al. (2016: 662), Day's close involvement in presidential affairs gave Barroso "leverage over policy planning and quality control mechanisms and, via the weekly directors-general meeting, chaired by the secretary general, a link to senior management." Yet the opposite conclusion is more persuasive: precisely due to this close involvement, Day acquired a pivotal position to exercise far-reaching influence on the Commission's top-level politicians and their decisions.

That Day could perform this pivotal role was also due to her personal qualities and her leadership style. An interviewee described her as a "tough personality," "quite authoritative," sometimes even "over-rigid" and "much more structured than Barroso" (Interview EU 1). This helped Day to direct "the whole administration and, with this, policymaking" (Interview EC 3). One interviewee described her as "a woman with an exceptional strong will" who transformed the SecGen "into a centralistic power machine" (Interview EC 9). Another observer noted she was "an absolute expert with incredibly sharp brains and very comprehensive knowledge ... yet she went far beyond her actual tasks and competences" (Interview EC 11). In short, "some found her a bit overbearing" (Interview EU 1).

However, interviewees also emphasize Day's conciliatory nature: "She was never unpleasant, never *blessant*, hurting people or being aggressive" (Interview EU 1). "She never demanded from people what she did not demand of herself, and when the political decision was different from hers, she accepted that; her ethics were exemplary" (Interview EU 2). "She was the best superior I ever had" (Interview EU 4). Clearly, Day's leadership style combined features that are usually considered "masculine" with others seen as "feminine" (Chapter 1 in this volume).

Day herself characterizes her leadership in pragmatic terms: "I was always very well prepared, collaborative, focused, reliable in that I always gave colleagues my honest assessment." "You need not be popular, but need to be respectful and re-spected." "Having been in different positions, I was able to bring all that together" (all citations Interview Day 4). An interviewee summarized: "Catherine has never sought a political role. Her influence stemmed from her unparalleled grasp of facts, figures and files; her superior knowledge of policy detail; her administrative and diplomatic experience; and her institutional loyalty" (Interview EU 2). In short, her leadership style, at once authoritative and conciliatory, was underpinned by expertise, hard work, and strong commitment.

Summing up, Day, though not empowered to set the Commission's agenda, nonetheless made a strong imprint on it by tightly structuring and supervising the process of agenda-setting and by shaping it in substantial terms. Regarding the services, she helped reduce the quantity and raise the quality of their agenda proposals. At the political level, she skillfully used persuasion to encourage the adoption of those proposals and to advance the Commission's priorities more broadly. She practiced a leadership style that combined both "masculine" and "feminine" features. She never openly intruded into the political role of the presi-dent and the College, but her agenda-shaping was political in the sense of pursuing the common good for the EU.

Mediating Conflicting Views and Positions

Day's pivotal position in multiple arenas of decision-making obviously confronted her with conflicting views or even open clashes between various actors. In such situations, she skillfully acted as mediator and broker. Within the Commission, she engaged in persuasion of all parties involved and consensus-building among them. In the legislative bodies, she mobilized followers behind the Commission's positions and shaped compromise solutions. Her personal views of conflict and consensus helped her to exercise these functions: "Different views [are] part of policymaking; you need the confrontation of ideas; the Commission must be as representative as possible; you have to arrive at compromises that will be appealing to a broad range of people" (Interview Day 3).

Mediating among the services came into play especially when elaborating the Commission's work program and deciding on legislative proposals and packages, usually affecting several DGs. Day in these situations engaged in intense debates, while insisting on defined priorities and basic principles. Regarding legislative proposals, the SecGen acted as "a significant power broker when other DGs clash[ed] over policy choices" (Hartlapp et al. 2014: 258). In developing legislative packages, Day had to conduct even more extensive talks. One such series of exchanges, with Energy and Environment, resulted in a comprehensive climate change package (Interview Day 2; for more examples, see Hartlapp et al. 2014).

At the political level, Day successfully forged compromises among the "big beasts" (Interview Day 2), the chefs de cabinet, so that oral procedures were often not needed. Though the share of written procedures was already high under Prodi, the Barroso Commission was able to increase their proportion even further (Hartlapp et al. 2014: 249). Day's mediating skills came particularly to the fore when elaborating the Multiannual Financial Framework (MFF) 2013–2020, a project involving nearly all the DGs. She managed to perfectly balance the differing interests of both the DGs and the responsible commissioners (Interviews EU 1 and 2).

For mediating among the other EU institutions, Day built close relationships with the respective top officials, while Barroso connected at the political level (Interview EU 2). The European Council was her primary concern (Interview Day 4). She was allowed to participate in its meetings, even after the Lisbon Treaty strictly limited the number of participants (Interviews EU 1 and 2). In difficult negotiations, she helped to propose compromise formula and elaborated the text of the conclusions in collaboration with the Council's secretary general (Interview EU 1). "I always tried to be reasonable," which increased the European Council's "willingness to take our views into account." The problem was "how to handle difficult questions of substance" and find "the rallying point that brings people together" (Interview Day 4). Day also collaborated with the permanent president of the European Council, Herman Van Rompuy, and his cabinet, as "they simply have not the same time available or sometimes not the expertise" to deal with policy substance and build compromises (Interview Day 4).

For the Council and Coreper (Committee of Permanent Representatives), dealing with sectoral issues, the SecGen staff bore responsibility. Yet when fundamental issues were at stake in the European Council, Day approached Coreper as the preparatory body. "When I did appear, they knew that the Commission is wanting to make progress or convey a serious message." The relationships with the EP were "much more difficult for me in a way, as a lot of work was done through the political groupings." In addition to the Council's secretary general, she thus also built a relationship with the EP's secretary general. "The three of us met quite often" to discuss "how to help ensure compromise on certain things" (all citations Interview Day 4).

Day also practiced a mediating style in relations with member states. A case in point is the European semester, where the Commission issues recommendations, which "member states did not like." "This is more policy than law; it is soft policy." In this context, Day tried "to understand member states' difficulties" rather than just impose recommendations. In cases of infringement procedures "we tried to be not over-legalistic; the aim was to solve the problem and to help them to sort it out" (all citations Interview Day 4).

Summarizing Day's performance in the face of conflicting views and positions, within the Commission she practiced a mediating and solution-driven leadership style; only on occasion did she use her authority to impose decisions. In the other EU institutions, she mainly collaborated with the administrative top level to reach compromises and "make things work" (Interview Day 4).

12.5 Conclusions: What Kind of Leadership?

Drawing conclusions about Day's leadership as secretary general of the Commission, it is first important to note that she excelled in the three functions of her office. She managed the services by structuring and innovating decision-making, reorganizing the SecGen, and transforming its mission into one involving a stronger political role. She shaped the Commission agenda by closely collaborating with the services, the College, and particularly the president, giving direction to decision-making, raising the quality and coherence of policy proposals, and overall improving the Commission's strategic capacity. She mediated conflicting views across EU institutions by extensively talking, persuading, and proposing compromise solutions and thus facilitating the adoption of policies. Her extraordinary influence in all these arenas was based on her capacity to manage procedures, her choice to prioritize policies and thus substantial issues, and her authoritative and at the same time collaborative and conciliatory leadership style. Together, these attributes allowed Day to make a strong imprint on the Commission's and, hence, the EU's policies.

Looking at the institutional and situational context of Day's tenure, she successfully used the available opportunities and overcame the constraints. She used the Kinnock reforms to innovate decision-making; the coordinative role of the SecGen to expand its mission toward a more political role; and, most importantly, Barroso's backing to pursue proactive agenda-shaping. She reacted to the enlarged Commission by centralizing decision-making, and mitigated the enhanced roles of the European Council and the EP through the establishment of cooperative relationships.

Her most important accomplishment lay in transforming the SecGen into an office not just close to the president, but in a pivotal position at the intersection between the Commission's political and administrative levels. This gave her, and the Commission administration more broadly, access to the power center. Conversely, it allowed her to use the power of the president and the College to direct and discipline the services and to ensure the consistency and coherence of the Commission agenda. This transformation was primarily Day's achievement—not

Barroso's, as Kassim et al. (2013, 2016) have suggested. She thus compensated in large part for the weaknesses of Barroso's presidency (Müller 2020). And Day's achievements are not limited to the Barroso era; many of them persist and have formed the basis for further advances, particularly the innovative procedures of decision-making and the pivotal position and role of the SecGen. Hence Day shaped and expanded not only her own strategic resources but also those of her successors and the Commission more broadly.

Assessing Day as an administrative leader, her behavior largely matches the definitions and normative claims presented early in this chapter. She did not act as an entrepreneurial leader or attempt to assume an explicit political role. She closely collaborated with the services and acted as a complement to the Commission's political level and especially its president, since they needed each other "to function, especially strategically" (Lemay 2009: 2). They joined forces "in the common pursuit of sound governance" (Svara 2001: 179). In sum, Day successfully performed the tightrope walk that highly qualified and committed administrative leaders face.

References

Aberbach, Joel, Robert Putnam, and Bert Rockman. 1981. *Bureaucrats and Politicians in Western Democracies*. Cambridge, MA: Harvard University Press.

Bauer, Michael. 2007. "The Politics of Reforming the European Commission Administration." In *Management Reforms in International Organizations*, eds. Michael Bauer and Christoph Knill, 51–69. Baden Baden: Nomos.

Bauer, Michael, and Jörn Ege. 2013. "Politicization within the European Commission's Bureaucracy." *International Review of Administrative Sciences* 78 (3): 403–424.

Bickerton, Christopher, Dermot Hodson, and Uwe Puetter, eds. 2015. *The New Intergovernmentalism: States and Supranational Actors in the Post-Maastricht Era*. Oxford: Oxford University Press.

Blondel, Jean. 1987. *Political Leadership: Towards a General Analysis*. London: Sage.

Burns, James MacGregor. 1978. *Leadership*. New York: Harper & Row.

Dinan, Desmond. 2010. "Institutions and Governance: A New Treaty, a Newly Elected Parliament, and a New Commission." *Journal of Common Market Studies* 48 (Annual Review): 95–118.

Elgie, Robert. 1995. *Political Leadership in Liberal Democracies*. Basingstoke, UK: Macmillan.

Ellinas, Antonis, and Ezra Suleiman. 2012. *The European Commission and Bureaucratic Autonomy: Europe's Custodians*. Cambridge, UK: Cambridge University Press.

Endo, Ken. 1999. *The Presidency of the European Commission under Jacques Delors: The Politics of Shared Leadership*. Basingstoke, UK: Macmillan.

Golberg, Elizabeth. 2018. 'Better Regulation': European Union Style. M-RCBG Associate Working Paper Series, No. 98.

Hartlapp, Miriam, Julia Metz, and Christian Rauh. 2014. *Which Policy for Europe: Power and Conflict inside the European Commission*. Oxford: Oxford University Press.

Hooghe, Liesbet. 2001. *The European Commission and the Integration of Europe: Images of Governance.* Cambridge, UK: Cambridge University Press.

Hooghe, Liesbet. 2012. "Images of Europe: How Commission Officials Conceive Their Institutions' Role." *Journal of Common Market Studies* 50 (1): 87–111.

Hooghe, Liesbet, and Christian Rauh. 2016. "The Commission Services: A Powerful Permanent Bureaucracy." In *Institutions of the European Union*, eds. Dermot Hodson and John Peterson, 187–212. Oxford: Oxford University Press.

Kassim, Hussein. 2004. "The Kinnock Reforms in Perspective: Why Reforming the Commission Is a Heroic, But Thankless, Task." *Public Policy and Administration* 19 (3): 25–41.

Kassim, Hussein. 2006. "The Secretariat General of the European Commission." In *The European Commission*, eds. David Spence and Geoffrey Edwards, 75–102. London: John Harper.

Kassim, Hussein. 2008. "'Mission Impossible', But Mission Accomplished: The Kinnock Reforms and the European Commission." *Journal of European Public Policy* 15 (5): 648–668.

Kassim, Hussein, Sara Connolly, Renaud Dehousse, Olivier Rozenberg, and Selma Bendjaballah. 2016. "Managing the House: The Presidency, Agenda Control and Policy Activism in the European Commission." *Journal of European Public Policy*, 24 (5): 653–674.

Kassim, Hussein, John Peterson, Michael Bauer, Sara Connolly, Renaud Dehousse, Liesbeth Hooghe, and Andrew Thompson. 2013. *The European Commission of the Twenty-first Century*. Oxford: Oxford University Press.

Kurpas, Sebastian, Caroline Grøn, and Piotr Kaczyński. 2008. *The European Commission after Enlargement: Does More Add Up to Less?* Brussels: Center for European Policy Studies.

Lemay, Lilly. 2009. "The Practice of Collective and Strategic Leadership in the Public Sector." *Innovation Journal: The Public Sector Innovation Journal* 14 (1): 1–19.

Müller, Henriette. 2020. *The Commission President and the Process of European Integration: Changing Patterns of Leadership Performance in Supranational Governance.* Oxford: Oxford University Press.

Nugent, Neill, and Mark Rhinard. 2019. "The 'Political' Roles of the European Commission." *Journal of European Integration* 41 (2): 203–220.

Nye, Joseph. 2008. *The Powers to Lead*. Oxford: Oxford University Press.

Orazi, Davide, Alex Turrini, and Giovanni Valotti. 2013. "Public Sector Leadership: New Perspectives for Research and Practice." *International Journal of Administrative Sciences* 79 (3): 486–504.

Peters, B. Guy. 2001. *The Politics of Bureaucracy*. 5th ed. London: Routledge.

Peterson, John. 2008. "Enlargement, Reform and the European Commission: Weathering a Perfect Storm?" *Journal of European Public Policy* 15 (5): 761–780.

Radaelli, Claudio, and Anne Meuwese. 2010. "Hard Questions, Hard Solutions: Proceduralisation through Impact Assessment in the EU." *West European Politics* 33 (1): 136–153.

Schön-Quinlivan, Emmanuelle. 2011. *Reforming the European Commission.* Basingstoke: Palgrave Macmillan.

Smeets, Sandrino, and Derek Beach. 2020. "Political and Instrumental Leadership in Major EU Reforms: The Role and Influence of the EU Institutions in Setting up the Fiscal Compact." *Journal of European Public Policy* 27 (1): 63–81.

Stevens, Handley, and Anne Stevens. 2006. "The Internal Reform of the Commission." In *The European Commission*, eds. David Spence and Geoffrey Edwards, 454–480. London: John Harper.

Svara, James. 2001. "The Myth of the Dichotomy: Complementarity of Politics and Administration in the Past and Future of Public Administration." *Public Administration Review* 61 (2): 176–183.

Terry, Larry D. 1998. "Administrative Leadership, Neo-Managerialism, and the Public Management Movement." *Public Administration Review* 58 (3): 194–200.

Tholoniat, Luc. 2009. "The Temporal Constitution of the European Commission: A Timely Investigation." *Journal of European Public Policy* 16 (2): 221–238.

Tömmel, Ingeborg. 2013. "The Presidents of the European Commission: Transactional or Transforming Leaders?" *Journal of Common Market Studies* 51 (4): 789–805.

Tömmel, Ingeborg. 2020. "Political Leadership in Times of Crisis: The Commission Presidency of Jean-Claude Juncker." *West European Politics* 43 (5): 1141–1162.

Trondal, Jarle. 2010. *An Emergent European Executive Order*. Oxford: Oxford University Press.

Wille, Anchrit. 2013. *The Normalization of the European Commission: Politics and Bureaucracy in the EU Executive*. Oxford: Oxford University Press.

List of Interviews

Interviews by the author with Catherine Day:
  Interview Day 1: 22.06.2020
  Interview Day 2: 20.07.2020
  Interview Day 3: 03.08.2020
  Interview Day 4: 04.09.2020

Interviews by the author with senior officials from the European Commission (three interviews) and the General Secretariat of the Council of the European Union (one interview):
  Interview EU 1: 19.12.2019
  Interview EU 2: 21.07.2020
  Interview EU 3: 14.08.2020
  Interview EU 4: 24.08.2020

Interviews by Henriette Müller with senior officials of the Commission (see Müller 2020: Appendix 2)
  Interview EC 3: 25.09.2013
  Interview EC 8: 21.10.2013
  Interview EC 11: 15.11.2013

Other Interviews:
  Interview Euractiv: Interview with European Commission Secretary-General Catherine Day, 26.09.2006 (updated 08.06.2007). www.euractiv.com/section/future-eu/interview/interview-with-european-commission-secretary-general-catherine-day
  Interview Elvert: Entretien avec Catherine Day par Jürgen Elvert, à Bruxelles le 9 septembre 2011. HISTCOM.2 (Histoire interne de la Commission européenne 1973–1986)

13

Women in EU Multilevel Administration

The Europeanization of Member-State Bureaucracies

Eva G. Heidbreder

13.1 Introduction: The Europeanization of Women's Leadership

European Union (EU) polity building has been a major driver of change inside the Union's member states. Polity, policies, and politics have been Europeanized through a wide range of mechanisms (Green Cowles et al. 2001; Featherstone and Radaelli 2003). Given that EU policies are implemented primarily by national bureaucracies, Europeanization has also substantially transformed national public administration (PA). Even though empirical evidence consistently shows the persistence of national administrative path dependencies, national PAs have been integrated into and adapted to the tightly interwoven system of EU multilevel administration both vertically (across levels, from the EU to the municipal) and horizontally (across states) (Olsen 2003). Against this backdrop, this chapter raises a key question about the positioning of women: Does EU integration cause changes in women's leadership in national PA?

In answering this question, the study pursues a theoretical and an empirical ambition. Theoretically, feminist approaches to PAs—developed in studies focusing on the USA—and conceptualizations of multilevel administration—developed in research on the EU—are brought together. Not least due to the focus on different polities, the USA and EU, the two research areas have not been linked. It is argued here that key insights about the role of women in PAs developed in the US context can inform our understanding of women in the EU's multilevel administration. The theoretical argument developed herein holds that new functional demands in EU multilevel administration are positively matched by feminist counterimages to standard PA dimensions. Hence, this chapter argues that the two literatures may be fruitfully combined to better understand the underlying assumptions that lead to particular behavioral expectations of women and the consequent impact on the leadership roles they attain—or fail to attain. The chapter's empirical contribution looks at the actual positioning of women in the EU's multilevel administration.

Eva G. Heidbreder, *Women in EU Multilevel Administration: The Europeanization of Member-State Bureaucracies.* In: *Women and Leadership in the European Union.* Edited by Henriette Müller and Ingeborg Tömmel, Oxford University Press.
© Oxford University Press (2022). DOI: 10.1093/oso/9780192896216.003.0014

Having theoretically established that multilevel administration creates functional demands that clash with prototype virtues promoted in modern PAs, we may expect a higher probability for women to attain a leadership position in EU-related than in state-centered PAs. To offer a probability probe of this expectation, the representation of women in German EU policy coordination is examined. Despite limitations in the empirical data, the results indeed indicate a slightly higher representation of women in leadership in EU-related policy coordination, even though women have entered leadership positions only recently and variance persists across policy areas. In contrast, in genuine EU administrative networks for which national administrations have created new leadership posts, women clearly dominate. As a first-cut plausibility probe, the study is limited to positional data, but the findings strongly suggest that further research should also invest in behavioral patterns, in particular to trace causal mechanisms that drive the observable changes.

The next section develops the theoretical argument. It first summarizes the main theoretical insights about EU multilevel administration and then asks what feminist PAs literature can add to better identify the functional implications of certain normative assumptions. This leads to the theoretical expectation that EU multilevel administration might offer more room for female-led PAs. The plausibility of this expectation is tested with original data from the two German ministries that coordinate EU policies and data from the Solvit (neologism for "solve it"), an EU-facilitated online service that interlinks national competent authorities, mainly online. While the empirical findings of this single country case cannot provide exhaustive explanations, they offer sufficient hints for further research into the impact of EU integration on female leadership positioning in PAs.

13.2 Theoretical Starting Points: Multilevel Administration as Trigger for New Administrative Norms?

To conduct a theory-guided empirical examination of positional leadership data on women in the EU, this section develops theoretical expectations about changes in women's leadership in national PAs triggered by EU integration. The research is problem driven and aims primarily at solving the empirical puzzle of whether Europeanization affects the appointment patterns of administrative leadership positions. Accordingly, core questions of feminist PA literature are not touched upon. In particular, the question of why we can observe differences in male and female representation is not dealt with. Attention is paid here to the findings about specific typical ideational features of modern PAs and how these normative underpinnings impact on behavior, that is, the functional consequences that a specific normative substructure entails and how these materialize in women's career paths.

To this end, first the main attributes of the EU multilevel administrative system are introduced to identify how EU PAs diverge from standard modern PAs. The chapter shows how crucial functional necessities of the EU multilevel administration challenge, and are partially even incompatible with, key working premises of state-centered PAs. Whereas this finding alone yields strong implications for leadership in national PAs, theoretical work on EU multilevel administration does not offer more specific insights into possible effects on women's leadership. Even though the theoretical and empirical findings of US feminist PA scholarship cannot be applied directly to the EU polity, the ideational prototypes of modern PA identified display significant overlaps that allow the formulation of more specific expectations about women's leadership in EU multilevel administration. The counterimages to male-dominated images in PAs can hence serve as conceptual/theoretical and prescriptive/normative models in the quest for norms of multilevel administration.

A Multilevel Perspective on the European Union's Administration

The EU is not a state. It does not operate as a hierarchical order based on the monopoly of power that characterizes modern statehood. In the realm of PAs, this feature is especially relevant because the EU lacks the command-and-control structures that are a key defining feature of modern administration in states (Weber 1980). Instead, national PAs implement the bulk of EU policies. Although the administrations of the EU member states remain formally independent and are not hierarchically subordinated to the European Commission as top executive, administrative practices have blurred these formal legalistic principles (Heidbreder 2011). Especially because competent authorities in the member states have to cater to new, greatly multiplied cross-border responsibilities, administrative practices create mutual dependencies. In essence, EU multilevel administration is a "system of vertically and horizontally networked administrative units that link actors on various levels (EU, state, sub-state), in different legal guises (public, semiautonomous, private), and under varying legal principles (direct or indirect effect of EU law, mutual recognition between member states, voluntary regulation) in autonomy-sharing procedures to administer all stages of EU policymaking" (Heidbreder 2019, own translation).

In line with this, during the past 10 years the European Commission has shifted its attention from the creation of an administrative center on the EU level to a decentralized and more bottom-up enabling of national PAs, as well as horizontal cooperation among national agencies, to ensure the effective functioning of the single market. Especially in the governance of the single market, the Commission has aimed at administrative capacity building on the (sub)national level, building up skills and capacities in the national systems to ensure the successful creation and implementation of EU policies by competent national authorities (Heidbreder 2014, 2019). This process indicates that the EU's multilevel administration differs substantially from and conflicts with the underlying principles of modern, state-bound PAs. In EU policymaking, national administrators have to constantly interact beyond the confinements of their state systems to ensure coherent EU policymaking. Most relevantly, these new cross-border practices clash with the concept of the command-and-control system that is typical for the hierarchically organized administrative state. Accordingly, EU policymaking is steered by multiple, interconnected competent authorities that cooperate within the EU legal framework without a top level that can issue direct instructions. In short, the EU's multilevel administration requires administrators to cater to mutual needs across borders. Hence, an ideal public administrator—from an EU perspective—is able to cater to demands from the different levels of the governance system, which involves individual skills such as an understanding of diverse PA systems and elaborate communication capabilities; not least, it also requires mutual trust between the vertically and horizontally interacting authorities. Crucial skills are enhanced by physically moving across levels, for example by secondment to the EU or another member state's administration. Yet such mobility does not correspond with traditional career paths that depend strongly on persistent visibility within and loyalty to the national system. In the daily handling of EU policies, both in administrative policy preparation and subsequent implementation, collaboration and participation move center stage. In the daily exercise of administrative duties, administrators thus increasingly depend on administrative exchange and assistance across member states. For example, under free movement of labor, national labor inspectorates need information about qualifications and social security obtained in other member states, which demands practicable access to data and constant interaction with other member states' administrations (Hartlapp and Heidbreder 2018).

In sum, multilevel administration in the EU creates demands on administrators that fundamentally differ from those in the prototypical modern administrative state. These new demands create a need for previously secondary skills and therefore qualities that ought to be rewarded in individuals' career paths. Perforating the closed, hierarchical structure of modern PAs, which is closely linked to the notion of the state, the demands of multilevel administration also challenge the underlying assumptions of modern PAs in very practical terms.

The Theoretical Take on the Role of Women in Public Administration

The crucial contribution of feminist PA theory to the study of women's leadership in the EU is that it offers theoretical counterimages that correspond with the functional demands of multilevel administration.[1] The historical evolution of PAs in the USA (Stivers 2000; see also McSwite 2004) shows that core traits attributed to modern PAs are strongly male-defined, while they exclude the experiences of women-led organizations that developed in parallel. To reform a spoils system of long standing into a modern PA, an impartial scientific approach and independent rational rule were used as legitimizing concepts. Accordingly, the widely accepted constituent elements of modern PAs were formulated in a specific historic context to overcome the principles of patronage in place. Against this background, Camilla Stivers has "argued persuasively that masculine perspectives have dominated the theory and practice of public administration" (Shields 2006: 418). The core features this literature identifies are scientific objectivity, professional autonomy, hierarchical authority, and professional like-mindedness (Miller 1993: 87). The following briefly summarizes Stivers feminist perspective on PA theory (1990), in which she conceptualizes counterimages to administrative neutrality, the model of the ideal public servant, administrative discretion, and the administrative state that speak to EU multilevel administration.

The first image is the quest for neutrality, which holds that administrators ought to act in an independent, rational, comprehensive, and efficient manner based on the liberal notion of individualism. The counterimage drawn by Stivers challenges that such neutrality could ever be possible, and she links the concept to "liberal individualism's insistence that the state maintain moral neutrality with respect to the preferences of autonomous persons" (1990: 53). Foregrounding the sorts of experiences socially associated with female roles underscores that, far from independent actors, people are mutually dependent. Applying this counterimage, "we might base the public interest dimensions of administrative decision-making as much on the discovery of mutual needs as on the adjudication of competing claims among disconnected utility-maximizers" (Stivers 1990: 54). Accordingly, PA cannot and should not aim for a neutral view to identify what serves individuals best. It should incorporate the diversity of perspectives in society and to use these as an opportunity for collaboration rather than considering diversity as a source of conflict (Stivers 1990: 55). Applied to multilevel administration, this counterimage conceptually pinpoints the conflict between cross-level administrative cooperation and autonomous administrative units. Replacing the image of neutrality with images of interconnectedness and collaboration thus resonates strongly with the specific demands of EU multilevel administration.

Second, the model of the ideal public servant is understood as a tool to build trust in administrators, rather than institutions. In the face of decreasing public

---

[1] To arrive at key insights applicable to EU multilevel administration, this chapter offers an interpretation of Camilla Stivers's counterimages that challenge commonly held male-dominated portrayals of PA. There is some relevant overlap between the feminist critique and critique raised in other streams of PA literature, especially in light of the new public management turn (for many Olsen 2006) that promises valuable insights.

trust in PAs, the question whether changing the underpinning imagery can rebuild trust becomes preeminent. For Stivers, "it appears that many of the modern images of the public administrator, such as the entrepreneur, the advocate, the decision-maker, derive their legitimacy and their appeal from their potential for individual visibility" (1990: 58). With visibility and individual recognition defined as public virtues, individuals try to comply and perform, which serves as a mechanism to stabilize the political order. Depicting a possible counterimage, "[t]he need to re-win the public's trust may call for more broadly interactive images" (Stivers 1990: 58), images that do not rest on individual achievement but interactive responsiveness. This shift speaks to shortcomings in EU multilevel administration in two ways. On the one hand, EU PAs—in particular the European Commission—is often alleged to act in ways particularly detached from citizens' concerns. On the other hand, the fact that improving skills in EU coordination through personal experience often reduces the visibility in the national reward system (especially secondments to EU institutions or other member states) makes engagement in EU coordination particularly unattractive to the "ideal" public servant. This raises the need for a positively defined counterimage that caters to the functional necessity of interactive responsiveness, not least to build trust in EU administration.

Third, administrative discretion is based on the ideal of PA independence from political interference. This image is contrasted with that of PA as an element of a larger governance system in which PA is intertwined with rather than separated from the political realm. Accordingly, instead of aiming for administrative discretion—i.e., the capacity of administrators to make independent judgments about the nature of the public interest—PA as administrative governance is "less hierarchical and more interactive, therefore less elitist and more democratic" (Stivers 1990: 59). Most relevantly, such a conceptual shift to a more bottom-up, democratic rather than top-down, elitist steering approach implies that "[c]ollaboration and participation thus become protection against bureaucratic pathology rather than a source of inefficiency" (Stivers 1990: 59). Notably, (voluntary) collaboration and participation are two of the most crucial functional needs that multilevel administration produces. Short of a system-embracing hierarchical administrative order, effective policy implementation can be achieved only if the (sub-)state-level competent authorities build trust and work in collaborative networks across borders and levels of governance—despite their high degree of discretion due to the lack of hierarchical EU-level authority.

Finally, the discussion of the administrative state highlights core issues involving the ends and means of PAs. Besides introducing for the first time "the idea that public administration theory is a theory of the state and administrative practice a form of statecraft" (Stivers 1990: 59), Stivers refers to Waldo's emphasis on the actual existence of a positive, intervening state with coercive powers to provide structure to a fragmented society (Waldo 1948). In the US-American understanding, this very ability of the state conflicts with the value of exercising full individual freedoms. For Stivers, the defense of freedom is accordingly key to our understanding of the administrative state. Freedom is assured by delineating the political arena and employing specific techniques of statecraft. To gain freedom, the modern state introduced a social, public space in opposition to the monarch. Historically, this was done by excluding women from the newly defined public and locating them in the private sphere. The correspondingly deployed technique to defend freedom is the ability to master public matters, procedural steering methods essentially independent of the content at stake. The feminist counterimage challenges, at first, the dichotomy between public and private, which is interpreted not as a solution to protect the freedom of all but as a source of oppression of many. As a consequence, the counterimage suggests "that our emphasis on the administrative state as virtue and administrative discretion as 'opportunity' for positive action in a fragmented polity, is our bid to establish and reserve to ourselves a sphere of freedom" (Stivers 1990: 63). This position recognizes that institutions, such as constitutions, laws, and norms, constrain action but recognizes that institutions, at the same time, enable "free" action (Stivers 1990: 63). In essence, the counterimage starts from the assumption that statecraft is the ability to interact, develop, and resolve people's needs rather than securing freedom for the few who dominate the public sphere, imposing solutions on the many. This discussion is admittedly complex and this condensed account is far from exhaustive. But even though the highly abstract counterimage does not offer ready-made models, it reveals the conceptual legacy that also obstructs a positive definition of what "multilevel administrative craft" might be. In the absence of hierarchically superior competences, EU multilevel administration falls by definition short of the tools of statecraft. In the EU even more than in a state, "public administrators need to consider the challenges represented in feminist theory, and use them as a source of creativity" (Stivers 1990: 64).

In a nutshell, the counterimages depict a redefined notion of public interest and how it can be served. Instead of scientific objectivity, professional autonomy, hierarchical authority, and professional like-mindedness, the counterimages highlight mutual needs, societal diversity that demands and enriches collaboration and participation, trust in administrative institutions, the interconnectedness between public and private spheres and thus interactive problem-solving. The counterimages do not amount to a concrete model of alternative PAs, but they sensitize one to the conceptual limitations of standard modern PAs. Equally, the counterimages do not automatically imply that women are more suited or even better in acting according to these alternative images. Indirectly, since these counterimages are derived from female experience, we may, with caution, expect that they more readily match the skills and professional expectations of women than those of men. This entails the empirical question of whether women do take different positions than men in EU multilevel administration.

Theoretical Expectations and Case Selection

While EU multilevel PA challenges the functioning modes of modern PAs, feminist PA thinking challenges the underpinning principles theoretically. The last section showed that shifting from the historically male-dominated PA images to more of a focus on female-shaped experience supports strong counterimages that correspond directly with the new functional demands of multilevel administration. The empirical question that ensues is whether the overlaps in hands-on functional demands and female-defined PA images affect the actual positioning of women. The EU's multilevel administration serves as an ideal case to probe this expectation because its very functional needs clash with key dimensions of the modern administrative state. As the feminist PA literature shows, the functional argument touches on skills and, more fundamentally, individual ambitions driven by career reward mechanisms in modern PAs.

Regarding personal skills, the abilities to interact, to be responsive, and to adapt to different contexts are important to successfully execute EU cross-border and cross-level policies. As much as such skills are honed when one spends part of one's career outside the national system, this clashes with the principles of neutrality and the ideal public servant. Since the EU itself does not replace state structures, it does not replicate career awards offered in state PAs to seconded officials. Therefore, experiences and expertise gained by administrators who leave their national context for a limited time are not systematically rewarded in the national nor in the EU PA system. The actual frame of reference of individual career paths remains national although the actual career path spans beyond these boundaries. In consequence, instead of creating trust in a larger EU system, sustaining the national PA as frame of reference while acting beyond this frame can generate the false image of an overly dominant EU bureaucracy that intervenes and dissolves long-standing legitimate and trusted national administration.

The formal persistence of the national administrative state combined with the actual dissolution of territorially delineated spheres of authority in multilevel PA therefore contradicts the administrative state and undermines legitimacy and trust. On the individual level, the ideal of a public servant lacks credibility in the EU because the system of shared authority blurs the role of the single administrator who interacts across levels. Hence, a set of alternative mechanisms to build trust and legitimacy is a structural feature of the multilevel PA because cross-level collaboration and participation are two of the most crucial functional needs that multilevel administration produces. Short of a system-embracing hierarchical administrative order, effective policy implementation can be achieved only if competent authorities with a high degree of discretion develop high levels of mutual trust and strong vertical and horizontal collaborative networks. On the ideational level, the alternative images of administrative governance match these demands much more closely than do the principles of the administrative state and thus offer interesting counterimages to the latter that can be empirically investigated.

In sum, given how the functional demands of multilevel administration clash with principles of modern PAs while they speak to the counterimages offered by feminist PA theory, we can expect more women in leadership in the administration of EU policies. For this expectation, it does not matter so much if the images or counterimages are indeed more "male" or "female"; it suffices that they are socially more strongly associated with men's or women's specific skills and experience.

There are a number of limitations to the empirical examination. Obviously, the effect of EU integration cannot be fully isolated but occurs in combination with various factors that hinder the advancement of women's leadership and thus influence the expected causal mechanism. The following therefore offers only a limited plausibility probe for the proposed expectation. First, rather than examining qualitatively if the images outlined match attitudes in national PAs, quantitative data on the positioning of women in leadership positions is analyzed. Admittedly, this is a rather crude check, but it offers basic information on whether changes have occurred and whether the expectation is generally supported by the positional data from national EU coordination in Germany. Furthermore, the study does not comprise qualitative data to uncover causal mechanisms. Thus, it cannot answer whether more women in EU-related leadership positions means that feminist counterimages have also gained practical relevance or whether traditional images prevail and therefore these particular positions are considered to have less—or even negative—career value in comparison to others.

Germany serves as a significant case for two reasons. On the one hand, due to the federalist state structure and high ministerial autonomy, German EU policy coordination is overly complex but at the same time highly effective (Beichelt 2009). Therefore, Germany has to meet even higher coordination demands than other, more centralized states. On the other hand, female representation in German PAs remains relatively low. In addition, it is a laggard in bringing women into administrative leadership positions (Biermann et al. 2018), which makes it a crucial case with which to probe the probability of the expectation. Finally, to have a benchmark that is less affected by specific national factors that hinder the advancement of women in EU-related leadership positions, the German data is contrasted with positional data from the Solvit network that interlinks national authorities for the sole purpose of resolving cross-border coordination problems.

13.3 Empirical Examination: The Placement of Women in New and Traditional PA Settings

Do we observe stronger female representation in leadership positions that deal directly with EU policymaking? Having established that functional necessities inherent to EU multilevel administration clash with standard images of rational, modern PAs and that multilevel administration fits much more easily with alternative images that conform more closely with qualities represented in female-defined organizations, this section examines various sources of data to answer the research question. Crucial for the data selection is that national PAs are responsible for the correct application of EU law and the enforcement of EU policies. The European Commission is responsible for overseeing and ensuring the correct application of EU law. Only in rare cases does the Commission execute policies directly. To ensure effective governance of the single market, the Commission therefore puts increasing effort into facilitating cross-country cooperation, Solvit being one of the key instruments to this end (Lottini 2010). In addition, the Commission has promoted administrative capacity building within member states (Heidbreder 2014). To account for the possible effects of the creation of new coordination instruments and changes inside member-state PAs, data on female representation in Solvit centers across 28 member states plus Iceland, Lichtenstein, and Norway (all participating in the single market) is contrasted with data from the two EU-coordinating German ministries, the Ministry for Economic Affairs and Energy (Bundesministerium für Wirtschaft und Energie, BMWi), and the Foreign Office (Auswärtiges Amt, AA). While the general expectation should hold across all three cases, the intervening effects that hinder women from attaining leadership positions should be more evident in the traditional line ministries that have successively taken on an increasing number of EU coordination tasks. The data offered by the European Commission and the ministries varies in scope and quality and thus offers only a tentative comparison. Central issues such as the career paths of women in the ministries and, in particular, qualitative data on the self-understanding and evaluation of women in EU policy coordination are not covered.

The study draws on original data collected and coded for it. The data on Solvit was received directly from the Commission. Earlier, qualitative research by the author pointed in a similar direction for the preceding years, indicating a persistent overrepresentation of women in EU-related positions. For the BMWi, organizational charts from 1952 (starting point of European coordination) through 2019 were analyzed to identify administrative leadership positions and women's leadership in these positions, as well as overall female administrative leadership positions (secretaries of state, heads of departments and units). From the AA, data on female office holders in EU-related leadership positions (heads of departments, units, and subunits) was provided for 2014–2019. This data is complemented by reports that the German Federal Statistical Agency (Statistisches Bundesamt) publishes annually, starting with data from 2015 (Meißmer 2016, 2017, 2018, 2019, 2020).

Descriptive Analysis: Solvit, the German Ministry for Economic Affairs, and the Foreign Office

Solvit is a network that links national competent authorities responsible for administering the single market. Based on the insight that misadministration often originates in coordination and technical administrative problems in cross-border

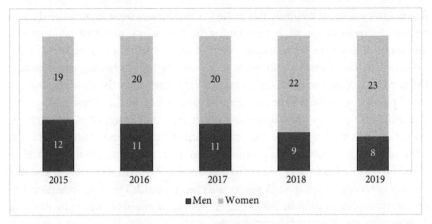

Fig. 13.1 Number of male/female Solvit officials in EU member states, 2015–2019
Sources: own graph; data retrieved from EU Commission.

cooperation, Solvit was created to resolve such problems early on and to prevent escalations resulting in formal infringement procedures.[2] All participating states have a so-called Solvit center to which complaints regarding the application of single market law can be addressed and that coordinates complaints inside the national PAs. Complaints are processed mostly digitally in the Solvit network. The Commission oversees incoming complaints and tracks if complaints are resolved within the statutory time frame of 10 weeks, but it does not get directly involved in handling the requests. Solvit thus represents a new institution that coordinates national PAs, facilitated and assisted but not actively steered by the European Commission. Since its inception in 2002, it has undergone some improvements that have led to a higher response rate and thus more effective problem-solving (Lottini 2020), but its basic functioning logic remains the same. Relevant here is that each national PA has created a Solvit center. In most participating states, the Solvit centers are placed in national core PAs—economic, foreign, or EU ministries—or specialized agencies (Moldoveanu and Nastase 2009). In Germany, Solvit is coordinated by a unit in the Ministry for Economic Affairs. The data presented in Figure 13.1 covers the years 2015–2019.

As the figure shows, of the total of 31, a minimum of 19 and maximum of 23 centers were headed by women, a share of 59%–71%. In Germany, the respective unit in the Ministry for Economic Affairs was consistently headed by a woman during this period.

On the state level, German EU policy coordination is handled by two lead ministries. While the Foreign Office deals with general affairs and foreign policy, the

---

[2] In cases of nonapplication of EU law, including misadministration of EU policies, the Commission can take a state to the Court of Justice of the EU in a so-called infringement procedure. In fact, the introduction of Solvit and the so-called EU Pilot, a network through which the Commission informally contacts national PAs to resolve administrative issues in case of misadministration of EU law, has led to a decrease in infringement procedures and higher compliance rates (Koops 2011).

Ministry for Economic Affairs coordinates all economic policies. To estimate how much the specific demands of EU policymaking affect the positioning of women, we have to look at their placement in these key ministries in the national system. For the BMWi, the most comprehensive dataset was analyzed (comprising organizational charts since 1949).

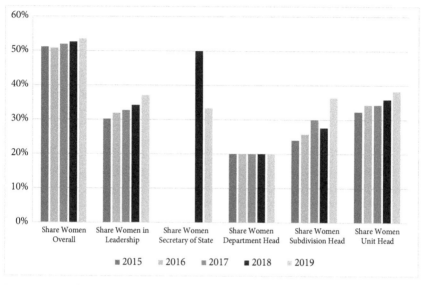

Fig. 13.2 Bundesministerium für Wirtschaft und Energie (Ministry for Economic Affairs and Energy): share of women's leadership according to position, 2015–2019
Sources: own table; data Meißmer (2016, 2017, 2018, 2019, 2020).

To contextualize the data on female leadership position holders, consider the overall share of women in the two ministries (see Figures 13.2 and 13.3). First, the overall share of women is higher in the BMWi, rising from 51% in 2015 to 53.6% in 2019, whereas it drops from 53.5% to 49% in the AA during the same period. The share of women in leadership positions in the BMWi ranges between 30.2% and 37.1%, with a consistent upward trend, while in the AA it ranges between 25.5% and 20.5%. In both ministries, the share of women is greater in lower-ranked leadership positions (head of units, Referatsleitung) than in those of higher rank (head of subdivision, Unterabteilungsleitung, and head of department, Abteilungsleitung). At the highest administrative level, the secretary of state (BMWi) or minister of state (AA), usually only two or three positions are available, to which women have recently begun to be appointed. Notably, the current female secretary of state in the BMWi, who took office in 2018, had previously been the head of the EU department (and a unit within the department) and had a full career in EU-related policy coordination in the BMWi.

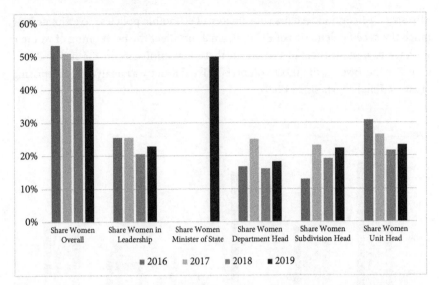

Fig. 13.3 Auswärtiges Amt (Foreign Office): share of women's leadership according to position, 2016–2019

Sources: own table; data Meißmer (2016, 2017, 2018, 2019, 2020).

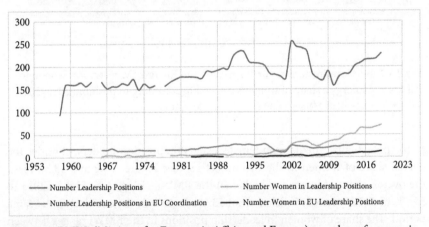

Fig. 13.4 BMWi (Ministry for Economic Affairs and Energy): number of women in leadership positions, general and EU related, 1953–2019

Sources: own chart; data BMWi.

Note: For each year, one organizational chart was coded, thus not all changes that occurred in a year are documented, the months coded varies pending on the data available. For 1965 and 1977 no data was available, other blanks in the graphs indicate that no women were represented in the respective year.

Figure 13.4 summarizes the data for the BMWi since the beginning of European policy coordination in 1952 (in absolute numbers). EU policy coordination is concentrated in special EU departments (with names and scopes of responsibility that change modestly over time) but is also exercised by single units in other departments. The figure shows the overall number of leadership positions in the ministry. Besides an overall increase of administrative staff, the numbers vary due to different portfolio assignments during certain periods and additional staffing during the era of German reunification. The number of women in all leadership positions ranges from zero throughout most of the 1950s and 1960s (with one exception) to low figures in the 1970s–1990s and significantly increases since. Within this group, the number of leadership positions related to EU policy coordination increased slightly after the Treaty of Maastricht in the 1990s and remains largely stable since (with the exception of the late 1990s). The figure shows, finally, that only very recently the number of female office holders in the EU-related units and departments doubled between 2010 and 2019.

In sum, the BMWi shows a significant and ongoing rise in female representation since 2005, with the share of female representation in EU-related areas indeed significantly higher than the overall average.

For the AA, the less comprehensive data allows only limited inferences. However, given that we can also expect here a significant increase of female representation in leadership positions only during the 2000s (see also the above data on the share of women in leadership positions in general), some valuable information can still emerge from the limited time frame. Figure 13.5 shows that as in the BMWi, we see an increase of women in EU-related leadership (from 11 or 12 to 20), which may be read as a slight trend in a similar direction. Overall, the share of women in EU-related leadership positions varies between 23.3% (2015, 2017) and 37.7% (2018). Relating this share back to the overall share of women in AA leadership positions, Figure 13.6 indicates higher female representation in

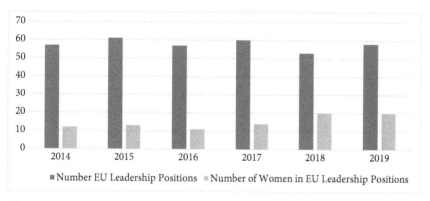

Fig. 13.5 Auswärtiges Amt (Foreign Office): number of women's leadership in EU coordination, 2014–2019

Sources: own graph; data by Auswärtiges Amt.

Note: Data on the entry and exit of women into office was transformed into one binary (m/f) data point per annum. Where an office was held by a man and a woman during a year, the longer-serving gender was coded.

EU-related areas since 2017. But, again, this finding should be taken with caution due to the very limited time period the data covers.

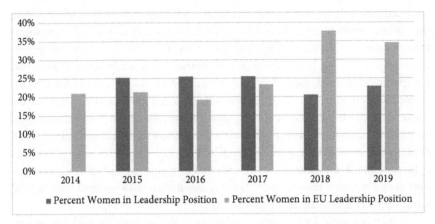

Fig. 13.6 Auswärtiges Amt (Foreign Office): share of women in leadership positions, overall and EU related, 2014–2019

Sources: own graph; data by Auswärtiges Amt; Meißmer (2016, 2017, 2018, 2019, 2020).

Note: Data on the entry and exit of women into office was transformed into one binary (m/f) data point per annum. Where an office was held by a man and a woman during a year, the longer-serving gender was coded.

To what degree do these results indicate more female leadership representation in EU policy coordination? In both German ministries, women were deeply underrepresented until the 2000s and continue to be underrepresented, especially in the AA. Female representation is obviously primarily affected by internal German factors rather than Europeanization. This said, inside the BMWi there is a consistent trend that supports the expectation that leadership positions in EU policy coordination are more open to women than leadership positions on average. In addition, in the BMWi the highest-ranking administrative posts, the head of department for EU coordination (since 2001) as well as the secretary of state (since 2017), are currently held by women. The fact that women are less strongly represented in EU coordination leadership positions in the AA may be explained by the different type of EU coordination carried out by the Foreign Office as well as the generally lower representation of women in leadership positions there. Whereas the BMWi coordinates all single market policies and is, accordingly, most occupied with the execution of the bulk of EU law, the AA coordinates all general affairs and foreign policy and is thus more concerned with high politics than the daily routines of single market execution. Contextualized as well by the substantial overrepresentation of women in the Solvit administrative coordination network, the data indicates that it is plausible to assume there is stronger female representation in leadership positions that coordinate standard

EU policies across member states. Yet we see that greater representation depends strongly on national factors—especially whether women are more generally represented in administrative leadership positions—and that in high politics access for women still appears to be restricted.

13.4 Conclusion: The Europeanization of Women's Administrative Leadership

Driven by the question of whether EU integration produces changes in women's leadership in national PAs, this chapter makes both a theoretical and an empirical contribution. The suggested link between the EU's multilevel administration and feminist PA theory offers a valuable path for further research. The literature on EU multilevel administration points to expected changes in national PAs but falls short of a uniform blueprint for an assimilated EU administrative model. This literature thus fails to identify which new images in PA shape or should shape multilevel administration. In other words, we know that national PAs change and we know which new functional demands occur in multilevel administration, but we lack alternative models. In addition, the empirical evidence does not show consistent patterns across member-state administrations. Theoretically, it is therefore fruitful to link the EU literature to US-focused feminist PA studies that formulate alternative images. The value added is that we can formulate positive expectations about how national PAs in the EU could adapt in the face of the new functional demands created by EU integration. Because the functional demands of multilevel administration clash with principles of modern PAs and because they speak to the counterimages offered by feminist PA theory, we can expect more leadership by women in the administration of EU policies. In a plausibility probe based on original data from two German ministries and an EU administrative coordination network, this expectation proved plausible in broad terms. However, women's leadership has reached truly significant levels only very late in the course of EU integration (after 2000) and still varies widely across policy areas. Besides a more thorough testing of female representation at all levels of multilevel administrative policy coordination and across member states, qualitative research on career paths, women's self-perception, and administrators' attitudes is needed to substantiate the research agenda proposed here. Addressing the question of whether changing functional demands due to EU integration have transformed the criteria for promotions in national administrations is not only a promising way forward to better understand the role of women in administrative leadership and the functioning logics of EU multilevel administration. It is also relevant in more general terms if we want to understand under which conditions EU multilevel administration transforms PAs and should transform modern PAs to successfully provide structure to a fragmented system.

References

Beichelt, Timm. 2009. "Delegation to the EU: Participation versus Efficiency in German EU-Policy." In *In Search of Legitimacy: Policy Making in Europe and the Challenge of Complexity*, ed. Ingolfur Blühdorn, 151–164. Opladen: Barbara Budrich.

Biermann, Kai, Geisler, Astrid, Polke-Majewski, Karsten, and Venohr, Sascha. 2018. "Die Hans-Bremse." *Die Zeit*, October 8.

Featherstone, Kevin, and Radaelli, Claudio M., eds. 2003. *The Politics of Europeanization*. Oxford: Oxford University Press.

Green Cowles, Maria, Caporaso, James, and Risse, Thomas, eds. 2001. *Transforming Europe: Europeanization and Domestic Change*. Ithaca, NY: Cornell University Press.

Hartlapp, Miriam, and Heidbreder, Eva G. 2018. "Mending the Hole in Multilevel Implementation: Administrative Cooperation Related to Worker Mobility." *Governance* 31 (1): 27–43.

Heidbreder, Eva G. 2019. "Europäischer Verwaltungsraum / Mehrebenenverwaltung". In *Handbuch zur Verwaltungsreform*, eds. Sylvia Veit, Christoph Reichard, and Göttrik Wewer, 77–85. Wiesbaden: Springer VS.

Heidbreder, Eva G. 2011. "Structuring the European Administrative Space: Policy Instruments of Multi-level Administration." *Journal of European Public Policy* 18 (5): 709–726.

Heidbreder, Eva G. 2014. "Administrative Capacities in the EU: Consequences of Multilevel Policy-Making." In *Governance Capacities of the Contemporary State*, eds. Martin Lodge and Kai Wegrich, 218–237. Oxford: Oxford University Press.

Koops, Catharina E. 2011. "EU Compliance Mechanisms: The Interaction between the Infringement Procedures, IMS, SOLVIT and EU-Pilot." Amsterdam Centre for European Law and Governance Working Paper Series 2011–08.

Lottini, Michaela. 2010. "Correct Application of EU Law by National Public Administrations and Effective Individual Protection: The SOLVIT Network." *Review of European Administrative Law* 3 (2): 5–26.

Lottini, Michaela. 2020. "The SOLVIT Network: State of the Art and Possible Future Developments." *Review of European Administrative Law* 1: 109–123.

McSwite, O. C. 2004. "Creating Reality through Administrative Practice: A Psychoanalytic Reading of Camilla Stivers' Bureau Men, Settlement Women." *Administration & Society* 36 (4): 406–426.

Miller, Hugh T. 1993. "Reviewed Work(s): Gender Images in Public Administration by Camilla Stivers." *Administrative Theory & Practice* 15 (2): 84–89.

Meißmer, Christian. 2016. *Gleichstellungsindex 2015: Gleichstellung von Frauen und Männern in den obersten Bundesbehörden*. Wiesbaden: Statistisches Bundesamt.

Meißmer, Christian. 2017. *Gleichstellungsindex 2016: Gleichstellung von Frauen und Männern in den obersten Bundesbehörden*. Wiesbaden: Statistisches Bundesamt.

Meißmer, Christian. 2018. *Gleichstellungsindex 2017: Gleichstellung von Frauen und Männern in den obersten Bundesbehörden*. Wiesbaden: Statistisches Bundesamt.

Meißmer, Christian. 2019. *Gleichstellungsindex 2018: Gleichstellung von Frauen und Männern in den obersten Bundesbehörden*. Wiesbaden: Statistisches Bundesamt.

Meißmer, Christian. 2020. *Gleichstellungsindex 2019: Gleichstellung von Frauen und Männern in den obersten Bundesbehörden*. Wiesbaden: Statistisches Bundesamt.

Moldoveanu, George and Nastase, Bogdan. 2009. "The Solvit National Coordination Mechanisms—An Organizational Analysis." *Transylvanian Review of Administrative Sciences*. https://www.rtsa.ro/tras/index.php/tras/article/view/208 (accessed August 5, 2020).

Olsen, Johan. 2003. "Towards a European Administrative Space?" *Journal of European Public Policy* 10 (4): 506–531.

Olsen, Johan. 2006. "Maybe It Is Time to Rediscover Bureaucracy." *Journal of Public Administration Research and Theory* 16 (1): 1–24.

Shields, Patricia M. 2006. "Democracy and the Social Feminist Ethics of Jane Addams: A Vision for Public Administration." *Administrative Theory & Praxis* 28 (3): 418–443.

Stivers, Camilla. 1990. "Toward a Feminist Perspective in Public Administration." *Women & Politics* 10 (4): 49–65.

Stivers, Camilla. 2000. *Bureau Men, Settlement Women: Constructing Public Administration in the Progressive Era*. Lawrence: University of Kansas Press.

Waldo, Dwight. 1948. *The Administrative State: A Study of the Political Theory of American Public Administration*. New York: Ronald Press.

Weber, Max 1980. *Wirtschaft und Gesellschaft. Grundriß der verstehenden Soziologie*. (Studienausgabe, 5. Aufl.) Tübingen: Mohr Siebeck.

PART VI
EXERCISING EXPERT LEADERSHIP

14

The Court of Justice of the European Union, Gender, and Leadership

Jessica Guth

14.1 Introduction

This chapter deals with an understudied area of European Union (EU)—law, policy, and politics—by examining the Court of Justice of the European Union (CJEU, the Court) from a leadership perspective.[1] In particular, it considers women's leadership and what that means in the case of the CJEU. The chapter first introduces the CJEU and its importance within the EU institutional framework and considers how leadership theories can be applied to it. The next section presents my arguments on positional leadership and details the number of women on the Court and the role women play within it. After presenting the rather bleak picture of women's significant underrepresentation, the section outlines some of the reasons for it. It explores the barriers women face in accessing the positions of leadership in the Court, focusing particularly on the appointment procedure. The chapter then turns to an examination of the women on the Court and the impact gender has on their work. The focus throughout this chapter is on positional leadership rather than behavioral leadership, asking questions about the number of women, access to positions, and volume and type of work, rather than about the extent to which female judges and Advocates General (AGs) carry out their functions differently.

14.2 The Court of Justice of the European Union: Multifaceted Leadership

The CJEU is the judicial branch of the EU. As an institution it has received comparatively little attention from political scientists and lawyers alike, although

[1] I would like to thank the participants at the workshop on Women and Leadership in the European Union, which took place in Osnabrück in January 2020, and Katherine Langley, Doug Morrison, and James Shipton for helpful comments and encouragement. Any errors or omissions remain my own. The role holders and numbers used in this chapter are correct as at November 6, 2021.

Jessica Guth, *The Court of Justice of the European Union, Gender, and Leadership.* In: *Women and Leadership in the European Union.* Edited by Henriette Müller and Ingeborg Tömmel, Oxford University Press.
© Oxford University Press (2022). DOI: 10.1093/oso/9780192896216.003.0015

lawyers of course spend a great deal of time analyzing its work (Alter 2009; Guth 2016a, 2016b; Guth and Elfving 2018). The Court, however, has always played an important role in the European project and some would argue has been a key driver in European integration (Garrett 1995; Alter 2009). Certainly, as I have argued elsewhere, the Court transformed the EU legal order into a system that allowed integration through law to proceed at pace (Guth 2016a). In this section I very briefly introduce the CJEU and the work it does. I then show how leadership as a concept and in particular the ideas of positional and behavioral leadership, which provide the thread running through this volume, can be applied in the context of the CJEU and its personnel.

The CJEU is made up of the Court of Justice (CoJ) and the General Court (GC, formerly Court of First Instance); between 2005 and 2016 it also included a Civil Service Tribunal that dealt with cases arising out of disputes between the EU and its civil service. The two current courts do not form a typical hierarchy as might be familiar from national systems. Instead they each have their own specific jurisdictions dealing with separate aspects of the EU legal system and policy portfolio and do not act as appeal courts for national legal systems. The GC deals principally with specific types of actions such as cases brought against the Commission by member states as well as direct actions brought against the EU institutions by natural or legal persons. It also has jurisdiction in cases relating to fact-intensive cases involving competition, state aid, trade, agriculture, and trademarks. The work of the CoJ encompasses all areas of EU law, such as constitutional cases involving free movement, fundamental rights, taxes, the environment, intellectual property, competition, state aid, and social policy. Although the CoJ acts as the court of first instance for certain matters, it is also the highest court for the EU, whereas the GC forms the lower level of the CJEU. Cases heard at the first instance by the GC may be subject to appeal to the CoJ on points of law only. The CoJ thus acts like a Constitutional Court or review court in many ways and is generally considered the more important and senior of the courts within the CJEU.

The CoJ deals with cases that are brought before it in two distinct ways. First, cases are referred to it by national courts via the preliminary reference procedure under Article 267 TFEU. Second, direct actions may be brought either by the Commission initiating infringement proceedings against member states for alleged failure to fulfil their Treaty obligations or by legal or natural persons bringing actions for annulment of EU law measures or actions for failure to act on the part of an EU institution, body, office, or agency. As such, the CJEU has a significant policymaking role that developed alongside its more traditional legal dispute resolution activities. Through the preliminary reference process in particular, the Court has had a significant impact on EU integration. By transforming the legal order (Guth 2016a) in such a way as to allow citizens to enforce their rights in their national courts and co-opting those courts into the enforcement of EU Law, it created a system by which EU integration could be significantly enhanced and sped up. The Court is therefore an important part of the EU institutional setup and the European project whether viewed from a legal or a political perspective.

To organize the work of the courts, judges are split into permanent chambers that hear the cases. In the GC, chambers are made up of five judges and from those chambers either three or all five judges will hear a case. In the CoJ, chambers comprise either three or five judges. In very important or complex cases it is possible that a grand chamber of 15 judges will sit and the full Court may hear particularly important cases. Each chamber has a president who is elected from among the members of the Court for a term of three years (five-judge chamber) or one year (three-judge chamber). The work of the judges on the CoJ is supported by 11 AGs. They are not linked to chambers. AGs are interesting for the discussion of judicial leadership precisely because they are not judges but have equivalent status to them and because more information about their work is publicly available. Their role is to assist the CoJ by providing a reasoned opinion in cases to which they are assigned and by taking on a great deal of the case management. Their opinions are published but they do not take part in deliberations or decision-making. AGs are full members of the Court and the rules treat them as equal to judges in all respects including qualifications needed for appointment and appointment process. We can therefore learn about gendered barriers to access and gendered impacts of work at the Court by looking at AGs. Research examining the role of AGs generally falls into two camps: First, those that try to ascertain the influence AGs have on the Court, often by statistically modeling the correlation between AG opinions and case outcomes (Arrebola 2016; Mortelmans 2005; Ritter 2006; Lazowski 2012; Carrubba et al. 2008; Carrubba and Gabel 2014). Second, those that take a more holistic view of the AG role as one which makes a contribution to the development of EU law as a whole (Albors-Llorens 2012; Sharpston 2008; see also Bobek 2012; Dashwood 1982; Tridimas 1997). In this latter work there is less of a focus on whether and to what extent the Court follows the AG's opinion and instead an examination of the arguments set out and the detail and persuasiveness of the opinions. What is clear, though, is that by virtue of the work that they do, AGs exercise considerable leadership. From a positional point of view, if it is true that the Court follows their opinions in a significant proportion of cases, then this can simply be categorized as positional leadership, with the CoJ as a follower of the AG. However, even where this is not the case, AGs often exercise leadership by using their opinions to fully set out the policy considerations as well as legal arguments, different possible solutions, and their interpretation of what the outcome should be. This is a much fuller consideration of the issues than can be found in CoJ judgments. The followers of AG leaders are therefore not just (or even at all) the judges in the case in question but judges of future cases as well as lawyers, policymakers, and even the public, as Laffranque (2004: 18) observes:

> In this context, opinions of the AG remain the only channel through which the public can learn about the controversies concerning the legal and factual issues of the case at hand. In contrast to the CJ and GC [...], the Advocates-General are more outspoken and often offer a more nuanced view of the controversies at hand, and their reasoning—even if not followed by the CJ—could come in handy later on.

This chapter therefore uses information about the AGs' work to shed some light on gender and women's leadership at the CJEU.

As many of the contributions to this volume note, there is no universally accepted definition of leadership. There certainly is not one of judicial leadership (Ryder and Hardy 2019); the limited literature on judicial leadership seems to focus on aspects like case management and "much judicial work is considered to be transactional" (Ryder and Hardy 2019: 42). For effective leadership to emerge in the judicial context, an element of both positional and behavioral leadership is necessary and, as Ryder and Hardy (2019: 42) argue, different theories of leadership applied to judicial leadership "illustrate the complex relationship between leadership theory, culture and organizational theory." This chapter follows the conceptualization of leadership as set out in the volume's Chapter 1. The positional leadership question thus deals with access to judicial positions on the CJEU and the difficulties women experience in accessing those positions, whereas behavioral leadership in this context is concerned with whether women lead or, in this case, carry out their judicial functions differently from men. The focus of this chapter is on the former. Positional leadership is often seen as the more straightforward conceptualization, with positional leaders simply being those who exercise authority over other people (Eagly and Carli 2007: 8). In the case of the Court of Justice, one might therefore argue that the CJEU in its entirety provides leadership as an institution in EU legal matters to the national courts of the member states, to the parties in any given case, to the other EU institutions, and in some cases to member states' governments. Alternatively, one could argue that all of the judges individually provide leadership because by virtue of being judges they have some authority over the parties to their cases, their staff, and each other and are indeed clarifying if not moving forward the interpretation of EU law. Similar arguments can be made about CoJ leading the GC or about the specific groupings of judges making up the chambers within the Court. On the most basic level one might classify just the presidents of the CoJ and the GC and maybe the vice-president of the CoJ as holding leadership positions or one might add the heads of chambers to that list. Depending on the context, all of these ways of thinking about leadership are potentially correct, so, in relation to the Court, even positional leadership is multifaceted and potentially complex because it depends on the context and on who, in that given context, we think of as followers or the intended audience or recipients of the judicial work in question.

Behavioral-leadership approaches would allow for the inclusion of a whole host of other actors in the Court who all potentially provide leadership. For example, some of the landmark cases relating to both the EU legal order and gender equality were championed by lawyers who set out to use EU law strategically to achieve legal change across the Union. Éliane Vogel-Polsky, one such example, certainly demonstrated a great deal of leadership in securing a case that raised the right issues and then framing the legal questions in such a way as to engage the full force of EU law.[2] In some cases, the national courts that decide whether or not to refer a question of EU law and how to frame the questions to be asked of the CoJ might be said to be exercising leadership. All of these interpretations of leadership are possible in the right contexts and worthy of further study in themselves. However, dealing with all these aspects is beyond the scope of this chapter and the focus here is thus on the positional leaders, the judges, and AGs of the Court.

14.3 A Story of Slow Progress: Gender and the Court of Justice of the European Union

Women remain woefully underrepresented throughout the CJEU. In the CoJ there are now 27 judges (one per member state) and 11 AGs, and on the GC there are two judges from each member state (54). Out of the current total of 92 judicial-level appointments, only 22 are women (seven in the CoJ and 15 in the GC) and historically very few women have been appointed, as can be seen in Table 14.1. The CJEU has always been and continues to be dominated by men. This becomes strikingly obvious when considering the chambers into which the courts are divided. In the CoJ, three of the 10 chambers do not have any women in them, two chambers have female presidents, and one chamber has two women out of its five judges. Each of the others has one woman. All chambers thus have a male majority and where three judges hear a case the judicial panel has a high likelihood of being all male. The GC does little better. Out of the 10 chambers, none have zero female representation, two have female presidents, and three even have a female majority (3:2), but mostly women make up one of the five judges that are grouped together to make the chambers and it is possible for an all-male panel of three to hear a case.

Table 14.1 shows us that the first woman to join the Court was Simone Rozès-Ludwig, who joined the then European Court of Justice as an AG in 1981. The president of the Court at the time noted the occasion:

It may have caused some surprise that as yet I have not mentioned the fact, and an important one in our eyes that it will be the first time that a woman has ever

---

[2] Readers interested in the role played by Éliane Vogel-Polsky might like to read Gubin, E. (2007).

Table 14.1 Women appointed to the Court by member state (present judges/AGs in bold)

Member State	GC Female Judges (including the former CFI and Civil Service Tribunal)	CoJ Female Judges Appointed	Female AG Appointed
Austria		Maria Berger (2009–2019)	Christine Stix-Hackl (2000–2006)
Belgium			
Bulgaria	Mariyana Kancheva (2011–present)		
Croatia	Vesna Tomljenović (2013–present) Tamara Perišin (2019–present)		Tamara Capeta (2001–present)
Cyprus	Anna Marcoulli (2016–present)		
Czech Republic	Irena Pelikánová (GC 2004–2019) Petra Škvařilová-Pelzl (2019–present)		
Denmark			
Estonia	Küllike Jürimäe (2004–2013)	Küllike Jürimäe (2013–present)	
Finland	Virpi Tiili (CFI 1995–2009) Tuula Riitta Pynnä (2019–present)		
France			Simone Rozès (1981–1984)
Germany	Waltraud Hakenberg (Registrar of the Civil Service Tribunal 2005–2016) Gabriele Steinfatt (2019–present)	Ninon Colneric (2000–2006)	Juliane Kokott (2003–present)
Greece			
Hungary			
Ireland		Fidelma O'Kelly Macken (1999–2004)	
Italy	Ornella Porchia (2019–present)	Lucia Serena Rossi (2018–present)	

Continued

Table 14.1 *Continued*

Member State	GC Female Judges (including the former CFI and Civil Service Tribunal)	CoJ Female Judges Appointed	Female AG Appointed
Latvia	Ingrida Labucka (2004–2020) **Inga Reine (2016–present)**	**Ineta Ziemele (2020–present)**	
Lithuania			
Luxembourg			
Malta	Ena Cremona (2004–2012) **Ramona Frendo (2019–present)**		
Netherlands		**Sacha Prechal (2010–present)**	
Poland	Irenan Boruta (Civil Service Tribunal 2005–2013) Irena Wiszniewska-Białecka (2004–2016) **Nina Półtorak (2016–present)** **Krystyna Kowalik-Bańczyk (2016–present)**		
Portugal	Maria Eugénia Martins de Nazaré Ribeiro (2003–2016) **Maria José Costeira (2016–present)**		
Romania	Octavia Spineanu-Matei (GC 2016–2021) **Mirela Stancu (GC 2019–present)**	Camelia Toader (2007–2021) **Octavia Spineanu-Matei (2021–present)**	
Slovakia			
Slovenia	Verica Trstebjak (CFI 2004–2006) **Maja Brkan (2021–present)**		Verica Trstebjak (2006–2012)
Spain	Maria Isabel Rofes i Pujol (Civil Service Tribunal 2009–2013)	Rosario Silva de Lapuerta (2003–2021) **Maria Lourdes Arastey Sahun (2021–present)**	
Sweden	Pernilla Lindh (CFI 1995–2006)	Pernilla Lindh (2006–2011)	
UK (no longer a MS)			Eleanor Sharpston (2006–2020)

Source: Collated from https://curia.europa.eu/jcms/jcms/j_6/en/

become part of this institution. It is not that the Court does not perceive the significance of that event, which is a reflection of the finest spirit of modern times. On the contrary, the case-law of the Court bears witness to the fact that, in so far as the Treaty calls upon it to do so, this institution watches attentively to ensure that the principle of equal treatment for men and women is observed.

(Mertens De Wilmars 1981: 76)

It was another 14 years before two further women joined the institution. This time, in 1995, judges from Finland and Sweden (Virpi Tilli and Pernilla Lindh, who later became a judge on the CoJ, respectively) joined what was then the Court of First Instance. Finally, in 1999, Fidelma O'Kelly Macken was the first woman to join the ECJ as a judge, followed by Nonin Colneric in 2000. The table highlights the several countries that have never had a female judge at the Court such as Belgium or Denmark, as well as, for example, Hungary. By contrast, Romania stands out as having had a female CoJ and two female GC judges in office; Poland and Croatia also have two female GC judges. Germany is the only country to have had a female judge in both Courts as well as an AG (though not all at the same time). The number of women overall is woefully low, even if there has been a slight improvement in the last four years.

The table may be surprising to some. It is difficult to explain why some member states have appointed more women than others. A 2017 report on gender equality in the legal professions across the EU for the JURI Committee (Galligan et al. 2017) helps explain some of the appointments. That study showed significant disparity between member states when it comes to women's representation in the judiciary at the national level, and one might expect those member states with higher proportions of women in the judiciary to also be more likely to appoint women to the CJEU. Given that the appointment to the CJEU requires the qualifications (CoJ) or ability (GC) to hold the highest judicial office in the member state, it is worth looking at the study's findings in relation to the senior judiciary. Only in Romania was the senior judiciary female dominated, with 85% of the judges being female. Luxembourg, Latvia, and Slovakia each had slightly more women than men in their higher courts, and Hungary and Greece were reported to have almost equal representation in 2014. Otherwise judges at the top level tend to be men, on average two-thirds, but with six member states reporting over 70% and three member states over 80% of the senior judicial posts occupied by men (Galligan et al. 2017: 51). These results perhaps explain Romania's appointment of women to the Court, but it does not hold true that those member states with more women in the national higher courts are more likely to appoint women to the CJEU. Out of the countries listed above, Hungary, Greece, Luxembourg, and Slovakia have not appointed any women and France, which had only a very slight underrepresentation of women at national level, has not appointed a woman to the Court since Simone Rozès-Ludwig was AG in the 1980s.

While the report highlights the use of gender quotas for the Belgian Constitutional Court, showing that there is an awareness of the need for gender balance (Galligan et al. 2017: 37), Belgium has never appointed a female judge to the CJEU. Given the lack of women in the senior judiciary in Belgium (less than 20%, according to Galligan et al. 2017), this is unsurprising. However, the reverse assumption to the one set out above, that member states which have low representation of women in the highest courts would also be unlikely to appoint women to the CJEU, does not hold universally true either. Estonia, Spain, and Portugal all have very low female representation in their highest courts but have still appointed women to the Court more than once (albeit, in Estonia's case the same woman, Küllike Jürimäe, was appointed first to the CFI and then the CoJ). The appointment of women to the CJEU can therefore not simply be explained by the feminization or otherwise of the legal profession and in particular the judiciary in member states, though it is unlikely to be completely irrelevant. Gill and Jensen (2020) also struggled to predict which member states would be more likely to appoint women to the Court based on fairly obvious assumptions about legal cultures and traditions and how they shape what member states see as essential requirements of senior judges. Gill and Jensen (2020: 128–129) hypothesized that "Member States with centralized constitutional review will be more likely to select an ECJ candidate with ministerial experience or with experience on the national constitutional court (as opposed to the ordinary courts) when compared to judicial review member states." This additional requirement would negatively impact on the likelihood of women being appointed because it narrows the pool of possible candidates, and women are less likely to be able to show all of the required experience. Their analysis, however, suggested that this is too simplistic: "Essentially, member states with centralized constitutional review tend to require their female ECJ appointees to have both a legal background and a policymaking background in the ministry or the constitutional court" (Gill and Jenson 2020: 136).

As is apparent from the preceding section, progress toward gender parity at the CJEU has been incredibly slow and may have even stagnated; female judges face many of the same barriers women encounter in other sectors and in particular in public life, and they are often required to explicitly show experience and skills that men are presumed to have (Gill and Jensen 2018). The first chapter of this volume has listed some of these barriers, noting the cultural assumptions and stereotypes about women, unequal access to resources, unequal family responsibilities, and absence of female role models. The report by Galligan et al. (2017: 31) similarly summarizes the barriers for women in the legal profession as including implicit gender bias, difficulties in balancing personal and professional life, a paucity of effective mentors and support networks, and hitting the glass ceiling (see also Schulz and Shaw 2013; Brenner 2014; Hunter 2015). As these barriers are well rehearsed in the literature, I do not propose to analyze them here in any detail beyond pointing out that they apply to the EU judiciary as much as they do in other sectors. An additional factor, however, has been identified in relation to the judiciary: transparency of the recruitment or appointment process (Galligan et al. 2017; International Commission of Jurists 2013; Schulz and Shaw 2013). There are significant differences between civil and common law countries in relation to the transparency of judicial appointments (Galligan et al. 2017), and the CJEU has been criticized for lacking a fair and transparent process, so this is worth further examination here.

Appointment processes undoubtedly impact on the access women have to positions on the Court (see Cohen 2010; Siebert 1997; Kenney 1998; Dumbrovský et al. 2014). The requirements for judicial appointments to the Court are set out in the treaties. Article 19 stipulates that a nominee's independence must be beyond doubt and Article 253 TFEU stipulates that the justices and AGs of the Court must:

> possess the qualifications required for appointment to the highest judicial offices in their respective countries or who are jurisconsults of recognised competence.

The conditions for the GC are almost identical, but here the requirement is only to "possess the ability required for appointment to high judicial office." Much of the research on the CJEU comments on the lack of transparency and the variety of ways in which judges are appointed in member states—which, given the limited criteria set out in the treaties and differing legal traditions, is perhaps obvious (Gill and Jensen 2018). The Treaty of Lisbon made some changes to the appointment process and added an EU-level panel that must give an opinion as to the suitability of a candidate (see Art. 255 TFEU; Solanke 2009; Bobek 2015). While the introduction of the panel has had an influence on some member states in terms of increasing transparency (Dumbrovský et al. 2014), it seems that the appointment of judges and AGs to the Court remains very much a member state-controlled exercise (Gill and Jensen 2018; Guth and Elfving 2018; Bobek 2015). This impacts on diversity. Turenne (2017: 572) notes: "At the level of the CJEU, diversity is the responsibility of every Member State, and consequently, individually that of no one." In fact, the Article 255 panel has declared that gender considerations are outside the scope of the panel (Sauvé 2019). The appointment process also means that the other key EU institutions, such as the Commission, have very little input in the process, despite having tried to drive gender mainstreaming of the institutions.

However, the importance of gender balance at the Courts, specifically in the future appointments to the GC, has been recognized in EU law in the form of Regulation 2015/2422/EU, which amended the Statute of the Court. Recital 11 of the Preamble to the Regulation states:

> It is of high importance to ensure gender balance within the General Court. In order to achieve that objective, partial replacements in that Court should be organised in such a way that the governments of Member States gradually begin to

nominate two Judges for the same partial replacement with the aim therefore of choosing one woman and one man, provided that the conditions and procedures laid down by the Treaties are respected.

Although it is too early to assess whether this notion is going to have the desired impact, Turenne is not optimistic:

> It is doubtful whether this provides the panel with any constraining power in relation to gender diversity—especially as the panel has previously stated that it does not have the competence to determine the composition of the Court of Justice or of the General Court.
>
> (2017: 572)

In fact, there may be reason to be a little more optimistic. The proportion of women on the GC is higher than on the CoJ (27.7% or 15 out of 54, compared to 23.68% or 9 out of 38), and, since 2016, 13 women have been appointed to the GC out of a total of 16 appointments, so maybe Recital 11 is being taken into consideration and progress is being made. However, clearly barriers remain and one of the key barriers is the requirement to possess the qualifications for appointment to the highest national judicial office. This requirement is couched in terms of merit. As Kenney demonstrates, the question of merit in the case of the CJEU is highly skewed:

> Choosing the best woman judge is no more antithetical to applying merit standards than choosing the best Cypriot judge. The difference is that requiring diversity of nationality or geography has been accepted as a representative restriction, whereas gender diversity has not.
>
> (2013: 128)

Further, as Lady Hale has argued in the context of the judiciary in the UK:

> It is always so much easier to recognise merit in people who are like the people who have always done the job, especially if they are people like oneself.
>
> (2017: 15)

Merit is a highly problematic and gendered concept and until unpacked sufficiently is likely to be little more than an excuse for the appointment of more men (Morison 2015; Castilla and Benard 2010). Further, Kenney (1998) has rightly noted that the appointments to the Court are political appointments and the requirement to demonstrate legal as well as policymaking expertise is highlighted by Gill and Jensen (2020). All of these issues have implications for gender because, as this volume illustrates, gender stereotypes and outmoded notions of what women should or should not do still shape their access to and experience of public life as well as our perception of their effectiveness, successes, or failures. "Given the persistent 'think leader, think male' culture, women are often ascribed less merit simply by not being male" (Galligan et al. 2017: 32). Increasing the transparency of the appointment process for judges and AGs to the CJEU in each member state and having a much clearer set of criteria that is more open to scrutiny would be a positive first step toward increasing the number of women appointed.

14.4 The Women of the Court of Justice: Who They Are and What They Do

It is a positive thing to be able to say that providing an introduction to all the women on the Court is beyond the scope of this chapter, because it means that there are finally more women on the Court than it is feasible to present here. Instead I present some brief comments on the women on the Court generally before focusing on the female AGs, past and present, to consider whether or not there is any evidence of men and women being asked to do the job differently.

For most of the women on the Court, very little information beyond the short presentation of them on the CJEU website is available. We can gain some understanding of their career, legal education, and professional experience prior to becoming a judge or AG. The available information suggests that the women on the Court are likely to have carried out postgraduate study and often doctoral-level work in law and/or related disciplines like political science and that they have judicial experience as well as experience as legal advisors or similar in government. Many also hold academic positions. In some cases, we can gain brief glimpses of their lives from sources such as newspapers. For example, an interview with Eleanor Sharpston (Maitland 2015) suggests that her early legal career as a barrister in the UK was difficult as "women were tolerated but not encouraged" and it was presumed that they would stick to areas such as family law. The interview also describes her relatively privileged position, which allowed her to hear "on the grapevine" about positions for law clerks at the ECJ and "drop in" to see Sir Gordon Slynn, who was the British Advocate General at the time, to secure one such job. We also know that Sharpston did not have to balance work and childcare commitments.

In contrast, Juliane Kokott is a mother of six, with an impressive legal and academic career. The publicly available information again reveals relative privilege, including studying in Bonn, Geneva, and Washington, DC, and significant international experience before going to the ECJ—a not uncommon profile. Sacha Prechal has a slightly different profile, having made her name in Dutch academia before going to the Court, while the first female vice-president (2018–2021) of the Court, Rosario Silva de Lapuerta, built her career in the Spanish State Legal Service before moving to the European Court. In general, though, very little about the lives, experiences, and views of these women is made public and even less is known about the barriers they may have faced in becoming judges and AGs of the Court or the way they approach the work there. We know, for example, that Christine Stix-Hackl was passed over for the judicial position on the ECJ twice. When her first term as AG expired and the Austrian judge on the ECJ was up for renewal at the same time, instead of appointing her, Austria opted to renew Peter Jann's term. Her supporters questioned why the term of a 71-year-old man was renewed whereas an equally qualified woman (aged around 50) was not even considered (Grimm and Kommenda 2018). The second occasion highlights the political nature of appointments: rumors circulated that Stix-Hackl used all her political capital and networks to put herself in the running for appointment to the CJEU in June 2018 to succeed Maria Berger (Grimm and Kommenda 2018) but again did not get the job. Detailed biographies of the members of the Court could help us to fully understand the pathways to the Court and the experiences of those pathways.

What is striking about the information available on the women in the Court and the snippets we can gather to gain insights into their lives is that they are so similar—similar to each other as well as similar to the men on the Court. There is nothing to suggest that men and women have significantly different career paths or significantly different experience that qualifies them for the judicial roles they hold. That is not to say, of course, that men and women do not experience those paths differently or that women have not had to overcome barriers that simply did not exist for men, and it does not mean that gender is not important in shaping these issues. The low number of women is testament to that and suggests that stereotypes, gendered conceptualizations of work and merit, and structural inequalities still make it difficult for women to access these positions. Those who do access them, though, have career paths that are remarkably similar to those of their male counterparts. These issues are important to unpack in terms of the impact on judging and they are being covered in the emerging literature on gender and judging (see Schulz and Shaw 2013, for example), but for the purposes of this chapter I now want to consider the extent to which gender impacts on the volume, type, and impact of the work carried out.

In 2006 Ritter published a paper analyzing the influence of AGs on the Court. The time frame of his analysis covers 2004 and 2005, a period where there were two female AGs at the Court (Stix-Hackl and Kokott). The analysis shows that all the AGs had a similar number of cases over the two years and there is certainly no gender difference in number of cases allocated. A similar picture emerges if we repeat that analysis now. In relation to opinions delivered in 2019, AGs Sharpston and Kokott were assigned a similar number of cases to their male counterparts. Sharpston delivered 23 and Kokott 29. Looking at only those AGs who were members of the Court for all of 2019 (thus excluding AG Bot, AG Wahl, and

AG Pikamäe), the highest number of opinions was delivered by AG Szpunar with 37 and the lowest by AG Tanchev with 20; the average was 29 (EUR-Lex; own analysis).

The analysis of the types of cases assigned further suggests that gender does not appear to influence the area of law or topic assigned. While Krook and O'Brien (2012) provide a list of policy fields considered as typically masculine, feminine, or neutral, this does not seem to be of relevance here. In 2019 both AG Sharpston and AG Kokott dealt with a variety of legal areas, ranging from consumer protection provisions to member states' failure to fulfil their EU law obligations in the wake of the migrant crisis (EUR-Lex; own analysis). While there may be some difference in the type of cases to which the two AGs are assigned, there is no evidence that their portfolio of cases is based on gendered assumptions made about typically masculine or feminine policy and legal areas.

The analysis undertaken by Ritter also shows the number of times a judgment cites the corresponding opinion at least once and again there appears to be no difference in terms of gender, with Stix-Hackl and Kokott coming at position 5 and 6 in the rankings (out of eight AGs at the time) and occupying the same position when multiple citations are taken into account (Ritter 2006: 22–24). This analysis has not been repeated, because it actually tells us very little about the influence of AG opinions on the Court and the relationship between opinion and judgment is complex and cannot be reduced to citations or mentions. Ritter's analysis showed that there was no gender difference, and the more qualitative analysis of policy areas undertaken by Guth and Elfving (2018) confirms that there is no evidence to suggest that the opinions of male and female AGs are treated or regarded any differently. This suggests that, while women continue to struggle to reach positions of leadership in the EU legal system, those that do attain such positions carry out the same volume of work as their male counterparts and do so with the same impact and effect. I accept that the analysis presented here is a fairly crude measure of gender differences, but it is useful to show that gender does not appear to be a factor in the assignment of cases nor does it seemingly have an impact on whether the Court will take an opinion into account and follow it fully or partially or not at all. This is a useful starting point from which future research can begin to explore questions of behavioral leadership.

14.5 Conclusions: Leadership in the Court

This chapter has shown that the CJEU can be analyzed from a leadership perspective and that this can provide important insights into the working of the Court and its personnel. It has argued that leadership in the Court is multifaceted, even where just positional leadership is considered. It shows that women remain woefully underrepresented and has considered the lack of transparency as well as the power member states have in the appointment process as contributing factors. However, the analysis also shows that the members of the Court are a very homogeneous group of people and that gender does not have an impact on the volume or type of work allocated or the impact of that work. This is not to suggest, though, that the underrepresentation of women at the CJEU is not important or in need of being urgently addressed. What this chapter does highlight is that while a women-and-leadership perspective on the Court adds another dimension to our knowledge of the CJEU as a legal and political institution, further work is needed to fully understand the complexities of it as a legal and political institution and of its personnel as judges, AGs, court staff, and people.

References

Albors-Llorens, Albertina. 2012. "Securing Trust in the Court of Justice of the EU: The Influence of the Advocates General." *Cambridge Yearbook of European Legal Studies* 14: 509–527.

Alter, Karen. 2009. *The European Court's Political Power*. Oxford: Oxford University Press.

Arrebola, Carlos, Ana Julia Mauricio, and Héctor Jiménez Portilla. 2016. "An Econometric Analysis of the Influence of the Advocate General on the Court of Justice of the European Union." *Cambridge Journal of Comparative and International Law* 5 (1): 82–112.

Bobek, Michal. 2012. "A Fourth in the Court: Why Are There Advocates General in the Court of Justice?" *Cambridge Yearbook of European Legal Studies* 14: 529–561.

Bobek, Michal, ed. 2015. *Selecting Europe's Judges*. Oxford: Oxford University Press.

Brenner, Hannah. 2014. "Expanding the Pathways to Gender Equality in the Legal Profession." *Legal Ethics* 17 (2): 261–280.

Carrubba, Clifford J., and Matthew Gabel. 2014. *International Courts and the Performance of International Agreements*. Cambridge, UK: Cambridge University Press.

Carrubba, Clifford J., Matthew Gabel, and Charles Hankla. 2008. "Judicial Behaviour under Political Constraints: Evidence from the European Court of Justice." *American Political Science Review* 102: 435.

Castilla, Emilio J., and Stephen Benard. 2010. "The Paradox of Meritocracy in Organizations." *Administrative Society Quarterly* 55 (4): 543–676.

Cohen, Antonin. 2010. "Ten Majestic Figures in Long Amaranth Robes: The Formation of the Court of Justice of the European Communities." *Revue française de science politique* 60 (2): 227–246.

Council of the European Union. Recommendation 96/694/EC of 2 December 1996 on the balanced participation of women and men in the decision-making process [1996] OJ L319/11.

Dashwood, Alan. 1982. "The Advocate General in the Court of Justice of the European Communities." *Legal Studies* 2 (2): 202–216.

Dumbrovský, Tomáš, Bilyana Petkova, and Marijn van der Sluis. 2014. "Judicial Appointments: The Article 255 TFEU Advisory Panel and Selection Procedures in the Member States." *Common Market Law Review* 51 (2): 455–482.

Eagly, Alice H., Carli, Linda L. 2007. *Through the Labyrinth: The Truth about How Women Become Leaders*. Boston, MA: Harvard Business School Press.

Galligan, Yvonne, et al. 2017. *Mapping the Representation of Women and Men in Legal Professions across the EU*. DG Internal Policies of the Union PE 596.804, available at www.europarl.europa.eu/RegData/etudes/STUD/2017/596804/IPOL_STU(2017)596804_EN.pdf.

Garrett, Geoffrey. 1995. "The Politics of Legal Integration in the European Union." *International Organization* 49 (1): 171–181.

Gill, Rebecca D., and Christian Jensen. 2020. "Where Are the Women? Legal Traditions and Descriptive Representation on the European Court of Justice." *Politics, Groups, and Identities* 8 (1): 122–142.

Grimm, Oliver, and Benedikt Kommenda. 2018. "Botschafterin Stix-Hackl verstorben." *Die Presse* [online], October 30, available at www.diepresse.com/5521767/botschafterin-stix-hackl-verstorben.

Gubin, E. 2007. *Éliane Vogel-Polsky: A Woman of Conviction*. Belgium: Institute for the Equality of Women and Men.

Guth, Jessica. 2016a. "Transforming the European Legal Order: The European Court of Justice at 60+." *Journal of Contemporary European Research* 12 (1): 455–466.

Guth, Jessica. 2016b. "Law as the Object and Agent of Integration: Gendering the Court of Justice of the European Union, Its Decisions and Their Impact." In *Gendering European Integration Theory*, eds. Gabriele Abels and Heather MacRae, 175–196. Opladen: Barbara Budrich.

Guth, Jessica, and Sanna Elfving. 2018. *Gender and the Court of Justice of the European Union*. Abingdon, UK: Routledge.

Hale, Brenda. 2017. "Judges, Power and Accountability: Constitutional Implications of Judicial Selection." Constitutional Law Summer School, University of Belfast. August 11, available at www.supremecourt.uk/docs/speech-170811.pdf.

Hunter, Rosemary. 2015. "More than Just a Different Face? Judicial Diversity and Decision-Making." *Current Legal Problems* 68: 119–141.

International Commission of Jurists. 2013. *Women and the Judiciary*. Geneva Forum Series no. 1. Materials relating to the 2013 Geneva Forum of Judges and Lawyers convened by the International Commission of Jurists.

Kenney, Sally J. 1998. "The Members of the Court of Justice of the European Communities." *Columbia Journal of European Law* 5: 101–133.

Kenney, Sally J. 2013. *Gender and Justice: Why Women in the Judiciary Really Matter*. Abingdon, UK: Routledge.

Laffranque, Julia. 2004. "Dissenting Opinion in the European Court of Justice: Estonia's Possible Contribution to the Democratisation of the European Union Judicial System." *Juridica International* 9: 14–23.

Lazowski, Adam. 2012. "Advocates General and Grand Chamber Cases: Assistance with the Touch of Substitution." *Cambridge Yearbook of European Legal Studies* 14: 635–662.

Maitland, A. 2015. 'Eleanor Sharpston'. The First 100 Years Available at https://first100years.org.uk/eleanor-sharpston/ [accessed 13th August 2021].

Mertens de Wilmars, Josse. 1981. President of the Court, on the occasion of the taking up of office by Mrs. Advocate General Simone Rozès. March 18, available at http://aei.pitt.edu/5165/1/5165.pdf.

Morison, John. 2015. "Finding Merit in Judicial Appointments: NIJAC and the Search for a New Judiciary in Northern Ireland." In *Criminal Justice in Transition: The*

Northern Ireland Context, eds. Anne-Marie McAlinden and Clare Dwyer, 31–156. Oxford: Hart.

Mortelmans, Kamiel. 2005. "The Court under the Influence of Its Advocates General: An Analysis of the Case Law on the Functioning of the Internal Market." *Yearbook of European Law* 24: 127–172.

Ritter, Cyril. 2006. "A New Look at the Role and Impact of Advocates General— Collectively and Individually." *Columbia Journal of European Law* 12: 751–776.

Ryder, Ernest, and Stephen Hardy. 2019. *Judicial Leadership: A New Strategic Approach.* Oxford: Oxford University Press.

Sauvé, Jean-Marc. 2015. "Selecting European Union's Judges: The Practice of the Article 255 Panel." In *Selecting Europe's Judges*, ed. Michal Bobek, 78–85. Oxford: Oxford University Press.

Schulz, Ulrike, and Gisela Shaw, eds. 2013. *Gender and Judging.* Oxford: Hart.

Sharpston, Eleanor. 2008. "The Changing Role of the Advocate General." In *Continuity and Change in EU Law: Essays in Honour of Sir Francis Jacobs*, eds. Anthony Arnull, Piet Eeckhout, and Takis Tridimas, 20–33. Oxford: Oxford University Press.

Siebert, Derk. 1997. *Die Auswahl der Richter am Gerichtshof der Europäischen Gemeinschaften: zu der erforderlichen Reform des Art 167 EGV.* Bern: Peter Lang.

Solanke, Iyiola. 2009. "Diversity and Independence in the European Court of Justice." *Columbia Journal of European Law* 15: 89–122.

Tridimas, Takis. 1997. "The Role of the Advocate General in the Development of Community Law: Some Reflections." *Common Market Law Review* 34: 1349–1387.

Turenne, Sophie. 2017. "Institutional Constraints and Collegiality at the Court of Justice of the European Union: A Sense of Belonging?" *Maastricht Journal of European and Comparative Law* 24 (4): 565–581.

15

Women's Leadership in the European Central Bank

Amy Verdun

15.1 Introduction

On November 1, 2019, Christine Lagarde took office as president of the European Central Bank (ECB). She is the first woman to serve in this role. Across the globe a very small number of women have ever served as central bank president, especially in advanced economies, and women are also severely underrepresented on central bank boards (Charléty et al. 2017).[1] In addition to being underrepresented in the very top position, women have also been notoriously underrepresented in other types of leadership roles in central banks. Employees of a central bank more often than not hold economics degrees. Economics has been a field more dominated by men than many other academic disciplines. In addition, central banking in particular has traditionally been seen as more male dominated than other professions or the discipline of economics more generally (OMFIF 2019).

The Governing Council is the main decision-making body of the ECB. To date it has been made up mostly of men, though a few women have served on it. It has 25 members (six members of the Executive Board and the Governors of the central banks of the 19 euro area countries). At the time of writing, it has only two female members—one of whom is the president. More women have held upper managerial positions in the ECB's administration. In its most recent annual report, the ECB recorded that about 30% of these senior positions were currently held by women (ECB 2020a: 109). This chapter provides a first analysis of women's leadership in the ECB. Central questions it addresses are: What have been the reasons for women's absence or presence in leadership positions in central banking in general and in the ECB in particular? What has been the behavioral leadership of Christine Lagarde, the first female ECB president?

---

[1] At the time that Janet Yellen was nominated for the position of chair of the Federal Reserve Bank (in 2013), the other female central bank presidents across the globe could be found in Argentina, Aruba, The Bahamas, Belarus, Botswana, Honduras, Kyrgyzstan, Lesotho, Malaysia, Russia, Samoa, São Tomé and Príncipe, Serbia, the Seychelles, Somalia, South Africa, and Tonga (Tsang 2013).

Amy Verdun, *Women's Leadership in the European Central Bank*. In: *Women and Leadership in the European Union*. Edited by Henriette Müller and Ingeborg Tömmel, Oxford University Press.
© Oxford University Press (2022). DOI: 10.1093/oso/9780192896216.003.0016

In keeping with the literature and Chapter 1 of this volume, this chapter assumes that gender roles are socially constructed (Elliott and Stead 2008; Ridgeway 2011). The chapter examines the setting of central banking and, within that, the specific situation at the ECB to explain the underrepresentation of women therein and to tease out a possible explanation thereof. The chapter seeks to investigate women's leadership of the ECB in the following way: Section 15.2 examines whether there is something special about central banking that obstructs women from rising to leadership roles in this profession. Section 15.3 looks at women in the ECB and their role as leaders in particular. This part of the chapter also examines policies of the ECB that have sought to improve its gender balance and eventually work toward greater gender equality at three levels of administration: the very top positions; the senior management; and the advancement of women versus men through the bureaucratic ranks into leadership positions. In addition, it also discusses a study by Hospido et al. (2019a, 2019b, 2020) of the ECB's gender performance and the reasons behind women's continued underrepresentation. Section 15.4 assesses the challenges around gender equality in the ECB based on interviews with key observers—six interviews with ECB personnel were conducted by the author for this study in November–December 2019 (see Appendix 15.1 of this chapter).[2] Section 15.5 examines the ascent to the ECB presidency by Christine Lagarde and discusses her behavioral leadership, thereby drawing on publicly available interviews given by the ECB president (see Appendix 15.2 of this chapter). The chapter concludes by offering some insights on positional leadership and the role of expertise in the leadership of central banks. It also advances a few observations about the behavioral leadership by President Lagarde to date, including the policies she has promoted, the particular focus of her public messaging, and her stance on women's leadership in the COVID-19 crisis.

15.2 Women in the Central Banking Profession

The ECB is one of the official European Union (EU) institutions. It is a supranational body that is responsible for the policies of the euro area, first and foremost to ensure price stability, and for EU economic and monetary policy; since 2013, it has also explicitly been tasked with banking supervision—both of these tasks in cooperation with national authorities. The ECB has a president at its helm and the most important decision-making body is its Governing Council which, as already mentioned, consists of an Executive Board (six members) and the Governors of the national central banks of the euro area countries (currently 19 countries).

[2] The author is grateful for financial support from Leiden University and her SSHRC Insight grant 435-2015-0943 to enable these interviews, and for the six interviewees to have made time available for her to ask questions and have conversations (five in person and one by phone). The interviewees have all asked not to be identified (for further details see Appendix 15.1).

The appointment of the members of the ECB Executive Board is ultimately approved by the European Council[3] whereas the Governors of the euro area national central banks are chosen at the national level. Another body is the General Council. It comprises the president and the vice-president of the ECB as well as the Governors of the national central banks of all 27 EU member states—also the EU member states that have not adopted the euro (currently eight states).[4] The ECB is able to affect gender issues only for its bureaucracy—not the very highest political positions.

The arrival of Christine Lagarde as president of the ECB has once again put the spotlight on the issue of gender and leadership in central banking (Hessler 2019; *Deutsche Welle* 2019). Central banks are important institutions that play a crucial role in overseeing the monetary system, whether at the national or international level. Directly and indirectly, they contribute to achieving economic growth, low inflation, employment, and currency stability. Traditionally, women were very much underrepresented in leadership positions in central banks. Diouf and Pépin (2017: 1), studying female central bank presidents, assert that "it seems that women have greater access to positions of responsibility in politics than in central banks where the *glass ceiling* is tougher." These findings are backed by professionals who keep track of the annual gender balance index in central banks. They find that in senior positions at public financial institutions around the globe, gender representation is even poorer than in other sectors that also have relatively poor gender representation such as politics and the private financial sector (OMFIF 2019: 1). In 2019, of the 173 central banks across the globe, only 14 were led by women, and in 20% of the cases (i.e., 35 central banks) there are no women in senior positions (OMFIF 2019: 1). Similarly, the ECB, with its 19 Governors of the national central banks of the euro area countries and its six Executive Board members in 2021, has (not counting the president) only one other woman member. It is noteworthy that the other female member is also a member of the ECB's Executive Board. Furthermore, in the two decades since the ECB's inception, there have only ever been two other female board members.

Some have argued that the low percentage of women in central banking may be caused by the reputation of and culture within the academic discipline of economics—the scientific field of study that provides most of the professional staff in central banks. Indeed, we do find low percentages of women in economics in past decades. Compared to the 1970s and 1980s, however, the field of economics has become more inclusive of women, though women's percentage in assistant

---

[3] The euro area member states propose candidates; these candidates are discussed in the Eurogroup. The Council agrees on a recommendation and after consultation with the European Parliament and the ECB Governing Council, the European Council makes the appointment (see https://www.consilium. europa.eu/de/infographics/ecb-executive-board-appointment-procedure/#).

[4] The composition of the ECB General Council is therefore the result of decisions of member states that independently appoint their own national central bank governors.

professorships and PhD programs has stagnated since the middle of the century's first decade (Lundberg 2020: 10). The American Economic Association (AEA) provides a yearly overview of women in the discipline (AEA 2018: 2). The data shows the loss of women scholars through the ranks. Gender scholars have called this phenomenon the "leaking pipeline" (see Bailyn 2003: 141). To address gender inequity in central banking, in a conference held at the ECB in Frankfurt in 2019, various facets of this conundrum were discussed (Ewing 2019). One such aspect is whether economics is a woman-friendly profession. Indeed, the culture in the economics discipline has been characterized as hostile to women, as demonstrated by a fairly aggressive seminar culture (Dupas et al. 2019). Researchers have also found evidence that scholars with female names are less likely to have paper proposals accepted at conferences (Hospido and Sanz 2019: 1). In sum, the relatively low number of women in both the economics profession and in academic positions in economics may impact the availability of suitable candidates for senior jobs in central banks, such as the ECB.

15.3 Positional Leadership: Women in the ECB

Let us now turn to the issue of how women are represented in the ECB administration and how they progress to senior ranks. There are about 3,500 staff working for the ECB which is located in Frankfurt am Main, Germany. The ECB is one of the newer EU institutions. Preceded by the European Monetary Institute (EMI), also located in Frankfurt, it was created in 1998. As noted above, in 2013, the ECB's remit was extended to include banking supervision. This expansion of responsibility led to a major hiring spree over a 12-month period, amounting to 770 supervisors and 230 support staff (Reuters 2013).[5] To land a job at the ECB as an economist,[6] the applicant more often than not has a doctoral degree in economics, is fluent in at least two European languages (one of them English), and aspires to climb the professional ladder. At the entry point, the profile of male and female professionals is very similar (Hospido et al. 2020). In 2010, the ECB formulated an active gender policy and the general promotion gap started to narrow from 2011 onward. In 2013, the ECB instituted a more explicit gender-equity policy with the clear goal of increasing the number of women in senior positions (ECB 2013). The policy was triggered in part by a politicized situation. In 2012, the European Parliament (EP) rejected the appointment of a member of the Executive Board of the ECB, stating

---

[5] The ECB reported 1,907 full-time equivalent permanent positions at the end of 2013 (an increase of 456.5 from the previous year), with the increase mostly due to the creation of the Single Supervisory Mechanism that would start on November 4, 2014 (ECB 2014: 10). The next annual report stated that the ECB had increased its staff to 2,577 by the end of 2014 (ECB 2015: 106).

[6] Although the job description "economist" suggests that these jobs are all "economists," some personnel have degrees in political science, law, or public administration.

that it was unacceptable that the Board, for the first time since its inception, would be all male (Chaffin 2012). This strong signal by the EP was seen as an appropriate occasion to revisit the ECB gender policy (Interview 5). At the time, 17% of management positions and 14% of senior management positions were held by women. The ECB's target was to increase those numbers to 35% and 28%, respectively, by 2019 (ECB 2013).

A study by Hospido et al. has taken the entire dataset of professional employees of the ECB to investigate how career progress worked between 2003 and 2017 (2019a, 2020). Expert staff starts at salary band F.[7] The proportion of women lessens with every step up the salary scale: 32% of those in salary bands F and G are women, but only 24% of those in salary band H and 17% in pay band I (Hospido et al. 2019a: 14). The results of the study suggest that since the gender-equity policies have been put in place, women have indeed improved their position in the ranks, though, as we will see below, they are still underrepresented.

Hospido et al. (2020) have sought to explain the underrepresentation of women in management positions in central banking. They examine four factors: (1) the pool is male dominated; (2) women do less well in competitive environments; (3) issues related to child-rearing and family versus career tradeoffs; and (4) gender-based discrimination in promotion decisions. Regarding the ECB, they find that women were less likely to be promoted before 2011. This situation was rectified in 2012–2017 when men and women were more or less equally likely to be promoted. The authors also find that women are less likely to apply for promotion than men. However, if women apply, they typically do so after they have been in their current pay band for a longer period of time than their male counterparts, which the authors attribute to women in this milieu as being more risk averse. Yet once they apply, the data show that their applications are more likely to be approved than those of their male colleagues, because they wait to put in their applications until they have more impressive CVs. Hospido and coauthors name this phenomenon the "gender applications gap" (Hospido et al. 2020: 22). The study also finds that, once promoted, women's pay increases faster, which the researchers attribute to female candidates having superior experience before they decide to apply for promotion. The study concludes that the ECB still suffers from a gender promotion gap, despite the success of its gender policies. The researchers recommend that more attention be paid to mentoring and childcare, and awareness that career progression typically slows down during the five years after a woman gives birth to her first child (Keloharju et al. 2019). The researchers emphasized that institutional efforts to reduce the gender promotion gap could include various

---

[7] During the period under study, job titles in salary bands F, G, and H included "economist," "senior economist," and "principal economist" (salary band depends also on seniority). Managerial salaries start at salary band I and can go up to L. It usually takes a minimum of seven years for an employee to move from salary band F to salary band H (Hospido et al. 2019a: 9–10). ECB positions were relabeled in 2020.

measures such as assertiveness training, enhanced child support, and efforts to reduce the "overly competitive" environment (Hospido et al. 2019b: 3).

The ECB gender policies have contributed to an increase in the share of women in senior management. Between 2011 and 2018, the number of women in senior management tripled with women now making up 30% of senior managers (ECB 2020a; ECB 2020b).[8] Although the increase in women in senior management of the bureaucracy is certainly important, the very senior roles in the ECB depend on political appointments by the member states or, in the case of the Executive Board, on approval by the European Council. Any achievement of gender equality in the staff of the ECB thus will not necessarily impact the appointments to the highest positions.

15.4 An Assessment of ECB Women's Advancement toward Leadership Positions

How and why have women experienced difficulties in advancing to senior management levels in the ECB? The very top jobs are political appointments and are therefore in the hands of member states. To determine what may be reasons for the lack of women in leading positions in the bureaucracy, I interviewed six professionals of the ECB in November and December 2019. These respondents included two men and four women, all with doctorates (three in economics, two in law, one in political science). They were selected from a range of seniorities, from lower professional to middle and higher professional ranks; one was in a very senior position. One person worked in research, one in communications, two in economic functions, and two as lawyers. Three of the interviews were based on a semi-structured questionnaire; the other three were more open-ended conversations about gender in the ECB.

From the interviews a number of factors that play a part in women's underrepresentation in leading positions became clear. When starting off in expert positions, the experience, skills, and training of men and women are largely similar. However, once in their positions, women face obstacles to career progress that are sometimes personal, but also more structural. A number of interviewees spelled out that women are sometimes less excited about putting all of their eggs in one basket when working toward job promotions. Compared to men, they are less willing to compromise everything for their careers, valuing a balance with their family lives (Interviews 3–6).

---

[8] Yet the pay gaps have remained. One reason is that as women wait to pursue promotions, their overall pay does not fully catch up. There are other factors that play a role in gender pay gaps (Haldane 2019). Haldane recommends central banking coordination, such as reporting on it with a view to disclosing pay gaps, which would lead to transparency, accountability, and action.

The respondents confirmed that there are structural factors involved that range from the lack of suitable childcare to cultural expectations about the role of women in society (women seen as either mothers or workers but not as those who would excel at both). Other points that were raised were the amount of time needed to do a professional job and whether women are able to combine that with caring roles. They also pointed to the fact that being one of the few women in a profession with mostly men can be "lonely," or that a position may demand that a female manager be "aggressive". Interviewee 3, however, stressed that in her opinion the ECB has excellent childcare facilities on the ground—even better than what is generally available in Frankfurt or other German cities—but that to have a successful career an ECB professional seems to need to work more than what a normal full-time job requires. Not all women are prepared to make that sacrifice.

Another factor that plays a role is that the environment is competitive. In such situations, a prospective female candidate is more likely than her male counterpart not to want to apply for the job at all. If she does, she will have made sure she meets all the criteria. This often means that she has been in the position longer, is being mentored by someone and encouraged to apply, and feels that if she applies, it will not be at the expense of someone else. This attitude toward promotions puts female candidates at a disadvantage as their male colleagues are more likely to apply even if they are uncertain to meet all the criteria (Interview 5). Hospido et al. (2020: 15) find that if women apply, they are in 13% of the cases likely to win the competition against 6% of the men. This finding is in line with the management research that shows women exhibit less self-confidence than men about their careers (Flynn et al. 2011) and with studies about promotions in academia (Bosquet et al. 2019).

The work climate in the institution is another challenge for women. Some men (and indeed some women) have a hard time imagining women as leaders. Interviewees who held senior positions indicated that, in their experience, those women who succeeded in the highest positions had a supervisor (boss) who was neutral or favorable to women in leading positions (Interviews 2 and 4). A male mentor or supervisor who is very encouraging facilitates women's success. Similarly, a male supervisor who does not care whether a person in a leadership role is a man or a woman is less likely to confirm stereotypes but rather allow men and women equal opportunities to excel. These anecdotal accounts suggest that women who have "made it" had male support at formative periods, which is related to the mentorship practices and culture of support in corporations. Yet many male mentors prefer not to be too close to junior women as they are concerned that others might perceive them as having a nonprofessional relationship (Swallow Prior 2012). Supporting young men is thus easier, with less risk of controversy, implying that male leaders have more opportunity to treat junior male colleagues as peers thereby doing more to facilitate their careers than those of women in similar positions (Swallow Prior 2012). Seeing that there are more senior men, there are fewer opportunities for women to be mentored by either women or men. This phenomenon was underscored by interviewees who indicated that for women to do well they need bosses who are open-minded and willing to support women.

All six interviewees expressed that it has been difficult for women to work in the highest positions if they have children, or for other social reasons. An interviewee suggested that once a woman has climbed the professional ladder, there is not much more she can "earn" in terms of reputation or social standing. Professional responsibilities can clash with caregiving roles, because the more senior positions demand long hours and considerable international and overnight travel, which impedes family roles. These challenges are noticeable in how some women perceive the attraction of obtaining higher-ranking jobs in the ECB. In this institution, these challenges are exacerbated because of the good working conditions. It leads to there being many competitive contenders for the jobs, the field is predominantly male, and the difficulty of maintaining a work–life balance can be intense especially because the environment is very international—more competition and less social infrastructure of usual social networks from the extended family. The ECB policies have been crucial in mitigating a number of these pressures so that more women can start to thrive in this environment.

Various interviewees also pointed to the fact that because of the very low number of women leaders in the ECB, there is rarely more than one woman in a senior management position in a given area, which does not do much to produce the benefits of true diversity (Interview 4). The International Labour Organization (ILO) recently confirmed that the effects of more balanced gender diversity start to become observable when 30% of the labor force (or, here, management board) is female (ILO 2019). The ILO follows insights from research that shows the effect of gender diversity starts to become effective when there are at least a few women in a committee or board (Konrad et al. 2008). This insight mirrors findings on corporate governance where solo women on boards also feel isolated and marginalized. They are more effective when they are not the only voice—meaning that a predominantly male culture can start to change after there are at least three women on a board, which is also true for other boards (Konrad and Kramer 2006). The fact that in most leadership functions in the ECB there are very few women means that it remains very difficult for those who are in leadership roles to have a strong impact on the gender balance.

Finally, the interviewees noted that the new policy of the ECB toward improving gender diversity in higher-ranking jobs has made a difference. And there is another element that may be making a difference. Since European banking supervision was delegated to the ECB, more women have been hired to execute tasks related to banking supervision. There seems to be a better female/male ratio in the banking supervision sections, particularly in those sections that have more lawyers rather than economists. Unsurprisingly, Sabine Lautenschläger, one of the members of the Executive Board, and Vice-Chair of the Supervisory Board (this double hat is a fixture of the role), has a background in financial supervision. She held the position from January 27, 2014 till October 31, 2019. The few women that reach the highest positions are often not trained economists.[9]

Turning to possible explanations for the relative dearth of women leaders in the ECB, we can connect the findings to existing theories. From theories of gendered bureaucratic ambition, we learn that the different genders respond differently to expert leadership, depending on the expectations of experiences in the career path (Maranto et al. 2019: 469; Henig 2002). Another explanation is that the lower level of women in leadership roles is due to women's choices (Rhode and Kellerman 2007). Researchers have a hard time sorting out the differences between nature and nurture in this regard and a challenge for researchers is that we have not reached the numbers to make complete comparisons. Clearly some of the factors could be either, and no matter how much one might try to offset the construction of identities and cultural expectations, there continue to be different stereotypes of men and women. A woman who is aggressive and ambitious is often seen in a more negative light than a man who manifests the same characteristics (Vasconcelos 2018; see also Rhode 2017; Eagly and Carli 2007).

15.5 Christine Lagarde—President of the ECB

Besides positional leadership, the recent appointment of Christine Lagarde offers an opportunity to explore behavioral leadership in the ECB. Lagarde became the president of the ECB in November 2019. She is a French citizen, trained as a lawyer. From July 2011 until a couple months before assuming the ECB presidency, she served as the managing director of the International Monetary Fund (IMF) in Washington, DC, where her legacy included achieving greater representation of emerging economies and developing countries (Interview B). Prior to that, she served in various capacities in the French government: as minister of the economy, finance, and industry from 2007 until 2011; minister of agriculture and fisheries (2007); and minister of commerce (2005–2007). She won a lot of praise for her ministerial work.[10] Before serving in these various government positions, she was a partner in a major international law firm, Baker McKenzie, from 1999 to 2004. She was the first woman to be minister of finance of a G-8 country, the first woman to lead the IMF, and is now the first woman to lead the ECB. In this position, she is the only woman on the 29-member ECB General Council—the

[9] Ms Danièle Nouy, who was chair of the Single Supervisory Mechanism, was trained in political science and law and worked in the Banque de France from 1974 until joining the ECB in January 2014 (Jones and Jenkins 2018).

[10] In November 2009, for example, the *Financial Times* praised her as the best finance minister in the euro area (Atkins et al. 2009).

Council that brings together the president and vice-president of the ECB as well as all the national governors of the central banks of all the member states of the EU.

Let us turn to the actual substance of monetary policy by Christine Lagarde during the first year of her time in office. The situation she has faced has been unusual given the circumstances of the COVID-19 pandemic that impacted her leadership of the ECB almost right from the start. For instance, there was one very politicized moment that is worth focusing on. On Thursday, March 12, 2020, at her regular news conference (held every six weeks), in which Lagarde explained the ECB policy around the COVID-19 crisis, she stated, "We are not here to close spreads" (CNBC 2020). She sought to emphasize that governments are responsible for fiscal spending, and to encourage the coordination of government fiscal policy. She really wanted to stress that point and did so several times during the press briefing. However, her "We are not here to close spreads" comment is said to have single-handedly set the Milan stock exchange into a nosedive (Hall et al. 2020). It recorded a decline of 17%—its biggest ever drop in a single day.[11] Although formally speaking not even wrong (the ECB's main goal is price stability), Lagarde quickly addressed the situation by apologizing to the ECB Governing Council the next day (Arnold 2020). Her actions backed up the retraction: by March 19, she had put forward an asset-purchasing program in response to the COVID-19 crisis worth €750 billion (ECB 2020c). In an interview on July 29, she indicated that this plan "was decided on 18 March 2020 at my kitchen table!" (Lagarde, Interview D). The location was caused by the change of workplace from office to home due to the pandemic—a shift that she had announced at the end of her March 12 press conference (CNBC 2020). By June this amount had been further increased to €1,350 billion (Reuters 2020). Lagarde chose to address the difficult situation that followed the market response to her comment and take bold action when she realized what the problem was, using additional communication to rectify the situation.

Lagarde has also alluded to the issue of gender equality (Interviews A, C, and D). One possible effect of the fact that she is a woman in terms of how she leads the ECB can be seen in how she manages her personnel (Interview 1). Right from the start, ECB employees noticed that Lagarde managed the organization differently from her predecessors. She has been explicit in addressing the lack of women in the central banking community. In her first speech to ECB staff, she pointed to this issue (Interview 1), as she has done on the record in a number

---

[11] The *Financial Times* stated the next day: "Christine Lagarde's comment that it was not the ECB's job to 'close the spreads' between 10-year Italian government bonds and German bonds—a measure of the risk differential between the two sovereign debts—caused it to spike by 60 basis points, the biggest daily increase on record. The FTSE MIB, Milan's blue-chip stock index, plummeted 17%, its biggest daily drop, out-slumping other equity markets on a terrible day for investors around the world" (Hall et al. 2020).

of high-profile interviews. In these interviews and other public speeches, Lagarde has focused on women's issues even if these were not central to her position or policies under discussion. She has called for increases in social spending to ensure and improve the health and well-being of women and girls (Interview A). Lagarde has also spoken publicly about the importance of having sufficient numbers of women in the highest positions and the benefits that result. She was reported as remarking:

> Adding one more woman in a firm's senior management or corporate board—while keeping the size of the board unchanged—is associated with an 8 to 13 basis-point higher return on assets... . If banks and financial supervisors increased the share of women in senior positions, the banking sector would be more stable too.
>
> (quoted in Seputyte and Eglitis 2019)

More recently, in a July 2020 interview with the *Washington Post*, she went a step further by singling out women leaders as having done a better job in dealing with the COVID-19 crisis:

> I'm going to be extremely biased, David, and I'm not going to be a central banker at this very moment, but I would say that for myself I've learned that women tend to do a better job [in dealing with the COVID-19 crisis]. It's quite fascinating, actually. When you look at those countries that were led by women and the path that they took and the policies that they adopted and the communication style that was in play was quite stunning. So, this is my woman's bias and I indulge in ceding to this bias.
>
> (Interview D)

She stated in the same interview that she felt that women leaders communicated well, adding, "It is essential that more women are included in politics and economics, including at the highest levels" (Interview D).

As a central bank president, she has been an outsider in more than one way. Not only is she the first female president, but she is also a lawyer rather than an economist. She is reportedly keen to assemble a team around her that she can trust so that she can make the right decisions (Interviews 1 and 2). Despite her lack of an economic doctorate and related criticisms voiced in the media (Arnold 2019; Chassany 2019; *Financial Times* 2019), none of those interviewed for this chapter expressed doubt about Lagarde's ability to lead the ECB. In fact, observers and journalists have pointed out that the role of the ECB is changing and that it may need to move closer to the political institutions of the EU (Hessler 2019). In comparison to Mario Draghi, her predecessor, who was seen as charismatic

(Tortola and Pansardi 2019) and said he would do "whatever it takes" to save the euro (Verdun 2017), Lagarde will face different challenges and may need to build bridges to other EU institutions. These challenges involve the fallout of the COVID-19 crisis, which is forecast to have a major impact on the global economy and especially the economies of the EU and the euro area, with their relatively elderly populations. Lagarde's political skills, developed while she was minister of finance of France and working at the helm of the IMF, and the fact that she represents a large EU member state are important assets that she can draw on to weather the COVID-19 storm (Howarth and Verdun 2020). With good news about vaccines having emerged in November 2020, the next phase of the economic crisis will need to be managed. The forecast is a gradual return to growth in 2021 but with some long-term damage to various economic sectors. Lagarde warned that the recovery may be bumpy until the vaccines have been administered widely (Associated Press 2020).

15.6 Conclusion

This chapter has examined the positional and, to a lesser extent, the behavioral leadership of women in the ECB. This study highlights a number of reasons why there still is an underrepresentation of women in the leadership of central banking in general and in the ECB in particular. Some are specific to the field of economics, in particular macroeconomics, and to central banking as a profession. These challenges are, for the most part, socially constructed and the behavior of colleagues, the bureaucracy, and society and its cultural expectations are important determinants of the situation. Over time the ECB has changed its approach to equity by considering not only the very senior positions, but also the whole bureaucratic process that underlies how professionals (men and women) rise to the top of the ECB bureaucracy. When it became clear that women were not rising to the top, the ECB responded by explicitly developing a gender-equity policy. This policy was partly triggered by pressure from the EP. Research into the effect of this policy suggests that more women have advanced to leadership positions in the past decade compared to the first period (the ECB predecessor having been established in 1994).

In terms of behavioral leadership, this chapter has offered a first, tentative analysis of the performance of Christine Lagarde as ECB president. She emphasizes women's issues, among others, and seeks to practice clear communication. The COVID-19 pandemic has provided the new ECB president with a steep learning curve and a major challenge. She has had to deal with a few difficulties in communication, but to date has weathered the first part of the storm well. However, the impact of the COVID-19 crisis is not yet over. It will be interesting to see whether under President Lagarde's leadership Europe can overcome the enormous challenges related to the COVID-19 crisis, and whether she may be able to include the gendered challenges that are connected to the crisis.

References

American Economic Association. 2018. *Reports from the American Economic Association's Committee on the Status of Women in the Economics Profession* 1. https://www.aeaweb.org/content/file?id=6388.

Arnold, Martin. 2019. "What Will Christine Lagarde's ECB Look Like?" *Financial Times*, October 27. https://www.ft.com/content/1683ea12-f4f7-11e9-a79c-bc9acae3b654.

Arnold, Martin. 2020. "Christine Lagarde Apologises for Botched Communication of ECB Strategy." *Financial Times*, March 15. https://www.ft.com/content/ce39716e-66c0-11ea-a3c9-1fe6fedcca75.

Associated Press. 2020. "The Latest: Lagarde: Recovery Bumpy until Vaccine Widespread." November 11. https://apnews.com/article/travel-virus-outbreak-england-united-nations-holiday-travel-c13572d2bf700fdbcf7e07d0643c7c98.

Atkins, Ralph, Andrew Whiffin, and FT Reporters. 2009. "FT Ranking of EU Finance Ministers." *Financial Times*, November 16. http://ig-legacy.ft.com/content/3f36c9c4-d2d0-11de-af63-00144feabdc0#axzz6aUBifqxh.

Bailyn, Lotte. 2003. "Academic Careers and Gender Equity: Lessons Learned from MIT." *Gender, Work and Organization* 10 (2): 137–153.

Bosquet, Clément, Pierre-Philippe Combes, and Cecilia García-Peñalosa. 2019. "Gender and Promotions: Evidence from Academic Economists in France." *Scandinavian Journal of Economics* 121 (3): 1020–1053.

Chaffin, Joshua. 2012. "MEPs Veto Mersch for ECB Board in Gender Stand-off." *Financial Times*, October 26. https://www.ft.com/content/4cdddfbe-1e99-11e2-be82-00144feabdc0.

Charléty, Patricia, Davide Romelli, and Estefania Santacreu-Vasut. 2017. "Appointments to Central Bank Boards: Does Gender Matter?" *Economics Letters* 155: 59–61.

Chassany, Anne-Sylvaine. 2019. "Christine Lagarde Shows How to Deal with the Imposter Syndrome." *Financial Times*, July 9. https://www.ft.com/content/13720bc4-a16e-11e9-a282-2df48f366f7d.

CNBC. 2020. "ECB's Christine Lagarde Speaks Following Decision to Hold Interest Rates." March 12. https://www.youtube.com/watch?v=W5uaKTWxbHc.

Deutsche Welle. 2019. "Christine Lagarde Nominated to Be the ECB's First Female Chief." July 2. https://www.dw.com/en/christine-lagarde-nominated-to-be-the-ecbs-first-female-chief/a-49446704.

Diouf, Ibrahima, and Dominique Pépin. 2017. "Gender and Central Banking" *Economic Modelling* 61: 193–206. https://doi.org/10.1016/j.econmod.2016.12.006. https://hal.archives-ouvertes.fr/hal-01224266v3/document.

Dupas, Pascaline, Alicia Modestino, Muriel Niederle, and Justin Wolfers. 2019. "Gender and the Dynamics of Economics Seminars." Paper presented at the Gender and Career Progression Conference of the Bank of England, Federal Reserve Board, and European Central Bank, October 21.

Eagly, Alice H., and Linda L. Carli. 2007. *Through the Labyrinth. The Truth about How Women Become Leaders*. Boston, MA: Harvard Business School Press.

Elliott, Carole, and Valerie Stead. 2008. "Learning from Leading Women's Experience: Towards a Sociological Understanding." *Leadership* 4 (2): 159–180.

European Central Bank. 2013. "ECB Aims to Double Share of Women in High-Ranking Positions." August 29. https://www.ecb.europa.eu/press/pr/date/2013/html/pr130829.en.html.

European Central Bank. 2014. *Annual Report 2013*. Frankfurt.

European Central Bank. 2015. *Annual Report 2014*. Frankfurt.

European Central Bank. 2019. "Why We Value Diversity." Frankfurt. https://www.ecb.europa.eu/careers/why-we-value-diversity/html/index.en.html.

European Central Bank. 2020a. *Annual Report 2019*. Frankfurt.

European Central Bank. 2020b. "ECB Announces New Measures to Increase Share of Female Staff Members." May 14. https://www.ecb.europa.eu/press/pr/date/2020/html/ecb.pr200514~94dbb7c109.en.html.

European Central Bank. 2020c. "ECB Announces €750 Billion Pandemic Emergency Purchase Programme (PEPP)." March 18. https://www.ecb.europa.eu/press/pr/date/2020/html/ecb.pr200318_1~3949d6f266.en.html.

European Personnel Selection Office. 2020. "Welcome to EU Careers." https://epso.europa.eu/home_en.

Ewing, Jack. 2019. "Women Are Missing at Central Banks." *New York Times*, October 22. https://www.nytimes.com/2019/10/22/business/women-central-banks.html.

Financial Times. 2019. "Brexit Is a Warning to Germany's ECB-Bashers: The Country Is Not Immune to the Disease of Mendacious Euroscepticism." November 5. https://www.ft.com/content/3ace340c-ff03-11e9-be59-e49b2a136b8d.

Flynn, Jill, Kathryn Heath, and Mary David Holt. 2011. "Four Ways Women Stunt Their Careers Unintentionally." *Harvard Business Review*, October 19. https://hbr.org/2011/10/four-ways-women-stunt-their-careers.

Haldane, Andrew G. 2019. "Understanding Pay Gaps." Paper presented at the Gender and Career Progression Conference of the Bank of England, Federal Reserve Board, and European Central Bank, October 21.

Hall, Ben, Miles Johnson, and Martin Arnold. 2020. "Italy Wonders Where Europe's Solidarity Is as Coronavirus Strains Show." *Financial Times*, March 13.

Henig, Simon. 2002. *Women and Political Power: Europe since 1945*. London: Routledge.

Hessler, Uwe. 2019. "Christine Lagarde Will Need All Her Skills to Steer ECB through Trying Times." *Deutsche Welle*, November 1. https://www.dw.com/en/christine-lagarde-will-need-all-her-skills-to-steer-ecb-through-trying-times/a-51046045.

Hospido, Laura, Luc Laeven, and Ana Lamo. 2019a. "The Gender Promotion Gap: Evidence from Central Banking." ECB Working Papers, No. 2265, April. https://www.ecb.europa.eu/pub/pdf/scpwps/ecb.wp2265~ad73fb9a6b.en.pdf.

Hospido, Laura, Luc Laeven, and Ana Lamo. 2019b. "The Gender Promotion Gap: What Holds Back Female Economists from Making a Career in Central Banking?" *ECB Research Bulletin* 63, October 14. https://www.ecb.europa.eu/pub/economic-research/resbull/2019/html/ecb.rb191014~7c79f5f557.en.html.

Hospido, Laura, Luc Laeven, and Ana Lamo. 2020. "The Gender Promotion Gap: Evidence from Central Banking" *Review of Economics and Statistics* [posted online] October 30. https://doi.org/10.1162/rest_a_00988.

Hospido, Laura, and Carlos Sanz. 2019. "Gender Gaps in the Evaluation of Research: Evidence from Submissions to Economics Conferences." Paper presented at the

Gender and Career Progression Conference of the Bank of England, Federal Reserve Board, and European Central Bank, October 21.

Howarth, David, and Amy Verdun. 2020. "Economic and Monetary Union at Twenty: A Stocktaking of a Tumultuous Second Decade: Introduction." *Journal of European Integration* 42 (3): 287–293.

International Labour Organization. 2019. "The Business Case for Change." Bureau for Employers' Activities/International Labour Organization Report, May 22. https://www.ilo.org/wcmsp5/groups/public/—dgreports/—dcomm/—publ/documents/publication/wcms_700953.pdf.

Jones, Claire, and Patrick Jenkins. 2018. "Eurozone Bank Supervisor Danièle Nouy: Building a Team from Scratch." *Financial Times*, December 15. https://www.ft.com/content/a614bc70-fd62-11e8-ac00-57a2a826423e.

Keloharju, Matti, Samuli Knüpfer, and Joacim Tåg. 2019. "What Prevents Women from Reaching the Top?" Paper presented at the Gender and Career Progression Conference of the Bank of England, Federal Reserve Board, and European Central Bank, October 21.

Konrad, Alison M., and Vicki W. Kramer. 2006. "How Many Women Do Boards Need?" *Harvard Business Review*, December. https://hbr.org/2006/12/how-many-women-do-boards-need.

Konrad, Alison M., Vicki W. Kramer, and Sumru Erkut. 2008. "Critical Mass: The Impact of Three or More Women on Corporate Boards." *Organizational Dynamics* 37 (2): 145–164.

Lundberg, Shelly, ed. 2020. *Women in Economics*. London: Centre for Economic Policy Research (CEPR) Press.

Maranto, Robert, Manuel P. Teodoro, Kristen Carroll, and Albert Cheng. 2019. "Gendered Ambition: Men's and Women's Career Advancement in Public Administration." *American Review of Public Administration* 49 (4): 469–481.

Marton, Kati. 2019. "The Merkel Model: The German Chancellor Has Shown How to Win and Keep Power in a Man's World." *Atlantic*, May 19. https://www.theatlantic.com/ideas/archive/2019/05/how-angela-merkel-keeps-power-mans-world/589675.

OMFIF [Official Monetary and Financial Institutions Forum]. 2019. "Gender Balance Index 2019. Banking on Balance. Diversity in central banks and public investment", London, UK: Official Monetary and Financial Institutions Forum. OMFIF.ORG (28 pages). https://www.omfif.org/gender-balance-index-2019.

Reuters. 2013. "Wanted: 770 ECB Banking Supervisors within a Year." October 22. https://ca.reuters.com/article/idUKBRE99L0XX20131022.

Reuters. 2020. "ECB Expands, Extends Bond-Buying Programme to Fight Pandemic." June 4. https://www.reuters.com/article/us-ecb-policy-rates/ecb-expands-extends-bond-buying-programme-to-fight-pandemic-idUSKBN23B1TT.

Rhode, Deborah L. 2017. *Women and Leadership*. Oxford: Oxford University Press.

Rhode, Deborah L., and Barbara Kellerman. 2007. "Women and Leadership: The State of Play." In *Women and Leadership: The State of Play and Strategies for Change*, eds. Barbara Kellerman and Deborah L. Rhode, 65–92. San Francisco, CA: Jossey-Bass.

Ridgeway, Cecilia L. 2011. *Framed by Gender: How Gender Inequality Persists in the Modern World*. Oxford: Oxford University Press.

Seputyte, Milda, and Aaron Eglitis. 2019. "Lagarde Is First Woman to Lead ECB But Men Rule the Rest of the Eurozone." Bloomberg, July 6. https://www.bloomberg.com

/news/articles/2019-07-06/lagarde-is-first-woman-to-lead-ecb-but-men-rule-rest-of-eurozone.

Swallow Prior, Karen. 2012. "Don't Let the Petraeus Affair Keep Men from Mentoring Women." *Atlantic*, November 19. https://www.theatlantic.com/sexes/archive/2012/11/dont-let-the-petraeus-affair-keep-men-from-mentoring-women/265407/.

Tortola, Pier Domenico, and Pamela Pansardi. 2019. "The Charismatic Leadership of the ECB Presidency: A Language-Based Analysis." *European Journal of Political Research* 58 (1): 96–116.

Tsang, Amie. 2013. "Women of the World's Central Banks." *Financial Times*, Opinion The World Blog, October 9.

Vasconcelos, Anselmo Ferreira. 2018. "Gender and Leadership Stereotypes Theory: Is It Reaching the Boundaries?" *Management Research Review* 41 (11): 1336–1355. https://doi-org.ezproxy.library.uvic.ca/10.1108/MRR-04-2017-0131.

Verdun, Amy. 2017. "Political Leadership of the European Central Bank." *Journal of European Integration* 39 (2): 207–221.

Interviews conducted by the author with ECB officials

Interviews 1–5, November 2019

Interview 6, December 2019

Public interviews conducted with Christine Lagarde cited above

- Interview A: Video interview with Christine Lagarde in her role as Managing Director of the IMF on the future of work and sustainable growth. Interviewed by Martin Murphy, Director of Communication of the ILO for the *ILC Daily Show*, June 18, 2019. https://www.youtube.com/watch?v=_JGGKp0RnSo.
- Interview B: Video interview with Christine Lagarde, at the time former managing director of the IMF, with *Xinhua* in Washington, DC, September 19, 2019. http://www.xinhuanet.com/english/2019-10/08/c_138455804.htm.
- Interview C: Video interview with Christine Lagarde, with Roula Khalaf of the *Financial Times*, on the COVID-19 crisis and the central bank response, July 8, 2020. https://www.ft.com/content/0c855423-a166-437d-8de3-e68154b50baa?FTCamp=engage/CAPI/website/Channel_muckrack//B2B.
- Interview D: Video interview with Christine Lagarde, President of the ECB, conducted by David Ignatius of the *Washington Post*, July 22, 2020. https://www-ecb-europa-eu.ezproxy.library.uvic.ca/press/inter/date/2020/html/ecb.in200723~0606f514ed.en.htm.
- Interview E: Interview with Christine Lagarde, conducted by Dominique Lecoq and Marc Aubault of *Le Courrier Cauchois*, July 29, 2020 (published July 31). https://www.ecb.europa.eu/press/inter/date/2020/html/ecb.in200731~7df348b85b.en.html.

PART VII

LOOKING AHEAD

Women at the Top of the EU

16

Strategic Leadership

Ursula von der Leyen as President of the European Commission

Henriette Müller and Ingeborg Tömmel

16.1 Introduction

On July 2, 2019, to the surprise of many, Ursula von der Leyen was nominated by the European Council for the office of President of the European Commission. She was the first woman to be considered for Europe's highest executive office. On July 16, she was elected Commission president by the European Parliament (EP) with the smallest margin to date, 383:327 votes and 22 abstentions. At the time of her nomination and election, she was relatively unknown to the European media and public. Significantly, she was not one of the selected *Spitzenkandidaten* of the European parties in the elections to the EP that had taken place in May 2019. The *Economist* greeted her election by opining that "it is hard to imagine a biography less suited to the mood of today's Europe than that of Ursula von der Leyen" (July 18, 2019).

Von der Leyen's turbulent ascendance to the Commission presidency could have been interpreted as foreshadowing a mediocre tenure. However, the political successes and policy results she achieved as president early in her term are remarkable within the context of the European Commission and the European Union (EU) more broadly. Taking into account her previous political career as well as the institutional–situational context of her tenure, this chapter provides a four-part assessment of Commission President von der Leyen by studying both her positional and behavioral leadership during roughly her first year in office.

First, it provides an overview of Ursula von der Leyen's late-blooming, but steeply ascending political career prior to becoming Commission president, evaluating her experiences, leadership style, and reputation. Second, it analyzes her appointment to the Commission presidency in light of the specific institutional–situational context, which was marked by sharp contestation between the European Council and the EP around the *Spitzenkandidaten* procedure. Third, the

Henriette Müller and Ingeborg Tömmel, *Strategic Leadership: Ursula von der Leyen as President of the European Commission*. In: *Women and Leadership in the European Union*. Edited by Henriette Müller and Ingeborg Tömmel, Oxford University Press. © Oxford University Press (2022). DOI: 10.1093/oso/9780192896216.003.0017

chapter studies von der Leyen's agenda-setting as president-elect and president of the European Commission, highlighting her priority-setting and venue shopping. Fourth, it focuses on her performance as Commission president under severe situational constraints—the COVID-19 crisis—examining her leadership in tackling the crisis and at the same time pushing forward her most salient agenda items.

Overall, the chapter concludes that von der Leyen's personal qualities—her high-flying ambitions, broad experiences in executive offices, concise communication style, bold handling of political debate and conflict, and, most importantly, her adherence to a political vision beyond narrow party politics—together allowed her to provide strategic leadership at the top of the European Commission. Favored by an enabling situational context, particularly the strong backing of the French–German tandem and the European Council, and a specific window of opportunity, the COVID-19 crisis, von der Leyen early on in her tenure succeeded in significantly expanding the powers and role of the European Commission and the Union as a whole.

16.2 Prior to the Commission Presidency: An Exceptional Political Career

The analysis of a politician's biographical background and previous career steps is important to illustrate an incumbent's understanding of a given office, his or her values, attitudes, and goal preferences, as well as his or her skills in and styles of providing leadership. In this regard, one can assume that the extent to which personal (pre)dispositions match the demands and context of a certain office provides insights into the actor's capacity to exert political leadership (Müller 2020). The following analysis focuses on von der Leyen's political ambitions, her evolving leadership capacities, and her political reputation.

Ursula von der Leyen was born on October 8, 1958 in Brussels. She grew up amid European political circles and attended the European School in Brussels (1964–1971). Her father, Ernst Albrecht, was an accomplished member of the European civil service in Brussels. In 1969, he returned to Germany and pursued a career in the Christian Democratic Union (CDU). From 1976 to 1990, he was State Premier of Lower Saxony.

Von der Leyen, after experiences in other university subjects and a semester abroad in London, turned in 1980 to the study of medicine at the Hanover Medical School (MHH), from which, in 1991, she obtained her doctorate. After a half-decade in the USA with her family (1992–1997), she worked until 2002 as a research fellow at the MHH (Rahlf 2009: 278). Thus, her early career, marked by delays and discontinuities, resembled that of many women who try to reconcile their professional ambitions with family life. This situation changed fundamentally when she entered politics in 2001.

Being in her early 40s, von der Leyen, despite having been a member of the CDU since 1990, was a latecomer to politics. At the same time, though, due to her father's career first in the European institutions and later in Lower Saxony, she had been exposed to politics, public media, and the public sphere since early on in life and was thus hardly a political outsider. In interviews, she has emphasized that she was strongly influenced by her father in developing a positive understanding of politics combined with a Christian–liberal values system (Rahlf 2009: 282–283).

Thus, in 2001, von der Leyen entered politics at the local and then, in 2003, the regional level. Her ambition was met with reservation by other politicians. Her candidacy for the Lower Saxon Parliament provoked intraparty controversy, since she defeated the long-term representative of the district in a runoff election (Rahlf 2009: 280). The CDU won a majority in the regional elections and von der Leyen became an MP. Soon thereafter, she was appointed minister of social affairs, women, family, and public health in the CDU-led state government.

Angela Merkel was one of her early supporters and sponsors within the CDU. Merkel recognized that von der Leyen's political competence and pragmatism as well as her biographical background could help the party's efforts to appeal to broader political strata (Rahlf 2009: 296). After the federal elections of 2005 and Merkel's assumption of the chancellorship, von der Leyen became federal minister for family, social affairs, women, and youth in the grand coalition. Between 2006 and 2009, she played a central role in two major policy initiatives that profoundly changed Germany's family planning and childcare apparatus.

These initiatives entailed: (1) the introduction of parental benefits based on income, including the amount of parental leave granted to fathers; and (2) the massive expansion of public childcare, with the states now obliged to provide a place for each child in a nursery. Von der Leyen encountered strong resistance to both initiatives from the conservatives within her party and the Christian Social Union (CSU), while the coalition partner, the Social Democrats, as well as the opposition supported her approach. She was able to take advantage of a favorable situational context marked by a broad societal consensus behind modernizing family policy, and she had the support of many stakeholders, most crucially the association of German employers. Still, the combination of von der Leyen's political leadership and her persistence in transforming her policy proposals into feasible implementation plans deserves much of the credit for yielding an effective program to modernize German family policy (Henninger and von Wahl 2010).

In 2009, von der Leyen was reappointed as family minister, but soon became minister for labor and social affairs. As labor minister, she was responsible for the introduction of a so-called education card (*Bildungskarte*) for children whose parents are dependent on state-based social welfare as well as the more contested new regulation of individual disbursements provided by the state (Dausend and Niejahr 2015: 50). In 2013, she became Germany's first female defense minister, taking over what had been a scandal-ridden ministry at the beginning of Merkel's third cabinet and remaining in the post into the fourth, serving until July 2019. During this time, she expanded arms and defense procurement and worked to increase the appeal of the German Bundeswehr as an employer, particularly in the wake of public revelations of sexual misconduct and illegal usage of Nazi symbols by army members. Although von der Leyen was the first defense minister since the 1990s to be reappointed to the position, her incumbency was not without controversy, especially concerning irregularities in spending on external consultancy contracts. Her performance as defense minister must thus be adjudged as mixed compared to her previous portfolios.

Regarding her political background, the following points are central: First, von der Leyen has always been convinced of her own capacities and ambitions, strategically using her convictions and public support as a compass for policy initiatives. Second, her ambitions are directed toward pragmatism rather than ideological or party-political stances. Third, this relative independence from narrow party politics has allowed her to gain support from diverse political and societal actors, even against resistance from within her own party—though it is important to note that Angela Merkel continuously supported her political endeavors. Fourth, political conflict has not prevented her from vigorously pursuing her goals. As the *Guardian* observed, "She has a reputation for resolve in the face of even the most aggressive opposition" (September 9, 2011).

In conclusion, von der Leyen's political reputation is characterized by ambition, determination, independence, and resoluteness in the face of conflict. While neither her biographical background nor her relative independence from party politics are exceptional in and of themselves, the combination of factors clearly is. All told, it is clear that von der Leyen has a highly effective leadership style both in terms of accessing leadership positions and in exercising leadership.

16.3 Becoming Commission President: A Pathway with Hurdles

Traditionally, the nomination of the Commission president, at least in terms of the EU's institutional structure, was a straightforward procedure: the European Council unanimously nominated the Commission President. As the powers of the EP expanded and the European Council was elevated to a formal EU institution, this institutional setting was gradually transformed, culminating in the regulations of the Lisbon Treaty. The Treaty entitles the European Council to propose, by qualified majority, a candidate for the office, yet the choice has to "take into account the elections to the European Parliament" (Art. 17(7) TEU). It stipulates: "This candidate shall be elected by the European Parliament" (Art. 17(7) TEU). Obviously, these regulations, which came into effect in 2014, leave much room for interpretation, and they politicized the procedure for nominating the Commission president.

The EP interpreted the new rules to its own advantage, while also aiming to give the European people a say in the choice of candidates. By nominating *Spitzenkandidaten* for each party group to the parliamentary elections, and by pledging that the candidate of the group winning the highest number of votes would be elected Commission president, the EP in fact deprived the European Council of its right of nomination. In 2014, this strategic move resulted in the appointment, only grudgingly accepted by the European Council, of Jean-Claude Juncker as Commission president (Hobolt 2014: 1537).

In 2019, however, the situational context was different. The European Council was determined to regain its prerogative of nominating the candidate and the procedure became subject to a power struggle with the EP (Cloos 2019; Heidbreder and Schade 2020; Müller-Gómez and Thieme 2020). Other situational factors were different as well, as Cloos (2019: 3–4), deputy secretary general of the Council, pointed out: none of the designated *Spitzenkandidaten* had Juncker's credentials; the liberal group Renew Europe declined to nominate a candidate, possibly under the influence of French President Emmanuel Macron; and, pivotally, after the elections the EP could not assemble a majority for any of its *Spitzenkandidaten*. Its members acted in line with party politics instead of forging a broad alliance vis-à-vis the European Council (Heidbreder and Schade 2020). Facing this stalemate, on July 2, 2019, the European Council nominated von der Leyen for the office of Commission president. This conveyed the power struggle between the EP and European Council *into* the EP, jeopardizing von der Leyen's election.

Why did the European Council nominate von der Leyen for the Commission presidency? While it reassumed its right to propose a candidate and thus stalled the potential transformation of the Union into a more representative system, it still had to respect the EP's right to elect the president and make concessions to the legislature. Negotiations over a suitable candidate put the French–German tandem in the driving seat, and package deals narrowed down the choice. As Macron was promoting Christine Lagarde for the presidency of the European Central Bank, it appeared fair to award Germany with the other top-level post, that of Commission president. As this meant bypassing the EPP's lead candidate, Manfred Weber, who was criticized for lacking experience in executive office (Belafi 2020: 30), only a well-experienced German member of the executive could be seriously considered for the position. Von der Leyen appeared to fulfill the criteria, and the heads of state and government (heads) without dissent nominated her for the office. This choice also meant matching certain EP preferences: first, by virtue of von der Leyen's membership in the EPP, the European Council acknowledged the party group's victory in the European election; second and more importantly, by nominating a woman, the European Council catered to the EP's persistent advocacy of gender balance in top EU positions. Against this background, von der Leyen's nomination for the presidency is less surprising than many in the media and other observers suggested.

In nominating candidates for other top positions in the EU, the European Council forged further compromises across member states and European parties and aimed to soothe the indignation of the EP about bypassing the *Spitzenkandidaten*. It chose a Belgian liberal as its president and a Spanish socialist as High Representative. It proposed elevating the bypassed lead candidates of the Socialists and Liberals, Frans Timmermans and Margrethe Vestager, to executive vice-presidents of the Commission, and elect Manfred Weber for a second two-and-a-half-year term as EP president (Müller Gómez and Thieme 2020: 187).

Obviously, the nomination for the Commission's top office maneuvered von der Leyen into a difficult, if not impossible position: although she had the backing of the heads, that of the EP was by no means secured. Many Members of Parliament (MEPs) were upset about the European Council's sidelining of the lead candidates, and the legislature was deeply divided over how to react to von der Leyen's candidacy. Von der Leyen, always highly ambitious but also experienced in open contests and unconstrained by narrow party-political positions, immediately took up the challenge to win the election in the EP. She pursued a twofold strategy: first, promptly drawing up an agenda for her presidency; second, convincing MEPs of her capacities.

In developing an agenda, von der Leyen consulted extensively with the Commission. This resulted in her setting forth a multifaceted yet focused agenda, encompassing six priorities: a "European Green Deal"; "an economy that works for people"; "a Europe fit for the digital age"; "protecting our way of life"; "a stronger Europe in the world"; and "a new push for democracy" (von der Leyen 2019a). This agenda was largely in line with the priorities of the Juncker Commission, particularly during the second half of its term, yet von der Leyen's ambitions and targets far surpassed earlier proposals (see next section).

Persuading MEPs to elect her was a much greater challenge. In extensive talks with the party groups, von der Leyen attempted to match the expectations of highly divergent ideological factions and promised to respect their preferences. This, however, led her to advocate contradictory proposals and make irreconcilable promises. For example, the European Green Deal particularly appealed to the Greens, as well as the Socialists and the Liberals, while the extreme right rejected it. Promising the Socialists Europe-wide minimum wages caused reservation among Conservatives. Advocating under a single rubric—"protecting our way of life"— both respect for the rule of law in the Union and a new migration policy, primarily involving stronger border controls against migrants, mirrored and at the same time contradicted claims of the extreme right as well as the values of liberal-minded MEPs. On top of this agenda, von der Leyen also made promises appealing to the EP in its entirety. Under the rubric of "a new push for democracy," she suggested to redefine the *Spitzenkandidaten* procedure, a right of initiative and full co-decision in all legislative affairs, and a citizen's Conference for the Future of

Europe, whose proposals could result in Treaty changes (von der Leyen 2019a: 19–20; Müller Gómez and Thieme 2020: 187–188).

The success of von der Leyen's strategy was at best mixed. Though the major pro-European party groups—the EPP, S&D (Socialists and Democrats), and Renew Europe—backed her candidacy, a significant number of MEPs from these groups did not vote for her. The Greens/EFA (European Free Alliance) and GUE/NGL (European United Left/Nordic Green Left) declared beforehand that they would not support her. In the end, the slight majority von der Leyen achieved depended on the votes of the right-wing ECR (European Conservatives and Reformists). Four months later, the EP accepted her college by a much greater margin, indicating that the process of her nomination rather than her candidacy as such had been the main point of contention.

In conclusion, the turbulence that affected von der Leyen's pathway to office was induced by the power struggle between the European Council and EP; doubts about the candidate's capacities played hardly a role. The ambiguities in the Lisbon regulations and the European Council's overturning of the *Spitzenkandidaten* procedure produced an enormous dilemma for the EP and threatened to undermine the candidate. Yet despite the political risks of a candidacy in such a situation, von der Leyen, thanks to her personal leadership capacities, succeeded. Her high ambitions, strong commitment, diligent handling of political conflict, and understanding of what was widely acceptable beyond narrow party-political positions secured her the support she needed.

16.4 Leading the Commission:
Setting and Promoting Europe's Agenda

This section focuses on the extent to which the six priorities von der Leyen laid out during her election campaign continued to be central to her agenda as president-elect and president. Making use of a total of 51 speeches retrieved from the website of the European Commission's press office, it examines the preference-setting and framing of topics, as well as the venues of speeches between November 1, 2019 and June 30, 2020.[1]

Due to the Commission's almost exclusive right to initiate legislation, shaping the EU's agenda through strategic agenda-setting is one of its president's primary political functions. The core tasks of any agenda setter comprise problem recognition and issue selection (Birkland 2007). In addition, it is important to focus on where and when to place an issue (i.e., venue strategies). It can be assumed

---

[1] Speeches were downloaded in July 2020 from the European Commission Press Release Database: https://ec.europa.eu/commission/presscorner/home/en.

that "the more the [issue appeals] to a wider range of relevant policy makers, the higher the issue will come onto the EU agenda" (Princen 2009: 42). Agenda setters thus strategically invest in the selection and framing of a concise number of topics as well as venue shopping to raise chosen political issues onto the agenda of a decision-making body.

Pursuant to these theoretical considerations, von der Leyen's speeches are analyzed by both topic and venue. The topical categories are: (1) Main Topics/Political Agenda; (2) Major Internal/External Events; and (3) Other Topics. The first refers to those topics and issue clusters she predominantly addressed, and as such formed her political agenda. The crucial characteristic of the main topics category is frequency, that is, how often von der Leyen addressed the respective issues.[2] Major Internal/External Events provides insight into when and how the president addressed important events at the European level, and to what extent this affected her own agenda-setting. The third category comprises those topics that were of minor importance to von der Leyen, based on the relative infrequency with which she mentioned them. The venue types are (1) EU institutions, e.g., the EP; (2) advocacy groups/civil society, e.g., interest and lobby groups, academic institutions, trade unions, foundations, and political or faith-based organizations; and (3) international conferences (e.g., a UN conference); (4) EU member states; and (5) non-member states.[3]

Starting with the delivery of speeches over time, we see that von der Leyen undertook a strong outreach approach early in her incumbency. Beginning with the Commission's inauguration on December 1, 2019, she gave nine speeches that month and 14 and 11, respectively, in the first two months of the new year. In comparison, her predecessor Jean-Claude Juncker (2014–2019), for example, gave a total of eight speeches in roughly his first six months in office (September 2014– March 2015).[4] However, von der Leyen's strategy was suddenly upended in March due to the outbreak of the COVID-19 pandemic in Europe. She delivered few speeches in the following months.

Turning to the content of speeches, the category of main topics comprises five issues that together form von der Leyen's political agenda (Figure 16.1). These main topics consist of: (1) the *European Green Deal/Climate Change* (21.35%); (2) the *Single Market* (16.29%); (3) *European Values/United Europe* (15.73%); (4) *Digitalization* (11.00%); (5) *Europe's Geostrategic Role* (6.74%). Together, these five topics comprised about 71% of the total topics addressed in her speeches. Von der Leyen's

---

[2] The threshold for frequency is 20 given codes for designation as a main topic, indicating that it has been addressed in more than a third of total speeches (N = 51). For an overview of the code system, see the Appendix 16.1 at the end of this chapter.
[3] The content analysis was conducted with the data analysis software MAXQDA. A given speech may have addressed more than one topic, but a given topic was coded only once per speech.
[4] European Commission Press Release Database: https://ec.europa.eu/commission/presscorner/home/en [accessed June 30, 2020].

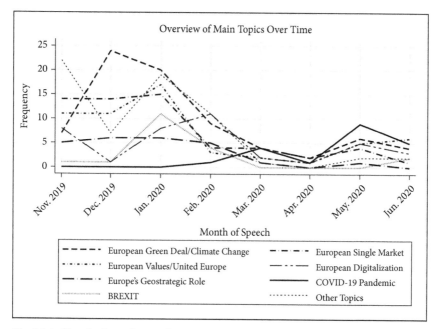

Fig. 16.1 Von der Leyen's agenda-setting: overview of main topics over time

agenda approach is thus concise and focused, concentrating on a small, yet comprehensive set of priorities. Apart from her main agenda, von der Leyen also referred to Brexit (5.34%) and the COVID-19 pandemic (5.62%)—major events comprising around 11% of her speech topics. She also addressed a cluster of other topics less frequently, such as globalization and European neighborhood and enlargement policies. These topics together comprised about 18% of the topics addressed in her speeches.

Zooming in on the main topics, the most dominant one is the European Green Deal, and the topic of climate change more broadly. The United Nation's Paris Agreement on climate change of 2015 and the heat waves that Europe experienced in 2018 and 2019, as well as the Friday for Future demonstrations by European youth since 2018, together generated a strong public movement across the European states, pressuring elites and policymakers to take serious action against climate change and to protect the environment. In light of this situational context, it was both an urgent but also strategic move by von der Leyen and the European Commission to place this topic at the front of the EU's agenda.

The framework of the European Green Deal, which was officially presented to the EP on December 11, 2019, entails a proposal for Europe's first (1) Climate Law, obliging EU members to stop carbon emissions on a net basis by 2050 (formally unveiled on March 5, 2020); (2) a Sustainable European Investment Plan; (3) a Carbon Border Tax; (4) a Just Transition Fund, which aims to balance out the costs of EU regions' compliance with climate change policies (European Commission 2019). While such steps were envisioned by the previous Commission (European Commission 2018), von der Leyen also boldly went beyond earlier proposals, for example, increasing the target for reducing carbon emissions by 50%–55% by 2030 compared to 1990, underscoring her commitment to climate change policy (European Commission 2019: 4).[5] Von der Leyen's appealing catch-phrase of the "European Green Deal," drawing on US President Franklin Delano Roosevelt's successful "New Deal" policies after the Great Depression in the 1930s, has provided a further, communicative boost for her most important agenda topic.

Although the European single market is her second-leading agenda topic (narrowly followed by her third main topic), it more resembles business as usual in any Commission agenda. In the context of Europe's industrial and trade policies, though, von der Leyen places stronger emphasis on EU–China interactions. She also proposed the concrete initiative of a European unemployment benefit reinsurance scheme to promote a stronger social market economy.

The third agenda topic concerns European values, appealing to Europe's unity and solidarity among citizens and countries. Here, she referred in particular to European integration and Europe's future, freedom, democracy, human rights, and, most importantly, commitment to the rule of law. It is apparent that the "renewed push for democracy," proclaimed as a priority during her candidacy (see section 16.3), did not emerge as a main topic on her agenda as incumbent but was, rather, more implicitly addressed in the context of European values. The same applies to her focus as a candidate on "protecting our way of life," a rubric that provoked widespread public and media criticism for the way in which it subsumed questions of migration (*New York Times*, September 12, 2019). She rarely spoke about migration and asylum policies in her early months as president, while she more explicitly embraced the topic of the rule of law.

Europe's digitalization and geostrategic role are her fourth and fifth most important agenda items. She has focused on digital transition and infrastructure, key technologies, and cybersecurity, as well as the general protection of personal data. Von der Leyen has also closely linked digitalization to the European Green Deal, framing it as a "twin digital and climate transition to strengthen our own industrial base and innovation potential" (von der Leyen 2019b: 5). Abels and Mushaben have pointed out that von der Leyen has also become known for coining the term "geopolitical Commission" (2020: 3). Von der Leyen understands the Commission as a decisively geopolitical institution and the EU as a geostrategic actor (von der Leyen 2019b: 2).

---

[5] In her state of the union address in 2020, Ursula von der Leyen dismissed the range of 50%–55% and confirmed the Commission's target of 55% by 2030, emphasizing that it would be the minimum for achieving climate neutrality by 2050 (von der Leyen 2020).

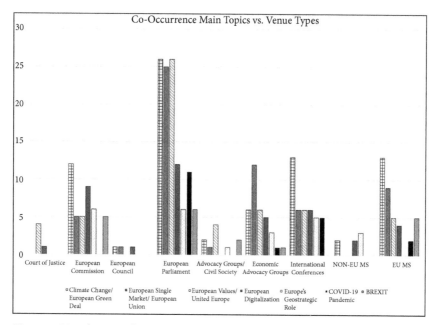

Fig. 16.2 Von der Leyen's agenda-setting: co-occurrence of main topics and venue types

From mid-March 2020, her agenda was at first sidelined completely by the dramatic spread of the coronavirus across Europe (Figure 16.1). Nonetheless, von der Leyen was quick to link her central topics prior to the crisis, the European Green Deal and digitalization in particular, to the pandemic recovery plan. While the European Green Deal was clearly overshadowed in the short term, it resurfaced from May onward in the context of the recovery plan, Next Generation EU (see next section).

Turning to venues, von der Leyen delivered about 59% of her speeches to EU institutions, and half of those to the EP (for a detailed overview of venues distribution, see Appendix 16.1 at the end of this chapter). Cross-analyzing the president's main topics with the venue types, a clear picture emerges. She addressed all five of her main topics in the EP. The European Green Deal, the single market, and European values stand out in particular, followed by digital transition and Europe's geostrategic role—topics that are central to but also the source of considerable controversy in the EP (Figure 16.2). This indicates that von der Leyen sees the EP as both the decision-making body where she expects most resistance to her agenda and a central arena in which to articulate that agenda to the larger European public spheres.

To sum up, the analysis of von der Leyen's agenda-setting between November 2019 and June 2020 provides four main results. First, given that successful supranational agenda-setting encourages a strong outreach strategy at the beginning of a term (Müller 2020), she fulfilled this demand, delivering a clear continuity of agenda from president-elect to president of the European Commission.

Second, supranational agenda-setting is more successful when it involves the selection and communication of a concise number of coherent topics that entail a push for greater European integration (Müller 2020). The Lisbon Treaty and the Parliament's increased role in electing the Commission president have led candidates since 2014 to lay out distinct agendas. While von der Leyen identified six priorities during her candidacy speech to the EP, she further streamlined her agenda, focusing on five main topics as president-elect and president. This indicates that von der Leyen has pushed an agenda that focuses on projects that have a high chance of achieving consensus support and thus implementation, while she has deemphasized more controversial issues and goals such as democratic reforms or "protecting our way of life."

Third, the concise roster of topics is reinforced through a clear communication style. Taking the example of the European Green Deal, while she did not invent the topic, her incisive rhetoric and application of catchwords has increased the attention paid to it among European audiences and beyond. However, at times her intense usage of catchphrases has backfired. This became apparent with the euphemistic term "relocation and/or return sponsorships," an essential component of the Commission's New Pact on Migration and Asylum (European Commission 2020a: 5). The phrasing was heavily criticized by the media and civil rights organizations, and in its German version was even selected most inappropriate word of 2020 (*Deutsche Welle*, January 21, 2021).

Finally, in relation to the COVID-19 recovery package, we see that von der Leyen reacted quickly to adapt her agenda, strategically realigning two of her main focuses—the European Green Deal and digitalization—to the changed situational context caused by the COVID-19 pandemic (see next section).

16.5   Empowering the Commission: Delivering on the Agenda by Tackling COVID-19

When Ursula von der Leyen assumed office, the situational context appeared relatively stable: she had the backing of the European Council, particularly the French–German tandem, and the respect of the EP. She therefore endeavored to swiftly deliver on her agenda (von der Leyen 2019a: 21). Soon, however, the outbreak of the COVID-19 crisis severely affected Europe and forced national executives to react on a day-to-day basis by imposing lockdowns, closing borders, safeguarding procurement of medical goods and equipment, and establishing various ad hoc instruments to stabilize their economies and secure their workforces. As health policies are national prerogatives, the Commission in this situation appeared to have no role.

Von der Leyen, though, immediately perceived the negative consequences that exclusively national efforts would have for the Union and recognized the window of opportunity that the crisis offered for entrepreneurial leadership at the European level. On March 2, she established a Corona Response Team, consisting of five commissioners responsible for medical issues, transnational mobility, as well as economic aspects of the crisis (European Commission 2020b). She also implemented emergency measures, such as coordination of procurement of medical goods and equipment, regulations to keep borders open to transnational trade, and the temporary relaxation of state aid rules (European Commission 2020c). In June 2020, she presented a "European strategy for the development, manufacturing and deployment of vaccines against COVID-19" and subsequently entered into contracts on behalf of the member states with medical firms producing such vaccines (European Commission 2021).

The situation was increasingly aggravated by the devastating economic consequences of the pandemic. Since member states were not evenly affected by the crisis, it became apparent that remedying the ensuing economic downturns was not only the responsibility of the respective governments, but required substantial European intervention and, as leaders at all government levels emphasized: *solidarity*. The discussion in Brussels quickly centered on providing financial assistance, particularly to those member states most seriously hit by the pandemic.

Von der Leyen swiftly responded to this shift in views with more forceful actions (Vitray and Lumet 2020: 6). Within the existing budget, she freed €37 billion for the Coronavirus Response Investment Initiative (European Commission 2020d). In addition, with an allocation of €100 billion, she established the SURE facility (Support to Mitigate Unemployment Risks in an Emergency), modeled on the German *Kurzarbeitergeld* (European Commission 2020e). Though von der Leyen introduced new initiatives, she kept them strictly within existing legal rules and practices. She thus mitigated possible resistance from member states and evaded lengthy decision-making procedures in the legislative bodies. In sum, early on in the crisis she developed strategies that were later pivotal to the successful launch of much more encompassing support packages at the European level.

While there was a consensus on massive financial support for the national economies, varying approaches were under consideration, such as Eurobonds or assistance by the European Stability Mechanism, with none attracting support from a majority of member states (Becker 2020). The situation changed when the French minister of finance launched a proposal that envisaged financial transfers funded through borrowing on financial markets. Soon after, a French–German initiative proposed a huge Recovery Fund of €500 billion as an instrument of European solidarity (Presse- und Informationsamt der Bundesregierung 2020). This audacious proposal, obviously at odds with the credo of avoiding any common debt in the EU, might well have encouraged the Commission president to come forward with a concept that went beyond even the French–German initiative. On May 27, von der Leyen submitted the proposal, under the title "The EU Budget Powering the Recovery Plan for Europe" (European Commission 2020f). It consisted of two pillars: first, an emergency European Recovery Instrument (ERI) under the aspirational rubric of a Next Generation EU (NGEU); second, a "reinforced" Multiannual Financial Framework (MFF) for 2021–2027.

The proposal included multiple innovations, most spectacularly a Recovery Fund of €750 billion in total, to be borrowed on financial markets under the aegis of the EU—€500 billion in grants and an additional €250 billion in loans. The proposal also envisaged administration of the whole fund by the Commission; integration of the Recovery Fund into the 2021–2027 MFF; national reform programs as condition for financial assistance, to be implemented within the European semester; and, finally, concentration of investment on the European Green Deal and digital transition.

Obviously, von der Leyen, besides promising huge amounts of financial transfers to the member states, employed strategic moves to make her proposal acceptable to the heads as well as the EP. By integrating the Recovery Fund into the MFF framework, she ensured that the transfers would work within existing rules. She anticipated that quick decisions would follow, as adopting the MFF was long overdue. The MFF framework also appealed to the EP, as it would allow the legislature to fully exert its budgetary powers (Becker 2020). Finally, by prioritizing the Green Deal and digital transition in EU spending, she also acted strategically on behalf of her own agenda.

In its meeting of June 2020, the European Council accepted the proposal with minor amendments. The decision came after extensive deliberation and debate (Becker 2020), with the "frugal four"—the Netherlands, Denmark, Sweden, and Austria—strongly against the proposal. In the crucial meeting, however, they could achieve no more than a small success. The overall amount of funds remained unchanged, with only the ratio of loans to grants shifting, the former raised from €250 to €360 billion and the latter reduced from €500 to €390 billion.

In December 2020, after further lengthy negotiations, the European Council and the EP finally adopted, with a few additional, again minor amendments, von der Leyen's rescue proposal and the integrated 2021–2027 MFF. The decision was preceded by a controversy over a resubmitted regulation, earlier proposed by the Juncker Commission, that envisaged making EU financial assistance to member states conditional on respect for the rule of law (Tömmel 2020: 1155–1156). After a stalemate between, on one side, Poland and Hungary, which threatened to veto the MFF, and, on the other, the EP, upholding the principle of the rule of law, the regulation was finally adopted by the Council and the EP. It will be applicable to all EU financial transfers to the member states.

The decision on the MFF and the enormous rescue package embedded within it is an astonishing result; some see it as historic (Vitray and Lumet 2020: 4). It marks a fundamental U-turn in European integration and in the stance of a majority of the heads. Fundamental principles vigorously upheld during the financial and sovereign debt crisis, such as avoiding common debt and financial transfers to member states, were set aside, as was the member states' usual reluctance to expand the powers of the EU and, especially, the Commission. In fact, the heads, in adopting this proposal, agreed to a strong move forward into unexplored directions of European integration.

Despite the various conflicts surrounding the agreement, von der Leyen achieved an exceptional victory at an early stage of her incumbency. The situational context was significant for this victory: the depth of the crisis, the threats linked to it, and its transnational nature made national governments more receptive to common solutions at the European level. Conversely, any state in opposition risked bearing the blame for massive economic losses and ensuing hardships for citizens across Europe, as Hungary and Poland experienced when they threatened to veto the MFF. It seems national governments have learned a lesson from the financial crisis: that strict austerity in times of crisis is counterproductive (Crespy 2020). Angela Merkel's U-turn to support an expansive investment policy based on common debt in the Union is particularly remarkable (see Chapter 10 in this volume). The consistent support from the EP as well as business representations, trade unions, and civil society actors for massive financial intervention further reinforced the broad consensus. Where such a consensus is absent, Commission proposals are easily shunted aside, as von der Leyen experienced with her New Pact for Migration and Asylum, submitted in September 2020 (European Commission 2020a).

Nevertheless, it was von der Leyen's proactive and strategic leadership, and that of the Commission more broadly, that provided the blueprint for the Union's decisions. By molding a proposal that boldly surpassed the French–German initiative, embedding it within basic principles and practices of European funding, and linking it to her agenda priorities, she significantly shaped the Union's decisions and pushed European integration into new territory.

Certain reservations are nonetheless justified. The Commission proposal, with its huge variety of new initiatives, funds, and facilities, each involving specific rules and conditions, is extremely complex (Pisani-Ferry 2020; Vitray and Lumet 2020: 6–8). This might constrain swift financial transfers and due implementation in the member states, as well as full respect for the rule of law and financial accountability (Alcidi et al. 2020). Some observers have expressed fears that fraud and corruption might ensue (Vitray and Lumet 2020: 7). Von der Leyen will thus have to prove that she is able not only to put forward ambitious proposals and get them adopted, but also to supervise their implementation to the benefit of the Union as a whole.

16.6 Conclusion

In drawing conclusions about Ursula von der Leyen's leadership as Commission president in roughly her first year in office, it is important to consider both her ascendance to as well as her performance in this top position.

Prior to the Commission presidency, von der Leyen enjoyed an exceptional career: although a latecomer to politics, she quickly climbed to and successively held increasingly powerful ministerial offices in the German government. Her personal capacities—ambition, determination, independence, and resoluteness—helped her to overcome the hurdles encountered in ascending to the Commission presidency. Even though her candidacy was highly contested in the EP, she succeeded in winning support in the assembly by advocating a comprehensive, yet focused agenda, appealing to MEPs far beyond her own party family.

Once in office, von der Leyen provided a concise agenda by specifying her priorities and defining steps toward implementation of her ambitious plans. When the COVID-19 crisis intervened, she quickly adapted and seized the opportunity to secure a role for the Union in addressing it. Starting with minor, yet crucial support measures, she soon took the lead in proposing an enormous rescue package and defining the rules and procedures for its implementation. In doing so, she significantly expanded the role of the European Commission and the Union as a whole.

Summarizing von der Leyen's successful leadership as Commission president, her personal capacities appear to be the most decisive factor in her success. Again, her high political ambitions, her purposeful goal orientation, her relative party-political independence, and her deft handling of debate stand out. Together, these capacities suggest why she has demonstrated strong political pragmatism and an ability to identify policy initiatives that are appealing to diverse societal and political strata. Von der Leyen is notable, as well, for her effective communication style, involving crisp language and pointed rhetoric. Altogether, her personal capacities have made her a highly productive political actor at the European level. It is true that the situational context has often enabled von der Leyen's initiatives, providing her room for political maneuver as Commission president. Still, she also endeavored to transcend her circumstances. Her proactive leadership, particularly in the face of the devastating COVID-19 crisis, has enabled her to further expand the Union's resources and opportunities for political action.

Yet, many politicians, the media, and the wider public in and beyond the EU member states do not share this positive assessment of von der Leyen's leadership. On the contrary, especially since the beginning of 2021, von der Leyen has received continuous criticism. In particular, she is considered to have failed in the negotiations around and acquisition of vaccines against the coronavirus. Her critics, however, overlook that von der Leyen made a huge, innovative leap in this case by proposing and undertaking joint action at the European level, instead of leaving member states to compete separately for the acquisition of vaccines. Her critics also forget that it was the heads in the European Council who only after great delay took the necessary decisions on this matter, and severely restricted the Commission's budgetary room of maneuver. The criticism of von der Leyen thus largely reflects national blame-shifting and scapegoating of the EU Commission and particularly its president rather than actual failure on their part (Hobolt and Tilley 2014).

Relating the insights presented in this chapter on von der Leyen's leadership to the function of the European Commission within the EU political system, her successes are actually not so surprising: The Commission's initiatives are not and should not be based on party-political ideologies or platforms; instead, they are and should be oriented around launching proposals for joint action and administering policies for the European common good. At the same time, the EU is an evolving polity, characterized by deep divergences among national governments, political parties, and increasingly also the European citizenry, with political contestation built into the system. Hence, while the *Economist* may have felt that Ursula von der Leyen's biography hardly suited the mood of Europe, it seems that her strategic leadership, showing the way forward and not shying from possible conflict, perfectly suits the contested European polity and the function of the Commission within it.

References

Abels, Gabriele, and Joyce M. Mushaben. 2020. "Great Expectations, Structural Limitations: Ursula von der Leyen and the Commission's New Equality Agenda." *Journal of Common Market Studies* 58 (1): 121–132.

Alcidi, Cinzia, Daniel Gros, and Francesco Corti. 2020. "Who Will Really Benefit from the Next Generation EU Funds?" *CEPS, Policy Insights*, October 25.

Becker, Peter. 2020. "Der Haushalt der EU als Chance in der Krise: Der Vorschlag der Kommission für einen neuen Finanzrahmen und einen Aufbaufonds." *SWP Aktuell* 56, June.

Belafi, Matthias, 2020. "Die Europäische Volkspartei nach der Europawahl 2019." In *Die Europawahl 2019: Ringen um die Zukunft Europas*, eds. Michael Kaeding, Manuel Müller, and Julia Schmälter, 27–37. Wiesbaden: Springer.

Birkland, Thomas A. 2007. "Agenda Setting in Public Policy." In *Handbook of Public Policy Analysis: Theory, Politics, and Methods*, eds. Frank Fischer, Gerald J. Miller, and Mara S. Sidney, 63–78. Boca Raton, FL: CRC Press.

Cloos, Jim. 2019. "Spitzenkandidaten: A Debate about Power and about the Future Development of the EU." *European Policy Brief* 56, September.

Crespy, Amandine. 2020. "The EU's Socioeconomic Governance 10 Years after the Crisis: Muddling Through and the Revolt against Austerity." *Journal of Common Market Studies* 58 (Annual Review): 133–146.

Dausend, Peter, and Elisabeth Niejahr. 2015. *Operation Röschen: Das System von der Leyen.* Frankfurt am Main: Campus Verlag [Kindle edition].

Deutsche Welle. 2021. "Gleich zwei Begriffe zum 'Unwort des Jahres 2020' gekührt." January 12. https://www.dw.com/de/gleich-zwei-begriffe-zum-unwort-des-jahres-2020-gek%C3%BCrt/a-56200161 (accessed January 24, 2021).

Economist. 2019. "Does Ursula von der Leyen Have the Right Skills for the EU Commission?" July 18. https://www.economist.com/europe/2019/07/18/does-ursula-von-der-leyen-have-the-right-skills-for-the-eu-commission?frsc=dg%7Ce (accessed July 20, 2020).

Euronews. 2020. "The EU's Rule of Law Budget Deal Saved Angela Merkel's Political Legacy." December 13. https://www.euronews.com/2020/12/13/the-eu-s-rule-of-law-budget-deal-saved-angela-merkel-s-political-legacy-view (accessed January 23, 2021).

European Commission. 2018. *A Clean Planet for All. A European Strategic Long-Term Vision for a Prosperous, Modern, Competitive and Climate Neutral Economy.* Brussels, November 28 [COM(2018)773 final].

European Commission. 2019. *The European Green Deal.* Brussels, December 11 [COM(2019) 640 final].

European Commission. 2020a. *New Pact on Migration and Asylum.* Brussels, September 23 [COM(2020) 609 final].

European Commission. 2020b. *Remarks by President von der Leyen at the Joint Press Conference with Commissioners Lenarčič, Kyriakides, Johansson, Vălean, and Gentiloni at the ERCC ECHO on the EU's Response to COVID-19.* Statement. Brussels, March 2.

European Commission. 2020c. *Communication from the Commission to the European Parliament, the European Council and the Council on Additional Covid-19 Response Measures* [COM(2020)687 final].

European Commission. 2020d. *Commission Acts to Make Available 37 Billion Euro from the EU Budget to Address the Coronavirus. News.* Brussels, March 13. https://ec.europa.eu/info/news/commission-acts-make-available-37-billion-euro-eu-budget-address-coronavirus-2020-mar-13_en (accessed January 20, 2021).

European Commission. 2020e. *SURE, the European Instrument for Temporary Support to Mitigate Unemployment Risks in an Emergency (SURE).* https://ec.europa.eu/info/business-economy-euro/economic-and-fiscal-policy-coordination/financial-assistance-eu/funding-mechanisms-and-facilities/sure_en (accessed January 22, 2021).

European Commission. 2020f. *Communication from the Commission to the European Parliament, the European Council, the Council, the European Economic and Social Committee and the Committee of the Regions: The EU Budget Powering the Recovery Plan for Europe* [COM(2020) 442 final].

European Commission. 2021. *Timeline of EU Action.* https://ec.europa.eu/info/liveworktraveleu/coronavirus-response/timeline-eu-action_en (accessed January 23, 2021).

Guardian. 2011. "Ursula von der Leyen: Germany's Next Chancellor?" September 9. https://www.theguardian.com/world/2011/sep/09/ursula-von-der-leyen-germany (accessed July 15, 2020).

Heidbreder, Eva G., and Daniel Schade. 2020. "Der institutionelle Wettstreit um die Spitzenkandidaten in der Europawahl 2019." In *Die Europawahl 2019: Ringen um die*

Zukunft Europas, eds. Michael Kaeding, Manuel Müller, and Julia Schmälter, 169–179. Wiesbaden: Springer.

Henninger, Annette, and Angelika von Wahl. 2010. "Das Umspiel von Veto-Spielern. Wie eine koservative Familienministerin den Familialismus des deutschen Wohlfahrtsstaates unterminiert." In *Die zweite Große Koalition. Eine Bilanz der Regierung Merkel 2006–2009*, eds. Christoph Egle and Reimut Zohnhöfer, 361–379. Wiesbaden: VS Verlag.

Hobolt, Sara B. 2014. "A Vote for the President? The Role of Spitzenkandidaten in the 2014 European Parliament Elections." *Journal of European Public Policy* 21 (10): 1528–1540.

Hobolt, Sara B. and James Tilley. 2014. *Blaming Europe? Responsibility without account-ability in the European Union*. Oxford: Oxford University Press.

Müller, Henriette. 2020. *Political Leadership and the European Commission Presidency*. Oxford: Oxford University Press.

Müller-Gomez, Johannes, and Alina Thieme. 2020. "The Appointment of the President of the European Commission 2019: A Toothless European Parliament?" In *Die Europawahl 2019: Ringen um die Zukunft Europas*, eds. Michael Kaeding, Manuel Müller, and Julia Schmälter, 181–190. Wiesbaden: Springer.

New York Times. 2019. "'Protecting Our European Way of Life'? Outrage Follows New E.U. Role." September 12. https://www.nytimes.com/2019/09/12/world/europe/eu-ursula-von-der-leyen-migration.html (accessed January 19, 2021).

Pisani-Ferry, Jean. 2020. "European Union Recovery Funds: Strings Attached, But Not Tied Up in Knots." *Bruegel, Policy Contribution* 19, October 2020.

Presse- und Informationsamt der Bundesregierung. 2020. "A French–German Initiative for the European Recovery from the Coronavirus Crisis." Pressemitteilung 173/20, May 18. https://www.bundesregierung.de/resource/blob/997532/1753772/414a4b5a1ca91d4f7146eeb2b39ee72b/2020-05-18-deutsch-franzoesischer-erklaerung-eng-data.pdf (accessed January 22, 2021).

Princen, Sebastiaan. 2009. *Agenda-Setting in the European Union*. New York: Palgrave Macmillan.

Rahlf, Katharina. 2009. "Ursula von der Leyen—Seiteneinsteigerin in zweiter Gen-eration." In *Seiteneinsteiger. Unkonventionelle Politiker-Karrieren in der Parteien-demokratie*, eds. Robert Lorenz and Matthias Micus, 274–300. Wiesbaden: VS Verlag.

Tömmel, Ingeborg. 2020. "Political Leadership in Times of Crisis: The Commission Presidency of Jean-Claude Juncker." *West European Politics* 43 (5): 1141–1162.

Vitray, Anne, and Sébastien Lumet. 2020. "Multi-annual Financial Framework and Next Generation EU: Review of an Unprecedented, Tumultuous European Bud-getary Chapter." *Fondation Robert Schuman, Policy Paper* 575, October 27.

Von der Leyen, Ursula. 2019a. *A Union That Strives for More: Political Guidelines for the Next European Commission 2019–2024*. Brussels: European Union.

Von der Leyen, Ursula. 2019b. *Speech by President-Elect von der Leyen in the European Parliament Plenary on the Occasion of the Presentation of her College of Commission-ers and their Programme*. Strasbourg, November 27 [SPEECH/19/6408].

Von der Leyen, Ursula. 2020. *State of the Union 2020*. Brussels, September 17 [IP/20/1599].

Code System for Agenda-Setting
of Ursula von der Leyen

Code System	Number of given codes/Frequency
Agenda-setting	*Total: 356*
(1) Main Topics/Political Agenda	
European Green Deal/Climate Change	76
European Single Market	58
European Values/United Europe	56
European Digitalization	39
Europe's Geostrategic Role	24
(2) Major Internal/External Events	
COVID-19 Pandemic	20
Brexit	19
(3) Other Topics	
European Neighborhood/Enlargement	16
Globalization/Global Challenges	16
Migration	12
Demography/Health	11
European Commission/Institutions	8
EU Member State Relations	1
Audience venues	*Total: 51 (Speeches, N = 51)*
(1) European Institutions	30
(2) Advocacy Groups/Civil Society	6
(3) International Conferences	8
(4) EU Member States	5
(5) Non-EU Member States	2

Women Leaders in the European Union

(as of October 2021)

European Commission

Commission Presidents

Name	Years of Position	Portfolio	Immediately Previous Position	Country	Entry Age
Von der Leyen, Ursula	2019–present	President of the European Commission	Federal Minister of Defense of Germany	Germany	60

Commissioners

Name	Years of Position	Portfolio	Immediately Previous Position	Country	Entry Age
Papandreou, Vasso	1989–1993	Employment, Industrial Relations and Social Affairs	Deputy Minister of Commerce in Greece	Greece	45
Scrivener, Christiane	1989–1995	Revenue Harmonization and Consumer Policies	Member of the European Parliament	France	63
Bonino, Emma	1994–1999	Consumer Policy, Fisheries and the European Community Humanitarian Office	Secretary of the Transnational Radical Party	Italy	47
Bjerregaard, Ritt	1995–1999	Environment	Vice-President of both OSCE's Parliamentary Assembly and Socialist International Women (SIW)	Denmark	53
Cresson, Edith	1995–1999	Research, Science and Technology	Prime Minister of France	France	60

Name	Years	Portfolio	Position	Country	Age
Gradin, Anita	1995–1999	Immigration, Home Affairs and Justice	Ambassador of Sweden to Austria and Slovenia	Sweden	61
Wulf-Mathies, Monika	1995–1999	Regional Policy	President of the Public Services, Transport and Traffic Union of Germany (ÖTV)	Germany	52
de Palacio, Loyola	1999–2004	Parliamentary Relations, Transport and Energy; Vice-President	Head of the Spanish Delegation in the European Parliament	Spain	49
Diamantopoulou, Anna	1999–2004	Employment and Social Affairs	Deputy Minister for Development of Greece	Greece	40
Reding, Viviane	1999–2004	Education and Culture	Member of the European Parliament	Luxembourg	48
Schreyer, Michaele	1999–2004	Budget	Member of the State Parliament of Berlin	Germany	48
Wallström, Margot Elisabeth	1999–2004	Environment	Minister of Social Affairs of Sweden	Sweden	45
Ferrero-Waldner, Benita	2004–2009	External Relations and the European Neighbourhood Policy	Minister of Foreign Affairs of Austria	Austria	56
Fischer Boel, Mariann	2004–2010	Agriculture and Rural Development	Minister for Food, Agriculture and Fisheries of Denmark	Denmark	61
Grybauskaitė, Dalia	2004–2009	Financial Programming and the Budget	Minister of Finance of Lithuania	Lithuania	48

Continued

Continued

Name	Years of Position	Portfolio	Immediately Previous Position	Country	Entry Age
Hübner, Danuta	2004–2009	Regional Policy	Minister for European Affairs of Poland	Poland	56
Kalniete, Sandra	2004–2004	Agriculture and Fisheries	Minister of Foreign Affairs of Latvia	Latvia	51
Kroes, Neelie	2004–2010	Competition	Adviser/board member to various (inter)national companies	Netherlands	63
Reding, Viviane	2004–2010	Information, Society and Media	European Commissioner for Education and Culture	Luxembourg	53
Wallström, Margot Elisabeth	2004–2010	Institutional Relations and Communication Strategy; First Vice-President	European Commissioner for Environment	Sweden	50
Kuneva, Meglena	2007–2010	Consumer Protection	Minister of European Affairs of Bulgaria	Bulgaria	49
Ashton, Catherine	2008–2009	Trade	Leader of the House of Lords of the United Kingdom	United Kingdom	52
Vassiliou, Androulla	2008–2009	Health	Chairperson of the Board of Trustees of the Cyprus Oncology Centre	Cyprus	65
Ferrero-Waldner, Benita	2009–2010	Trade	European Commissioner for External Relations and the European Neighbourhood Policy	Austria	61
Damanaki, Maria	2010–2014	Maritime Affairs and Fisheries	Member of the Greek Parliament	Greece	57

Name	Years	Portfolio	Position	Country	Age
Geoghegan-Quinn, Máire	2010–2014	Research, Innovation and Science	Member of the European Court of Auditors	Ireland	59
Georgieva, Kristalina	2010–2014	International Cooperation, Humanitarian Aid and Crisis Management	Vice-President and Corporate Secretary of the World Bank Group	Bulgaria	57
Hedegaard, Connie	2010–2014	Climate Action	Minister of Climate and Energy of Denmark	Denmark	59
Kroes, Neelie	2010–2014	Digital Agenda; Vice-President	European Commissioner for Competition	Netherlands	69
Malmström, Cecilia	2010–2014	Home Affairs	Minister for EU-Affairs of Sweden	Sweden	41
Reding, Viviane	2010–2014	Justice, Fundamental Rights and Citizens; Vice-President	European Commissioner for Information, Society and Media	Luxembourg	58
Vassiliou, Androulla	2010–2014	Education, Culture, Multilingualism	European Commissioner for Health	Cyprus	67
Bieńkowska, Elżbieta Ewa	2014–2019	Internal Market, Industry, Entrepreneurship and SMEs	Deputy Prime Minister and Minister of Infrastructure and Development of Poland	Poland	52
Bulc, Violeta	2014–2019	Transport	Deputy Prime Minister, Minister for Development, Strategic Projects and Cohesion of Slovenia	Slovenia	50
Crețu, Corina	2014–2019	Regional Policy	Vice-President of the European Parliament	Romania	46
Georgieva, Kristalina	2014–2016	Budget und Human Resources	European Commissioner for International Cooperation, Humanitarian Aid and Crisis Management	Bulgaria	61

Continued

Continued

Name	Years of Position	Portfolio	Immediately Previous Position	Country	Entry Age
Jourová, Věra	2014–2019	Justice, Consumers and Gender Equality	Minister for Regional Development of the Czech Republic	Czech Republic	50
Malmström, Cecilia	2014–2019	Trade	European Commissioner for Home Affairs	Sweden	41
Reicherts, Martine	2014–2014	Justice, Fundamental Rights and Citizenship	Director General Publications Office	Luxembourg	57
Thyssen, Marianne	2014–2019	Employment, Social Affairs, Skills and Labour Mobility	Head of the Belgian delegation of the EPP Group in the European Parliament	Belgium	58
Vestager, Margrethe	2014–2019	Competition	Minister for Economic Affairs and the Interior of Denmark	Denmark	46
Gabriel, Mariya	2017–2019	Digital Economy and Society	Vice-President of the EPP Group in the European Parliament	Bulgaria	38
Dalli, Helena	2019–present	Equality	Minister for European Affairs and Equality of Malta	Malta	57
Ferreira, Elisa	2019–present	Cohesion and Reforms	Vice-Governor of Banco de Portugal	Portugal	64

Name	Dates	Portfolio	Background	Country	Age
Gabriel, Mariya	2019–present	Innovation and Youth	European Commissioner for Digital Economy and Society	Bulgaria	38
Johansson, Ylva	2019–present	Home Affairs	Minister for Employment and Integration of Sweden	Sweden	55
Jourová, Věra	2019–present	Values and Transparency; Vice-President	European Commissioner for Justice, Consumers and Gender Equality	Czech Republic	50
Kyriakidou, Stella	2019–present	Health and Food Safety	Member of the House of Representatives of Cyprus	Cyprus	63
Simson, Kadri	2019–present	Energy	Minister of Economic Affairs and Infrastructure of Estonia	Estonia	42
Šuica, Dubravka	2019–present	Democracy and Demography; Vice-President	Vice-Chair of the EPP Group in the European Parliament	Croatia	62
Urpilainen, Jutta	2019–present	International Partnerships	Member of the Finnish Parliament	Finland	44
Vălean, Adina	2019–present	Transport	Member of the European Parliament	Romania	46
Vestager, Margrethe	2019–present	A Europe Fit for the Digital Age and Competition, Executive Vice-President	European Commissioner for Competition	Denmark	46
McGuinness, Mairead	2020–present	Financial Stability, Financial Services and the Capital Markets Union	Vice-President of the European Parliament	Ireland	61

Secretaries General

Name	Years of Position	Portfolio	Immediately Previous Position	Country	Entry Age
Day, Catherine	2005–2015	Secretary General of the European Commission	Director General DG Environment	Ireland	51
Juhansone, Ilze	2020–present	Secretary General of the European Commission	Deputy Secretary General of the European Commission	Latvia	49

Directors General

Name	Years of Position	Portfolio	Immediately Previous Position	Country	Entry Age
Flesch, Colette	1990–1997	DG Information, Communication, Culture, Media and Sports	Member of the European Parliament	Luxembourg	53
Ventura, Isabelle	1996–1999	DG Financial Stability, Financial Services and Capital Markets Union	N.A.	N.A.	51
Flesch, Colette	1997–1999	DG Translation and Information Technologies	Director General DG Information, Communication, Culture, Media and Sports	Luxembourg	60

Name	Years	DG	Position	Country	Age
Day, Catherine	2002–2005	DG Environment	Deputy Director General, DG External Relations	Ireland	47
Quintin, Odile	2002–2005	DG Employment, Social Affairs and Equal Opportunities	Acting Deputy Director General DG Employment, Social Affairs and Equal Opportunities	France	55
Quintin, Odile	2005–2010	DG Education and Culture	Director General DG Employment, Social Affairs and Equal Opportunities	France	60
Reicherts, Martine	2007–2015	DG Publications Office	Head of Service of the Office for Infrastructure and Logistics in Luxembourg	Luxembourg	50
Durand, Claire-Françoise	2008–2009	DG Legal Services	Deputy Director General DG Legal Services	France	62
Souka, Irene	2009–2020	DG Human Resources and Security	Deputy Director General DG Personnel and Administration	Greece	55
Ewans, Lowri	2010–2015	DG Fisheries and Maritime Affairs	Deputy Director General DG Competition	United Kingdom	52
Le Bail, Françoise	2010–2014	DG Justice	Deputy Director General DG Enterprise and Industry	France	60
Testori Coggi, Paola	2010–2014	DG Health and Consumers	Deputy Director General DG Health and Consumers	Italy	57
Calviño Santamaria, Nadia Maria	2014–2018	DG Budget	Deputy Director General DG Internal Market and Services	Spain	46

Continued

Continued

Name	Years of Position	Portfolio	Immediately Previous Position	Country	Entry Age
Ewans, Lowri	2015–2019	DG Internal Market, Industry, Entrepreneurship and SMEs	Director General DG Fisheries and Maritime Affairs	United Kingdom	57
Pariat, Monique	2015–2020	DG Humanitarian Aid and Civil Protection	Deputy Director General, DG Agriculture and Rural Development	France	57
Reicherts, Martine	2015–2018	DG Education and Culture	Director General Publications Office	Luxembourg	57
Astola, Tiina	2016–2020	DG Justice and Consumers	Permanent Secretary of the Finnish Ministry of Justice	Finland	63
Fink-Hooijer, Florika	2016–present	DG Interpretation	Director for Strategy, Policy and International Cooperation DG Humanitarian Aid and Civil Protection	Germany	54
Ingestad, Gertrud	2016–2020	DG Informatics	Director for Digital Business Solutions DG Digit	Sweden	58
Bucher, Anne	2018–present	DG Health and Food Safety	Chair of Regulatory Scrutiny Board	France	60
Christophidou, Themis	2018–present	DG Education, Youth, Sport and Culture	Head of Cabinet of Commissioner Christos Stylianides	Cyprus	57
Kotzeva, Mariana	2018–present	DG Eurostat	Deputy Director General Eurostat	Bulgaria	51
Michou, Paraskevi	2018–2020	DG Migration and Home Affairs	Deputy Secretary General of the European Commission	Greece	63
Ahrenkilde Hansen, Pia	2019–present	DG Communication	Deputy Secretary General of the European Commission	Denmark	56

Name	Years	Department	Position	Country	Age
Juul Jørgensen, Ditte	2019–present	DG Energy	Head of Cabinet of Commissioner Vestager	Denmark	58
Weyand, Sabine	2019–present	DG Trade	Deputy Chief Negotiator of the Task Force for the preparation and conduct of the negotiations with the United Kingdom under Art. 50 TEU	Germany	55
Ingestad, Gertrud	2020–present	DG Human Resources and Security	Director General DG Informatics	Sweden	58
Jorna, Kerstin	2020–present	DG Internal Market, Industry, Entrepreneurship and SMEs	Deputy Director General DG Economic and Financial Affairs	Germany	58
Michou, Paraskevi	2020–present	DG Humanitarian Aid and Civil Protection	Director General DG Migration and Home Affairs	Greece	
Pariat, Monique	2020–present	DG Migration and Home Affairs	Director General DG Humanitarian Aid and Civil Protection	France	57
Saastamoinen, Salla	2020–present	DG Justice and Consumers	Director for Civil and Commercial Justice, DG Justice and Consumers	Finland	57
Vitcheva, Charlina	2020–present	DG Maritime Affairs and Fisheries	Deputy Director General of the Joint Research Centre	Bulgaria	57

European External Action Service

High Representatives of the Union for Foreign Affairs and Security Policies

Name	Years of Position	Immediately Previous Position	Country	Entry Age
Ashton, Catherine	2009–2014	European Commissioner for Trade	United Kingdom	53
Mogherini, Federica	2014–2019	Minister of Foreign Affairs and International Cooperation of Italy	Italy	41

Secretaries General of the EEAS

Name	Years of Position	Immediately Previous Position	Country	Entry Age
Schmid, Helga	2016–2020	Deputy Secretary General of the European External Action Service	Germany	55

European Council

Heads of State or Government

Name	Years of Position	Position	Immediately Previous Position	Country	Entry Age
Thatcher, Margaret	1979–1990	Prime Minister of the UK	Leader of the Conservative Party of the United Kingdom	United Kingdom	53
Jäätteenmäki, Anneli	2003–2003	Prime Minister of Finland	Chairwoman of the Centre Party of Finland	Finland	48
Merkel, Angela	2005–2021	Chancellor of Germany	Leader of the Christian Democratic Union of Germany	Germany	51
Grybauskaitė, Dalia	2009–2019	President of Lithuania	European Commissioner for Financial Programming and the Budget	Lithuania	53
Kiviniemi, Mari	2010–2011	Prime Minister of Finland	Minister for Public Administration and Local Government of Finland	Finland	41
Radičová, Iveta	2010–2012	Prime Minister of Slovakia	Member of the Slovakian Parliament	Slovakia	53
Thorning-Schmidt, Helle	2011–2015	Prime Minister of Denmark	Leader of the Social Democratic Party of Denmark	Denmark	44

Continued

Continued

Name	Years of Position	Position	Immediately Previous Position	Country	Entry Age
Bratušek, Alenka	2013–2014	Prime Minister of Slovenia	Member of the National Assembly of Slovenia	Slovenia	42
Kopacz, Ewa	2014–2015	Prime Minister of Poland	Marshal of the Sejm of Poland	Poland	57
Straujuma, Laimdota	2014–2016	Prime Minister of Latvia	Minister for Agriculture of Latvia	Latvia	63
Szydło, Beata	2015–2017	Prime Minister of Poland	Treasurer of the Law and Justice party of Poland	Poland	52
Bierlein, Brigitte	2019–2020	Chancellor of Austria	President of the Constitutional Court of Austria	Austria	69
Frederiksen, Mette	2019–present	Prime Minister of Denmark	Leader of the Social Democratic Party of Denmark	Denmark	41
Marin, Sanna	2019–present	Prime Minister of Finland	Minister of Transport and Communications of Finland	Finland	34
Wilmès, Sophie	2019–2020	Prime Minister of Belgium	Minister of Budget of Belgium	Belgium	44
Andersson, Magdalena	2021–present	Prime Minister of Sweden	Finance Minister of Sweden	Sweden	54

European Parliament

Presidents

Name	Years of Position	Political Group	Immediately Previous Position	Country	Entry Age
Veil, Simone	1979–1982	ELDR	Minister of Health in France	France	52
Fontaine, Nicole	1999–2002	EPP	Vice-President of the European Parliament	France	57

Vice-Presidents

Name	Years of Position	Political Group	Immediately Previous Position	Country	Entry Age
Péry, Nicole	1984–1997	S&D	Member of the European Parliament	France	41
Flesch, Colette	1985–1990	ALDE	Member of the European Parliament	Luxembourg	48
Fontaine, Nicole	1989–1994	EPP	Member of the European Parliament	France	47
Isler Béguin, Marie Anne	1992–1994	Greens/EFA	Member of the European Parliament	France	35
Noya, Maria Magnani	1992–1994	S&D	Member of the European Parliament	Italy	60
Fontaine, Nicole	1994–1999	EPP	Vice-President of the European Parliament	France	52
Schleicher, Ursula	1994–1999	EPP	Member of the European Parliament	Germany	61
Hoff, Magdalene	1997–1997	S&D	Member of the European Parliament	Germany	53

Continued

Continued

Name	Years of Position	Political Group	Immediately Previous Position	Country	Entry Age
Lienemann, Marie-Noëlle	1999–2001	S&D	Member of the European Parliament	France	50
Kaufmann, Sylvia-Yvonne	2004–2007	GUE/NGL	Member of the European Parliament	Germany	49
Roth-Behrendt, Dagmar	2004–2007	S&D	Member of the European Parliament	Germany	51
Neyts-Uyttebroeck, Annemie	2005–2011	ALDE	Member of the European Parliament	Belgium	61
Kratsa-Tsagaropoulou, Rodi	2007–2012	EPP	Member of the European Parliament	Greece	53
Morgantini, Luisa	2007–2009	GUE/NGL	Member of the European Parliament	Italy	66
Rothe, Mechtild	2007–2009	S&D	Member of the European Parliament	Germany	61
Wallis, Diana	2007–2012	ALDE	Member of the European Parliament	United Kingdom	52
Angelilli, Roberta	2009–2014	EPP	Member of the European Parliament	Italy	44
Durant, Isabelle	2009–2014	Greens/EFA	Member of the European Parliament	Belgium	54
Koch-Mehrin, Silvana	2009–2011	ALDE	Member of the European Parliament	Germany	38
Roth-Behrendt, Dagmar	2009–2012	S&D	Member of the European Parliament	Germany	56
Podimata, Anni	2011–2014	S&D	Member of the European Parliament	Greece	48
Crețu, Corina	2014–2014	S&D	Member of the European Parliament	Romania	46
Guillaume, Sylvie	2014–2019	S&D	Member of the European Parliament	France	52
Lunacek, Ulrike	2014–2017	Greens/EFA	Member of the European Parliament	Austria	57
McGuinness, Mairead	2014–2017	EPP	Member of the European Parliament	Ireland	55
Vălean, Adina	2014–2017	EPP	Member of the European Parliament	Romania	46
Gebhardt, Evelyn	2017–2019	S&D	Member of the European Parliament	Germany	60
Hautala, Heidi	2017–present	Greens/EFA	Member of the European Parliament	Finland	61
Járóka, Lívia	2017–2019	EPP	Member of the European Parliament	Hungary	43

Name	Years of Position	Political Group	Immediately Previous Position	Country	Entry Age
McGuinness, Mairead	2017–2020	EPP	Vice-President of the European Parliament	Ireland	58
Barley, Katharina	2019–present	S&D	Minister of Justice and Consumer Protection of Germany	Germany	50
Beer, Nicola	2019–present	RE	Member of the German Parliament	Germany	49
Charanzová, Dita	2019–present	RE	Member of the European Parliament	Czech Republic	44
Dobrev, Klára	2019–present	S&D	CEO of the Altus Ltd.	Hungary	47
Járóka, Lívia	2019–present	EPP	Vice-President of the European Parliament	Hungary	45
Kopacz, Ewa	2019–present	EPP	Prime Minister of Poland	Poland	63

Presidents of Party Groups

Name	Years of Position	Political Group	Immediately Previous Position	Country	Entry Age
Green, Pauline	1994–1999	S&D	Leader of the European Parliamentary Labour Party	United Kingdom	45
Hautala, Heidi	1999–2002	Greens/EFA	Member of the European Parliament	Finland	43
Frassoni, Monica	2002–2009	Greens/EFA	Member of the European Parliament	Italy	39
Harms, Rebecca	2009–2014	Greens/EFA	Member of the European Parliament	Germany	52
Zimmer, Gabi	2012–2019	GUE/NGL	Member of the European Parliament	Germany	57
Le Pen, Marine	2016–2017	ENF/ED	Member of the European Parliament	France	48
Keller, Ska	2016–present	Greens/EFA	Member of the European Parliament	Germany	34
Aubry, Manon	2019–present	GUE/NGL	Member of the European Parliament	France	29
Garcia Perez, Irtaxe	2019–present	S&D	Member of the European Parliament	Spain	44

Court of Justice of the European Union

Court of Justice

Judges

Name	Years of Position	Immediately Previous Position	Country	Entry Age
O'Kelly Macken, Fidelma	1999–2004	Judge of the High Court in Ireland	Ireland	57
Colneric, Ninon	2000–2006	President of the Landesarbeitsgericht Schleswig-Holstein, Germany	Germany	51
De Lapuerta, Rosario Silva	2003–2021	Deputy Director General for Community and International Legal Assistance of the Public Prosecutor's Office at the Spanish Ministry of Justice	Spain	49
Lindh, Pernilla	2006–2011	Judge at the Court of First Instance	Sweden	61
Toader, Camelia	2007–2021	Judge at the High Court of Cassation and Justice of Romania	Romania	43
Berger, Maria	2009–2019	Member of the European Parliament	Austria	53
Prechal, Alexandra	2010–present	Professor of European Law at the University of Utrecht, Netherlands	Netherlands	51
Jürimäe, Küllike	2013–present	Judge at the General Court	Estonia	51
Rossi, Lucia Serena	2018–present	Representative of the Italian Government on the Governing Board of the Academy of European Law	Italy	60
Ziemele, Ineta	2020–present	President of the Constitutional Court of the Republic of Latvia (2017–2020)	Latvia	50
Arastey Sahún, Maria Lourdes	2021–present	Judge at the Tribunal Supremo (Supreme Court); Judge at the North Atlantic Treaty Organization (NATO) Administrative Tribunal (Brussels, Belgium) (2013–2021)	Spain	62
Spineanu-Matei, Octavia	2021–present	Judge at the General Court, CJEU	Romania	54

Advocates General

Name	Years of Position	Immediately Previous Position	Country	Entry Age
Rozès, Simone	1981–1984	President of the Tribunal de Grande Instance de Paris, France	France	60
Stix-Hackl, Christine	2000–2006	Head of the European Union-Legal Service in the Ministry of Foreign Affairs of Austria	Austria	43
Kokott, Juliane	2003– present	Director of the Institute for European and International Business Law at the University of St Gallen	Germany	46
Sharpston, Eleanor	2006– present	Senior Research Fellow and Affiliated Lecturer at the Centre for European Legal Studies of the University of Cambridge	United Kingdom	50
Trstenjak, Verica	2006–2012	Judge at the Court of First Instance	Slovenia	43
Ćapeta, Tamara	2021– present	Professor of Law, University of Zagreb	Croatia	54

Court of First Instance (1989–2009)/General Court (2009–present)

Judges

Name	Years of Position	Immediately Previous Position	Country	Entry Age
Lindh, Pernilla	1995–2006	Director and Director General for Legal Affairs, at the Ministry of Foreign Affairs of Sweden	Sweden	49
Tiili, Virpi	1995–2009	Director General of the Office for Consumer Protection, Finland	Finland	52
Martins de Nazaré Ribeiro, Maria Eugénia	2003–2016	Legal Secretary to the President of the Court of First Instance	Portugal	47
Cremona, Ena	2004–2012	Member of the European Commission against Racism and Intolerance	Malta	68
Labucka, Ingrida	2004–2020	Member of the International Court of Arbitration in The Hague and Member of the Latvian Parliament	Latvia	41
Pelikánová, Irena	2004–2019	Member of the Legislative Council of the Government of the Czech Republic	Czech Republic	55
Trstenjak, Verica	2004–2006	Associate Professor of Legal Theory, Civil Law and Corporate Law at the University of Maribor, Slovenia	Slovenia	41
Wiszniewska-Białecka, Irena	2004–2016	Judge at the Supreme Administrative Court of Poland	Poland	57
Kancheva, Mariyana	2011–present	Lawyer in Sofia and Brussels	Bulgaria	53
Jürimäe, Küllike	2004–2013	Judge at the Tallinn Court of Appeal	Estonia	42
Tomljenović, Vesna	2013–present	Professor at the Faculty of Law, University of Rijeka, Croatia	Croatia	57
José Costeira, Maria	2016–present	Judge at the Commercial Court, Lisbon	Portugal	49
Kowalik-Bańczyk, Krystyna	2016–present	Associate Professor at the Institute for Legal Studies of the Polish Academy of Sciences	Poland	43

Name	Years	Position	Country	Age
Marcoulli, Anna	2016–present	Member of the Legal Service of the European Commission	Cyprus	42
Półtorak, Nina	2016–present	Director of the EU Law Department, Supreme Administrative Court and Judge at the Regional Administrative Court, Kraków, Poland	Poland	45
Reine, Inga	2016–present	Legal adviser at the Permanent Representation of Latvia to the European Union	Latvia	41
Spineanu-Matei, Octavia	2016–2021	Judge at the High Court of Cassation and Justice of Romania	Romania	49
Frendo, Ramona	2019–present	Legal expert at the courts of Valletta, Malta and member of the panel of national arbitrators of Malta	Malta	48
Perišin, Tamara	2019–present	Special Adviser to the Ministry of Science and Education, Croatia	Croatia	40
Porchia, Ornella	2019–present	Legal Adviser to the Permanent Representation of Italy to the European Union	Italy	53
Pynnä, Tuula Riitta	2019–present	Judge at the Supreme Court of Finland	Finland	61
Škvařilová-Pelzl, Petra	2019–present	Research and Documentation Directorate General of the Court of Justice of the European Union	Czech Republic	44
Stancu, Mirela	2019–present	Judge at the Tribunal of Bucharest, Romania	Romania	45
Steinfatt, Gabriele	2019–present	Judge at the Higher Administrative Court, Bremen, Germany	Germany	42
Brkan, Maja	2021–present	Associate Professor of EU Law, University of Maastricht	Slovenia	42

European Central Bank

Presidents

Name	Years of Position	Immediately Previous Position	Country	Entry Age
Lagarde, Christine	2019–present	Managing Director of the IMF	France	63

Members of the Executive Board

Name	Years of Position	Immediately Previous Position	Country	Entry Age
Hämäläinen, Sirkka	1998–2003	Governor of the Central Bank of Finland	Finland	59
Tumpel-Gugerell, Gertrude	2003–2011	Vice-Governor of the Austrian Central Bank	Austria	50
Lautenschläger, Sabine	2014–2019	Vice-President of the Deutsche Bundesbank	Germany	49
Schnabel, Isabel	2020–present	Professor of Finance at the University of Bonn, Member of the German Council of Economic Experts	Germany	49

Members of the Governing Council

Name	Years of Position	Position	Immediately Previous position	Country	Entry Age
Georghadji, Chrystalla	2014–2019	Governor of the Central Bank of Cyprus / Member of the Governing Council of the European Central Bank	President of the Court of Auditors of Cyprus	Cyprus	58

Directors General

Name	Years of Position	Position	Immediately Previous Position	Country	Entry Age
Zilioli, Chiara	2014–present	DG Legal Services	Deputy Director General DG Legal Services	Italy	N.A.
Catherine, Anne-Sylvie	2016–present	DG Human Resources	Head of the Human Resources Department, CERN	France	46
Bausback, Anna Maria	2018–present	Directorate Finance	Corporate Development Board Office at Aareal Bank AG	Germany	N.A.
Mann, Claudia	2018–present	Directorate Internal Audit	Deputy Director General Finance	Germany	40

Continued

Continued

Name	Years of Position	Position	Immediately Previous Position	Country	Entry Age
Rahmouni-Rousseau, Imène	2019–present	DG Market Operations	Director of Markets at the Banque de France	France	43
San Agapito, Cristina	2019–present	Directorate Administration	Deputy Chief People and Organization Officer at CELSA Group	Spain	N.A.
Senkovic, Petra	2019–present	DG Secretariat	Director General Secretariat and Secretary to the Supervisory Board	N.A.	49
Stapel-Weber, Silke	2019–present	DG Statistics	Director National Accounts, Prices and Key Indicators at Eurostat	Germany	55

Index

Tables and figures are indicated by an italic *t* and *f* following the page number; 'n' after the page number indicates the footnote.